PhonicsWorks™
Lesson Guide Basic

Book 2

Book Staff and Contributors

Kristen Kinney   *Director, Primary Literacy*
Lenna King, Amy Rauen   *Instructional Designers*
Mary Beck Desmond   *Senior Text Editor*
Jill Tunick   *Text Editor*
Suzanne Montazer   *Creative Director, Print and ePublishing*
Sasha Blanton   *Senior Print Visual Designer*
David Batchelor, Carol Leigh   *Print Visual Designers*
Kim Barcas, Stephanie Williams   *Cover Designers*
Amy Eward   *Senior Manager, Writers*
Susan Raley   *Senior Manager, Editors*
Deanna Lacek   *Project Manager*

Maria Szalay   *Senior Vice President for Product Development*
John Holdren   *Senior Vice President for Content and Curriculum*
David Pelizzari   *Vice President, Content and Curriculum*
Kim Barcas   *Vice President, Creative*
Laura Seuschek   *Vice President, Instructional Design and Evaluation & Research*
Aaron Hall   *Vice President, Program Management*

Lisa Dimaio Iekel   *Production Manager*
John Agnone   *Director of Publications*

Credits

About K12 Inc.

K12 Inc., a technology-based education company, is the nation's leading provider of proprietary curriculum and online education programs to students in grades K–12. K^{12} provides its curriculum and academic services to online schools, traditional classrooms, blended school programs, and directly to families. K12 Inc. also operates the K^{12} International Academy, an accredited, diploma-granting online private school serving students worldwide. K^{12}'s mission is to provide any child the curriculum and tools to maximize success in life, regardless of geographic, financial, or demographic circumstances. K12 Inc. is accredited by CITA. More information can be found at www.K12.com.

ISBN-13: 978-1-60153-127-8
ISBN-10: 1-60153-127-3
Printed by RR Donnelley, Roanoke, VA, USA, July 2011, Lot 072011

Contents

Digraphs *wh* and *ch*

Getting Stronger: Letter Sounds

Trigraph −*tch* and Ending −*ck*

Getting Stronger: Digraphs, Trigraph −*tch*, and Ending −*ck*

Review Digraphs and the Trigraph –*tch*

Getting Stronger: Digraphs and the Trigraph –*tch*

Telling and Asking Sentences

Getting Stronger: Short Vowels, Digraphs, and Sentences

Endings –s and –es

Getting Stronger: Vowels

Endings –ff, –ll, –ss, –zz, and –all

Compound Words

Getting Stronger: Sentences, Endings, and Compound Words

Words, Letters & Sounds, and Sentences

Introduction

This book provides the following information for K[12] PhonicsWorks:

- About K[12] PhonicsWorks
- Lesson Guide
- Activity Book
- Assessments Book
- PhonicsWorks Readers
- PhonicsWorks Online

The Lesson Guide contains detailed lesson plans for each day and is organized by unit. The lesson plans are placed in the order in which you will use them. Activity Book and Unit Checkpoint Answer Keys are included for you in the lesson plans.

The Activity Book supplements the Lesson Guide and provides an opportunity for students to do some work on their own. While many of the Activity Book pages can be completed independently, we recommend that you provide instruction and guidance (for instance, reviewing the instructions and sample task together) as necessary.

Note that the pages in the Lesson Guide and the Activity Book are also available online in the Materials list. The online version will match the book version unless it has an "update" label.

K¹² PhonicsWorks™ Program Overview

Reading is the most important skill for success in school and society.
— SUSAN L. HALL AND LOUISA C. MOATS, *STRAIGHT TALK ABOUT READING*

Introduction

You *can* teach your child to read!

The K¹² PhonicsWorks™ program is based on the best current research and years of firsthand experience. K¹²'s approach is—

- Explicit; lessons directly address relationships between sounds and letters.
- Systematic; lessons build logically, sequentially, and step by step.
- Multisensory; lessons engage students in a variety of visual, auditory, and tactile activities.

The PhonicsWorks program is organized into two parts—Basic and Advanced—typically completed over the course of two grades. When combined with instruction in literature (such as K¹² Language Arts Literature and Comprehension program for Kindergarten and K¹² Language Arts program for Grade 1), PhonicsWorks offers a comprehensive and balanced approach to help students acquire the critical skills and knowledge required for reading and literacy.

General Objectives

PhonicsWorks is designed to help students achieve these important goals:

- Recognize the relationship between sounds and letters.
- Blend sounds represented by letters into words.
- Read and spell longer, unfamiliar words by breaking them into syllables.
- Read grade-level text with fluency (appropriate speed and accuracy).
- Read "sight words" (high-frequency words such as *said* or *was*; many of these words do not follow the patterns that have been taught).

Before You Begin

Before you get started, familiarize yourself with the PhonicsWorks program.

Standard Curriculum Materials (K¹² Supplied)

PhonicsWorks Basic includes the following materials:

- *K¹² PhonicsWorks* DVD training video
- K¹² PhonicsWorks Basic Kit
- *K¹² PhonicsWorks Readers Basic*
- *K¹² PhonicsWorks Basic Lesson Guide Book 1* and *Book 2*
- *K¹² PhonicsWorks Basic Activity Book*
- *K¹² PhonicsWorks Basic Assessments Book 1* and *Book 2*
- Online activities

PhonicsWorks Advanced includes all of the materials in the Basic course, as well as an Advanced Tile Kit.

Additional Materials (Learning Coach Supplied)

You will need to have the following materials on hand, which are labeled "Also Needed" in offline and online Materials lists:

- 3½ x 5-inch index cards
- Index card file box
- Black, nontoxic marker
- Dictation notebook (either loose-leaf paper in a binder or a spiral-bound notebook)
- Pencils
- Folder with loose-leaf paper (for portfolio materials and notes on student progress)

Prepare in Advance

When it's time to begin instruction, you will be well prepared if you take the time to *watch the video, read the lesson plans, and practice using the Tile Kit.* The *K¹² PhonicsWorks* DVD introduces the PhonicsWorks program, shows you how to use the Tile Kit, and explains teaching procedures.

Sounds and Letters: Basics of Phonics

Printed words are made up of letters that represent sounds. When we read words, we turn the letters into their corresponding speech sounds.

Consider the word *cat*, which has three letters:

c a t

The word *cat* also has three speech sounds, or phonemes (FO-neemz), which are written as follows:

/k/ /ă/ /t/

You will notice that sounds are written within slashes that we call *sound boxes.* The *K¹² PhonicsWorks* DVD provides a guide to pronouncing basic phonemes in the English language.

Let's look at one more word. Consider the word *boat*, which has four letters:

b o a t

Although the word *boat* has four letters, it has only three sounds:

/b/ /ō/ /t/

Over the course of the PhonicsWorks program, students will learn the following relationships between sounds and letters:

- Some sounds are represented by only one letter. For example, the sound /m/, as in <u>m</u>ouse, is almost always spelled with the letter *m*.
- Some sounds are represented by a combination of letters. For example, the sound /ch/, as in <u>ch</u>ip, is almost always spelled with the letters *ch*.
- Some sounds can be spelled more than one way. For example, the sound /k/ can be spelled *c*, as in <u>c</u>at; *k*, as in <u>k</u>ite; or *ck*, as in chi<u>ck</u>. The long o sound, /ō/, can be spelled *o*, as in n<u>o</u>; *oa*, as in b<u>oa</u>t; *oe*, as in t<u>oe</u>; *ow*, as in sn<u>ow</u>; and *o-e*, as in h<u>o</u>m<u>e</u>.

Course Instruction Guide

Number of Lessons

K[12] PhonicsWorks covers a total of 360 lessons: 180 in the Basic course and 180 in the Advanced course. Lessons are organized into groups of five lessons. Every fifth lesson presents online review activities and an assessment.

Lesson Time

These lesson times are estimates. You and students might take more or less time per lesson. Feel free to split the lessons into smaller segments and provide breaks for students as needed.

- **Basic:** 180 lessons; 30 minutes offline, 20 minutes online
- **Advanced:** 180 lessons; 30 minutes offline, 20 minutes online during the first semester and 15 minutes offline, 15 minutes online during the second semester.

Working Offline and Online

In the printed Lesson Guide, you will find step-by-step guidance for the offline portion of each lesson. These direct, explicit, and systematic lessons help students build a strong foundation of letter–sound knowledge. After the offline portion of the lesson is finished, students are ready to work independently online to reinforce, through engaging review and practice, the core lesson content. Some students may benefit from a short break between the offline and online portions of each lesson.

PhonicsWorks Basic Program: Lesson Guide Components

Unit Overview and Lesson Overview

Each new unit begins with a Unit Overview to help you understand the topics to be covered in the unit. A unit covers five days of instruction. Each day, the first page of the lesson plan indicates the materials; objectives; and any advance preparation, keywords, or Big Ideas you will need to be familiar with before you begin teaching.

Sight Words

Typically, students learn three new sight words every other week. Do not worry if students are unable to master all of the words for the week, because later lessons provide many opportunities to review them.

It is recommended that students work on no more than five sight words at a time. For example, if students master two of the three words for a given week, it is fine to add the third word to the following week's list, for a total of four words. However, if students are unable to master all three of the words, do not add all three to the following week's words.

Preparing sight word cards: You will need two sets of sight word cards to complete the Sight Words activities. One set of cards is supplied in your PhonicsWorks Kit. For the second set, you may either create your own using index cards or print a set from the online lesson and cut them into cards. If you create a set using index cards, you will need 3½ x 5-inch index cards and the list of words found in this section of the program overview. Use a bold black marker and print each word in neat, large, lowercase letters. Keep the two sets of cards somewhere convenient. As you work through the Phonics lessons, you will gradually add these cards to the file box (sight words box).

Here are the sight words in the Basic course:

- the, and, is
- on, to, in
- it, he, was
- says, have, with
- where, from, there
- that, of, put
- two, they, both
- you, went, we

- what, their, want
- said, your, so
- who, see, or
- for, she, her
- does, why, one
- were, my, are
- Mr., Mrs., Dr.

Get Ready

These activities help students review previously taught sounds and letters, and reinforce skills and concepts from earlier lessons.

Learn

In this section of the lesson, new concepts are introduced and practiced through a variety of multisensory activities, including the following:

- Listening to sounds in words
- Manipulating letter tiles
- Completing Activity Book pages with fun written activities
- Writing words and sentences that you dictate

In the first eight units, students practice phonological awareness. Phonological awareness is the ability to recognize and distinguish sounds of speech in language. We learn to speak before we learn to read; we learn to hear sounds before we learn which letters represent those sounds. Accordingly, in the first eight units of PhonicsWorks Basic, students focus on phonological awareness activities, distinguishing and manipulating sounds. Activities include Sound Chains; Finger Stretching; and Head, Waist, Toes.

Be patient. Do these activities thoroughly and well. Research has shown that explicit phonological awareness instruction leads to better reading.

Try It

This section of the lesson asks students to apply their new knowledge of a concept in a variety of ways. They may be asked to read from a PhonicsWorks Reader, write words or sentences in a Dictation activity, or complete an Activity Book page.

- **PhonicsWorks Readers:** The K[12] PhonicsWorks Readers are "decodable readers" with a carefully controlled vocabulary almost exclusively made up of letter–sound patterns and sight words students have already studied. Even though these stories are written in words students have studied, most beginning readers still need plenty of time to figure out the words. When students read the stories, you serve as a guide to help them when they have difficulty. The lessons offer detailed suggestions about how to help students read accurately and sound out challenging words.

Monitor progress: As students read, it is very important that you sit next to them and carefully observe their progress. Lesson plans provide instructions for taking notes while you listen to students read. These notes will help you decide which letters and sounds students still need to work on and which sight words are still difficult for them. You may want to keep a small notebook in which you can write the title of the reading assignment, the date, a list of skills students have mastered, and what they need to work on.

▶ **Dictation:** Early in the PhonicsWorks program, students will use letter tiles to create words dictated to them. As students' skills progress, students move to writing words and then sentences. It is important that you follow the instructions for Dictation as outlined in the Lesson Guide. Research indicates that these steps are the most effective for reinforcing students' letter–sound knowledge.

▶ **Activity Book Pages:** Students will complete two to four pages in each unit of PhonicsWorks. In most cases, after you have read the directions to students and observed them complete one or two examples, they may finish the page independently. Be sure to review students' completed work, making note of any letters and sounds they still need to work on and which sight words have yet to be mastered.

Online Overview

The last section of the Lesson Guide provides an overview of what students will accomplish during their online, independent review and practice of concepts taught to date. You may choose to sit with students during this time, but these activities were designed with plenty of audio and engaging animation to help them work independently.

Unit Checkpoint

Every fifth lesson in the PhonicsWorks program provides a Unit Checkpoint to help you determine how well students have learned the skills covered in the unit. On Unit Checkpoint days, students begin by spending time online completing review and practice activities. The activities provide a fun, interactive way to review concepts from the unit.

Unit Checkpoints and Answer Keys: You will find the Unit Checkpoint assessment pages in *K¹² PhonicsWorks Assessments.* You will find Answer Keys in the Lesson Guide. You can also print both the Unit Checkpoint pages and the Answer Key from the online lesson.

Please note: Throughout the PhonicsWorks program, the Lesson Guide for Unit Checkpoints contain test exercises that are not listed on students' Unit Checkpoint pages. This is not an error. The exercises printed only in the Lesson Guide are for you to assess students' listening skills. Please follow the directions and note students' verbal responses on the Unit Checkpoint page to use later when scoring the Checkpoint.

After you have scored the Unit Checkpoint, remember to **return to the computer and enter the results**.

"Getting Stronger" Units

After the tenth unit of the Basic course, every other unit is called a "Getting Stronger" unit. These units are designed to strengthen students' skills through review and practice. If students are consistently scoring 100 percent on the Unit Checkpoints in prior units, you may choose to skip the Getting Stronger units. Before skipping the unit, have students take the Unit Checkpoint to make sure they have truly mastered the content. ***Please note: If you choose to skip these units, you will need to return to the computer and mark all the lessons in the unit as "completed."***

Should you skip ahead? Each student learns to read at his or her own pace. This variation is natural and is generally not a cause for concern. We have designed PhonicsWorks to meet the needs of a broad range of students, and we believe most students will benefit from working through all lessons in the program.

While some students might be able to skip some of the Getting Stronger lessons, most students will benefit from the review and practice. This practice helps ensure that they have thoroughly mastered early reading skills and that they are making progress toward achieving what cognitive psychologists call "automaticity." That is, they are on their way to becoming skilled readers who can automatically turn printed letters into their corresponding speech sounds without having to linger over individual letters and sounds. It's like reaching the point in math when students can quickly add and subtract mentally without having to count on their fingers, or in music when they can play "Twinkle, Twinkle, Little Star" on the piano without having to search for the notes.

Most students need repeated review and practice to achieve automaticity. When you come to the Getting Stronger lessons, however, you may feel that students have sufficiently mastered the skills taught in prior lessons. If they are consistently achieving perfect or near-perfect scores on the Unit Checkpoints and if you feel that they will not benefit from further review and practice, then you may skip the Getting Stronger lessons and move to the next unit.

Keep a Portfolio

To document students' progress, we recommend that you keep a portfolio of their work. You can compile a comprehensive portfolio by keeping all of the following items:

- ▶ The box of sight word cards
- ▶ Completed Activity Book pages and Dictation activities
- ▶ Your notes from Try It activities
- ▶ Completed Unit Checkpoint pages

PhonicsWorks Advanced Program: Lesson Components

In the Advanced course, lessons are presented much like the lessons in the Basic course (see above). The first four units of the Advanced course review the content of PhonicsWorks Basic, and the remaining units provide instruction in more advanced phonics concepts, such as blends, long vowels, and difficult spelling patterns.

Sight Words

The first four units of the Advanced course cover the 45 sight words from the Basic course. During this time, students will work on approximately 12 words per week. As in the Basic course, two sets of sight word cards are required. One set can be found in your PhonicsWorks Kit, and you may either make the second set yourself using index cards or print the second set from the online lesson. Here are the other sight words for the Advanced course:

- ▶ too, walk, talk
- ▶ again, out, pull
- ▶ next, my, friend
- ▶ goes, anything, begin
- ▶ down, know, after
- ▶ mother, father, only
- ▶ even, look, gone
- ▶ love, very, some
- ▶ none, more, held
- ▶ would, could, should
- ▶ brother, sister, baby

- ▶ many, animal, while
- ▶ together, people, other
- ▶ above, here, move
- ▶ these, against, now
- ▶ every, neighbor, behind
- ▶ once, come, about
- ▶ please, follow, saw
- ▶ everything, under, whether
- ▶ nothing, over, almost
- ▶ children, write, number
- ▶ because, its, first

The Tile Kit:
Multisensory Instruction

PhonicsWorks lessons incorporate *multisensory* instruction. Lesson activities ask students to look, listen, touch, move, and speak.

The Tile Kit is at the core of this multisensory instruction. The Tile Kit contains letters and letter combinations that represent sounds. Students use the magnetized tiles to manipulate sounds and letters in fun activities that combine visual, auditory, tactile, and oral learning.

How to Use the Tile Kit

The Tile Kit is used for a variety of gentle, interactive procedures, such as "build words," "touch and say," and "word chains." Detailed instructions for these procedures are provided in the lessons. (You can also see the Tile Kit used in the *K¹² PhonicsWorks* DVD.) The more you use the kit, the less you will need to consult the instructions, although the instructions are always available for you to use.

The Tile Kit helps students understand how speech is represented in print. For example, consider how we use the tiles to build the word *chin*. When students first build the word *chin*, they will be guided to select three tiles:

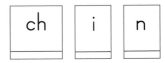

The single sound /ch/ is represented by two letters, *c* and *h*. Because those two letters are printed on a single tile, students get both visual and tactile reinforcement of the simple but important concept that two letters can represent one sound.

Basic Letter Tiles

In the PhonicsWorks Basic course, you receive the Tile Kit, which consists of a binder with pages for the Basic letter tiles. These tiles include the following:

- ► Color tiles
- ► All uppercase (capital) letters
- ► All lowercase letters (multiple tiles provided for each letter)
- ► Digraphs *sh*, *ch*, *th*, *wh*, *ph*, and *ck* and trigraph *tch* (multiple tiles provided for each)
- ► Common word endings –*s*, –*es*, –*ed*, –*ing*, –*er*, and –*est*
- ► Double letter endings –*ff*, –*ll*, –*ss*, –*zz*, and –*all*
- ► Basic punctuation marks: period, question mark, exclamation point, comma, and apostrophe
- ► Vowels printed in red (to provide a visual cue for identifying those letters)

Advanced Letter Tiles

In PhonicsWorks Advanced, you receive the PhonicsWorks Basic course Tile Kit and the Advanced letter tile pages, which include letter tiles with common spellings for sounds that can be spelled in more than one way. The pages are organized to group together the various letters or combinations of letters that represent one sound.

For example, in one section of the binder you will find the following tiles for the long *o* vowel sound:

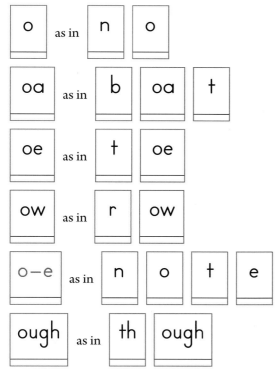

In another section you will find the following tiles to represent the consonant sound /j/:

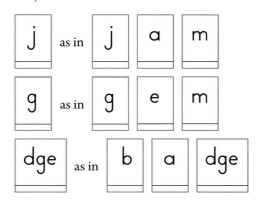

Here is the complete list of what you will receive (some tiles in multiples):

- All PhonicsWorks Basic tiles
- Word endings *ng, ang, ing, ong, ung*
- Word endings *nk, ank, ink, onk, unk*
- Long vowel sound /ā/: *a, e, ai, ay, eigh, a–e, ea*
- Long vowel sound /ē/: *e, e, ee, ea, ie, y, e–e*
- Long vowel sound /ī/: *i, e, ie, y, igh, i–e, y–e*
- Long vowel sound /ō/: *o, e, ow, oa, oe, o–e, ough*
- Long vowel sound /ū/: *u, e, u–e, ew, eu*
- Long double *o* sound (/o͞o/): *oo, e, u, ue, ew, u–e, ough*
- Short double *o* sound (/o͝o/): *oo, u, ou*
- Schwa sound: /ə/
- R-controlled vowels: *ar, or, er, ir, ur, ear, oar, ore*

My Accomplishments! Chart

Research shows that rewarding students for quality work can increase their motivation. To aid you in rewarding students, you will receive a My Accomplishments! chart and sticker sheet for use throughout the course. This chart gives students a tangible and concrete representation of their progress and accomplishments throughout the PhonicsWorks course (and other courses in which they may be enrolled), which they can proudly display and share with others. When students score 80% or above on a Unit Checkpoint, have them add a sticker for that unit to the My Accomplishments! chart. Encourage students to set goals and watch their stickers accumulate. Verbally reinforce their progress to help them understand the connection between their own growing skill set and the My Accomplishments! chart.

How to Correct Errors: "Accentuate the Positive"

All students will make mistakes as they learn to read. They may have to try repeatedly to grasp concepts that strike experienced readers as painfully obvious. When correcting mistakes, we need to remain patient and encouraging.

PhonicsWorks lessons suggest specific phrases for you to use when students make an error. These suggestions are meant to help make the experience of learning to read a positive one that focuses on success.

For example, imagine that you ask students to touch the letter *b* and they touch the letter *d*. You want to avoid a negative (and potentially discouraging) response such as, "No, that's not right. Try again." Instead, say, "You touched the letter *d*. This is the letter *b*. Touch this letter and say *b*." These words inform students that they did indeed touch a letter, and they serve as a reminder of the name of the letter touched. They also provide immediate and gentle guidance about how to give the right answer.

PhonicsWorks Keywords

accent – the emphasis, by stress or pitch, on a word or syllable. For example, in the word *garden*, the accent falls on the first syllable, *gar*.

base word – the part of a word that contains a prefix, suffix, or both. A base word can stand on its own.

blend – a combination of two or three consonants in which you hear the sound of each consonant; for example, the two letters *st* can each be heard in the word *stop*, and the three letters *str* can each be heard in the word *string*.

compound word – a word made from two smaller words (for example, baseball)

decode – the ability to translate written forms into their corresponding speech sounds. For example, students decode when they recognize that *d* represents /d/, *o* represents /ŏ/, *g* represents /g/, and therefore that combination of letters (*d-o-g*) is the word *dog*.

digraph – two letters together that make one sound. For example, the two letters *sh* in the word *fish* make one sound.

onset – the part of a word preceding the first vowel. For example, in the word *smart*, *sm* is the onset.

phonemes – the smallest units of sound. Phonemes are combined to make words.

phonological awareness – the ability to identify and manipulate sound parts in words. The ability to identify similar sounds in words, create rhyming words, and count syllables are all signs of phonological awareness.

rime – the part of a word that includes the first vowel and what follows it. For example, in the word *smart*, *art* is the rime.

schwa – an unstressed vowel indistinct in pronunciation, often similar to short *u*. In the word *garden*, the unstressed syllable *den* contains the schwa sound. In the word *alone*, the unstressed syllable *a* is the schwa sound. The schwa sound is represented by the symbol ə.

trigraph – three letters together that make one sound. For example, the three letters *tch* in the word *match* make one sound.

Review Short Vowels (A)

Unit Overview

In this unit, students will
- ▶ Learn the sight words *two*, *they*, and *both*.
- ▶ Review the short vowel sounds /ă/, /ĕ/, /ĭ/, /ŏ/, and /ŭ/ for the letters *a*, *e*, *i*, *o*, and *u*.
- ▶ Build words.
- ▶ Practice reading and writing.

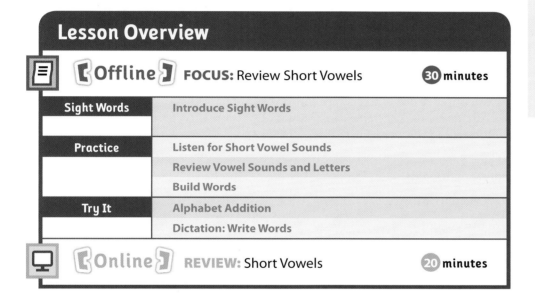

Lesson Overview

Offline FOCUS: Review Short Vowels		**30** minutes
Sight Words	Introduce Sight Words	
Practice	Listen for Short Vowel Sounds	
	Review Vowel Sounds and Letters	
	Build Words	
Try It	Alphabet Addition	
	Dictation: Write Words	
Online REVIEW: Short Vowels		**20** minutes

Advance Preparation

If you have not already done so, create a second set of the sight words cards either by writing words on 3½ x 5-inch index cards (the list of words can be found in the Sight Words section of the Lesson Guide introduction) or printing a set from the online lesson. In addition, you will be instructed throughout the semester to make a series of word cards for individual activities. Save these cards for further use.

 **30 minutes**

FOCUS: Review Short Vowels

Work **together** with students to complete offline Sight Words, Practice, and Try It activities.

Sight Words

Introduce Sight Words

Help students learn the sight words *two*, *they*, and *both*.

1. Gather the sight word cards *two*, *they*, and *both*.

2. Show students the *two* card.

3. **Say:** This is the word *two*, as in the number *two*. We see this word so often that we want to be able to read and spell it quickly without thinking about it. Look closely at the word *two*. Spell the word *two* aloud. Take a picture of the word *two* in your mind. When you think you can spell *two* yourself, turn the card over and use your letter tiles to spell the word *two*. Check the card to see if you spelled the word *two* correctly. Read aloud the word you spelled with the letter tiles.

4. Repeat the activity with the remaining sight words.

5. Chart students' progress on the back of each card.

   ► Divide the back of the card into two columns.
   ► Label the first column "Read" and the second column "Spell."
   ► Record the dates that students read or spell the word correctly. When students can read and spell the word correctly three times in a row, they have mastered the word. You may want to put a star or sticker on their card when they have mastered that word.

6. Add the cards to students' sight words box.

 Sight words can be very difficult for some students. It's important to let students work at their own pace and really master these words, as they occur frequently in reading and writing.

Objectives
- Read sight words.
- Spell sight words.

Practice

Listen for Short Vowel Sounds

Say words with the sounds /ă/, /ĕ/, /ĭ/, /ŏ/, and /ŭ/ to help students identify the difference between short vowels sounds in words.

1. **Say:** I'm going to say a word. You'll listen for the **vowel sounds /ă/, /ĕ/, /ĭ/, /ŏ/, or /ŭ/** in the word. Tell me the vowel sound that you hear. For example, if I say *mop*, you'll say /ŏ/ because the vowel sound you hear in *mop* is /ŏ/.

2. Guide students with these questions if they have difficulty identifying the vowel sound:
   - ▶ What is the sound you hear in the middle of the word? Answers will vary.
   - ▶ Do you hear the sound [target sound] in the word? Listen to the word [target word] again.
   - ▶ Can you think of another word that has the sound [target sound]? Answers will vary.

3. Say each word. Have students identify the vowel sound in the word.
   - ▶ *pit* /ĭ/
   - ▶ *Pam* /ă/
   - ▶ *pun* /ŭ/
   - ▶ *pop* /ŏ/
   - ▶ *got* /ŏ/
   - ▶ *vet* /ĕ/
   - ▶ *sat* /ă/
   - ▶ *red* /ĕ/
   - ▶ *fun* /ŭ/
   - ▶ *sip* /ĭ/

Objectives
- Identify short vowel sounds.
- Identify and use the sound /ă/.
- Identify and use the sound /ĕ/.
- Identify and use the sound /ĭ/.
- Identify and use the sound /ŏ/.
- Identify and use the sound /ŭ/.
- Given the letter, identify the most common sound.
- Given the sound, identify the most common letter or letters.
- Blend sounds to create words.
- Identify individual sounds in words.
- Write words by applying grade-level phonics knowledge.

Review Vowel Sounds and Letters

Help students review vowel sounds and letters.

1. Place the following letter tiles on students' whiteboard: *a, e, i, o,* and *u,* plus any letters that are confusing for them.

2. **Say:** I am going to point to each letter. Tell me a sound for that letter.

3. **Say:** I am going to say a sound. Repeat the sound and touch its letter.

4. Point to some letters two or three times, so students don't think that once they have named a sound they are finished with it.

5. Redirect students if they name the letter and not its sound.

   Say: You are right that the name of the letter is [letter]. We want the sound for this letter. What is the sound?

6. Redirect students if they name the sound incorrectly.

   Say: That is the sound of another letter.

7. Provide additional guidance if students touch the wrong letter tile during the review.

   Say: That is the letter tile for the sound [sound for incorrect letter tile]. We are looking for the letter tile for the sound [target sound].

8. If students touch the wrong letter again, point to the correct letter.

   Say: This is the letter tile for the sound [target sound]. Touch this letter tile and say its sound.

Build Words
Help students use letters and sounds to build words.

1. Place the following letter tiles at the top of students' whiteboard: *a, e, g, i, n, o, p, s, t,* and *u.*

2. Draw three horizontal lines across the middle of students' whiteboard to represent the sounds in a word.

3. **Say:** Let's use letters and sounds to build the word *top.*

4. Have students finger stretch the sounds in *top.*

5. Have students

   ▸ Identify the first, next, and last sounds in *top.*
   ▸ Choose the corresponding letter for each of the sounds.
   ▸ Move the letters to the correct lines on their whiteboard.

6. Guide students with these questions:

   ▸ What is the first sound in *top*? /t/
     Which line does the letter for that sound go on? the first one
   ▸ What is the next sound in *top*? /ŏ/
     Which line does the letter for that sound go on? the second one
   ▸ What's the last sound in *top*? /p/
     Which line does the letter for that sound go on? the last one

7. Redirect students if they select the incorrect letter.

   Say: That sound is in the word [word], and it is the [first, second, third] sound. We want the sound [target sound].

   Continue until students select the correct letter.

8. Have students touch and say the word.

9. Have them say the word as they use a dry-erase marker to write the word on the whiteboard.

10. Repeat the activity to build the following words:

    ▸ *pat* /p/ /ă/ /t/
    ▸ *sip* /s/ /ĭ/ /p/
    ▸ *pen* /p/ /ĕ/ /n/
    ▸ *tug* /t/ /ŭ/ /g/

Try It

Alphabet Addition

Have students complete page PH 53 in *K¹² PhonicsWorks Basic Activity Book* for more practice with words that have short vowel sounds. First have students add the parts of the word together to make a new word. Then have them write the word, read the word aloud, and read the silly sentence.

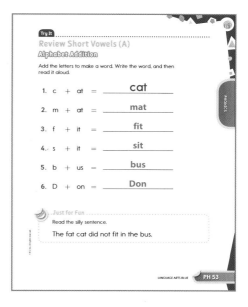

Dictation: Write Words

Have students practice identifying sounds and writing words.

1. Gather a pencil and the dictation notebook. Say the word *pet*. Then give these directions to students:

   ▶ Repeat the word.
   ▶ Write the word in your notebook.
   ▶ Read the word aloud.

2. When students have finished, write the following word on your whiteboard: *pet*.

3. Have them compare their answer to your correct version.

4. Repeat this procedure with the words *tug* and *sit*.

   ▶ If students make an error and don't see it, help them correct their mistake by having them finger stretch the sounds in the word they missed.
   ▶ If students are having difficulty selecting the correct letters or sounds, review those letters or sounds that are confusing them.
   ▶ If students have difficulty with first, middle, and last sounds, have them finger stretch the sounds in words.

 **20 minutes**

REVIEW: Short Vowels

Students will work online independently to

▸ Practice the short vowel sounds /ă/, /ĕ/, /ĭ/, /ŏ/, and /ŭ/ made by the letters *a*, *e*, *i*, *o*, and *u*.

▸ Practice decoding text by reading a story.

Help students locate the online activities and provide support as needed.

Offline Alternative

No computer access? Have students point out and name things or words that contain the short vowel sounds /ă/, /ĕ/, /ĭ/, /ŏ/, and /ŭ/, such as *cap*, *pet*, *kit*, *top*, and *rug*. You might also ask students to spell simple words that contain the sounds /ă/, /ĕ/, /ĭ/, /ŏ/, and /ŭ/ made by the letters *a*, *e*, *i*, *o*, and *u* and other letters they have learned.

Objectives

- Identify short vowel sounds.
- Given the letter, identify the most common sound.
- Given the sound, identify the most common letter or letters.
- Identify and use the sound /ă/.
- Identify and use the sound /ĕ/.
- Identify and use the sound /ĭ/.
- Identify and use the sound /ŏ/.
- Identify and use the sound /ŭ/.
- Identify individual sounds in words.
- Read aloud grade-level text with appropriate automaticity, prosody, accuracy, and rate.
- Decode words by applying grade-level word analysis skills.

Review Short Vowels (B)

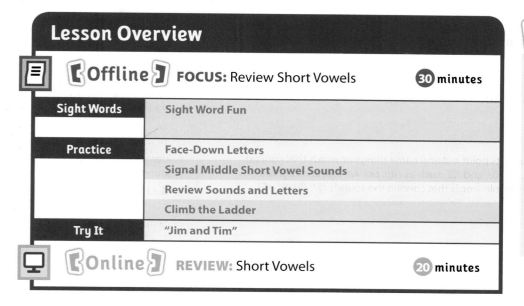

Lesson Overview

Offline FOCUS: Review Short Vowels — **30** minutes

Sight Words	Sight Word Fun
Practice	Face-Down Letters
	Signal Middle Short Vowel Sounds
	Review Sounds and Letters
	Climb the Ladder
Try It	"Jim and Tim"

Online REVIEW: Short Vowels — **20** minutes

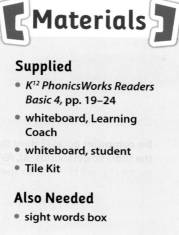

Materials

Supplied
- *K¹² PhonicsWorks Readers Basic 4*, pp. 19–24
- whiteboard, Learning Coach
- whiteboard, student
- Tile Kit

Also Needed
- sight words box

Advance Preparation

Place lowercase letter tiles in alphabetical order on your whiteboard.

 **Offline** **30 minutes**

FOCUS: Review Short Vowels

Work **together** with students to complete offline Sight Words, Practice, and Try It activities.

Sight Words •

Sight Word Fun

Help students learn the sight words *two, they,* and *both,* and up to two additional sight words they have yet to master.

1. Gather the sight word cards *two, they,* and *both,* and up to two additional sight word cards.

2. Choose one sight word card to begin.

   Say: Look at this word and take a picture of it in your mind. When you think you can spell the word yourself, turn the card over and use your letter tiles to spell the word.

3. After students spell the word, have them check the card to see if they spelled the word correctly.

   Say: Read aloud the word you spelled with the letter tiles.

4. Repeat the activity with the remaining sight words.

   TIP Sight words can be very difficult for some students. Let students work at their own pace and really master these words.

Objectives
- Read sight words.
- Spell sight words.

Practice ••

Face-Down Letters

To help students master the ability to recognize the letters of the alphabet, have them practice identifying and naming letters. Grab your whiteboard with letters placed in alphabetical order.

1. Lay your whiteboard down on a flat surface and flip over the letter tiles *e, h, j, n, o, s, v,* and *x* so they are face down on the whiteboard.

2. **Say:** These letters are face down. We are looking at the back of them. Name each letter and then turn it over to see if you were right.

TIP If students miss any of the letters, have them turn over the missed ones and try again.

Signal Middle Short Vowel Sounds

Use a special signal to help students identify **middle short vowel sounds** in words.

1. **Say:** I'm going to tell you a special sound, and then I'll say some words. Repeat each word I say and make a special signal to tell me where the special sound is. If the special vowel sound is at the middle of the word, clap your hands. If the special vowel sound is **not** at the middle of the word, just smile at me. For example,

   ▸ If I ask you to listen for the sound /ă/ and I say the word *mat*, you'll repeat the word *mat* and clap your hands because *mat* has the sound /ă/ in the middle.

   ▸ If I say the word *pop*, you'll repeat the word *pop* and smile at me because *pop* has the sound /ŏ/, not /ă/, in the middle.

2. Say each sound and group of words. Have students make the special signal to identify the middle sound.

   ▸ /ŏ/: *tan, hop, gas, tot, cog, tin* clap: *hop, tot, cog*
   ▸ /ĭ/: *pit, set, sat, sit* clap: *pit, sit*
   ▸ /ă/: *gas, had, jet, hop, tag* clap: *gas, had, tag*
   ▸ /ŭ/: *sop, sun, fed, bud, tug* clap: *sun, bud, tug*

3. Guide students with these questions if they have difficulty identifying the vowel sound:

   ▸ What is the sound you hear in the middle of the word? Answers will vary.
   ▸ Do you hear the sound [target sound] in the word? Listen to the word [target word] again.
   ▸ Can you think of another word that has the sound [target sound]? Answers will vary.

TIP If students can't identify the middle sound of each word, say the word again and emphasize the middle sound by stretching it out (for example, *baaaaat*). If necessary, have students look at your mouth while you stretch the sounds.

Objectives

- Identify letters of the alphabet.
- Identify middle sounds in words.
- Identify short vowel sounds.
- Identify and use the sound /ă/.
- Identify and use the sound /ĕ/.
- Identify and use the sound /ĭ/.
- Identify and use the sound /ŏ/.
- Identify and use the sound /ŭ/.
- Given the letter, identify the most common sound.
- Given the sound, identify the most common letter or letters.
- Identify the new word when one sound is changed in a word.
- Identify words that rhyme.

Review Sounds and Letters

Help students review sounds for the letters *m, n, o, p, qu, r, s, t, u, v, w, x, y,* and *z,* plus any letters that are confusing for them.

1. Place the following letter tiles in random order on students' whiteboard: *m, n, o, p, qu, r, s, t, u, v, w, x, y,* and *z,* plus any letters that are confusing.

2. **Say:** Let's go over some letters and sounds.

3. Point to each letter tile and have students say a sound that letter or letters make.

   - *x* /ks/
   - *n* /n/
   - *z* /z/
   - *p* /p/
   - *t* /t/
   - *r* /r/
   - *s* /s/

   - *qu* /kw/
   - *u* /ŭ/
   - *v* /v/
   - *w* /w/
   - *m* /m/
   - *y* /y/
   - *o* /ŏ/

4. Say each of the following sounds. Have students repeat the sound and touch the corresponding letter tile.

   - /ks/ *x*
   - /n/ *n*
   - /z/ *z*
   - /p/ *p*
   - /t/ *t*
   - /r/ *r*
   - /s/ *s*

   - /kw/ *qu*
   - /ŭ/ *u*
   - /v/ *v*
   - /w/ *w*
   - /m/ *m*
   - /y/ *y*
   - /ŏ/ *o*

5. As you do the activity, point to some letter tiles two or three times so that students don't think they are finished with a sound after they have named it.

6. Redirect students if they say an incorrect sound when you point to a letter tile.

   Say: That's the sound of another letter. What is the sound for this letter?

7. Help students if they touch the wrong letter tile after they repeat a sound.

   Say: That letter goes with the sound [sound for incorrect letter tile]. We're looking for the letter that goes with the sound [target sound].

Climb the Ladder

Help students use letters to build words.

1. On students' whiteboard or a sheet of paper, draw a ladder with five or more rungs.

2. Write the word *man* on the bottom rung.

3. Point to the word *man*.

   Say: I can make the word *pan* by changing one letter in this word.

4. Write the word *pan* on the second rung of the ladder.

   Say: Think of a word that you can make by changing only one letter in *pan*. Tell me the word and write it on the next step on the ladder.

5. If students struggle, coach them to change the first letter in each word.

   Say: Read the word on the bottom rung. What sound do you hear at the beginning of the word? What letter has that sound?

   Say: Name a word that rhymes with the word at the bottom. What sound do you hear at the beginning of the rhyming word? What letter has that sound? Make a new word by using the new letter. Read the new word.

6. Continue the process until students reach the top of the ladder. Remind students that they may change only one sound: the beginning, middle, or last sound.

7. Redirect students if they select a word that changes more than one letter.

   Say: How many letters changed from the last word to your new word? Try to think of a word that has only one letter change.

8. Redirect students if they spell a word incorrectly, but the sounds they spell are correct (such as *ruf* for *rough*).

   Say: You have the sounds and letters right, but that word doesn't follow our spelling rules. We will learn how to spell it later. Try another word.

(TIP) If students have difficulty thinking of real words, have them use nonsense words.

Try It

"Jim and Tim"

Have students read "Jim and Tim" on page 19 of *K¹² PhonicsWorks Readers Basic 4.*

   Students should read the story silently once or twice before reading the story aloud. When students miss a word that can be sounded out, point to it and give them three to six seconds to try the word again. If students still miss the word, tell them the word so the flow of the story isn't interrupted.

   After reading the story, make a list of all the words students missed, and go over those words with them. You may use letter tiles to show students how to read the words.

Objectives

- Read aloud grade-level text with appropriate automaticity, prosody, accuracy, and rate.
- Decode words by applying grade-level word analysis skills.
- Track text from left to right.
- Turn pages sequentially.

 **20 minutes**

REVIEW: Short Vowels

Students will work online independently to

▶ Practice the short vowel sounds /ă/, /ĕ/, /ĭ/, /ŏ/, and /ŭ/ for the letters *a, e, i, o,* and *u.*

Help students locate the online activities and provide support as needed.

Offline Alternative

No computer access? Have students point out and name things or words that begin with the short vowel sounds /ă/, /ĕ/, /ĭ/, /ŏ/, and /ŭ/, such as *and, egg, it, on,* and *up.* You might also ask students to spell simple words that contain the sounds /ă/, /ĕ/, /ĭ/, /ŏ/, and /ŭ/ made by the letters *a, e, i, o,* and *u* and other letters they have learned.

 Objectives

- Identify short vowel sounds.
- Given the letter, identify the most common sound.
- Given the sound, identify the most common letter or letters.
- Identify and use the sound /ă/.
- Identify and use the sound /ĕ/.
- Identify and use the sound /ĭ/.
- Identify and use the sound /ŏ/.
- Identify and use the sound /ŭ/.
- Identify individual sounds in words.

Review Short Vowels (C)

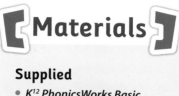
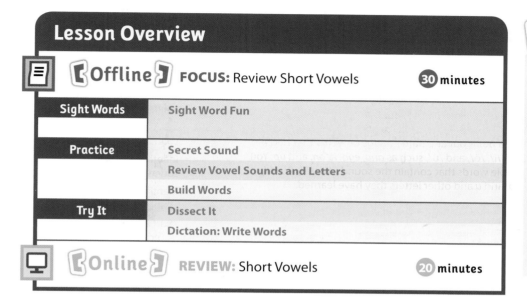

Lesson Overview

☰ 〖 Offline 〗 **FOCUS:** Review Short Vowels   **30** minutes

Sight Words	Sight Word Fun
Practice	Secret Sound
	Review Vowel Sounds and Letters
	Build Words
Try It	Dissect It
	Dictation: Write Words

💻 〖 Online 〗 **REVIEW:** Short Vowels   **20** minutes

〖 Materials 〗

Supplied
- *K¹² PhonicsWorks Basic Activity Book*, p. PH 54
- whiteboard, Learning Coach
- whiteboard, student
- Tile Kit

Also Needed
- sight words box
- dictation notebook

 **Offline** 🔟 **minutes**

FOCUS: Review Short Vowels

Work **together** with students to complete offline Sight Words, Practice, and
Try It activities.

Sight Words •

Sight Word Fun

Help students learn the sight words *two, they,* and *both,* and up to two additional sight
words they have yet to master.

1. Gather the sight word cards *two, they,* and *both,* and up to two additional sight
   word cards.

2. Choose one sight word card to begin.

   Say: Look at this word and take a picture of it in your mind. When you think
   you can spell the word yourself, turn the card over and use your letter tiles to
   spell the word.

3. After students spell the word, have them check the card to see if they spelled
   the word correctly.

   Say: Read aloud the word you spelled with the letter tiles.

4. Repeat the activity with the remaining sight words.

   TIP Sight words can be very difficult for some students. Let students work at their
   own pace and really master these words.

Objectives
- Read sight words.
- Spell sight words.

Practice ••

Secret Sound

Say groups of words to help students recognize **middle sounds** in words.

1. **Say:** I am going to say some groups of words. Listen for a secret sound in the middle of each word. Then tell me what sound you hear in the middle of each group of words.

2. Say each of the following groups of words. Have students identify the secret sound in each group.

   ▸ *sip, lid, nit, rip* /ĭ/
   ▸ *pat, gas, nap, sad* /ă/
   ▸ *tub, gut, sub, buff* /ŭ/
   ▸ *pop, hot, fog, sop* /ŏ/
   ▸ *get, Ted, bed, red* /ĕ/

TIP If students can't identify the secret sound, have them listen while you say each word again and then have them repeat each word. Have them say what sound they hear in the middle of each word.

Review Vowel Sounds and Letters

Help students review vowel sounds and letters.

1. Place the following letter tiles on students' whiteboard: *a, e, i, o,* and *u,* plus any letters that are confusing for them.

2. **Say:** I am going to point to each letter. Tell me a sound for that letter.

3. **Say:** I am going to say a sound. Repeat the sound and touch its letter.

4. Point to some letters two or three times, so students don't think that once they have named a sound they are finished with it.

5. Redirect students if they name the letter and not its sound.

   Say: You are right that the name of the letter is [letter]. We want the sound for this letter. What is the sound?

6. Redirect students if they name the sound incorrectly.

   Say: That is the sound of another letter.

7. Provide additional guidance if students touch the wrong letter tile during the review.

   Say: That is the letter for the sound [sound for incorrect letter tile]. We are looking for the letter for the sound [target sound].

8. If students touch the wrong letter again, point to the correct letter.

   Say: This is the letter tile for the sound [target sound]. Touch this letter tile and say its sound.

Objectives

- Identify middle sounds in words.
- Identify short vowel sounds.
- Identify and use the sound /ă/.
- Identify and use the sound /ĕ/.
- Identify and use the sound /ĭ/.
- Identify and use the sound /ŏ/.
- Identify and use the sound /ŭ/.
- Given the letter, identify the most common sound.
- Given the sound, identify the most common letter or letters.
- Identify the new word when one sound is changed in a word.
- Identify individual sounds in words.
- Write words by applying grade-level phonics knowledge.

Build Words

Help students use letters and sounds to build words.

1. Place the following letter tiles at the top of students' whiteboard: *a, b, d, e, g, m, o, r, s,* and *u.*

2. Draw three horizontal lines across the middle of students' whiteboard to represent the sounds in a word.

3. **Say:** Let's use letters and sounds to build the word *beg.*

4. Have students finger stretch the sounds in *beg.*

5. Have students
   ▶ Identify the first, next, and last sounds in *beg.*
   ▶ Choose the corresponding letter for each of the sounds.
   ▶ Move the letters to the correct lines on students' whiteboard.

6. Guide students with these questions:
   ▶ What is the first sound in *beg*? /b/
      Which line does the letter for that sound go on? the first one
   ▶ What is the next sound in *beg*? /ĕ/
      Which line does the letter for that sound go on? the second one
   ▶ What's the last sound in *beg*? /g/
      Which line does the letter for that sound go on? the last one

7. Redirect students if they select the incorrect letter.

   Say: That sound is in the word [word], and it is the [first, second, third] sound. We want the sound [target sound].

   Continue until students select the correct letter.

8. Have students touch and say the word.

9. Have them say the word as they use a dry-erase marker to write the word on the whiteboard.

10. Repeat the activity to build the following words:
    ▶ *sad* /s/ /ă/ /d/
    ▶ *gum* /g/ /ŭ/ /m/
    ▶ *rod* /r/ /ŏ/ /d/

Try It

Dissect It

Have students complete page PH 54 in *K¹² PhonicsWorks Basic Activity Book* for more practice identifying vowels. Have students draw a circle around the vowel, read the word aloud, and write the word. Finally have them read the word aloud again.

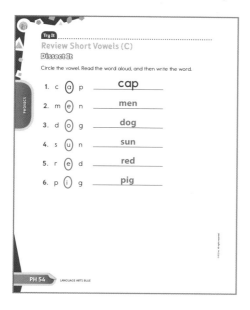

Dictation: Write Words

Have students practice identifying sounds and writing words.

1. Gather a pencil and the dictation notebook. Say the word *gum*. Then give these directions to students:

   ► Repeat the word.
   ► Write the word in your notebook.
   ► Read the word aloud.

2. When students have finished, write the following word on your whiteboard: *gum*.

3. Have them compare their answer to your correct version.

4. Repeat this procedure with the words *rod* and *pig*.

   ► If students make an error and don't see it, help them correct their mistake by having them finger stretch the sounds in the word they missed.
   ► If students are having difficulty selecting the correct letters or sounds, review those letters or sounds that are confusing them.
   ► If students have difficulty with first, middle, and last sounds, have them finger stretch the sounds in words.

 **minutes**

REVIEW: **Short Vowels**

Students will work online independently to

▶ Practice the short vowel sounds /ă/, /ĕ/, /ĭ/, /ŏ/, and /ŭ/ for the letters *a, e, i, o,* and *u.*

▶ Practice decoding text by reading a story.

Help students locate the online activities and provide support as needed.

Offline Alternative

No computer access? Have students point out and name things or words that begin with the short vowel sounds /ă/, /ĕ/, /ĭ/, /ŏ/, and /ŭ/, such as *and, egg, it, on,* and *up.* You might also ask students to spell simple words that contain the sounds /ă/, /ĕ/, /ĭ/, /ŏ/, and /ŭ/ made by the letters *a, e, i, o,* and *u* and other letters they have learned.

Objectives

- Identify short vowel sounds.
- Given the letter, identify the most common sound.
- Given the sound, identify the most common letter or letters.
- Identify and use the sound /ă/.
- Identify and use the sound /ĕ/.
- Identify and use the sound /ĭ/.
- Identify and use the sound /ŏ/.
- Identify and use the sound /ŭ/.
- Identify individual sounds in words.
- Read aloud grade-level text with appropriate automaticity, prosody, accuracy, and rate.
- Decode words by applying grade-level word analysis skills.

Review Short Vowels (D)

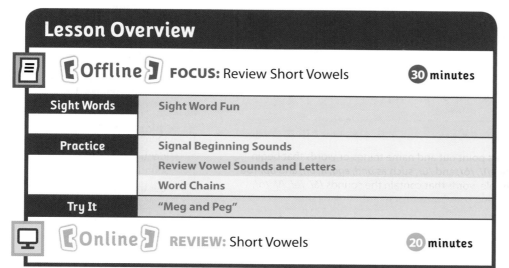

Lesson Overview

Offline **FOCUS:** Review Short Vowels — **30** minutes

Sight Words	Sight Word Fun
Practice	Signal Beginning Sounds
	Review Vowel Sounds and Letters
	Word Chains
Try It	"Meg and Peg"

Online **REVIEW:** Short Vowels — **20** minutes

Materials

Supplied
- *K¹² PhonicsWorks Readers Basic 4*, pp. 25–30
- whiteboard, student
- Tile Kit

Also Needed
- sight words box

 **Offline** **30 minutes**

FOCUS: Review Short Vowels

Work **together** with students to complete offline Sight Words, Practice, and Try It activities.

Practice ·

Sight Word Fun

Help students learn the sight words *two*, *they*, and *both*, and up to two additional sight words them have yet to master.

1. Gather the sight word cards *two*, *they*, and *both*, and up to two additional sight word cards.

2. Choose one sight word card to begin.

   Say: Look at this word and take a picture of it in your mind. When you think you can spell the word yourself, turn the card over and use your letter tiles to spell the word.

3. After students spell the word, have them check the card to see if they spelled the word correctly.

   Say: Read aloud the word you spelled with the letter tiles.

4. Repeat the activity with the remaining sight words.

TIP Sight words can be very difficult for some students. Let students work at their own pace and really master these words.

 Objectives
- Read sight words.
- Spell sight words.

Practice ••

Signal Beginning Sounds

Use a special signal to help students identify **beginning sounds** in words.

1. **Say:** I'm going to tell you a special sound, and then I'll say some words. Repeat each word I say and make a special signal to tell me where the special sound is. If the special sound is at the beginning of the word, tug your ear. If the special sound is **not** at the beginning of the word, just smile at me. For example,

   ▸ If I ask you to listen for the sound /ă/ and I say the word *apple*, you'll repeat the word *apple* and tug your ear because *apple* has the sound /ă/ at the beginning.

   ▸ If I say the word *odd*, you'll repeat the word *odd* and smile at me because *odd* has the sound /ŏ/, not /ă/, at the beginning.

2. Say each sound and group of words. Have students make the special signal to identify the beginning sound.

   ▸ /ă/: *antics, ask, end, into, asp* tug ear: *antics, ask, asp*
   ▸ /ĕ/: *edge, Edward, Ellen, Ollie, octopus* tug ear: *edge, Edward, Ellen*
   ▸ /ĭ/: *into, elbow, igloo, is, if* tug ear: *into, igloo, is, if*
   ▸ /ŭ/: *offer, under, up, ugly, egg,* tug ear: *under, up, ugly*
   ▸ /ŏ/: *under, operation, otter, antics, off* tug ear: *operation, otter, off*

TIP If students can't identify the beginning sound of each word, say the word again and emphasize the beginning sound by repeating it three times (for example, /t/ /t/ /t/, *taste*). You can also draw out the beginning sound when you say the word (for example, *mmmommy*). If necessary, have students look at your mouth while you repeat the sounds.

Review Vowel Sounds and Letters

Help students review vowel sounds and letters.

1. Place the following letter tiles on students' whiteboard: *a, b, c, d, e, f, g, h, i, j, k,* and *l,* plus any letters that are confusing for them.

2. **Say:** I am going to point to each letter. Tell me a sound for that letter.

3. **Say:** I am going to say a sound. Repeat the sound and touch its letter. Tell me whether the sound is a vowel or a consonant. vowels: *a, e,* and *i*   consonants: *b, c, d, f, g, h, j, k,* and *l*

4. Point to some letters two or three times, so students don't think that once they have named a sound they are finished with it.

5. Redirect students if they name the letter and not its sound.

   Say: You are right that the name of the letter is [letter]. We want the sound for this letter. What is the sound?

Objectives

- Identify beginning sounds in words.
- Identify short vowel sounds.
- Identify and distinguish between and consonants and vowels.
- Given the letter or letters, identify the most common sound.
- Given the sound, identify the most common letter or letters.
- Identify the new word when one sound is changed in a word.
- Identify individual sounds in words.

6. Redirect students if they name the sound incorrectly.

   Say: That is the sound of another letter.

7. Provide additional guidance if students touch the wrong letter tile during the review.

   Say: That is the letter tile for the sound [sound for incorrect letter tile]. We are looking for the letter tile for the sound [target sound].

8. If students touch the wrong letter tile again, point to the correct letter.

   Say: This is the letter tile for the sound [target sound]. Touch this letter tile and say its sound.

Word Chains

Have students build words by adding and changing letters to help them recognize and use individual sounds in words.

1. Place the following letters at the top of students' whiteboard: *a, b, d, e, h, i, m, o, s, t,* and *u.*

2. **Say:** I am going to build the first word in a chain. The word is *ham.*

   ‣ I will pull down the letters for the sounds /h/, /ă/, and /m/ to spell the word *ham.*

   ‣ I will touch and say *ham.* To change *ham* to *hat,* I will think about which sound is changed from the word *ham* to *hat.* I will need to replace the letter *m* at the end of the word with the letter *t.*

   ‣ Touch and say the word *hat.* Now it's your turn to change *hat* to *pat.* You can spell *hot* by making only one change. Touch and say the new word.

3. Redirect students if they select the incorrect letter for any sound.

   Say: That letter is for the sound [incorrect sound]. We want the letter for the sound [target sound]. What letter makes that sound? Answers will vary.

4. Redirect students if they name the sound incorrectly.

   Say: To change the word [first word] to [target word], we need the letter for the sound [target sound].

   Show students how to make the change. Have them touch and say the new word after they move the letters.

5. Follow this procedure to make the following words: *hut, hit, hid, bid, bed, bad, sad.*

6. For every new word, have students add, replace, or remove only one letter.

TIP If students struggle, review the sounds and letters that are confusing them.

Try It

"Meg and Peg"

Have students read "Meg and Peg" on page 25 of *K¹² PhonicsWorks Readers Basic 4.*

    Students should read the story silently once or twice before reading the story aloud. When students miss a word that can be sounded out, point to it and give them three to six seconds to try the word again. If students still miss the word, tell them the word so the flow of the story isn't interrupted.

    After reading the story, make a list of all the words students missed, and go over those words with them. You may use letter tiles to show students how to read the words.

Objectives

- Read aloud grade-level text with appropriate automaticity, prosody, accuracy, and rate.
- Decode words by applying grade-level word analysis skills.
- Track text from left to right.
- Turn pages sequentially.

Online   20 minutes

REVIEW: Short Vowels

Students will work online independently to

▸ Practice the short vowel sounds /ă/, /ĕ/, /ĭ/, /ŏ/, and /ŭ/ for the letters *a, e, i, o,* and *u.*

Help students locate the online activities and provide support as needed.

Objectives

- Identify short vowel sounds.
- Given the letter, identify the most common sound.
- Given the sound, identify the most common letter or letters.
- Identify and use the sound /ă/.
- Identify and use the sound /ĕ/.
- Identify and use the sound /ĭ/.
- Identify and use the sound /ŏ/.
- Identify and use the sound /ŭ/.
- Identify individual sounds in words.

Offline Alternative

No computer access? Have students point out and name things or words that contain with the short vowel sounds /ă/, /ĕ/, /ĭ/, /ŏ/, and /ŭ/, such as *jam, pen, hip, job,* and *tub.* You might also ask students to spell simple words that contain the sounds /ă/, /ĕ/, /ĭ/, /ŏ/, and /ŭ/ made by the letters *a, e, i, o,* and *u* and other letters they have learned.

Unit Checkpoint

Lesson Overview

 **Online** REVIEW: Short Vowels **20** minutes

Offline UNIT CHECKPOINT: Review Short Vowels **30** minutes

Materials

Supplied

- K¹² PhonicsWorks Basic Assessments, pp. PH 103–108

Objectives

- Identify and use the sound /ă/.
- Identify and use the sound /ĕ/.
- Identify and use the sound /ĭ/.
- Identify and use the sound /ŏ/.
- Identify and use the sound /ŭ/.
- Identify and use vowels and vowel sounds.
- Identify short vowel sounds.
- Read, write, and spell words containing short vowel sounds.
- Identify individual sounds in words.
- Given the letter or letters, identify the most common sound.
- Given the sound, identify the most common letter or letters.
- Read instructional-level text with 90% accuracy.
- Read aloud grade-level text with appropriate automaticity, prosody, accuracy, and rate.
- Write words by applying grade-level phonics knowledge.
- Write sight words.
- Read sight words.

Online **20** minutes

REVIEW: **Short Vowels**

Students will review short vowel sounds to prepare for the Unit Checkpoint. Help students locate the online activities and provide support as needed.

 **30 minutes**

UNIT CHECKPOINT: Review Short Vowels

Explain that students are going to show what they have learned about sounds, letters, and words.

1. Give students the Unit Checkpoint pages for the Review Short Vowels unit and print the Unit Checkpoint Answer Key, if you'd like.

2. Use the instructions below to help administer the Checkpoint to students. On the Answer Key or another sheet of paper, note student answers to oral response questions to help with scoring the Checkpoint later.

3. Use the Answer Key to score the Checkpoint, and then enter the results online.

Part 1. Say Sounds Have students read across the rows from left to right and say a sound that each letter makes. Note any sounds they say incorrectly.

Part 2. Word Dissection For each word, say the sound students should identify. Have them read the word aloud and circle the letter or group of letters that spells the requested sound.

19. *middle sound*

20. *ending sound*

21. *beginning sound*

22. *ending sound*

23. *middle sound*

Part 3. Finger Stretching Say each word to students. Have them say each word and finger stretch the sounds. Note any words they finger stretch incorrectly.

24. *Rex*　　　　　　　　27. *top*

25. *pan*　　　　　　　　28. *mug*

26. *wet*

Part 4. Dictation Say each word to students. Have them repeat and write the word.

29. *fit*　　　　　　　　31. *cut*

30. *mad*　　　　　　　　32. *pop*

Part 5. Read Aloud Listen to students read the sentences aloud. Count and note the number of words they read correctly.

Part 6. Say Letters Say each sound. Have students say a letter or letters that make that sound. Note any incorrect responses.

34. /w/

35. /d/

36. /ĭ/

37. /y/

38. /z/

39. /ă/

40. /b/

41. /k/

42. /v/

43. /ŭ/

44. /f/

45. /ŏ/

46. /p/

47. /r/

48. /ĕ/

49. /kw/

50. /z/

51. /t/

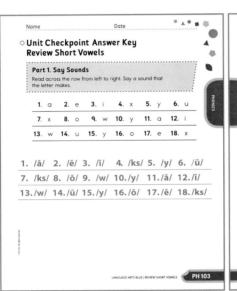

Unit Checkpoint Answer Key
Review Short Vowels

Part 1. Say Sounds
Read across the row from left to right. Say a sound that the letter makes.

1. a   2. e   3. i   4. x   5. y   6. u
7. x   8. o   9. w   10. y   11. a   12. i
13. w   14. u   15. y   16. o   17. e   18. x

1. /ă/   2. /ĕ/   3. /ĭ/   4. /ks/   5. /y/   6. /ŭ/
7. /ks/   8. /ŏ/   9. /w/   10. /y/   11. /ă/   12. /ĭ/
13. /w/   14. /ŭ/   15. /y/   16. /ŏ/   17. /ĕ/   18. /ks/

PH 103

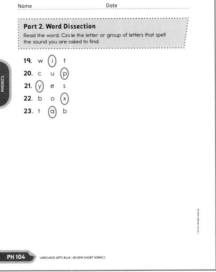

Part 2. Word Dissection
Read the word. Circle the letter or group of letters that spell the sound you are asked to find.

19. w (i) t
20. c u (p)
21. (y) e s
22. b o (x)
23. t (a) b

PH 104

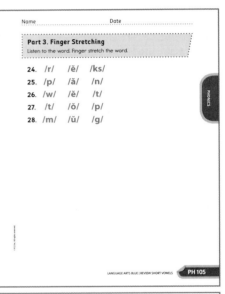

Part 3. Finger Stretching
Listen to the word. Finger stretch the word.

24. /r/   /ĕ/   /ks/
25. /p/   /ă/   /n/
26. /w/   /ĕ/   /t/
27. /t/   /ŏ/   /p/
28. /m/   /ŭ/   /g/

PH 105

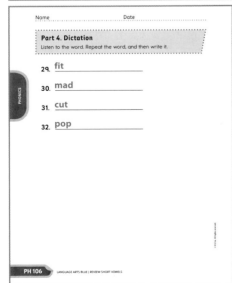

Part 4. Dictation
Listen to the word. Repeat the word, and then write it.

29. fit
30. mad
31. cut
32. pop

PH 106

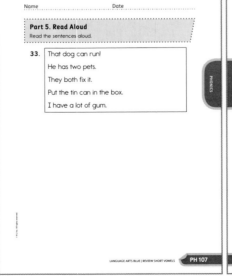

Part 5. Read Aloud
Read the sentences aloud.

33. That dog can run!
He has two pets.
They both fix it.
Put the tin can in the box.
I have a lot of gum.

PH 107

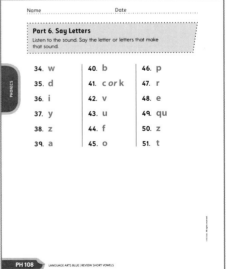

Part 6. Say Letters
Listen to the sound. Say the letter or letters that make that sound.

34. w   40. b   46. p
35. d   41. c or k   47. r
36. i   42. v   48. e
37. y   43. u   49. qu
38. z   44. f   50. z
39. a   45. o   51. t

PH 108

Getting Stronger: Short Vowels (A)

Unit Overview

In this unit, students will
- Review sight words.
- Practice the short vowel sounds /ă/, /ĕ/, /ĭ/, /ŏ/, and /ŭ/ for the letters *a*, *e*, *i*, *o*, and *u*.
- Build words.
- Practice reading and writing.

[Materials]

Supplied
- *K¹² PhonicsWorks Basic Activity Book,* p. PH 55
- whiteboard, student
- Tile Kit

Also Needed
- sight words box

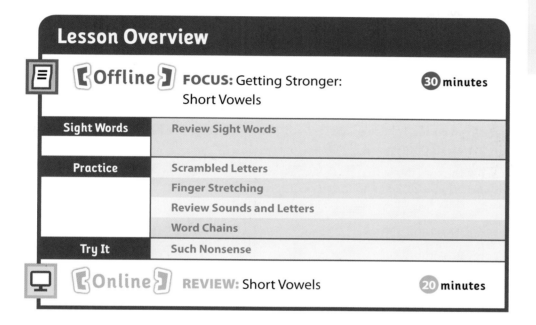

Lesson Overview

[Offline] FOCUS: Getting Stronger: Short Vowels	30 minutes

Sight Words	Review Sight Words
Practice	Scrambled Letters
	Finger Stretching
	Review Sounds and Letters
	Word Chains
Try It	Such Nonsense

[Online] REVIEW: Short Vowels	20 minutes

 **30 minutes**

FOCUS: Getting Stronger: Short Vowels

Work **together** with students to complete offline Sight Words, Practice, and Try It activities.

Sight Words

Review Sight Words

Help students learn to recognize sight words.

Objectives
- Read sight words.
- Spell sight words.
- Write sight words.

1. Gather all the sight word cards students have yet to master from their sight words box. Stack the cards on the table face down.

2. Have students pick up a word and read it to you.

3. If they read it quickly and correctly, put the card in one stack. If they hesitate or do not read the word correctly, put it in another stack. The second stack should have words that they will review again.

4. Take the stack of words that students read correctly and dictate each word to them. They may choose to either write the word or spell it aloud.

5. If students spell the word correctly, put the card in the first stack because they have mastered the word. If they misspell the word, add it to the stack of cards to review again.

6. Chart students' progress on the back of each card.

   ▸ Divide the back of the card into two columns.
   ▸ Label the first column "Read" and the second column "Spell."
   ▸ Record the dates that students read or spell the word correctly. When students can read and spell the word correctly three times in a row, they have mastered the word. You may want to put a star or sticker on their card when they have mastered that word.

TIP Even if students can read and spell all the words correctly, it is still beneficial for them to review sight words. Choose as many additional words as you would like for each subsequent activity.

Practice ·

Scrambled Letters

To help students master the alphabet, have them practice identifying and naming letters.

1. Place the following letter tiles in random order on students' whiteboard: *b, f, i, k, n, p, r, s, u,* and *w.*

2. Have students arrange the letters in alphabetical order.

 TIP Students may find this activity easier if they slowly sing "The Alphabet Song" to themselves as they work.

Finger Stretching

Use finger stretching to help students identify individual sounds in words.

1. **Say:** Let's review finger stretching. In the word *led,* the first sound is /l/, the next sound is /ĕ/, and the last sound is /d/. I will finger stretch each sound as I say it. Then I'll say the word while pulling my fist toward my body.

2. Finger stretch the word *led* for students.

3. **Say:** I'm going to say words with several sounds in them. You'll say each word, and then finger stretch it while you say each sound in the word.

4. Say the following words and have students finger stretch them. After they finger stretch each word, ask them the question for that word.

   ▸ *pod* /p/ /ŏ/ /d/   What is the middle sound? /ŏ/
   ▸ *tax* /t/ /ă/ /ks/   What is the last sound? /ks/
   ▸ *pig* /p/ /ĭ/ /g/   What is the middle sound? /ĭ/
   ▸ *tug* /t/ /ŭ/ /g/   What is the first sound? /t/
   ▸ *bog* /b/ /ŏ/ /g/   What is the middle sound? /ŏ/

TIP Refer to the *K¹² PhonicsWorks* DVD for a demonstration of finger stretching.

Review Sounds and Letters

Help students review sounds for the letters *b, e, f, g, m, o, t, u,* and *w,* plus any letters that are confusing for them.

1. Place the following letter tiles in random order on students' whiteboard: *b, e, f, g, m, o, t, u,* and *w,* plus any letters that are confusing.

2. **Say:** Let's go over some letters and sounds.

3. Point to each letter tile and have students say a sound that letter makes.

   ▸ *b* /b/   ▸ *m* /m/
   ▸ *u* /ŭ/   ▸ *e* /ĕ/
   ▸ *f* /f/   ▸ *g* /g/
   ▸ *t* /t/   ▸ *w* /w/
   ▸ *o* /ŏ/

 Objectives
- Identify letters of the alphabet.
- Identify individual sounds in words.
- Identify short vowel sounds.
- Identify and use the sound /ă/.
- Identify and use the sound /ĕ/.
- Identify and use the sound /ĭ/.
- Identify and use the sound /ŏ/.
- Identify and use the sound /ŭ/.
- Given the letter, identify the most common sound.
- Given the sound, identify the most common letter or letters.
- Identify the new word when one sound is changed in a word.

4. Say each of the following sounds. Have students repeat the sound and touch the corresponding letter tile.

- ▸ /b/ *b*
- ▸ /ŭ/ *u*
- ▸ /f/ *f*
- ▸ /t/ *t*
- ▸ /ŏ/ *o*

- ▸ /m/ *m*
- ▸ /ĕ/ *e*
- ▸ /g/ *g*
- ▸ /w/ *w*

5. As you do the activity, point to some letter tiles two or three times so that students don't think they are finished with a sound after they have named it.

6. Redirect students if they say an incorrect sound when you point to a letter tile.

   Say: That's the sound of another letter. What is the sound for this letter?

7. Help students if they touch the wrong letter tile after they repeat a sound.

   Say: That letter tile goes with the sound [sound for incorrect letter tile]. We're looking for the letter tile that goes with the sound [target sound].

Word Chains

Have students build words by adding and changing letters to help them recognize and use individual sounds in words.

1. Place the following letters at the top of students' whiteboard: *a, b, e, f, g, h, i, s, t,* and *u.*

2. **Say:** I am going to build the first word in a chain. The word is *bat.*

   - ▸ I will pull down the letters for the sounds /b/, /ă/, and /t/ to spell the word *bat.*
   - ▸ I will touch and say *bat.* To change *bat* to *bet,* I will think about which sound is changed from the word *bat* to *bet.* I will need to replace the letter *a* with the letter *e.*
   - ▸ Touch and say the word *bet.* Now it's your turn to change *bet* to *set.* You can spell *set* by making only one change. Touch and say the new word.

3. Redirect students if they select the incorrect letter for any sound.

   Say: That letter is for the sound [incorrect sound]. We want the letter for the sound [target sound]. What letter makes that sound? Answers will vary.

4. Redirect students if they name the sound incorrectly.

   Say: To change the word [first word] to [target word], we need the letter for the sound [target sound].

   Show students how to make the change. Have them touch and say the new word after they move the letters.

5. Follow this procedure to make the following words: *sit, fit, fat, hat, hut, hug, bug, beg, bag, big*.

6. For every new word, have students add, replace, or remove only one letter.

Try It

Such Nonsense

Have students complete page PH 55 in *K¹² PhonicsWorks Basic Activity Book* for more practice with words that have short vowel sounds. First have students read each group of words aloud. Then have them draw a picture that they think will go with the underlined nonsense word.

Objectives
• Read aloud grade-level text with appropriate automaticity, prosody, accuracy, and rate.

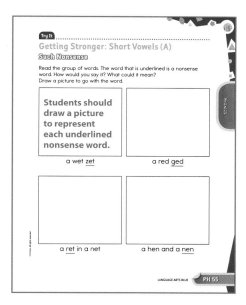

 **20** minutes

REVIEW: **Short Vowels**

Students will work online independently to

► Practice the short vowel sounds /ă/, /ĕ/, /ĭ/, /ŏ/, and /ŭ/ made by the letters *a, e, i, o,* and *u.*

► Practice decoding text by reading a story.

Help students locate the online activities and provide support as needed.

Offline Alternative

No computer access? Have students point out and name things or words that contain the short vowel sounds /ă/, /ĕ/, /ĭ/, /ŏ/, and /ŭ/, such as *has, pen, fish, shop,* and *rush.* You might also ask students to spell simple words that contain the sounds /ă/, /ĕ/, /ĭ/, /ŏ/, and /ŭ/ made by the letters *a, e, i, o,* and *u* and other letters they have learned.

 Objectives

- Identify short vowel sounds.
- Given the letter, identify the most common sound.
- Given the sound, identify the most common letter or letters.
- Identify and use the sound /ă/.
- Identify and use the sound /ĕ/.
- Identify and use the sound /ĭ/.
- Identify and use the sound /ŏ/.
- Identify and use the sound /ŭ/.
- Identify individual sounds in words.
- Read aloud grade-level text with appropriate automaticity, prosody, accuracy, and rate.
- Decode words by applying grade-level word analysis skills.

Getting Stronger: Short Vowels (B)

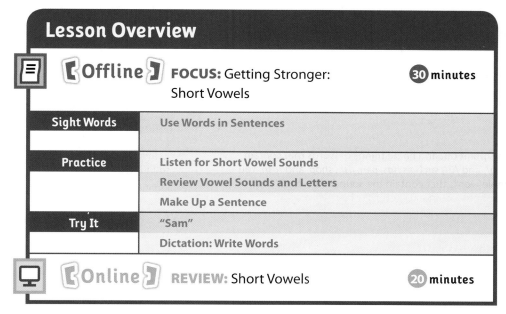

Lesson Overview

Offline FOCUS: Getting Stronger: Short Vowels — **30** minutes

Sight Words	Use Words in Sentences
Practice	Listen for Short Vowel Sounds
	Review Vowel Sounds and Letters
	Make Up a Sentence
Try It	"Sam"
	Dictation: Write Words

Online REVIEW: Short Vowels — **20** minutes

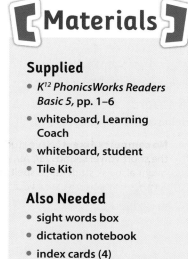

Materials

Supplied
- *K¹² PhonicsWorks Readers Basic 5*, pp. 1–6
- whiteboard, Learning Coach
- whiteboard, student
- Tile Kit

Also Needed
- sight words box
- dictation notebook
- index cards (4)

Advance Preparation

For Make Up a Sentence, print each of the following words on index cards, using one card per word: *kid*, *sun*, *cut*, and *fin*.

 **Offline** **30 minutes**

FOCUS: Getting Stronger: Short Vowels

Work **together** with students to complete offline Sight Words, Practice, and Try It activities.

Sight Words

Use Words in Sentences

Help students use sight words in sentences.

1. Gather all the sight word cards students have yet to master from their sight words box. Spread the sight word cards on the table.

2. **Say:** Let's use sight words in sentences.

3. Have students

   ▸ Touch each card and read the word on it.
   ▸ Make up a sentence using the word.
   ▸ Put the card in a pile after using the word in a sentence.
   ▸ Go through the pile of cards and read each sight word again.
   ▸ Spell each word.

TIP If students have difficulty with any of the sight words, place those cards in a pile to review again.

> **Objectives**
> • Read sight words.
> • Spell sight words.

Practice

Listen for Short Vowel Sounds

Say words with the sounds /ă/, /ĕ/, /ĭ/, /ŏ/, and /ŭ/ to help students identify the difference between short vowels sounds in words.

1. **Say:** I'm going to say a word. You'll listen for the **vowel sounds /ă/, /ĕ/, /ĭ/, /ŏ/, or /ŭ/** in the word. Tell me the vowel sound that you hear. For example, if I say *him*, you'll say /ĭ/ because the vowel sound you hear in *him* is /ĭ/.

2. Guide students with these questions if they have difficulty identifying the vowel sound:

   ▸ What is the sound you hear in the middle of the word? Answers will vary.
   ▸ Do you hear the sound [target sound] in the word? Listen to the word [target word] again.
   ▸ Can you think of another word that has the sound [target sound]? Answers will vary.

3. Say each word. Have students identify the vowel sound in the word.

   ▸ *ham* /ă/   ▸ *bud* /ŭ/
   ▸ *fix* /ĭ/   ▸ *bed* /ĕ/
   ▸ *fox* /ŏ/   ▸ *tub* /ŭ/
   ▸ *bet* /ĕ/   ▸ *tab* /ă/
   ▸ *bit* /ĭ/

> **Objectives**
> • Identify short vowel sounds.
> • Identify and use the sound /ă/.
> • Identify and use the sound /ĕ/.
> • Identify and use the sound /ĭ/.
> • Identify and use the sound /ŏ/.
> • Identify and use the sound /ŭ/.
> • Given the letter, identify the most common sound.
> • Given the sound, identify the most common letter or letters.
> • Read aloud grade-level text with appropriate automaticity, prosody, accuracy, and rate.
> • Identify complete sentences.

Review Vowel Sounds and Letters

Help students review vowel sounds and letters.

1. Place the following letter tiles on students' whiteboard: *a, e, i, o,* and *u,* plus any letters that are confusing for them.

2. **Say:** I am going to point to each letter. Tell me a sound for that letter.

3. **Say:** I am going to say a sound. Repeat the sound and touch its letter.

4. Point to some letters two or three times, so students don't think that once they have named a sound they are finished with it.

5. Redirect students if they name the letter and not its sound.

   Say: You are right that the name of the letter is [letter]. We want the sound for this letter. What is the sound?

6. Redirect students if they name the sound incorrectly.

   Say: That is the sound of another letter.

7. Provide additional guidance if students touch the wrong letter tile during the review.

   Say: That is the letter tile for the sound [sound for incorrect letter tile]. We are looking for the letter tile for the sound [target sound].

8. If students touch the wrong letter again, point to the correct letter.

   Say: This is the letter tile for the sound [target sound]. Touch this letter tile and say its sound.

Make Up a Sentence

Help students use words to make sentences.

1. Gather the index cards you prepared, and place them face down on the table in one pile.

2. Have students
   - ▸ Select a card.
   - ▸ Read the word.
   - ▸ Use the word in an interesting, fun, or silly sentence.

TIP If students read a word incorrectly, have them finger stretch the sounds in the word or use letter tiles to spell the word and touch and say.

Try It

"Sam"

Have students read "Sam" on page 1 of *K¹² PhonicsWorks Readers Basic 5*.

Students should read the story silently once or twice before reading the story aloud. When students miss a word that can be sounded out, point to it and give them three to six seconds to try the word again. If students still miss the word, tell them the word so the flow of the story isn't interrupted.

After reading the story, make a list of all the words students missed, and go over those words with them. You may use letter tiles to show students how to read the words.

Dictation: Write Words

Have students practice identifying sounds and writing words.

1. Gather a pencil and the dictation notebook. Say the word *fin*. Then give these directions to students:

   ▸ Repeat the word.
   ▸ Write the word in your notebook.
   ▸ Read the word aloud.

2. When students have finished, write the following word on your whiteboard: *fin*.

3. Have them compare their answer to your correct version.

4. Repeat this procedure with the words *top*, *jet*, and *gum*.

   ▸ If students make an error and don't see it, help them correct their mistake by having them finger stretch the sounds in the word they missed.
   ▸ If students are having difficulty selecting the correct letters or sounds, review those letters or sounds that are confusing them.
   ▸ If students have difficulty with first, middle, and last sounds, have them finger stretch the sounds in words.

Objectives

- Read aloud grade-level text with appropriate automaticity, prosody, accuracy, and rate.
- Decode words by applying grade-level word analysis skills.
- Track text from left to right.
- Turn pages sequentially.
- Write words by applying grade-level phonics knowledge.
- Follow three-step directions.

 **20 minutes**

REVIEW: **Short Vowels**

Students will work online independently to

▶ Practice the short vowel sounds /ă/, /ĕ/, /ĭ/, /ŏ/, /ŭ/ for the letters *a, e, i, o,* and *u.*

Help students locate the online activities and provide support as needed.

Offline Alternative

No computer access? Have students point out and name things or words that contain with the short vowel sounds /ă/, /ĕ/, /ĭ/, /ŏ/, and /ŭ/, such as *rag, net, quiz, log,* and *cup.* You might also ask students to spell simple words that contain the sounds /ă/, /ĕ/, /ĭ/, /ŏ/, and /ŭ/ made by the letters *a, e, i, o,* and *u* and other letters they have learned.

Objectives

- Identify short vowel sounds.
- Given the letter, identify the most common sound.
- Given the sound, identify the most common letter or letters.
- Identify and use the sound /ă/.
- Identify and use the sound /ĕ/.
- Identify and use the sound /ĭ/.
- Identify and use the sound /ŏ/.
- Identify and use the sound /ŭ/.
- Identify individual sounds in words.

Getting Stronger: Short Vowels (C)

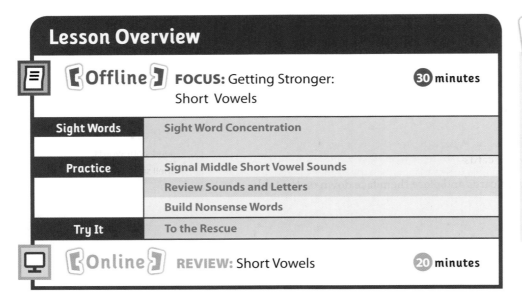

Lesson Overview

Offline FOCUS: Getting Stronger: Short Vowels **30** minutes

Sight Words	Sight Word Concentration
Practice	Signal Middle Short Vowel Sounds
	Review Sounds and Letters
	Build Nonsense Words
Try It	To the Rescue

Online REVIEW: Short Vowels **20** minutes

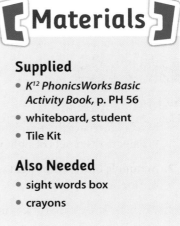

Materials

Supplied
- *K¹² PhonicsWorks Basic Activity Book,* p. PH 56
- whiteboard, student
- Tile Kit

Also Needed
- sight words box
- crayons

Advance Preparation

Gather two sets of the sight word cards that students have yet to master.

 **Offline** **30** minutes

FOCUS: Getting Stronger: Short Vowels

Work **together** with students to complete offline Sight Words, Practice, and Try It activities.

Sight Words

Sight Word Concentration

Help students review sight words.

Objectives
- Read sight words.
- Spell sight words.
- Write sight words.

1. Gather the two sets of sight word cards.

2. Scramble both sets of sight word cards and place them face down on the table or floor.

3. Turn over two cards at a time; take turns with students. If the cards match, the person turning over the matching cards reads the word and uses it in a sentence. If the cards don't match, the person turns them back over.

4. Remove and save the matching cards.

5. Continue the activity until all the cards are paired.

6. Have students read all the words.

7. Take the stack of words that students read correctly and dictate each word to them.

8. Have students write each word or spell it aloud.

TIP If students have difficulty with any sight words, let them work at their own pace to really master these words.

Practice ....

Signal Middle Short Vowel Sounds

Use a special signal to help students identify **middle vowel sounds** in words.

1. **Say:** I'm going to tell you a special sound, and then I'll say some words. Repeat each word I say and make a special signal to tell me where the special sound is. If the special vowel sound is at the middle of the word, pinch your chin. If the special vowel sound is **not** at the middle of the word, just smile at me. For example,

   ▸ If I ask you to listen for the sound /ă/ and I say the word *mat*, you'll repeat the word *mat* and pinch your chin because *mat* has the sound /ă/ in the middle.

   ▸ If I say the word *pop*, you'll repeat the word *pop* and smile at me because *pop* has the sound /ŏ/, not /ă/, in the middle.

2. Say each sound and group of words. Have students make the special signal to identify the middle sound.

   ▸ /ĭ/: *tin, pot, mist, rip, with* pinch chin: *tin, mist, rip, with*
   ▸ /ŏ/: *that, Ron, lost, jig, soft* pinch chin: *Ron, lost, soft*
   ▸ /ĕ/: *left, sit, Ken, tub, bed* pinch chin: *left, Ken, bed*
   ▸ /ŭ/: *tan, tug, gum, just, pin* pinch chin: *tug, gum, just*
   ▸ /ă/: *man, gas, bus, boss, band* pinch chin: *man, gas, band*

3. Guide students with these questions if they have difficulty identifying the vowel sound:

   ▸ What is the sound you hear in the middle of the word? Answers will vary.
   ▸ Do you hear the sound [target sound] in the word? Listen to the word [target word] again.
   ▸ Can you think of another word that has the sound [target sound]? Answers will vary.

TIP If students can't identify the middle sound of each word, say the word again and emphasize the middle sound by stretching it out (for example, *baaaaat*). If necessary, have students look at your mouth while you stretch the sounds.

Objectives

- Identify middle sounds in words.
- Identify short vowel sounds.
- Identify and use the sound /ă/.
- Identify and use the sound /ĕ/.
- Identify and use the sound /ĭ/.
- Identify and use the sound /ŏ/.
- Identify and use the sound /ŭ/.
- Given the letter, identify the most common sound.
- Given the sound, identify the most common letter or letters.
- Identify the new word when one sound is changed in a word.
- Identify individual sounds in words.
- Write words by applying grade-level phonics knowledge.

Review Sounds and Letters

Help students review sounds for the letters *a, c, e, m, p, r, s,* and *x,* plus any letters that are confusing for them.

1. Place the following letter tiles in random order on students' whiteboard: *a, c, e, m, p, r, s,* and *x,* plus any letters that are confusing.

2. **Say:** Let's go over some letters and sounds.

3. Point to each letter tile and have students say a sound that letter makes.

   ▸ *a* /ă/   ▸ *e* /ĕ/
   ▸ *x* /ks/   ▸ *r* /r/
   ▸ *p* /p/   ▸ *s* /s/
   ▸ *m* /m/   ▸ *c* /k/

4. Say each of the following sounds. Have students repeat the sound and touch the corresponding letter tile.

- ► /ă/ *a*
- ► /ks/ *x*
- ► /p/ *p*
- ► /m/ *m*

- ► /ĕ/ *e*
- ► /r/ *r*
- ► /s/ *s*
- ► /k/ *c* or *k*

5. As you do the activity, point to some letter tiles two or three times so that students don't think they are finished with a sound after they have named it.

6. Redirect students if they say an incorrect sound when you point to a letter tile.

   Say: That's the sound of another letter. What is the sound for this letter?

7. Help students if they touch the wrong letter tile after they repeat a sound.

   Say: That letter tile goes with the sound [sound for incorrect letter tile]. We're looking for the letter tile that goes with the sound [target sound].

Build Nonsense Words

Help students use letters and sounds to build nonsense words.

1. Place the following letter tiles at the top of students' whiteboard: *a, b, e, f, g, h, i, m, o, p, r, u,* and *z*.

2. Draw three horizontal lines across the middle of students' whiteboard to represent the sounds in a word.

3. **Say:** Some words don't have any meaning. We call these **nonsense words**. Even though we don't know what a word means, we can still read it. Nonsense words will be very important when we read longer words. When we break longer words into parts, sometimes the parts are nonsense words.

4. **Say:** Let's use letters and sounds to build the word *gup*.

5. Have students finger stretch the sounds in *gup*.

6. Have students

   - ► Identify the first, next, and last sounds in *gup*.
   - ► Choose the corresponding letter for each of the sounds.
   - ► Move the letters to the correct lines on their whiteboard.

7. Guide students with these questions:

   - ► What is the first sound in *gup*? /g/
     Which line does the letter for that sound go on? the first one
   - ► What is the next sound in *gup*? /ŭ/
     Which line does the letter for that sound go on? the second one
   - ► What's the last sound in *gup*? /p/
     Which line does the letter for that sound go on? the last one

8. Redirect students if they select the incorrect letter.

   Say: That sound is in the word [word], and it is the [first, second, third] sound. We want the sound [target sound].

   Continue until students select the correct letter.

9. Have students touch and say the word.

10. Have them say the word as they use a dry-erase marker to write the word on the whiteboard.

11. Repeat the activity to build the following words:

   ▶ *rom* /r/ /ŏ/ /m/
   ▶ *bez* /b/ /ĕ/ /z/
   ▶ *fap* /f/ /ă/ /p/
   ▶ *hib* /h/ /ĭ/ /b/

Try It

To the Rescue

Have students complete page PH 56 in *K¹² PhonicsWorks Basic Activity Book* for more practice with short vowels. Have students read each word aloud and color the boxes that name real words to help the rabbit find the path to the log.

Objectives
- Read aloud grade-level text with appropriate automaticity, prosody, accuracy, and rate.

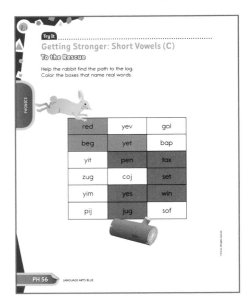

Try It

Getting Stronger: Short Vowels (C)

To the Rescue

Help the rabbit find the path to the log.
Color the boxes that name real words.

red	yev	gol
beg	yet	bap
yit	pen	tax
zug	coj	set
yim	yes	win
pij	jug	sof

PH 56   LANGUAGE ARTS BLUE

 **20 minutes**

REVIEW: **Short Vowels**

Students will work online independently to

▸ Practice the short vowel sounds /ă/, /ĕ/, /ĭ/, /ŏ/, and /ŭ/ for the letters *a, e, i, o,* and *u.*

▸ Practice decoding text by reading a story.

Help students locate the online activities and provide support as needed.

Offline Alternative

No computer access? Have students point out and name things or words that begin with the short vowel sounds /ă/, /ĕ/, /ĭ/, /ŏ/, and /ŭ/, such as *and, egg, it, on,* and *up.* You might also ask students to spell simple words that contain the sounds /ă/, /ĕ/, /ĭ/, /ŏ/, and /ŭ/ made by the letters *a, e, i, o,* and *u* and other letters they have learned.

Objectives

- Identify short vowel sounds.
- Given the letter, identify the most common sound.
- Given the sound, identify the most common letter or letters.
- Identify and use the sound /ă/.
- Identify and use the sound /ĕ/.
- Identify and use the sound /ĭ/.
- Identify and use the sound /ŏ/.
- Identify and use the sound /ŭ/.
- Identify individual sounds in words.
- Read aloud grade-level text with appropriate automaticity, prosody, accuracy, and rate.
- Decode words by applying grade-level word analysis skills.

Getting Stronger: Short Vowels (D)

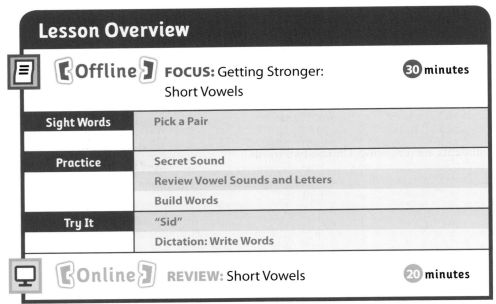

Lesson Overview

[Offline] **FOCUS:** Getting Stronger: Short Vowels — **30 minutes**

Sight Words	Pick a Pair
Practice	Secret Sound
	Review Vowel Sounds and Letters
	Build Words
Try It	"Sid"
	Dictation: Write Words

[Online] **REVIEW:** Short Vowels — **20 minutes**

Materials

Supplied
- *K12 PhonicsWorks Readers Basic 5*, pp. 7–12
- whiteboard, Learning Coach
- whiteboard, student
- Tile Kit

Also Needed
- sight words box
- dictation notebook

 **30** minutes

FOCUS: Getting Stronger: Short Vowels

Work **together** with students to complete offline Sight Words, Practice, and Try It activities.

Sight Words

Pick a Pair

Play a card game with students for more practice with sight words.

1. Gather the sight word cards that students are reviewing. Choose two words and place the cards on the table.

2. Ask questions to help students identify each word. For example, if the words are *or* and *one*, you could ask, "Which word names a number?" If the words are *on* and *but*, you could ask, "Which word is the opposite of *off*?"

3. Continue the activity until students identify all the words.

4. Take the stack of words that students read correctly and dictate each word to them.

5. Have students write each word or spell it aloud.

Objectives

- Read sight words.
- Spell sight words.
- Write sight words.

Practice

Secret Sound

Say groups of words to help students recognize **middle sounds** in words.

1. **Say:** I am going to say some groups of words. Listen for a secret sound in the middle of each word. Then tell me what sound you hear in the middle of each group of words.

2. Say each of the following groups of words. Have students identify the secret sound in each group.

   ▸ *pot, hop, cod, rob* /ŏ/
   ▸ *Ned, beg, net, set* /ĕ/
   ▸ *run, duck, bug, dug* /ŭ/
   ▸ *rip, hid, lit, quit* /ĭ/
   ▸ *gap, sad, pan, that* /ă/

TIP If students can't identify the secret sound, have them listen while you say each word again and then have them repeat each word. Have students say what sound they hear in the middle of each word.

Review Vowel Sounds and Letters

Help students review vowel sounds and letters.

1. Place the following letter tiles on students' whiteboard: *a, e, i, o,* and *u,* plus any letters that are confusing for them.

2. **Say:** I am going to point to each letter. Tell me a sound for that letter.

3. **Say:** I am going to say a sound. Repeat the sound and touch its letter.

4. Point to some letters two or three times, so students don't think that once they have named a sound they are finished with it.

5. Redirect students if they name the letter and not its sound.

   Say: You are right that the name of the letter is [letter]. We want the sound for this letter. What is the sound?

6. Redirect students if they name the sound incorrectly.

   Say: That is the sound of another letter.

7. Provide additional guidance if students touch the wrong letter tile during the review.

   Say: That is the letter tile for the sound [sound for incorrect letter tile]. We are looking for the letter tile for the sound [target sound].

8. If students touch the wrong letter again, point to the correct letter.

   Say: This is the letter tile for the sound [target sound]. Touch this letter tile and say its sound.

Objectives

- Identify middle sounds in words.
- Identify short vowel sounds.
- Identify and use the sound /ă/.
- Identify and use the sound /ĕ/.
- Identify and use the sound /ĭ/.
- Identify and use the sound /ŏ/.
- Identify and use the sound /ŭ/.
- Given the letter, identify the most common sound.
- Given the sound, identify the most common letter or letters.
- Blend sounds to create words.
- Identify individual sounds in words.
- Write words by applying grade-level phonics knowledge.

Build Words

Help students use letters and sounds to build words.

1. Place the following letter tiles at the top of students' whiteboard: *a, b, d, e, g, i, j, n, o, r, t, u, w,* and *x*.

2. Draw three horizontal lines across the middle of students' whiteboard to represent the sounds in a word.

3. **Say:** Let's use letters and sounds to build the word *wax*.

4. Have students finger stretch the sounds in *wax*.

5. Have students

   ▸ Identify the first, next, and last sounds in *wax*.
   ▸ Choose the corresponding letter for each of the sounds.
   ▸ Move the letters to the correct lines on their whiteboard.

6. Guide students with these questions:

   ▸ What is the first sound in *wax*? /w/
     Which line does the letter for that sound go on? the first one
   ▸ What is the next sound in *wax*? /ă/
     Which line does the letter for that sound go on? the second one
   ▸ What's the last sound in *wax*? /ks/
     Which line does the letter for that sound go on? the last one

7. Redirect students if they select the incorrect letter.

   Say: That sound is in the word [word], and it is the [first, second, third] sound. We want the sound [target sound].

   Continue until students select the correct letter.

8. Have students touch and say the word.

9. Have them say the word as they use a dry-erase marker to write the word on the whiteboard.

10. Repeat the activity to build the following words:

    ▸ *jug* /j/ /ŭ/ /g/
    ▸ *bet* /b/ /ě/ /t/
    ▸ *rod* /r/ /ŏ/ /d/
    ▸ *win* /w/ /ĭ/ /n/

Try It

"Sid"

Have students read "Sid" on page 7 of *K¹² PhonicsWorks Readers Basic 5.*

Students should read the story silently once or twice before reading the story aloud. When students miss a word that can be sounded out, point to it and give them three to six seconds to try the word again. If students still miss the word, tell them the word so the flow of the story isn't interrupted.

After reading the story, make a list of all the words students missed, and go over those words with them. You may use letter tiles to show students how to read the words.

Dictation: Write Words

Have students practice identifying sounds and writing words.

1. Gather a pencil and the dictation notebook. Say the word *Ted.* Then give these directions to students:

    ▸ Repeat the word.
    ▸ Write the word in your notebook.
    ▸ Read the word aloud.

2. When students have finished, write the following word on your whiteboard: *Ted.*

3. Have them compare their answer to your correct version.

4. Repeat this procedure with the words *rut, wax,* and *pup.*

    ▸ If students make an error and don't see it, help them correct their mistake by having them finger stretch the sounds in the word they missed.
    ▸ If students are having difficulty selecting the correct letters or sounds, review those letters or sounds that are confusing them.
    ▸ If students have difficulty with first, middle, and last sounds, have them finger stretch the sounds in words.

TIP Remind students that the word *Ted* is a proper noun. Have them write the word with a beginning capital letter.

Objectives

- Read aloud grade-level text with appropriate automaticity, prosody, accuracy, and rate.
- Decode words by applying grade-level word analysis skills.
- Track text from left to right.
- Turn pages sequentially.
- Write words by applying grade-level phonics knowledge.
- Follow three-step directions.

 **20 minutes**

REVIEW: **Short Vowels**

Students will work online independently to

▶ Practice the short vowel sounds /ă/, /ĕ/, /ĭ/, /ŏ/, /ŭ/ for the letters *a, e, i, o,* and *u.*

Help students locate the online activities and provide support as needed.

Offline Alternative

No computer access? Have students point out and name things or words that contain the short vowel sounds /ă/, /ĕ/, /ĭ/, /ŏ/, and /ŭ/, such as *bat, bed, tin, hop,* and *jug.* You might also ask students to spell simple words that contain the sounds /ă/, /ĕ/, /ĭ/, /ŏ/, and /ŭ/ made by the letters *a, e, i, o,* and *u* and other letters they have learned.

Objectives

- Identify short vowel sounds.
- Given the letter, identify the most common sound.
- Given the sound, identify the most common letter or letters.
- Identify and use the sound /ă/.
- Identify and use the sound /ĕ/.
- Identify and use the sound /ĭ/.
- Identify and use the sound /ŏ/.
- Identify and use the sound /ŭ/.
- Identify individual sounds in words.

Unit Checkpoint

Lesson Overview

 **Online**   **REVIEW:** Short Vowels   **20** minutes

Offline   **UNIT CHECKPOINT:** Getting Stronger: Short Vowels   **30** minutes

Materials

Supplied

- *K¹² PhonicsWorks Basic Assessments,* pp. PH 109–113

Objectives

- Identify and use the sound /ă/.
- Identify and use the sound /ĕ/.
- Identify and use the sound /ĭ/.
- Identify and use the sound /ŏ/.
- Identify and use the sound /ŭ/.
- Identify and use vowels and vowel sounds.
- Identify short vowel sounds.
- Read, write, and spell words containing short vowel sounds.
- Identify individual sounds in words.
- Given the letter, identify the most common sound.
- Given the sound, identify the most common letter or letters.
- Read instructional-level text with 90% accuracy.
- Read aloud grade-level text with appropriate automaticity, prosody, accuracy, and rate.
- Write words by applying grade-level phonics knowledge.
- Write sight words.
- Read sight words.

Online   **20** minutes

REVIEW: Short Vowels

Students will review the short vowel sounds /ă/, /ĕ/, /ĭ/, /ŏ/, and /ŭ/ for the letters *a, e, i, o,* and *u* to prepare for the Unit Checkpoint. Help students locate the online activities and provide support as needed.

[Offline] 30 minutes

UNIT CHECKPOINT: Getting Stronger: Short Vowels

Explain that students are going to show what they have learned about sounds, letters, and words.

1. Give students the Unit Checkpoint pages for the Getting Stronger: Short Vowels unit and print the Unit Checkpoint Answer Key, if you'd like.

2. Use the instructions below to help administer the Checkpoint to students. On the Answer Key or another sheet of paper, note student answers to oral response questions to help with scoring the Checkpoint later.

3. Use the Answer Key to score the Checkpoint, and then enter the results online.

Part 1. Say Sounds Have students read across the rows from left to right and say a sound that each letter makes. Note any sounds they say incorrectly.

Part 2. Word Dissection For each word, say the sound students should identify. Have them read the word aloud and circle the letter or group of letters that spells the requested sound.

19. *middle sound*

20. *ending sound*

21. *beginning sound*

22. *ending sound*

23. *middle sound*

Part 3. Finger Stretching Say each word to students. Have them say each word and finger stretch the sounds. Note any words they finger stretch incorrectly.

24. *yet*   27. *rub*

25. *fad*   28. *yip*

26. *log*

Part 4. Dictation Say each word to students. Have them repeat and write the word.

29. *bet*   31. *bun*

30. *wax*   32. *hip*

Part 5. Read Aloud Listen to students read the sentences aloud. Count and note the number of words they read correctly.

Name _____ Date _____

○ Unit Checkpoint Answer Key
Getting Stronger: Short Vowels

Part 1. Say Sounds
Read across the row from left to right. Say a sound that the letter makes.

1. a	2. e	3. i	4. o	5. u	6. y
7. w	8. x	9. z	10. e	11. y	12. o
13. i	14. u	15. y	16. w	17. u	18. x

1. /ă/ 2. /ĕ/ 3. /ĭ/ 4. /ŏ/ 5. /ŭ/ 6. /y/
7. /w/ 8. /ks/ 9. /z/ 10. /ĕ/ 11. /y/ 12. /ŏ/
13. /ĭ/ 14. /ŭ/ 15. /y/ 16. /w/ 17. /ŭ/ 18. /ks/

Name _____ Date _____

Part 2. Word Dissection
Read the word. Circle the letter or group of letters that spell the sound you are asked to find.

19. b (u) n
20. s i (x)
21. (y) e s
22. b o (x)
23. w (e) b

Name _____ Date _____

Part 3. Finger Stretching
Listen to the word. Finger stretch the word.

24. /y/   /ĕ/   /t/
25. /f/   /ă/   /d/
26. /l/   /ŏ/   /g/
27. /r/   /ŭ/   /b/
28. /y/   /ĭ/   /p/

Name _____ Date _____

Part 4. Dictation
Listen to the word. Repeat the word, and then write it.

29. bet _____
30. wax _____
31. bun _____
32. hip _____

Name _____ Date _____

Part 5. Read Aloud
Read the sentences aloud.

33.
> Ten men can run.
> The bed is in the den.
> Tim fed his pup.
> Did Dan let Ted in yet?
> Kim can get in.

Introduce Digraph *sh*

Unit Overview

In this unit, students will

- Learn the sight words *you*, *went*, and *we*.
- Identify letters and sounds in the alphabet.
- Learn the digraphs *sh* and *th*.
- Identify beginning and ending sounds in words.
- Build words.

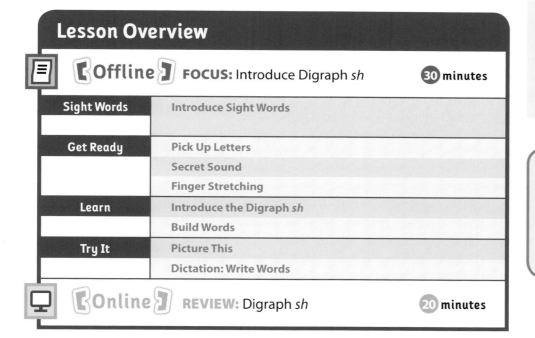

Lesson Overview

☰	**〖Offline〗** FOCUS: Introduce Digraph *sh*	**30** minutes
Sight Words	Introduce Sight Words	
Get Ready	Pick Up Letters	
	Secret Sound	
	Finger Stretching	
Learn	Introduce the Digraph *sh*	
	Build Words	
Try It	Picture This	
	Dictation: Write Words	
🖥	**〖Online〗** REVIEW: Digraph *sh*	**20** minutes

〖Materials〗

Supplied

- *K¹² PhonicsWorks Basic Activity Book,* p. PH 57
- whiteboard, Learning Coach
- whiteboard, student
- Tile Kit

Also Needed

- sight words box
- dictation notebook

Keywords

digraph – two letters together that make one sound. *Di* means "two" and *graph* means "written." Common digraphs include *sh*, *th*, *ch*, and *wh*.

[Offline] ⏱ 30 minutes

FOCUS: Introduce Digraph *sh*

Work **together** with students to complete offline Sight Words, Get Ready, Learn, and Try It activities.

Sight Words

Introduce Sight Words

Help students learn the sight words *you*, *went*, and *we*.

1. Gather the sight word cards *you*, *went*, and *we*.

2. Show students the *you* card.

3. **Say:** This is the word *you*. We see this word so often that we want to be able to read and spell *you* quickly without thinking about it. Look closely at the word *you*. Spell the word *you* aloud. Take a picture of the word *you* in your mind. When you think you can spell *you* yourself, turn the card over and use your letter tiles to spell the word *you*. Check the card to see if you spelled the word *you* correctly. Read aloud the word you spelled with the letter tiles.

4. Repeat the activity with the remaining sight words.

5. Chart students' progress on the back of each card.

   ▸ Divide the back of the card into two columns.
   ▸ Label the first column "Read" and the second column "Spell."
   ▸ Record the dates that students read or spell the word correctly. When students can read and spell the word correctly three times in a row, they have mastered the word. You may want to put a star or sticker on the card when they have mastered that word.

6. Add the cards to students' sight words box.

TIP Sight words can be very difficult for some students. Let students work at their own pace and really master these words, as they occur frequently in reading and writing.

> ⭐ **Objectives**
> • Read sight words.
> • Spell sight words.

Get Ready

Pick Up Letters

Help students use letters and sounds to make words and sentences.

1. Place the following letter tiles on students' whiteboard: *b, c, d, qu, r, s,* and *z*.

2. **Say:** Let's play a game with these letters.

3. Pick up the letter tile for *b*.

4. **Say:** I chose the letter *b*. The sound is /b/. A word that starts with the sound /b/ is *bash*. A sentence using that word is *My party was a bash*. Now it's your turn.

> ⭐ **Objectives**
> • Identify letters of the alphabet.
> • Given the letter, identify the most common sound.
> • Identify ending sounds in words.
> • Identify individual sounds in words.
> • Identify and use the sound /sh/.

5. Continue taking turns until all the letter tiles have been chosen.

6. Have students answer the following questions for each letter or group of letters:

   ▸ What is (are) the letter(s)?
   ▸ What is the sound?
   ▸ What is a word that starts with that sound?
   ▸ What sentence can you make with that word?

7. Redirect students if they name a word that starts with the sound, but not the letter (such as *knob*).

   Say: That is a word that doesn't follow the rules that we know for spelling. Try another word.

8. Prompt students if they have trouble matching the sounds with words. For example,

   Say: That's the sound /j/, as in *jelly*. Can you think of another word that starts with that sound?

Secret Sound

Say groups of words to help students recognize **ending sounds** in words.

1. **Say:** I am going to say some groups of words. Listen for a secret sound at the end of each word. Then tell me what sound you hear at the end of each group of words.

2. Say each of the following groups of words. Have students identify the secret sound in each group.

   ▸ *back, stick, bake, sneak* /k/
   ▸ *mash, fish, crush, lash* /sh/
   ▸ *with, both, math, truth* /th/

TIP If students can't identify the secret sound, have them listen while you say each word again and then have them repeat each word. Have students say what sound they hear at the end of each word.

Finger Stretching

Use finger stretching to help students identify individual sounds in words.

1. **Say:** Let's review finger stretching. In the word *ship*, the first sound is /sh/, the next sound is /ĭ/, and the last sound is /p/. I will finger stretch each sound as I say it. Then I'll say the word while pulling my fist toward my body.

2. Finger stretch the word *ship* for students.

3. **Say:** I'm going to say words with several sounds in them. You'll say each word and then finger stretch it while you say each sound in the word.

4. Say the following words and have students finger stretch them. After they finger stretch each word, ask them the question for that word.

- ▶ *rash* /r/ /ă/ /sh/   What is the first sound? /r/
- ▶ *ship* /sh/ /ĭ/ /p/   What is the middle sound? /ĭ/
- ▶ *dish* /d/ /ĭ/ /sh/   What is the first sound? /d/
- ▶ *smash* /s/ /m/ /ă/ /sh/   What is the last sound? /sh/
- ▶ *bud* /b/ /ŭ/ /d/   What is the middle sound? /ŭ/
- ▶ *mesh* /m/ /ĕ/ /sh/   What is the first sound? /m/
- ▶ *shut* /sh/ /ŭ/ /t/   What is the middle sound? /ŭ/

 Refer to the *K¹² PhonicsWorks* DVD for a demonstration of finger stretching.

Learn

Introduce the Digraph *sh*

To help students learn the digraph *sh*, have them practice identifying and naming words that have the digraph *sh* for the sound /sh/.

1. Place the following letter tile on students' whiteboard: *sh*.

2. **Say:** You've learned all the letters of the alphabet and the sounds that go with them. Now we're going to learn about a sound that is spelled with two letters. This sound is spelled *sh*.

3. Point to the *sh* tile.

   Say: When we see *sh*, we read the sound /sh/. Touch the *sh* tile and say /sh/.

4. **Say:** Two letters that make one sound are called a **digraph**. Let's practice the sound /sh/ and the letters *sh*.

5. **Say:** The sound for the digraph *sh* is /sh/, as in the word *ship*. Can you think of some more words that have the sound /sh/ spelled *sh*?

6. Help students if they can't think of any words. Examples include *shin, shop, sash, cash, fish,* and *dish*.

Objectives

- Identify and use the sound /sh/.
- Identify the letters, given the sound /sh/.
- Identify and use the digraph *sh*.
- Write words by applying grade-level phonics knowledge.
- Identify individual sounds in words.
- Blend sounds to create words.

Build Words

Help students use letters and sounds to build words.

1. Place the following letter tiles at the top of students' whiteboard: *a, i, m, o, p, sh,* and *w*.

2. Draw three horizontal lines across the middle of students' whiteboard to represent the sounds in a word.

3. **Say:** Let's use letters and sounds to build the word *mash*.

4. Have students finger stretch the sounds in *mash*.

5. Have students

   ▸ Identify the first, next, and last sounds in *mash*.
   ▸ Choose the corresponding letter for each of the sounds.
   ▸ Move the letters to the correct lines on their whiteboard.

6. Guide students with these questions:

   ▸ What is the first sound in *mash*? /m/
     Which line does the letter for that sound go on? the first one
   ▸ What is the next sound in *mash*? /ă/
     Which line does the letter for that sound go on? the second one
   ▸ What's the last sound in *mash*? /sh/
     Which line do the letters for that sound go on? the last one

7. Redirect students if they select the incorrect letter.

   Say: That sound is in the word [word], and it is the [first, second, third] sound. We want the sound [target sound].

   Continue until students select the correct letter.

8. Have students touch and say the word.

9. Have them say the word as they use a dry-erase marker to write the word on the whiteboard.

10. Repeat the activity to build the following words:

    ▸ *shop* /sh/ /ŏ/ /p/
    ▸ *wish* /w/ /ĭ/ /sh/

Try It

Picture This

Have students complete page PH 57 in *K¹² PhonicsWorks Basic Activity Book* for more practice with the digraph *sh*. Have students write the digraph *sh* in the blank to complete the word and read the word aloud.

Objectives

- Read aloud grade-level text with appropriate automaticity, prosody, accuracy, and rate.
- Identify and use the sound /sh/.
- Identify the letters, given the sound /sh/.
- Identify and use the digraph *sh*.
- Write words by applying grade-level phonics knowledge.
- Follow three-step directions.

Dictation: Write Words

Have students practice identifying sounds and writing words.

1. Gather a pencil and the dictation notebook. Say the word *ship*. Then give these directions to students:

   ▸ Repeat the word.
   ▸ Write the word in your notebook.
   ▸ Read the word aloud.

2. When students have finished, write the following word on your whiteboard: *ship*.

3. Have them compare their answer to your correct version.

4. Repeat this procedure with the words *shut*, *shop*, *dash*, *fish*, and *ash*.

   ▸ If students make an error and don't see it, help them correct their mistake by having them finger stretch the sounds in the word they missed.
   ▸ If students are having difficulty selecting the correct letters or sounds, review those letters or sounds that are confusing them.
   ▸ If students have difficulty with first, middle, and last sounds, have them finger stretch the sounds in words.

   **minutes**

REVIEW: Digraph *sh*

Students will work online independently to

▸ Practice the digraph *sh*.
▸ Practice decoding text by reading sentences.

Help students locate the online activities and provide support as needed.

Offline Alternative

No computer access? Have students point out and name things or words that contain the sound *sh* (for example, *shad* or *rash*). You might also ask students to spell words that contain the digraph *sh*.

> **Objectives**
>
> - Identify and use the sound /sh/.
> - Identify the letters, given the sound /sh/.
> - Identify and use the digraph *sh*.
> - Identify individual sounds in words.
> - Read aloud grade-level text with appropriate automaticity, prosody, accuracy, and rate.
> - Decode words by applying grade-level word analysis skills.

Practice Digraph *sh*

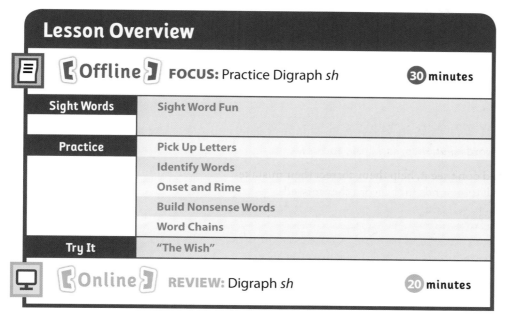

Lesson Overview

Offline — **FOCUS:** Practice Digraph *sh* — **30** minutes

Sight Words	Sight Word Fun
Practice	Pick Up Letters
	Identify Words
	Onset and Rime
	Build Nonsense Words
	Word Chains
Try It	"The Wish"

Online — **REVIEW:** Digraph *sh* — **20** minutes

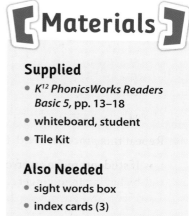

Materials

Supplied
- *K¹² PhonicsWorks Readers Basic 5*, pp. 13–18
- whiteboard, student
- Tile Kit

Also Needed
- sight words box
- index cards (3)

 **30 minutes**

FOCUS: Practice Digraph *sh*

Work **together** with students to complete offline Sight Words, Practice, and Try It activities.

Sight Words

· ·

Sight Word Fun

Help students learn the sight words *you, went,* and *we,* and up to two additional sight words they have yet to master.

1. Gather the sight word cards *you, went,* and *we,* and up to two additional sight word cards.

2. Choose one sight word card to begin.

   Say: Look at this word and take a picture of it in your mind. When you think you can spell the word yourself, turn the card over and use your letter tiles to spell the word.

3. After students spell the word, have them check the card to see if they spelled the word correctly.

   Say: Read aloud the word you spelled with the letter tiles.

4. Repeat the activity with the remaining sight words.

TIP Sight words can be very difficult for some students. Let them work at their own pace and really master these words.

Objectives
- Read sight words.
- Spell sight words.

....

Pick Up Letters

Help students use letters and sounds to make words and sentences.

1. Place the following letter tiles on students' whiteboard: *a , b, e, sh, u, w,* and *x.*

2. **Say:** Let's play a game with these letters.

3. Pick up the letter tile for *a.*

4. **Say:** I chose the letter *a.* The sound is /ă/. A word that starts with the sound /ă/ is *ash.* A sentence using that word is *The campfire put ash into the air.* Now it's your turn.

5. Continue taking turns until all the letter tiles have been chosen.

6. Have students answer the following questions for each letter or group of letters:

   ▸ What is (are) the letter(s)?
   ▸ What is the sound?
   ▸ What is a word that starts with that sound?
   ▸ What sentence can you make with that word?

7. Redirect students if they name a word that starts with the sound, but not the letter (such as *knob*).

   Say: That is a word that doesn't follow the rules that we know for spelling. Try another word.

8. Prompt students if they have trouble matching the sounds with words. For example,

   Say: That's the sound /j/, as in *jelly.* Can you think of another word that starts with that sound?

Objectives

- Identify letters of the alphabet.
- Given the letter, identify the most common sound.
- Identify and use the sound /sh/.
- Identify the letters, given the sound /sh/.
- Identify and use the digraph *sh.*
- Identify a word when given the onset and rime.
- Identify individual sounds in words.
- Write words by applying grade-level phonics knowledge.
- Blend sounds to create words.
- Identify the new word when one sound is changed in a word.

Identify Words

Help students identify the number of words in a phrase or sentence.

1. Gather three index cards.

2. **Say:** A sentence is made up of words. A phrase is a part of a sentence. We read words in a sentence or phrase from left to right.

3. **Say:** Let's use index cards to stand for words in phrases.

   ▸ The phrase *my red hat* has three words, so I'll place three index cards on the table and put them next to each other.
   ▸ I'll say *my* as I touch the first card, *red* as I touch the second card, and *hat* as I touch the third card.
   ▸ Now you touch the cards and say the words *my red hat.*

4. Remove the cards from the table. Give students the stack of cards.

5. Say the following words and phrases. Have students put one card on the table for each word you say. Have them repeat each word as they put down each card. Have students pick up the cards between each example.

  ▸ *cup*
  ▸ *plastic cup*
  ▸ *tall plastic cup*
  ▸ *shirt*
  ▸ *blue shirt*
  ▸ *old blue shirt*
  ▸ *pie*
  ▸ *cherry pie*
  ▸ *juicy cherry pie*

TIP If students can't identify the number of words in a phrase, say the phrase again and lay down an index card for each word you say. Have students count the cards and say how many words are in the phrase.

Onset and Rime

In a word, the part of the syllable before the first vowel sound is the **onset**. The part of the syllable after the first vowel sound is the **rime**. For example, in *shift*, /sh/ is the onset and *ift* is the rime. Help students put together words that are broken down into parts by onset and rime.

1. **Say:** I'm going to break a word into two parts. Your job is to put the parts together and say the word. If the first part of a word is /sh/ and the last part of the word is *ift*, then the whole word is *shift*: /sh/ . . . *ift* . . . *shift*.

2. Say the following pairs of word parts. Have students tell you the word that each pair forms.

  ▸ /sh/ . . . *elf* shelf
  ▸ /ă/ . . . *sh* ash
  ▸ /h/ . . . *ush* hush

Build Nonsense Words

Help students use letters and sounds to build nonsense words.

1. Place the following letter tiles at the top of students' whiteboard: *a, d, e, f, n, sh,* and *u.*

2. Draw three horizontal lines across the middle of students' whiteboard to represent the sounds in a word.

3. **Say:** Some words don't have any meaning. We call these **nonsense words**. Even though we don't know what a word means, we can still read it. Nonsense words will be very important when we read longer words. When we break longer words into parts, sometimes the parts are nonsense words.

4. **Say:** Let's use letters and sounds to build the word *fash.*

5. Have students finger stretch the sounds in *fash.*

6. Have students

   ▸ Identify the first, next, and last sounds in *fash*.
   ▸ Choose the corresponding letter for each sound.
   ▸ Move the letters to the correct lines on their whiteboard.

7. Guide students with these questions:

   ▸ What is the first sound in *fash*? /f/
     Which line does the letter for that sound go on? the first one
   ▸ What is the next sound in *fash*? /ă/
     Which line does the letter for that sound go on? the second one
   ▸ What's the last sound in *fash*? /sh/
     Which line do the letters for that sound go on? the last one

8. Redirect students if they select the incorrect letter.

   Say: That sound is in the word [word], and it is the [first, second, third] sound. We want the sound [target sound].

   Continue until students select the correct letter.

9. Have students touch and say the word.

10. Have them say the word as they use a dry-erase marker to write the word on the whiteboard.

11. Repeat the activity to build the following words:

    ▸ *shud* /sh/ /ŭ/ /d/
    ▸ *shen* /sh/ /ĕ/ /n/

Word Chains

Have students build words by adding and changing letters to help them recognize and use individual sounds in words.

1. Place the following letters at the top of students' whiteboard: *a, b, c, d, l, m, s,* and *sh*.

2. **Say:** I am going to build the first word in a chain. The word is *mash*.

   ▸ I will pull down the letters for the sounds /m/, /ă/, and /sh/ to spell the word *mash*.
   ▸ I will touch and say *mash*. To change *mash* to *dash*, I will think about which sound is changed from the word *mash* to *dash*. I will need to replace the letter *m* with the letter *d*.
   ▸ Touch and say the word *dash*. Now it's your turn to change *dash* to *lash*. You can spell *lash* by making only one change. Touch and say the new word.

3. Redirect students if they select the incorrect letter for any sound.

   Say: That letter is for the sound [incorrect sound]. We want the letter for the sound [target sound]. What letter makes that sound? Answers will vary.

4. Redirect students if they name the sound incorrectly.

    Say: To change the word [first word] to [target word], we need the letter for the sound [target sound].

    Show students how to make the change. Have them touch and say the new word after they move the letters.

5. Follow this procedure to make the following words: *cash*, *bash*, *sash*.

6. For every new word, have students add, replace, or remove only one letter tile.

 If students struggle, review the sounds and letters that are confusing them.

"The Wish"

Have students read "The Wish" on page 13 of *K¹² PhonicsWorks Readers Basic 5*.

Students should read the story silently once or twice before reading the story aloud. When students miss a word that can be sounded out, point to it and give them three to six seconds to try the word again. If students still miss the word, tell them the word so the flow of the story isn't interrupted.

After reading the story, make a list of all the words students missed, and go over those words with them. You may use tiles to show students how to read the words.

> **Objectives**
> - Read aloud grade-level text with appropriate automaticity, prosody, accuracy, and rate.
> - Decode words by applying grade-level word analysis skills.

 Online **20** minutes

REVIEW: Digraph *sh*

Students will work online independently to

▶ Practice the digraph *sh*.

Help students locate the online activities and provide support as needed.

Offline Alternative

No computer access? Have students point out and name things or words that contain the sound *sh* (for example, *shop* or *rash*). You might also ask students to spell words that contain the digraph *sh*.

> **Objectives**
> - Identify and use the sound /sh/.
> - Identify the letters, given the sound /sh/.
> - Identify and use the digraph *sh*.
> - Identify individual sounds in words.

Introduce Digraph *th*

Lesson Overview

[Offline] FOCUS: Introduce Digraph *th*   **30** minutes

Sight Words	Sight Word Fun
Get Ready	Review Sounds and Letters
	Secret Sound
	Finger Stretching
Learn	Introduce the Digraph *th*
	Build Words
Try It	Go Fish!
	Dictation: Write Words

[Online] REVIEW: Digraph *th*   **20** minutes

Supplied
- *K¹² PhonicsWorks Basic Activity Book,* p. PH 58
- whiteboard, Learning Coach
- whiteboard, student
- Tile Kit

Also Needed
- sight words box
- dictation notebook
- crayons

 **Offline** **30 minutes**

FOCUS: Introduce Digraph *th*

Work **together** with students to complete offline Sight Words, Get Ready, Learn, and Try It activities.

Sight Words

Sight Word Fun

Help students learn the sight words *you, went,* and *we,* and up to two additional sight words they have yet to master.

1. Gather the sight word cards *you, went,* and *we,* and up to two additional sight word cards.

2. Choose one sight word card to begin.

   Say: Look at this word and take a picture of it in your mind. When you think you can spell the word yourself, turn the card over and use your letter tiles to spell the word.

3. After students spell the word, have them check the card to see if they spelled the word correctly.

   Say: Read aloud the word you spelled with the letter tiles.

4. Repeat the activity with the remaining sight words.

TIP Sight words can be very difficult for some students. Let them work at their own pace and really master these words.

> **Objectives**
> • Read sight words.
> • Spell sight words.

Get Ready

Review Sounds and Letters

Help students review sounds for the letters and digraph *c, e, f, j, p, sh,* and *t,* plus any letters that are confusing for them.

1. Place the following letter tiles in random order on students' whiteboard: *c, e, f, j, p, sh,* and *t,* plus any letters that are confusing.

2. **Say:** Let's go over some letters and sounds.

3. Point to each letter tile and have students say a sound that letter or letters make.

   ▸ *e* /ĕ/
   ▸ *sh* /sh/
   ▸ *f* /f/
   ▸ *c* /k/
   ▸ *j* /j/
   ▸ *p* /p/
   ▸ *t* /t/

> **Objectives**
> • Identify letters of the alphabet.
> • Given the letter, identify the most common sound.
> • Given the sound, identify the most common letter or letters.
> • Identify beginning sounds in words.
> • Identify individual sounds in words.
> • Identify and use the sound /th/.
> • Identify and use the sound /<u>th</u>/.

4. Say each of the following sounds. Have students repeat the sound and touch the corresponding letter tile.

   ▶ /ĕ/ *e*
   ▶ /sh/ *sh*
   ▶ /f/ *f*
   ▶ /k/ *c*
   ▶ /j/ *j*
   ▶ /p/ *p*
   ▶ /t/ *t*

5. As you do the activity, point to some letter tiles two or three times so that students don't think they are finished with a sound after they have named it.

6. Redirect students if they say an incorrect sound when you point to a letter tile.

   Say: That's the sound of another letter. What is the sound for this letter?

7. Help students if they touch the wrong letter tile after they repeat a sound.

   Say: That letter tile goes with the sound [sound for incorrect letter tile]. We're looking for the letter tile that goes with the sound [target sound].

Secret Sound

Say groups of words to help students recognize **beginning sounds** in words.

1. **Say:** I am going to say some groups of words. Listen for a secret sound in the beginning of each word. Then tell me what sound you hear in the beginning of each group of words.

2. Say each of the following groups of words. Have students identify the secret sound in each group.

   ▶ *shift, sharp, shadow, shape* /sh/
   ▶ *mud, much, math, mash* /m/
   ▶ *do, dive, date, dash* /d/

   (TIP) If students can't identify the secret sound, have them listen while you say each word again and then have them repeat each word. Have students say what sound they hear at the beginning of each word.

Finger Stretching

Use finger stretching to help students identify individual sounds in words.

1. **Say:** Let's review finger stretching. In the word *shock*, the first sound is /sh/, the next sound is /ŏ/, and the last sound is /k/. I will finger stretch each sound as I say it. Then I'll say the word while pulling my fist toward my body.

2. Finger stretch the word *shock* for students.

3. **Say:** I'm going to say words with several sounds in them. You'll say each word and then finger stretch it while you say each sound in the word.

4. Say the following words and have students finger stretch them. After they finger stretch each word, ask them the question for that word.

 ▸ *fan* /f/ /ă/ /n/   What is the first sound? /f/
 ▸ *path* /p/ /ă/ /th/   What is the middle sound? /ă/
 ▸ *with* /w/ /ĭ/ /th/   What is the first sound? /w/
 ▸ *moth* /m/ /ŏ/ /th/   What is the last sound? /th/
 ▸ *thick* /th/ /ĭ/ /k/   What is the first sound? /th/
 ▸ *thin* /th/ /ĭ/ /n/   What is the middle sound? /ĭ/
 ▸ *bath* /b/ /ă/ /th/   What is the first sound? /b/

TIP Refer to the *K¹² PhonicsWorks* DVD for a demonstration of finger stretching.

Learn

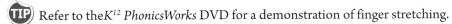

Introduce the Digraph *th*

To help students learn the digraph *th*, have them practice identifying and naming words that have the letters *th* for the sounds /th/ and /<u>th</u>/.

1. Place the following letter tile on students' whiteboard: *th*.

2. **Say:** We're going to learn about another sound like the sound /sh/. Because it's one sound made with two letters, it's also called a **digraph**, just like *sh*. This sound is spelled *th*.

3. Point to the *th* tile.

4. **Say:** To make the sound /th/ as in the word *thumb*, stick your tongue out, put your teeth on your tongue, and blow. Do it again and touch the *th* tile as you make the sound /th/. Sometimes when we see *th*, we read the sound /th/. Touch the *th* tile and say /th/.

5. **Say:** Sometimes the digraph *th* makes another sound, too. You must listen carefully to hear the difference between the two sounds.

 ▸ Say *thumb*.
 ▸ Listen to the sound /th/ at the beginning of the word *thumb*.
 ▸ Touch your throat as you say *thumb*. Your throat is silent and still.

6. **Say:** Now listen to the beginning sound in the word *that*.

 ▸ Say *that*.
 ▸ Listen to the sound /<u>th</u>/ at the beginning of the word *that*.
 ▸ Touch your throat as you say *that*. Your throat vibrates because you are making noise this time when you say /<u>th</u>/.

7. **Say:** When we see the letters *th*, we read either the sound /th/ or /<u>th</u>/. Both sounds are spelled with the same letters.

 ▸ Touch the *th* tile and say the sound /th/, as in *thumb*, which is quiet.
 ▸ Touch the *th* tile again, and this time say the sound /<u>th</u>/, as in *that*, which is noisy.

Objectives
- Identify and use the sound /th/.
- Identify and use the sound /<u>th</u>/.
- Identify the letters, given the sound /th/.
- Identify the letters, given the sound /<u>th</u>/.
- Identify and use the digraph *th*.
- Identify individual sounds in words.
- Blend sounds to create words.
- Write words by applying grade-level phonics knowledge.

Build Words

Help students use letters and sounds to build words.

1. Place the following letter tiles at the top of students' whiteboard: *a, i, n, p, s, t,* and *th*.

2. Draw three horizontal lines across the middle of students' whiteboard to represent the sounds in a word.

3. **Say:** Let's use letters and sounds to build the word *thin*.

4. Have students finger stretch the sounds in *thin*.

5. Have students

   ▸ Identify the first, next, and last sounds in *thin*.
   ▸ Choose the corresponding letter tile for each of the sounds.
   ▸ Move the letters to the correct lines on their whiteboard.

6. Guide students with these questions:

   ▸ What is the first sound in *thin*? /th/
      Which line do the letters for that sound go on? the first one
   ▸ What is the next sound in *thin*? /ĭ/
      Which line does the letter for that sound go on? the second one
   ▸ What's the last sound in *thin*? /n/
      Which line does the letter for that sound go on? the last one

7. Redirect students if they select the incorrect letter.

   Say: That sound is in the word [word], and it is the [first, second, third] sound. We want the sound [target sound].

   Continue until students select the correct letter.

8. Have students touch and say the word.

9. Have them say the word as they use a dry-erase marker to write the word on the whiteboard.

10. Repeat the activity to build the following words:

    ▸ *this* /th/ /ĭ/ /s/
    ▸ *that* /th/ /ă/ /t/
    ▸ *path* /p/ /ă/ /th/

Try It

Go Fish!

Have students complete page PH 58 in *K¹² PhonicsWorks Basic Activity Book* for more practice with the sounds /sh/ and /th/ for the digraphs *sh* and *th*. Have students read the word aloud and color the fish yellow for words that contain the sound /sh/ and pink for words that contain the sound /th/.

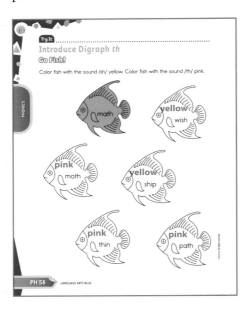

Dictation: Write Words

Have students practice identifying sounds and writing words.

1. Gather a pencil and the dictation notebook. Say the word *thin*. Then give these directions to students:

   ▸ Repeat the word.
   ▸ Write the word in your notebook.
   ▸ Read the word aloud.

2. When students have finished, write the following word on your whiteboard: *thin*.

3. Have them compare their answer to your correct version.

4. Repeat this procedure with the words *with* and *this*.

   ▸ If students make an error and don't see it, help them correct their mistake by having them finger stretch the sounds in the word they missed.
   ▸ If students are having difficulty selecting the correct letters or sounds, review those letters or sounds that are confusing them.
   ▸ If students have difficulty with first, middle, and last sounds, have them finger stretch the sounds in words.

 **20 minutes**

REVIEW: Digraph *th*

Students will work online independently to

▸ Practice the digraph *th*.
▸ Practice decoding text by reading a story.

Help students locate the online activities and provide support as needed.

Offline Alternative

No computer access? Have students point out and name things or words that contain the sound *th* or *th* (for example, *math* or *this*). You might also ask students to spell words that contain the digraph *th*.

Objectives

- Identify and use the sound /th/.
- Identify and use the sound /th/.
- Identify the letters, given the sound /th/.
- Identify the letters, given the sound /th/.
- Identify and use the digraph *th*.
- Identify individual sounds in words.
- Read aloud grade-level text with appropriate automaticity, prosody, accuracy, and rate.
- Decode words by applying grade-level word analysis skills.

Practice Digraphs *sh* and *th*

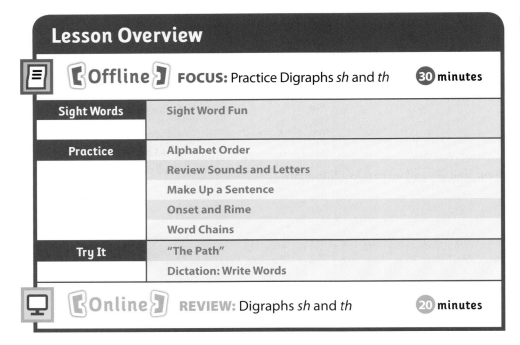

Lesson Overview

Offline FOCUS: Practice Digraphs *sh* and *th*   **30** minutes

Sight Words	Sight Word Fun
Practice	Alphabet Order
	Review Sounds and Letters
	Make Up a Sentence
	Onset and Rime
	Word Chains
Try It	"The Path"
	Dictation: Write Words

Online REVIEW: Digraphs *sh* and *th*   **20** minutes

Materials

Supplied
- *K¹² PhonicsWorks Readers Basic 5*, pp. 19–24
- whiteboard, Learning Coach
- whiteboard, student
- Tile Kit

Also Needed
- sight words box
- dictation notebook
- index cards (3)

Advance Preparation

Place lowercase letters in alphabetical order on your whiteboard.

For Make Up a Sentence, print the following words on index cards, using one index card per group of words: *red hat*, *big ship*, and *the path*.

 **30 minutes**

FOCUS: Practice Digraphs *sh* and *th*

Work **together** with students to complete offline Sight Words, Practice, and Try It activities.

Sight Words

Sight Word Fun

Help students learn the sight words *you*, *went*, and *we*, and up to two additional sight words they have yet to master.

Objectives
- Read sight words.
- Spell sight words.

1. Gather the sight word cards *you*, *went*, and *we*, and up to two additional sight word cards.

2. Choose one sight word card to begin.

   Say: Look at this word and take a picture of it in your mind. When you think you can spell the word yourself, turn the card over and use your letter tiles to spell the word.

3. After students spell the word, have them check the card to see if they spelled the word correctly.

   Say: Read aloud the word you spelled with the letter tiles.

4. Repeat the activity with the remaining sight words.

TIP Sight words can be very difficult for some students. Let them work at their own pace and really master these words.

Practice

Alphabet Order

Review alphabetic order with students.

1. Place the lowercase letter tiles *a* through *z* on students' whiteboard.

2. **Say:** Let's review the order of some letters in the alphabet.

3. Without looking at the whiteboard, have students

   ► Name the letter before *k*.
   ► Name the letter after *n*.
   ► Name any letter that comes before *f*.
   ► Name any letter that comes after *h*.
   ► Name any two letters that come before *m*.
   ► Name any two letters that come after *m*.

 If students hesitate, have them check the letters on the whiteboard.

Review Sounds and Letters

Help students review sounds for the letters and digraphs *d, e, l, o, r, sh, th,* and *x,* plus any letters that are confusing for them.

1. Place the following letter tiles in random order on students' whiteboard: *d, e, l, o, r, sh, th,* and *x,* plus any letters that are confusing.

2. **Say:** Let's go over some letters and sounds.

3. Point to each letter tile and have students say a sound that letter or letters make.

   ► *sh* /sh/   ► *o* /ŏ/
   ► *e* /ĕ/   ► *l* /l/
   ► *r* /r/   ► *d* /d/
   ► *th* /th/ or /<u>th</u>/   ► *x* /ks/

4. Say each of the following sounds. Have students repeat the sound and touch the corresponding letter tile.

   ► /sh/ *sh*   ► /ŏ/ *o*
   ► /ĕ/ *e*   ► /l/ *l*
   ► /r/ *r*   ► /d/ *d*
   ► /th/ *th*   ► /ks/ *x*
   ► /<u>th</u>/ *th*

5. As you do the activity, point to some letter tiles two or three times so that students don't think they are finished with a sound after they have named it.

6. Redirect students if they say an incorrect sound when you point to a letter tile.

   Say: That's the sound of another letter. What is the sound for this letter?

7. Help students if they touch the wrong letter tile after they repeat a sound.

   Say: That letter tile goes with the sound [sound for incorrect letter tile]. We're looking for the letter tile that goes with the sound [target sound].

Make Up a Sentence

Help students use words to make sentences.

1. Gather the index cards you prepared, and place them face down on the table in one pile.

2. Have students

   ► Select a card.
   ► Read the words.
   ► Use the words in an interesting, fun, or silly sentence.

TIP If students read a word incorrectly, have them finger stretch the sounds in the word.

Onset and Rime

In a word, the part of the syllable before the first vowel sound is the **onset**. The part of the syllable after the first vowel sound is the **rime**. For example, in *thump*, /th/ is the onset and *ump* is the rime. Help students put together words that are broken down into parts by onset and rime.

1. **Say:** I'm going to break a word into two parts. Your job is to put the parts together and say the word. If the first part of a word is /th/ and the last part of the word is *ump*, then the whole word is *thump*: /th/ ... *ump* ... *thump*.

2. Say the following pairs of word parts. Have students tell you the word that each pair forms.

   ► /th/ ... *ink* think
   ► /th̲/ ... *ose* those
   ► /b/ ... *ath* bath
   ► /t/ ... *enth* tenth

Word Chains

Have students build words by adding and changing letters to help them recognize and use individual sounds in words.

1. Place the following letter tiles at the top of students' whiteboard: *a, b, d, m, sh,* and *th.*

2. **Say:** I am going to build the first word in a chain. The word is *math.*

   ▸ I will pull down the letters for the sounds /m/, /ă/, and /th/ to spell the word *math.*

   ▸ I will touch and say *math.* To change *math* to *bath,* I will think about which sound is changed from the word *math* to *bath.* I will need to replace the letter *m* with the letter *b.*

   ▸ Touch and say the word *bath.* Now it's your turn to change *bath* to *bash.* You can spell *bash* by making only one change. Touch and say the new word.

3. Redirect students if they select the incorrect letter for any sound.

   Say: That letter is for the sound [incorrect sound]. We want the letter for the sound [target sound]. What letter makes that sound? Answers will vary.

4. Redirect students if they name the sound incorrectly.

   Say: To change the word [first word] to [target word], we need the letter for the sound [target sound].

   Show students how to make the change. Have them touch and say the new word after they move the letters.

5. Follow this procedure to make the following words: *dash* and *dab.*

6. For every new word, have students add, replace, or remove only one letter tile.

TIP If students struggle, review the sounds and letters that are confusing them.

Try It ....

"The Path"

Have students read "The Path" on page 19 of *K¹² PhonicsWorks Readers Basic 5.*

Students should read the story silently once or twice before reading the story aloud. When students miss a word that can be sounded out, point to it and give them three to six seconds to try the word again. If students still miss the word, tell them the word so the flow of the story isn't interrupted.

After reading the story, make a list of all the words students missed, and go over those words with them. You may use tiles to show students how to read the words.

Dictation: Write Words

Have students practice identifying sounds and writing words.

1. Gather a pencil and the dictation notebook. Say the word *that.* Then give these directions to students:

   ► Repeat the word.
   ► Write the word in your notebook.
   ► Read the word aloud.

2. When students have finished, write the following word on your whiteboard: *that.*

3. Have them compare their answer to your correct version.

4. Repeat this procedure with the words *then* and *math.*

   ► If students make an error and don't see it, help them correct their mistake by having them finger stretch the sounds in the word they missed.
   ► If students are having difficulty selecting the correct letters or sounds, review those letters or sounds that are confusing them.
   ► If students have difficulty with first, middle, and last sounds, have them finger stretch the sounds in words.

Objectives

- Read aloud grade-level text with appropriate automaticity, prosody, accuracy, and rate.
- Decode words by applying grade-level word analysis skills.
- Track text from left to right.
- Turn pages sequentially.
- Write words by applying grade-level phonics knowledge.
- Follow three-step directions.
- Identify and use the sound /th/.
- Identify and use the sound /th/.
- Identify the letters, given the sound /th/.
- Identify the letters, given the sound /th/.
- Identify and use the digraph *th.*
- Identify and use the sound /sh/.
- Identify the letters, given the sound /sh/.
- Identify and use the digraph *sh.*

 **20 minutes**

REVIEW: Digraphs *sh* and *th*

Students will work online independently to

▶ Practice the digraph *th*.

Help students locate the online activities and provide support as needed.

Offline Alternative

No computer access? Have students point out and name things or words that contain the sounds *th*, <u>*th*</u>, and *sh* (for example, *moth*, *then*, and *shop*). You might also ask students to spell words that contain the digraph *th* or *sh*.

Objectives
- Identify and use the sound /th/.
- Identify and use the sound /<u>th</u>/.
- Identify the letters, given the sound /th/.
- Identify the letters, given the sound /<u>th</u>/.
- Identify and use the digraph *th*.
- Identify and use the sound /sh/.
- Identify the letters, given the sound /sh/.
- Identify and use the digraph *sh*.
- Identify individual sounds in words.

Unit Checkpoint

Lesson Overview

🖥️ **〖Online〗** REVIEW: Digraphs *sh* and *th* **⓴ minutes**

📄 **〖Offline〗** UNIT CHECKPOINT: Digraphs **㉚ minutes**
sh and *th*

〖Materials〗

Supplied

• *K¹² PhonicsWorks Basic Assessments,* pp. PH 115–120

Objectives

- Identify and use the sound /<u>th</u>/.
- Identify and use the sound /th/.
- Identify and use the digraph *th*.
- Identify the letters, given the sound /<u>th</u>/.
- Identify the letters, given the sound /th/.
- Identify and use the sound /sh/.
- Identify and use the digraph *sh*.
- Identify the letters, given the sound /sh/.
- Identify letters of the alphabet.
- Identify individual sounds in words.
- Given the letter, identify the most common sound.
- Given the sound, identify the most common letter or letters.
- Read sight words.
- Read instructional-level text with 90% accuracy.
- Read aloud grade-level text with appropriate automaticity, prosody, accuracy, and rate.
- Write words by applying grade-level phonics knowledge.

 **⓴ minutes**

REVIEW: Digraphs *sh* and *th*

Students will review the digraphs *sh* and *th* to prepare for the Unit Checkpoint. Help students locate the online activities and provide support as needed.

Offline **30** minutes

UNIT CHECKPOINT: Digraphs *sh* and *th*

Explain that students are going to show what they have learned about letters, sounds, and words.

1. Give students the Unit Checkpoint pages for the Digraphs *sh* and *th* unit and print the Unit Checkpoint Answer Key, if you'd like.

2. Use the instructions below to help administer the Checkpoint to students. On the Answer Key or another sheet of paper, note student answers to oral response questions to help with scoring the Checkpoint later.

3. Use the Answer Key to score the Checkpoint, and then enter the results online.

Part 1. Say Sounds Have students read across the rows from left to right and say the sound or sounds that each letter, letters, or word part makes. Note any sounds they say incorrectly.

Part 2. Word Dissection For each word, say the sound students should identify. Have them read the word aloud and circle the letter or group of letters that spells the requested sound.

19. *ending sound*

20. *beginning sound*

21. *ending sound*

22. *middle sound*

23. *beginning sound*

Part 3. Finger Stretching Say each word to students. Have them say each word and finger stretch the sounds. Note any words they finger stretch incorrectly.

24. *ship*   27. *moth*

25. *this*   28. *with*

26. *shed*   29. *bath*

Part 4. Dictation Say each word to students. Have them repeat and write the word.

30. *fish*   32. *this*

31. *ship*   33. *bath*

Part 5. Read Aloud Listen to students read the sentences aloud. Count and note the number of words they read correctly.

Getting Stronger: Short Vowels (B)

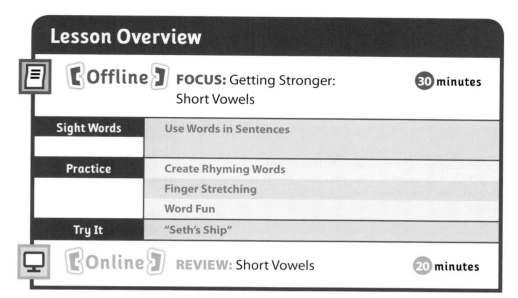

Lesson Overview

Offline **FOCUS:** Getting Stronger: Short Vowels — **30** minutes

Sight Words	Use Words in Sentences
Practice	Create Rhyming Words
	Finger Stretching
	Word Fun
Try It	"Seth's Ship"

Online **REVIEW:** Short Vowels — **20** minutes

Materials

Supplied
- *K¹² PhonicsWorks Readers Basic 5,* pp. 25–30

Also Needed
- sight words box
- index cards (10)

Advance Preparation

For Word Fun, print the following words on index cards, using one card per word: *rug, pan, dish, cup, nut, can, map, gum, tub,* and *hat.*

 **Offline** ⏲ **30 minutes**

FOCUS: Getting Stronger: Short Vowels

Work **together** with students to complete offline Sight Words, Practice, and Try It activities.

Sight Words ••

Use Words in Sentences

Help students use sight words in sentences.

1. Gather all the sight word cards students have yet to master from their sight words box. Spread the sight word cards on the table.

2. **Say:** Let's use sight words in sentences.

3. Have students

   ▸ Touch each card and read the word on it.
   ▸ Make up a sentence using the word.
   ▸ Put the card in a pile after using the word in a sentence.
   ▸ Go through the pile of cards and read each sight word again.
   ▸ Spell each word.

TIP If students have difficulty with any of the sight words, place those cards in a pile to review again.

Objectives
- Read sight words.
- Spell sight words.

Practice ••

Create Rhyming Words

Have students combine word parts and make words that rhyme.

1. **Say:** I'm going to break a word into two parts. Your job is to put the parts back together and say the word.

   ▸ For example, if the first part of the word is /p/ and the last part is /ăt/, then you'll say *pat*: /p/ . . . /ăt/ . . . *pat*.
   ▸ Next you'll add a new **beginning sound** to make a word that rhymes. For example, you'll use the same last part, /ăt/, and add a new first sound, like /m/. The rhyming word is /m/ . . . /ăt/ . . . *mat*.

2. **Say:** Now it's your turn: /f/ . . . /ăt/.

   ▸ What's the word? *fat*
   ▸ Now use the same last part, /ăt/, but add a new sound, /k/, at the beginning. What word did you make? *cat*

3. Say the two word parts. Have them say the word the parts form. Have them add a new beginning sound to the last part of the word to make rhyming words: /k/ . . . /ăt/ *cat*   Possible rhyming words: *rat, sat, bat, hat*

Objectives
- Identify words that rhyme.
- Identify short vowel sounds.
- Identify and use the sound /ă/.
- Identify and use the sound /ĕ/.
- Identify and use the sound /ĭ/.
- Identify and use the sound /ŏ/.
- Identify and use the sound /ŭ/.
- Given the letter, identify the most common sound.
- Given the sound, identify the most common letter or letters.
- Read aloud grade-level text with appropriate automaticity, prosody, accuracy, and rate.
- Identify complete sentences.

Finger Stretching

Use finger stretching to help students identify individual sounds in words.

1. **Say:** Let's review finger stretching. In the word *than*, the first sound is /<u>th</u>/, the next sound is /ă/, and the last sound is /n/. I will finger stretch each sound as I say it. Then I'll say the word while pulling my fist toward my body.

2. Finger stretch the word *than* for students.

3. **Say:** I'm going to say words with several sounds in them. You'll say each word and then finger stretch it while you say each sound in the word.

4. Say the following words and have students finger stretch them. After they finger stretch each word, ask them the question for that word.

   ► *hush* /h/ /ŭ/ /sh/   What is the middle sound? /ŭ/
   ► *wish* /w/ /ĭ/ /sh/   What is the first sound? /w/
   ► *ship* /sh/ /ĭ/ /p/   What is the last sound? /p/
   ► *gush* /g/ /ŭ/ /sh/   What is the middle sound? /ŭ/
   ► *this* /<u>th</u>/ /ĭ/ /s/   What is the first sound? /<u>th</u>/
   ► *shed* /sh/ /ĕ/ /d/   What is the middle sound? /ĕ/
   ► *than* /<u>th</u>/ /ă/ /n/   What is the first sound? /<u>th</u>/

 Refer to the *K¹² PhonicsWorks* DVD for a demonstration of finger stretching.

Word Fun

Have students practice reading words and identifying names of common objects.

1. Gather the index cards you prepared and place them face down in one pile.

2. **Say:** You are going to practice reading and writing some words.

   ► You will choose a card from the pile and read the word on it.
   ► Then you are going to flip the card over and write the word on the backside of the card.
   ► I'll try first.

3. Choose a card from the pile, and say and write the word.

   Say: Now it's your turn. Choose a card and read it to me.

4. If time permits, have students choose two words and draw a picture of those words on the back of the card.

 If students stumble over any words, have them touch and say the words. Touch and say these words along with them.

Try It

"Seth's Ship"

Have students read the "Seth's Ship" story on page 25 of *K¹² PhonicsWorks Readers Basic 5*.

Students should read the story silently once or twice before reading the story aloud. When students miss a word that can be sounded out, point to it and give them three to six seconds to try the word again. If students still miss the word, tell them the word so the flow of the story isn't interrupted.

After reading the story, make a list of all the words students missed, and go over those words with them. You may use letter tiles to show students how to read the words.

Objectives
- Read aloud grade-level text with appropriate automaticity, prosody, accuracy, and rate.
- Decode words by applying grade-level word analysis skills.
- Track text from left to right.
- Turn pages sequentially.

 **20 minutes**

REVIEW: Short Vowels

Students will work online independently to

▶ Practice the short vowel sounds /ă/, /ĕ/, /ĭ/, /ŏ/, /ŭ/ for the letters *a, e, i, o,* and *u.*

Help students locate the online activities and provide support as needed.

Offline Alternative

No computer access? Have students point out and name things or words that contain the short vowel sounds /ă/, /ĕ/, /ĭ/, /ŏ/, and /ŭ/, such as *path, Beth, thin, moth,* or *mush.* You might also ask students to spell simple words that contain the sounds /ă/, /ĕ/, /ĭ/, /ŏ/, and /ŭ/ made by the letters *a, e, i, o,* and *u* and other letters they have learned.

Objectives
- Identify short vowel sounds.
- Given the letter, identify the most common sound.
- Given the sound, identify the most common letter or letters.
- Identify and use the sound /ă/.
- Identify and use the sound /ĕ/.
- Identify and use the sound /ĭ/.
- Identify and use the sound /ŏ/.
- Identify and use the sound /ŭ/.
- Identify individual sounds in words.

Getting Stronger: Digraphs (A)

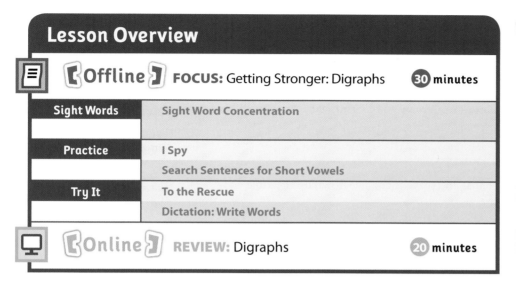

Lesson Overview

[Offline] **FOCUS:** Getting Stronger: Digraphs **30** minutes

Sight Words	Sight Word Concentration
Practice	I Spy
	Search Sentences for Short Vowels
Try It	To the Rescue
	Dictation: Write Words

[Online] **REVIEW:** Digraphs **20** minutes

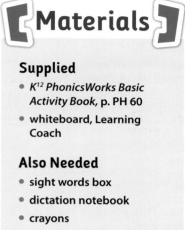

Materials

Supplied
- *K¹² PhonicsWorks Basic Activity Book*, p. PH 60
- whiteboard, Learning Coach

Also Needed
- sight words box
- dictation notebook
- crayons

Advance Preparation

Gather two sets of the sight word cards that students have yet to master.

 **Offline** **30** minutes

FOCUS: Getting Stronger: Digraphs

Work **together** with students to complete offline Sight Words, Practice, and Try It activities.

Sight Words

Sight Word Concentration
Help students review sight words.

1. Gather the two sets of sight word cards.

2. Scramble both sets of sight word cards and place them face down on the table or floor.

3. Turn over two cards at a time; take turns with students. If the cards match, the person turning over the matching cards reads the word and uses it in a sentence. If the cards don't match, the person turns them back over.

4. Remove and save the matching cards.

5. Continue the activity until all the cards are paired.

6. Have students read all the words.

7. Take the stack of words that students read correctly and dictate each word to them.

8. Have students write each word or spell it aloud.

TIP If students have difficulty with any sight words, let them work at their own pace to really master these words.

 Objectives
- Read sight words.
- Spell sight words.
- Write sight words.

Practice

I Spy
Have students name and use common objects to help them recognize individual sounds in words.

1. Explain to students that you will be playing I Spy and show them how to use the thumb and index finger to make a circle, simulating a spyglass.

2. **Say:** I say, "I spy, with my little eye, something that starts with the sound /l/." Your job is to guess what I spy. What I had in mind was the *light*. *Light* begins with the sound /l/.

3. Repeat Step 2 with a different object in the room.

4. **Say:** Are you ready to begin? I spy, with my little eye, something that starts with the sound [target sound]. Can you guess what it is?

 Objectives
- Identify individual sounds in words.
- Identify and use the digraph *sh*.
- Identify and use the digraph *th*.
- Identify short vowel sounds.
- Identify and use the sound /ă/.
- Identify and use the sound /ĕ/.
- Identify and use the sound /ĭ/.
- Identify and use the sound /ŏ/.
- Identify and use the sound /ŭ/.

5. After students have guessed the object, repeat Step 4 until you have spied six objects, or until students tire of the game. Possible words to use are *shoe, shirt, shadow, bath, math book, radio, telephone, dish, hair, table, floor, book, paper, computer, cup,* and *rug.*

6. Redirect students if they name an object with an incorrect sound.

   Say: The sound that begins the word [word] is [sound]. We're looking for the sound [target sound]. What is a word that begins with that sound? Now look around the room. What do you see that begins with that sound?

7. Narrow down the search to a certain part of the room if students become frustrated. If they continue to have trouble, narrow down the search to two objects.

   Say: What is the beginning sound of [target word]? What is the beginning sound of [another word]? Which one starts with the sound [target sound]?

Search Sentences for Short Vowels

Have students practice identifying **vowel sounds** in words that are in a sentence.

1. **Say:** I'm going to say a special sound that is in a word. You will repeat that sound and the word. The first sound is /ŭ/, as in the word *bump.*

2. Have students say the target sound /ŭ/ and the word *bump.*

3. **Say:** Now I will read a sentence. Repeat the sentence and tell me the word that has the same sound. The first sentence is *Ross likes to run.* Which word in the sentence has the special sound? *run*

4. Have students repeat the sentence and say the word.

5. Redirect students if they don't name the correct word.

   Say: Let me say the sentence again. Remember, you're listening for the sound [special sound].

6. Guide students if they have difficulty. Say two words from the sentence and have them choose the one with the target vowel sound.

7. Use the same procedure with the following words and sentences:

   ▸ /ŏ/, as in *top*   *Dan sat on the mat.* on
   ▸ /ĕ/, as in *then*   *Tim met Kim at the hut.* met
   ▸ /ŭ/, as in *shut*   *Sit on the rug.* rug
   ▸ /ĭ/, as in *pin*   *Gus did hug the pup.* did
   ▸ /ă/, as in *sat*   *Lynn did nab the fish.* nab

Try It

To the Rescue

Have students complete page PH 60 in *K¹² PhonicsWorks Basic Activity Book* for more practice with digraphs. Have students read each word and color the boxes that name real words to help the rabbit find the path to the log.

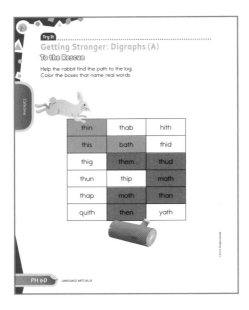

Dictation: Write Words

Have students practice identifying sounds and writing words.

1. Gather a pencil and the dictation notebook. Say the word *dish*. Then give these directions to students:

   ▸ Repeat the word.
   ▸ Write the word in your notebook.
   ▸ Read the word aloud.

2. When students have finished, write the following word on your whiteboard: *dish*.

3. Have them compare their answer to your correct version.

4. Repeat this procedure with the words *shut*, *that*, and *bath*.

   ▸ If students make an error and don't see it, help them correct their mistake by having them finger stretch the sounds in the word they missed.
   ▸ If students are having difficulty selecting the correct letters or sounds, review those letters or sounds that are confusing them.
   ▸ If students have difficulty with first, middle, and last sounds, have them finger stretch the sounds in words.

 **20 minutes**

REVIEW: Digraphs

Students will work online independently to

▶ Practice the digraphs *sh* and *th*.
▶ Practice decoding text by reading a story.

Help students locate the online activities and provide support as needed.

Offline Alternative

No computer access? Have students point out and name things or words that contain the digraphs *sh* and *th*, such as *fish*, *path*, and *then*. You might also ask students to spell simple words that contain the sounds /sh/, /th/, and /th/.

Objectives

- Identify and use the sound /sh/.
- Identify the letters, given the sound /sh/.
- Identify and use the digraph *sh*.
- Identify and use the sound /th/.
- Identify and use the sound /th/.
- Identify the letters, given the sound /th/.
- Identify the letters, given the sound /th/.
- Identify and use the digraph *th*.
- Identify individual sounds in words.
- Read aloud grade-level text with appropriate automaticity, prosody, accuracy, and rate.
- Decode words by applying grade-level word analysis skills.

Getting Stronger: Digraphs (B)

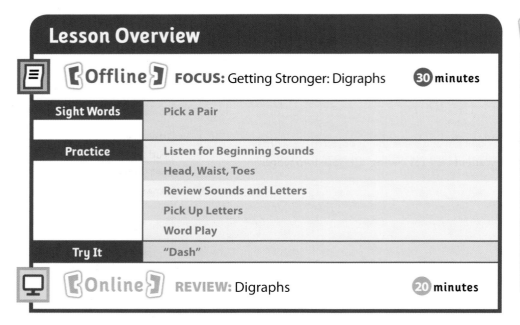

Lesson Overview

[Offline] **FOCUS:** Getting Stronger: Digraphs   **30** minutes

Sight Words	Pick a Pair
Practice	Listen for Beginning Sounds
	Head, Waist, Toes
	Review Sounds and Letters
	Pick Up Letters
	Word Play
Try It	"Dash"

[Online] **REVIEW:** Digraphs   **20** minutes

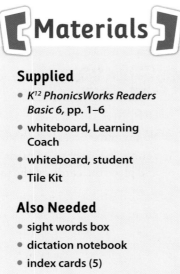

Materials

Supplied
- *K¹² PhonicsWorks Readers Basic 6*, pp. 1–6
- whiteboard, Learning Coach
- whiteboard, student
- Tile Kit

Also Needed
- sight words box
- dictation notebook
- index cards (5)

Advance Preparation

For Word Play, print each of the following words on index cards, using one card per word: *pup, dig, fish, dot,* and *that.*

 **30 minutes**

FOCUS: Getting Stronger: Digraphs

Work **together** with students to complete offline Sight Words, Practice, and Try It activities.

Sight Words

Pick a Pair

Play a card game with students for more practice with sight words.

1. Gather the sight word cards that students are reviewing. Choose two words and place the cards on the table.

2. Ask questions to help students identify each word. For example, if the words are *or* and *one*, you could ask, "Which word names a number?" If the words are *on* and *but*, you could ask, "Which word is the opposite of *off*?"

3. Continue the activity until students identify all the words.

4. Take the stack of words that students read correctly and dictate each word to them.

5. Have students write each word or spell it aloud.

Objectives
- Read sight words.
- Spell sight words.
- Write sight words.

Practice

Listen for Beginning Sounds

Help students identify beginning sounds in words.

1. **Say:** I'm going to say a word. Listen for the beginning sound. Then tell me the sound.

   ▸ For example, if I say *shine*, you will say /sh/ because the first sound you hear in *shine* is /sh/.
   ▸ Now it's your turn. Listen to the word I say. You repeat the word and then tell me the first sound in the word.

2. Repeat the procedure, using the following words to help students recognize beginning sounds:

   ▸ *balloon* /b/
   ▸ *vase* /v/
   ▸ *then* /th/
   ▸ *shed* /sh/
   ▸ *think* /th/
   ▸ *shape* /sh/
   ▸ *never* /n/

Objectives
- Identify beginning sounds in words.
- Identify individual sounds in words.
- Identify and use the digraph *sh*.
- Identify and use the digraph *th*.
- Identify and use the digraph *ch*.
- Identify short vowel sounds.
- Given the letter, identify the most common sound.
- Given the sound, identify the most common letter or letters.
- Read aloud grade-level text with appropriate automaticity, prosody, accuracy, and rate.
- Write words by applying grade-level phonics knowledge.

Head, Waist, Toes

Help students practice identifying the sounds in words.

1. **Say:** Let's identify sounds in words by touching parts of our body as we say each sound. For example, I'll say *can*, which has three sounds, and you'll repeat the word. Do these steps with me:

    ▸ The first sound in *can* is /k/, so I touch my head as I say /k/.
    ▸ The middle sound is /ă/, so I touch my waist as I say /ă/.
    ▸ The last sound is /n/, so I touch my toes as I say /n/.

2. Say the words below. Have students repeat each word and then touch their head, waist, and toes as they say each sound in the word. After they say the sounds in each word, ask them the question for that word.

    ▸ thin /th/ /ĭ/ /n/   What is the first sound? /th/
    ▸ rush /r/ /ŭ/ /sh/   What is the last sound? /sh/
    ▸ cab /k/ /ă/ /b/   What is the first sound? /k/
    ▸ thud /th/ /ŭ/ /d/   What is the first sound? /th/
    ▸ shot /sh/ /ŏ/ /t/   What is the first sound? /sh/
    ▸ sit /s/ /ĭ/ /t/   What is the middle sound? /ĭ/

(TIP) If students have difficulty with this activity, be sure they can identify beginning, middle, and end. If students still have difficulty with this activity, try finger stretching the words instead.

Review Sounds and Letters

Help students review sounds for the letters *e, g, h, j, o, p, qu, s,* and *w,* plus any letters that are confusing for them.

1. Place the following letter tiles in random order on students' whiteboard: *e, g, h, j, o, p, qu, s,* and *w,* plus any letters that are confusing.

2. **Say:** Let's go over some letters and sounds.

3. Point to each letter tile and have students say a sound that letter or letters make.

    ▸ *g* /g/   ▸ *w* /w/
    ▸ *j* /j/   ▸ *qu* /kw/
    ▸ *o* /ŏ/   ▸ *p* /p/
    ▸ *h* /h/   ▸ *e* /ĕ/
    ▸ *s* /s/

4. Say each of the following sounds. Have students repeat the sound and touch the corresponding letter tile.

    ▸ /g/ *g*   ▸ /w/ *w*
    ▸ /j/ *j*   ▸ /kw/ *qu*
    ▸ /ŏ/ *o*   ▸ /p/ *p*
    ▸ /h/ *h*   ▸ /ĕ/ *e*
    ▸ /s/ *s*

5. As you do the activity, point to some letter tiles two or three times so that students don't think they are finished with a sound after they have named it.

6. Redirect students if they say an incorrect sound when you point to a letter tile.

   Say: That's the sound of another letter. What is the sound for this letter?

7. Help students if they touch the wrong letter tile after they repeat a sound.

   Say: That letter tile goes with the sound [sound for incorrect letter tile]. We're looking for the letter tile that goes with the sound [target sound].

Pick Up Letters

Help students use letters and sounds to make words and sentences.

1. Place the following letter tiles on students' whiteboard: *b, e, p, sh, th,* and *z.*

2. **Say:** Let's play a game with these letters.

3. Pick up the letter tile for *sh.*

4. **Say:** I chose the letters for the digraph *sh.* The sound is /sh/. A word that starts with the sound /sh/ is *shine.* A sentence using that word is *I see the sun shine in the sky.* Now it's your turn.

5. Continue taking turns until all the letter tiles have been chosen.

6. Have students answer the following questions for each letter or group of letters.

   ▸ What is (are) the letter(s)?
   ▸ What is the sound?
   ▸ What is a word that starts with that sound?
   ▸ What sentence can you make with that word?

7. Redirect students if they name a word that starts with the sound, but not the letter (such as *knob*).

   Say: That is a word that doesn't follow the rules that we know for spelling. Try another word.

8. Prompt students if they have trouble matching the sounds with words. For example,

   Say: That's the sound /j/, as in *jelly.* Can you think of another word that starts with that sound?

Word Play

Have students practice reading and writing words and sentences.

1. Gather the index cards you prepared.

2. **Say:** You are going to read a set of words, and choose one of the words and use it in a sentence. You will make up the sentence and write in on your whiteboard.

3. Have students touch and say each word.

4. Help students to use proper capitalization and punctuation in the sentence that they write.

 ·

"Dash"

Have students read "Dash" on page 1 of *K*[12] *PhonicsWorks Readers Basic 6*.

Students should read the story silently once or twice before reading the story aloud. When students miss a word that can be sounded out, point to it and give them three to six seconds to try the word again. If students still miss the word, tell them the word so the flow of the story isn't interrupted.

After reading the story, make a list of all the words students missed, and go over those words with them. You may use letter tiles to show students how to read the words.

Objectives
- Read aloud grade-level text with appropriate automaticity, prosody, accuracy, and rate.
- Decode words by applying grade-level word analysis skills.
- Track text from left to right.
- Turn pages sequentially.

 Online 🔟 **minutes**

REVIEW: Digraphs

Students will work online independently to

▶ Practice the digraphs *sh* and *th*.

Help students locate the online activities and provide support as needed.

Objectives
- Identify and use the sound /sh/.
- Identify the letters, given the sound /sh/.
- Identify and use the digraph *sh*.
- Identify and use the sound /th/.
- Identify and use the sound /th/.
- Identify the letters, given the sound /th/.
- Identify the letters, given the sound /th/.
- Identify and use the digraph *th*.
- Identify individual sounds in words.

Offline Alternative

No computer access? Have students point out and name things or words that contain the digraphs *sh* and *th*, such as *sash*, *bath*, and *that*. You might also ask students to spell simple words that contain the sounds /sh/, /th/, and /th/.

Unit Checkpoint

Lesson Overview

[Online] **REVIEW:** Short Vowels and Digraphs — **20** minutes

 [Offline] **UNIT CHECKPOINT:** Getting Stronger: Short Vowels and Digraphs — **30** minutes

[Materials]

Supplied

- *K¹² PhonicsWorks Basic Assessments,* pp. PH 121–126

Objectives

- Identify and use the sound /ă/.
- Identify and use the sound /ĕ/.
- Identify and use the sound /ĭ/.
- Identify and use the sound /ŏ/.
- Identify and use the sound /ŭ/.
- Identify short vowel sounds.
- Identify and use the sound /<u>th</u>/.
- Identify and use the sound /th/.
- Identify and use the digraph *th.*
- Identify the letters, given the sound /<u>th</u>/.
- Identify the letters, given the sound /th/.
- Identify and use the sound /sh/.
- Identify and use the digraph *sh.*
- Identify the letters, given the sound /sh/.
- Read, write, and spell words containing short vowel sounds.

- Identify individual sounds in words.
- Given the letter, identify the most common sound.
- Given the sound, identify the most common letter or letters.
- Read instructional-level text with 90% accuracy.
- Read aloud grade-level text with appropriate automaticity, prosody, accuracy, and rate.
- Write words by applying grade-level phonics knowledge.
- Write sight words.
- Read sight words.

 **20** minutes

REVIEW: Short Vowels and Digraphs

Students will review the short vowel sounds /ă/, /ĕ/, /ĭ/, /ŏ/, and /ŭ/ for the letters *a, e, i, o,* and *u* and the digraphs *sh* and *th* to prepare for the Unit Checkpoint. Help students locate the online activities and provide support as needed.

 **30 minutes**

UNIT CHECKPOINT: Getting Stronger: Short Vowels and Digraphs

Explain that students are going to show what they have learned about sounds, letters, and words.

1. Give students the Unit Checkpoint pages for the Getting Stronger: Short Vowels and Digraphs unit and print the Unit Checkpoint Answer Key, if you'd like.

2. Use the instructions below to help administer the Checkpoint to students. On the Answer Key or another sheet of paper, note student answers to oral response questions to help with scoring the Checkpoint later.

3. Use the Answer Key to score the Checkpoint, and then enter the results online.

Part 1. Say Sounds Have students read across the rows from left to right and say the sound or sounds that each letter, letters, or word part makes. Note any sounds they say incorrectly.

Part 2. Word Dissection For each word, say the sound students should identify. Have them read the word aloud and circle the letter or group of letters that spells the requested sound.

19. *ending sound*

20. *beginning sound*

21. *ending sound*

22. *middle sound*

23. *middle sound*

Part 3. Finger Stretching Say each word to students. Have them say each word and finger stretch the sounds. Note any words they finger stretch incorrectly.

24. *shop*   27. *moth*

25. *dash*   28. *with*

26. *shed*   29. *thud*

Part 4. Dictation Say each word to students. Have them repeat and write the word.

30. *wish*   32. *that*

31. *shut*   33. *math*

Part 5. Read Aloud Listen to students read the sentences aloud. Count and note the number of words they read correctly.

Part 6. Say Letters Say each sound. Have students say a letter or letters that make that sound. Note any incorrect responses.

35. /th/	44. /ă/
36. /sh/	45. /ĕ/
37. /kw/	46. /sh/
38. /ŏ/	47. /ŭ/
39. /r/	48. /<u>th</u>/
40. /ŭ/	49. /ĭ/
41. /ĭ/	50. /l/
42. /ks/	51. /w/
43. /ĕ/	52. /ŏ/

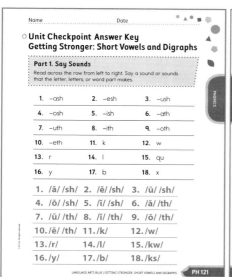

○ **Unit Checkpoint Answer Key**
Getting Stronger: Short Vowels and Digraphs

Part 1. Say Sounds
Read across the row from left to right. Say a sound or sounds that the letter, letters, or word part makes.

1. –ash	2. –esh	3. –ush
4. –osh	5. –ish	6. –ath
7. –uth	8. –ith	9. –oth
10. –eth	11. k	12. w
13. r	14. l	15. qu
16. y	17. b	18. x

1. /ă/ /sh/	2. /ĕ/ /sh/	3. /ŭ/ /sh/
4. /ŏ/ /sh/	5. /ĭ/ /sh/	6. /ă/ /th/
7. /ŭ/ /th/	8. /ĭ/ /th/	9. /ŏ/ /th/
10. /ĕ/ /th/	11. /k/	12. /w/
13. /r/	14. /l/	15. /kw/
16. /y/	17. /b/	18. /ks/

LANGUAGE ARTS BLUE | GETTING STRONGER: SHORT VOWELS AND DIGRAPHS   PH 121

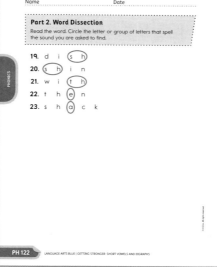

PH 122   LANGUAGE ARTS BLUE | GETTING STRONGER: SHORT VOWELS AND DIGRAPHS

Part 2. Word Dissection
Read the word. Circle the letter or group of letters that spell the sound you are asked to find.

19. d i (s h)
20. (s h) i n
21. w i (t h)
22. t h (e) n
23. s h (a) c k

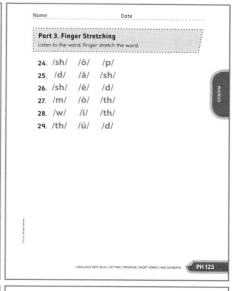

Part 3. Finger Stretching
Listen to the word. Finger stretch the word.

24. /sh/ /ŏ/ /p/
25. /d/ /ă/ /sh/
26. /sh/ /ĕ/ /d/
27. /m/ /ŏ/ /th/
28. /w/ /ĭ/ /th/
29. /th/ /ŭ/ /d/

LANGUAGE ARTS BLUE | GETTING STRONGER: SHORT VOWELS AND DIGRAPHS   PH 123

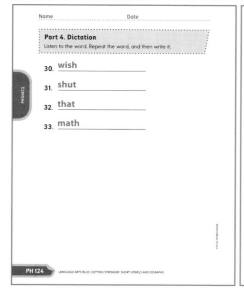

Part 4. Dictation
Listen to the word. Repeat the word, and then write it.

30. wish
31. shut
32. that
33. math

PH 124   LANGUAGE ARTS BLUE | GETTING STRONGER: SHORT VOWELS AND DIGRAPHS

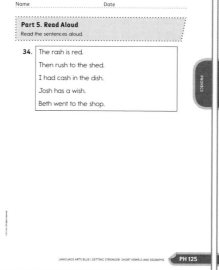

Part 5. Read Aloud
Read the sentences aloud.

34.
> The rash is red.
> Then rush to the shed.
> I had cash in the dish.
> Josh has a wish.
> Beth went to the shop.

LANGUAGE ARTS BLUE | GETTING STRONGER: SHORT VOWELS AND DIGRAPHS   PH 125

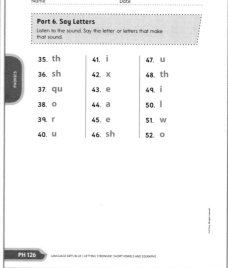

Part 6. Say Letters
Listen to the sound. Say the letter or letters that make that sound.

35. th	41. i	47. u
36. sh	42. x	48. th
37. qu	43. e	49. i
38. o	44. a	50. l
39. r	45. e	51. w
40. u	46. sh	52. o

PH 126   LANGUAGE ARTS BLUE | GETTING STRONGER: SHORT VOWELS AND DIGRAPHS

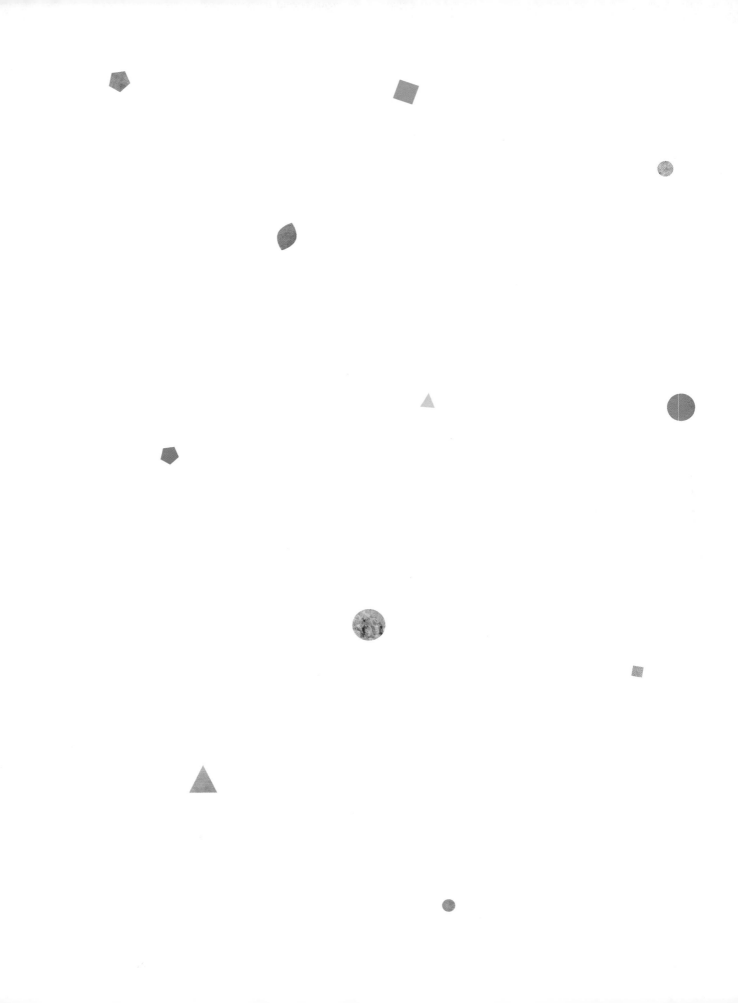

Introduce Digraph *wh*

Unit Overview

In this unit, students will
- ▶ Learn the sight words *what*, *their*, and *want*.
- ▶ Identify letters and sounds in the alphabet.
- ▶ Learn the digraphs *wh* and *ch*.
- ▶ Identify beginning and ending sounds in words.
- ▶ Build words.

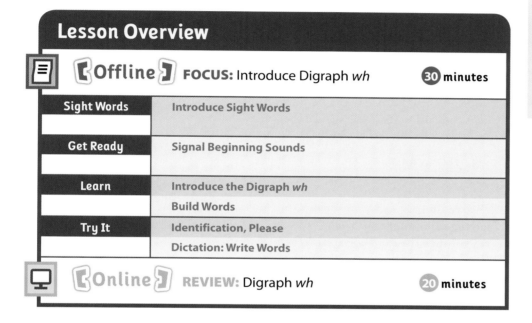

Lesson Overview

Offline FOCUS: Introduce Digraph *wh* **30** minutes

Sight Words	Introduce Sight Words
Get Ready	Signal Beginning Sounds
Learn	Introduce the Digraph *wh*
	Build Words
Try It	Identification, Please
	Dictation: Write Words

Online REVIEW: Digraph *wh* **20** minutes

Materials

Supplied
- *K¹² PhonicsWorks Basic Activity Book,* p. PH 61
- whiteboard, Learning Coach
- whiteboard, student
- Tile Kit

Also Needed
- sight words box
- dictation notebook

 **Offline** **30 minutes**

FOCUS: Introduce Digraph *wh*

Work **together** with students to complete offline Sight Words, Get Ready, Learn, and Try It activities.

Sight Words

Introduce Sight Words

Help students learn the sight words *what*, *their*, and *want*.

1. Gather the sight word cards *what*, *their*, and *want*.

2. Show students the *what* card.

3. **Say:** This is the word *what*. We see this word so often that we want to be able to read and spell *what* quickly without thinking about it. Look closely at the word *what*. Spell the word *what* aloud. Take a picture of the word *what* in your mind. When you think you can spell *what* yourself, turn the card over and use your letter tiles to spell the word *what*. Check the card to see if you spelled the word *what* correctly. Read aloud the word you spelled with the letter tiles.

4. Repeat the activity with the remaining sight words.

5. Chart students' progress on the back of each card.

   ► Divide the back of the card into two columns.
   ► Label the first column "Read" and the second column "Spell."
   ► Record the dates that students read or spell the word correctly. When students can read and spell the word correctly three times in a row, they have mastered the word. You may want to put a star or sticker on the card when they have mastered that word.

6. Add the cards to students' sight words box.

 TIP Sight words can be very difficult for some students. Let students work at their own pace and really master these words, as they occur frequently in reading and writing.

Objectives
- Read sight words.
- Spell sight words.

Get Ready

Signal Beginning Sounds

Use a special signal to help students identify **beginning sounds** in words.

1. **Say:** I'm going to tell you a special sound, and then I'll say some words. Repeat each word I say and make a special signal to tell me where the special sound is. If the special sound is at the beginning of the word, pat your cheek. If the special sound is **not** at the beginning of the word, just smile at me. For example,

   ▸ If I ask you to listen for the sound /th/ and I say the word *think*, you'll repeat the word *think* and pat your cheek because *think* has the sound /th/ at the beginning.

   ▸ If I say the word *blink*, you'll repeat the word *blink* and smile at me because *blink* has the sound /b/, not /th/, at the beginning.

2. Say each sound and group of words. Have students make the special signal to identify the beginning sound.

   ▸ /th/: *think, blink, thirsty, first, shift, three* pat cheek: *think, thirsty, three*
   ▸ /w/: *think, whisper, whistle, munch, while* pat cheek: *whisper, whistle, while*
   ▸ /sh/: *show, crisp, stomp, shy, shadow,* pat cheek: *show, shy, shadow*

TIP If students can't identify the beginning sound of each word, say the word again and emphasize the beginning sound by repeating it three times (for example, /t/ /t/ /t/ *taste*). You can also draw out the beginning sound when you say the word (for example, *mmmommy*). If necessary, have students look at your mouth while you repeat the sounds.

Objectives
- Identify beginning sounds in words.

Learn

Introduce the Digraph *wh*

To help students learn the digraph *wh*, have them practice identifying and naming words that have the letters *wh* for the sound /w/.

1. Place the following letter tile on students' whiteboard: *wh*.

2. **Say:** You've learned all the letters of the alphabet and the sounds that go with them. Now we're going to learn about a sound that is spelled with two letters. This sound is spelled *wh*.

3. Point to the *wh* tile.

   Say: When we see *wh*, we read the sound /w/. Touch the *wh* tile and say /w/.

4. **Say:** Two letters that make one sound are called a **digraph**. Let's practice the sound /w/ and the letters *wh*.

Objectives
- Identify and use the digraph *wh*.
- Identify the sound /w/, given the digraph *wh*.
- Identify the digraph *wh*, given the sound /w/.
- Write words by applying grade-level phonics knowledge.
- Identify individual sounds in words.
- Blend sounds to create words.

5. **Say:** The sound for the digraph *wh* is /w/, as in the word *when*. Can you think of some more words that have the sound /w/ spelled *wh*?

6. Help students if they can't think of any words. These words are often question words. Examples include *when*, *what*, *why*, and *where*.

(TIP) *K[12] PhonicsWorks* early reading program teaches that the digraph *wh* and the consonant *w* make the same sound, which is /w/. Teaching students that *wh* makes a different sound from *w* would not conform to the pronunciation of words in twenty-first-century American English.

Build Words

Help students use letters and sounds to build words.

1. Place the following letter tiles at the top of students' whiteboard: *e, i, n, p,* and *wh.*

2. Draw three horizontal lines across the middle of students' whiteboard to represent the sounds in a word.

3. **Say:** Let's use letters and sounds to build the word *when.*

4. Have students finger stretch the sounds in *when.*

5. Have students
   ▸ Identify the first, next, and last sounds in *when.*
   ▸ Choose the corresponding letter for each of the sounds.
   ▸ Move the letters to the correct lines on their whiteboard.

6. Guide students with these questions:
   ▸ What is the first sound in *when*? /w/
     Which line do the letters for that sound go on? the first one
   ▸ What is the next sound in *when*? /ĕ/
     Which line does the letter for that sound go on? the second one
   ▸ What's the last sound in *when*? /n/
     Which line does the letter for that sound go on? the last one

7. Redirect students if they select the incorrect letter.

   Say: That sound is in the word [word], and it is the [first, second, third] sound. We want the sound [target sound].

   Continue until students select the correct letter.

8. Have students touch and say the word.

9. Have them say the word as they use a dry-erase marker to write the word on the whiteboard.

10. Repeat the activity to build the word *whip.* /w/ /ĭ/ /p/

Try It

Identification, Please

Have students complete page PH 61 in *K¹² PhonicsWorks Basic Activity Book* for more practice with digraphs. Have students read each word part or letter aloud and circle the digraphs *wh*, *sh*, and *th*.

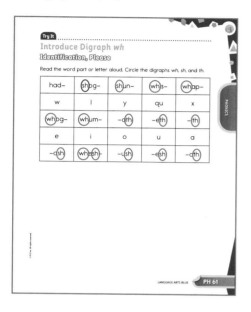

Dictation: Write Words

Have students practice identifying sounds and writing words.

1. Gather a pencil and the dictation notebook. Say the word *when*. Then give these directions to students:
   - Repeat the word.
   - Write the word in your notebook.
   - Read the word aloud.

2. When students have finished, write the following word on your whiteboard: *when*.

3. Have them compare their answer to your correct version.

4. Repeat this procedure with the words *whip* and *which*.
   - If students make an error and don't see it, help them correct their mistake by having them finger stretch the sounds in the word they missed.
   - If students are having difficulty selecting the correct letters or sounds, review those letters or sounds that are confusing them.
   - If students have difficulty with first, middle, and last sounds, have them finger stretch the sounds in words.

 **20 minutes**

REVIEW: Digraph *wh*

Students will work online independently to

▶ Practice the digraph *wh*.

▶ Practice decoding text by reading a story.

Help students locate the online activities and provide support as needed.

Offline Alternative

No computer access? Have students point out and name things or words that contain the spelling *wh* for the sound /w/ (for example, *whiz* or *whim*). You might also ask students to spell words that contain the digraph *wh*.

 Objectives

• Identify and use the digraph *wh*.

• Identify the sound /w/, given the digraph *wh*.

• Identify the digraph *wh*, given the sound /w/.

• Identify individual sounds in words.

• Read aloud grade-level text with appropriate automaticity, prosody, accuracy, and rate.

• Decode words by applying grade-level word analysis skills.

Practice Digraph *wh*

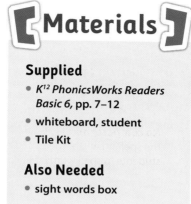
Lesson Overview

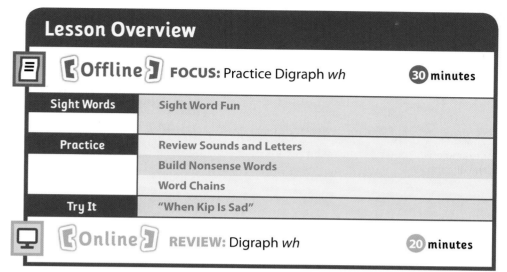

⟨Offline⟩ FOCUS: Practice Digraph *wh*   **30** minutes

Sight Words	Sight Word Fun
Practice	Review Sounds and Letters
	Build Nonsense Words
	Word Chains
Try It	"When Kip Is Sad"

⟨Online⟩ REVIEW: Digraph *wh*   **20** minutes

Materials

Supplied
- *K¹² PhonicsWorks Readers Basic 6*, pp. 7–12
- whiteboard, student
- Tile Kit

Also Needed
- sight words box

 **30 minutes**

FOCUS: Practice Digraph *wh*

Work **together** with students to complete offline Sight Words, Practice, and Try It activities.

Sight Words

Sight Word Fun

Help students learn the sight words *what, their,* and *want,* and up to two additional sight words they have yet to master.

1. Gather the sight word cards *what, their,* and *want,* and up to two additional sight word cards.

2. Choose one sight word card to begin.

   Say: Look at this word and take a picture of it in your mind. When you think you can spell the word yourself, turn the card over and use your letter tiles to spell the word.

3. After students spell the word, have them check the card to see if they spelled the word correctly.

   Say: Read aloud the word you spelled with the letter tiles.

4. Repeat the activity with the remaining sight words.

TIP Sight words can be very difficult for some students. Let them work at their own pace and really master these words.

Objectives
- Read sight words.
- Spell sight words.

Practice

Review Sounds and Letters

Help students review sounds for the letters and digraphs *b, j, s, sh, th, w,* and *wh,* plus any letters that are confusing for them.

1. Place the following letter tiles in random order on students' whiteboard: *b, j, s, sh, th, w,* and *wh,* plus any letters that are confusing.

2. **Say:** Let's go over some letters and sounds.

3. Point to each letter tile and have students say a sound the letter or letters make.

   ▸ *sh* /sh/
   ▸ *s* /s/
   ▸ *th* /th/ or /th/
   ▸ *wh* /w/
   ▸ *b* /b/
   ▸ *j* /j/
   ▸ *w* /w/

Objectives
- Given the letter, identify the most common sound.
- Given the sound, identify the most common letter or letters.
- Identify individual sounds in words.
- Blend sounds to create words.
- Identify the digraph *wh,* given the sound /w/.
- Identify the sound /w/, given the digraph *wh.*
- Identify and use the digraph *wh.*
- Identify the new word when one sound is changed in a word.

4. Say each of the following sounds. Have students repeat the sound and touch the corresponding letter tile.

- ► /sh/ *sh*
- ► /s/ *s*
- ► /th/ or /<u>th</u>/ *th*
- ► /w/ *wh* or *w*
- ► /b/ *b*
- ► /j/ *j*

5. As you do the activity, point to some letter tiles two or three times so that students don't think they are finished with a sound after they have named it.

6. Redirect students if they say an incorrect sound when you point to a letter tile.

   Say: That's the sound of another letter. What is the sound for this letter?

7. Help students if they touch the wrong letter tile after they repeat a sound.

   Say: That letter tile goes with the sound [sound for incorrect letter tile]. We're looking for the letter tile that goes with the sound [target sound].

Build Nonsense Words

Help students use letters and sounds to build nonsense words.

1. Place the following letter tiles at the top of students' whiteboard: *d, i, s,* and *wh.*

2. Draw three horizontal lines across the middle of students' whiteboard to represent the sounds in a word.

3. **Say:** Some words don't have any meaning. We call these **nonsense words**. Even though we don't know what a word means, we can still read it. Nonsense words will be very important when we read longer words. When we break longer words into parts, sometimes the parts are nonsense words.

4. **Say:** Let's use letters and sounds to build the word *whis.*

5. Have students finger stretch the sounds in *whis.*

6. Have students

   - ► Identify the first, next, and last sounds in *whis.*
   - ► Choose the corresponding letter for each sound.
   - ► Move the letters to the correct lines on their whiteboard.

7. Guide students with these questions:

   - ► What is the first sound in *whis*? /w/
     Which line do the letters for that sound go on? the first one
   - ► What is the next sound in *whis*? /ĭ/
     Which line does the letter for that sound go on? the second one
   - ► What's the last sound in *whis*? /s/
     Which line does the letter for that sound go on? the last one

8. Redirect students if they select the incorrect letter.

   Say: That sound is in the word [word], and it is the [first, second, third] sound. We want the sound [target sound].

   Continue until students select the correct letter.

9. Have students touch and say the word.

10. Have them say the word as they use a dry-erase marker to write the word on the whiteboard.

11. Repeat the activity to build the word *whid*. /w/ /ĭ/ /d/

Word Chains

Have students build words by adding and changing letters to help them recognize and use individual sounds in words.

1. Place the following letters at the top of students' whiteboard: *B, b, d, e, n, t, th,* and *wh*.

2. **Say:** I am going to build the first word in a chain. The word is *when*.

   ▸ I will pull down the letters for the sounds /w/, /ĕ/, and /n/ to spell the word *when*.
   ▸ I will touch and say *when*. To change *when* to *then*, I will think about which sound is changed from the word *when* to *then*. I will need to replace the letters *wh* with the letters *th*.
   ▸ Touch and say the word *then*. Now it's your turn to change *then* to *den*. You can spell *den* by making only one change. Touch and say the new word.

3. Redirect students if they select the incorrect letter for any sound.

   Say: That letter is for the sound [incorrect sound]. We want the letter for the sound [target sound]. What letter makes that sound? Answers will vary.

4. Redirect students if they name the sound incorrectly.

   Say: To change the word [first word] to [target word], we need the letter for the sound [target sound].

   Show students how to make the change. Have them touch and say the new word after they move the letters.

5. Follow this procedure to make the following words: *Ben, Beth, bet*.

6. For every new word, have students add, replace, or remove only one letter tile.

(TIP) For the proper name word, replace the lowercase letter with a capital letter. Remember to change back to the lowercase letter for the next word in the chain. If students struggle, review the sounds and letters that are confusing them.

Try It ....

"When Kip Is Sad"

Have students read "When Kip Is Sad" on page 7 of *K¹² PhonicsWorks Readers Basic 6.*

Students should read the story silently once or twice before reading the story aloud. When students miss a word that can be sounded out, point to it and give them three to six seconds to try the word again. If students still miss the word, tell them the word so the flow of the story isn't interrupted.

After reading the story, make a list of all the words students missed, and go over those words with them. You may use tiles to show students how to read the words.

Objectives

- Read aloud grade-level text with appropriate automaticity, prosody, accuracy, and rate.
- Decode words by applying grade-level word analysis skills.
- Track text from left to right.
- Turn pages sequentially.

 **20 minutes**

REVIEW: Digraph *wh*

Students will work online independently to

▶ Practice the digraph *wh.*

Help students locate the online activities and provide support as needed.

***

Offline Alternative

No computer access? Have students point out and name things or words that contain the spelling *wh* for the sound /w/ (for example, *what* or *whap*). You might also ask students to spell words that contain the digraph *wh.*

Objectives

- Identify and use the digraph *wh.*
- Identify the sound /w/, given the digraph *wh.*
- Identify the digraph *wh*, given the sound /w/.
- Identify individual sounds in words.
- Read aloud grade-level text with appropriate automaticity, prosody, accuracy, and rate.
- Decode words by applying grade-level word analysis skills.

Introduce Digraph *ch*

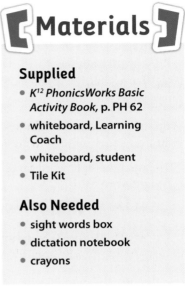

Lesson Overview

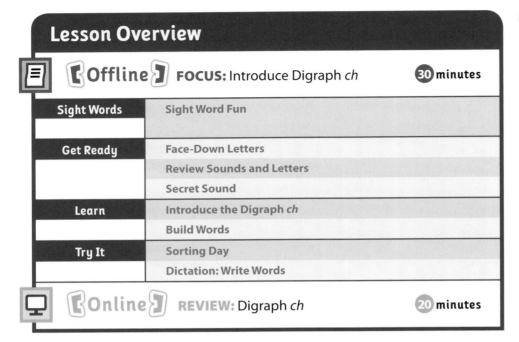

Offline	FOCUS: Introduce Digraph *ch*	30 minutes

Sight Words	Sight Word Fun
Get Ready	Face-Down Letters
	Review Sounds and Letters
	Secret Sound
Learn	Introduce the Digraph *ch*
	Build Words
Try It	Sorting Day
	Dictation: Write Words

Online	REVIEW: Digraph *ch*	20 minutes

Materials

Supplied
- *K¹² PhonicsWorks Basic Activity Book*, p. PH 62
- whiteboard, Learning Coach
- whiteboard, student
- Tile Kit

Also Needed
- sight words box
- dictation notebook
- crayons

Advance Preparation

Place lowercase letter tiles in alphabetical order on your whiteboard.

〔Offline〕 **30** minutes

FOCUS: Introduce Digraph *ch*

Work **together** with students to complete offline Sight Words, Get Ready, Learn, and Try It activities.

Sight Words
••

Sight Word Fun

Help students learn the sight words *what*, *their*, and *want*, and up to two additional sight words they have yet to master.

1. Gather the sight word cards *what*, *their*, and *want*, and up to two additional sight word cards.

2. Choose one sight word card to begin.

   Say: Look at this word and take a picture of it in your mind. When you think you can spell the word yourself, turn the card over and use your letter tiles to spell the word.

3. After students spell the word, have them check the card to see if they spelled the word correctly.

   Say: Read aloud the word you spelled with the letter tiles.

4. Repeat the activity with the remaining sight words.

TIP Sight words can be very difficult for some students. Let them work at their own pace and really master these words.

Objectives
- Read sight words.
- Spell sight words.

Get Ready
••

Face-Down Letters

To help students master the ability to recognize the letters of the alphabet, have them practice identifying and naming letters. Grab your whiteboard with letters placed in alphabetical order.

1. Lay your whiteboard down on a flat surface and flip over the following letter tiles so they are face down on the whiteboard: *d*, *g*, *h*, *p*, *r*, *t*, *x*, and *z*.

2. **Say:** These letters are face down. We are looking at the back of them. Name each letter and then turn it over to see if you were right.

TIP If students miss any of the letters, have them turn over the missed ones and try again.

Objectives
- Identify letters of the alphabet.
- Given the letter, identify the most common sound.
- Given the sound, identify the most common letter or letters.
- Identify beginning sounds in words.
- Identify individual sounds in words.
- Identify and use the sound /ch/.

Review Sounds and Letters

Help students review sounds for the letters and digraphs *c, d, j, k, s, sh, th,* and *wh,* plus any letters that are confusing for them.

1. Place the following letter tiles in random order on students' whiteboard: *c, d, j, k, s, sh, th,* and *wh,* plus any letters that are confusing.

2. **Say:** Let's go over some letters and sounds.

3. Point to each letter tile and have students say a sound that letter or letters make.

   - *wh* /w/
   - *sh* /sh/
   - *th* /th/ or /<u>th</u>/
   - *k* /k/
   - *c* /k/
   - *d* /d/
   - *s* /s/
   - *j* /j/

4. Say each of the following sounds. Have students repeat the sound and touch the corresponding letter tile.

   - /w/ *wh*
   - /sh/ *sh*
   - /th/ or /<u>th</u>/ *th*
   - /k/ *c* or *k*
   - /d/ *d*
   - /s/ *s*
   - /j/ *j*

5. As you do the activity, point to some letter tiles two or three times so that students don't think they are finished with a sound after they have named it.

6. Redirect students if they say an incorrect sound when you point to a letter tile.

   Say: That's the sound of another letter. What is the sound for this letter?

7. Help students if they touch the wrong letter tile after they repeat a sound.

   Say: That letter tile goes with the sound [sound for incorrect letter tile]. We're looking for the letter tile that goes with the sound [target sound].

Secret Sound

Say groups of words to help students recognize **beginning sounds** in words.

1. **Say:** I am going to say some groups of words. Listen for a secret sound in the beginning of each word. Then tell me what sound you hear in the beginning of each group of words.

2. Say each of the following groups of words. Have students identify the secret sound in each group.

   - *whisper, which, whistle, while* /w/
   - *think, thud, thorn, thin* /th/
   - *child, chicken, church, check* /ch/

TIP If students can't identify the secret sound, have them listen while you say each word again and then have them repeat each word. Have students say what sound they hear in the beginning of each word.

Learn

Introduce the Digraph *ch*

To help students learn the digraph *ch*, have them practice identifying and naming the letters *ch* for the sound /ch/.

1. Place the following letter tile on students' whiteboard: *ch*.

2. **Say:** You've learned all the letters of the alphabet and the sounds that go with them. Now we're going to learn about another sound. It's like the /sh/, /th/, /t̲h̲/, and /wh/ sounds you've learned.

3. Point to the *ch* tile.

   Say: When we see *ch*, we read the sound /ch/. Touch the *ch* tile and say the sound /ch/.

4. **Say:** Two letters that make one sound are called a **digraph**. Let's practice the sound /ch/ and the letters *ch*.

5. **Say:** The sound for the digraph *ch* is /ch/, as in the word *chip*. Can you think of some more words that have the sound /ch/ spelled *ch*?

6. Help students if they can't think of any words. Examples include *chin, chop, chap, chug, rich, much,* and *which*.

Objectives

- Identify and use the sound /ch/.
- Identify the letters, given the sound /ch/.
- Identify and use the digraph *ch*.
- Identify individual sounds in words.
- Blend sounds to create words.
- Write words by applying grade-level phonics knowledge.

Build Words

Help students use letters and sounds to build words.

1. Place the following letter tiles at the top of students' whiteboard: *ch, i, n, p, r, s, u,* and *wh*.

2. Draw three horizontal lines across the middle of students' whiteboard to represent the sounds in a word.

3. **Say:** Let's use letters and sounds to build the word *chin*.

4. Have students finger stretch the sounds in *chin*.

5. Have students

   ▸ Identify the first, next, and last sounds in *chin*.
   ▸ Choose the corresponding letter for each of the sounds.
   ▸ Move the letters to the correct lines on their whiteboard.

6. Guide students with these questions:

   ▸ What is the first sound in *chin*? /ch/
     Which line do the letters for that sound go on? the first one
   ▸ What is the next sound in *chin*? /ĭ/
     Which line does the letter for that sound go on? the second one
   ▸ What's the last sound in *chin*? /n/
     Which line does the letter for that sound go on? the last one

7. Redirect students if they select the incorrect letter.

    Say: That sound is in the word [word], and it is the [first, second, third] sound. We want the sound [target sound].

    Continue until students select the correct letter.

8. Have students touch and say the word.

9. Have them say the word as they use a dry-erase marker to write the word on the whiteboard.

10. Repeat the activity to build the following words:

    ▸ *chip* /ch/ /ĭ/ /p/
    ▸ *which* /w/ /ĭ/ /ch/
    ▸ *such* /s/ /ŭ/ /ch/
    ▸ *rich* /r/ /ĭ/ /ch/

Try It

Sorting Day

Have students complete page PH 62 in *K¹² PhonicsWorks Basic Activity Book* for more practice with digraphs. Have students read the word aloud and color the box blue for words that contain the digraph *wh* and pink for words that contain the digraph *ch*.

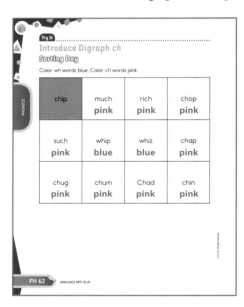

Objectives

- Identify and use the sound /wh/.
- Identify and use the sound /ch/.
- Identify the letters, given the sound /ch/.
- Identify and use the digraph *ch*.
- Identify individual sounds in words.
- Write words by applying grade-level phonics knowledge.
- Follow three-step directions.

Dictation: Write Words

Have students practice identifying sounds and writing words.

1. Gather a pencil and the dictation notebook. Say the word *chip*. Then give these directions to students:

   ▶ Repeat the word.
   ▶ Write the word in your notebook.
   ▶ Read the word aloud.

2. When students have finished, write the following word on your whiteboard: *chip*.

3. Have them compare their answer to your correct version.

4. Repeat this procedure with the words *chap* and *much*.

   ▶ If students make an error and don't see it, help them correct their mistake by having them finger stretch the sounds in the word they missed.
   ▶ If students are having difficulty selecting the correct letters or sounds, review those letters or sounds that are confusing them.
   ▶ If students have difficulty with first, middle, and last sounds, have them finger stretch the sounds in words.

   **minutes**

REVIEW: Digraph *ch*

Students will work online independently to

▶ Practice the digraph *ch*.
▶ Practice decoding text by reading a story.

Help students locate the online activities and provide support as needed.

Offline Alternative

No computer access? Have students point out and name things or words that contain the digraph *ch* (for example, *chum* or *rich*). You might also ask students to spell words that contain the digraph *ch*.

Objectives

- Identify and use the sound /ch/.
- Identify the letters, given the sound /ch/.
- Identify and use the digraph *ch*.
- Identify individual sounds in words.
- Read aloud grade-level text with appropriate automaticity, prosody, accuracy, and rate.
- Decode words by applying grade-level word analysis skills.

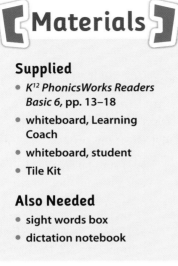

Practice Digraphs *wh* and *ch*

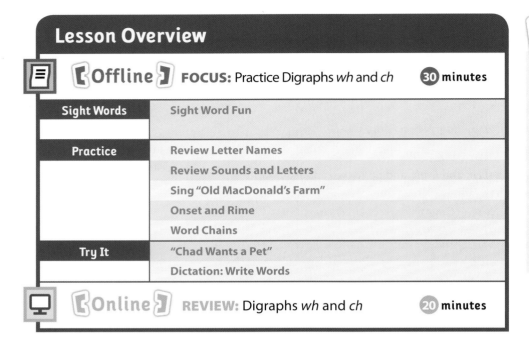

Lesson Overview

Offline FOCUS: Practice Digraphs *wh* and *ch*   **30** minutes

Sight Words	Sight Word Fun
Practice	Review Letter Names
	Review Sounds and Letters
	Sing "Old MacDonald's Farm"
	Onset and Rime
	Word Chains
Try It	"Chad Wants a Pet"
	Dictation: Write Words

Online REVIEW: Digraphs *wh* and *ch*   **20** minutes

Materials

Supplied
- *K¹² PhonicsWorks Readers Basic 6,* pp. 13–18
- whiteboard, Learning Coach
- whiteboard, student
- Tile Kit

Also Needed
- sight words box
- dictation notebook

Advance Preparation

Place lowercase letters in alphabetical order and digraphs on your whiteboard.

[Offline] 30 minutes

FOCUS: Practice Digraphs *wh* and *ch*

Work **together** with students to complete offline Sight Words, Practice, and Try It activities.

Sight Words

Sight Word Fun

Help students learn the sight words *what, their,* and *want,* and up to two additional sight words they have yet to master.

1. Gather the sight word cards *what, their,* and *want,* and up to two additional sight word cards.

2. Choose one sight word card to begin.

   Say: Look at this word and take a picture of it in your mind. When you think you can spell the word yourself, turn the card over and use your letter tiles to spell the word.

3. After students spell the word, have them check the card to see if they spelled the word correctly.

   Say: Read aloud the word you spelled with the letter tiles.

4. Repeat the activity with the remaining sight words.

TIP Sight words can be very difficult for some students. Let them work at their own pace and really master these words.

Objectives
- Read sight words.
- Spell sight words.

Practice

Review Letter Names

To help students master the alphabet, have them practice identifying and naming the letters *e, f, g, h, i, j,* and *z.* Grab your whiteboard with letters.

1. Point to each letter and have students touch and name each one.

   e   f   g   h   i   j   z

2. Say the name of each letter. After each one, have students repeat the name and touch the tile.

   e   f   g   h   i   j   z

3. Redirect students if they name a letter incorrectly.

   ‣ Name the letter students missed.
   ‣ Have them touch the letter and say its name.
   ‣ Have students trace the shape of the letter with their finger on the brown side of their board, and have them say the letter's name as they trace the shape.
   ‣ If students name a letter incorrectly twice, point to the letter and tell them its name. Have students touch the letter and say its name.

Review Sounds and Letters

Help students review sounds for the letters and digraphs *ch, e, h, k, m, qu, th, u,* and *wh,* plus any letters that are confusing for them.

1. Place the following letter tiles in random order on students' whiteboard: *ch, e, h, k, m, qu, th, u,* and *wh,* plus any letters that are confusing.

2. **Say:** Let's go over some letters and sounds.

3. Point to each letter tile and have students say a sound that letter or letters make.

   ‣ *wh* /w/
   ‣ *ch* /ch/
   ‣ *e* /ĕ/
   ‣ *th* /th/ or /<u>th</u>/
   ‣ *u* /ŭ/
   ‣ *m* /m/
   ‣ *qu* /kw/
   ‣ *k* /k/
   ‣ *h* /h/

4. Say each of the following sounds. Have students repeat the sound and touch the corresponding letter tile.

   ‣ /w/ *wh*
   ‣ /ch/ *ch*
   ‣ /ĕ/ *e*
   ‣ /th/ *th*
   ‣ /<u>th</u>/ *th*
   ‣ /ŭ/ *u*
   ‣ /m/ *m*
   ‣ /kw/ *qu*
   ‣ /k/ *k*
   ‣ /h/ *h*

5. As you do the activity, point to some letter tiles two or three times so that students don't think they are finished with a sound after they have named it.

6. Redirect students if they say an incorrect sound when you point to a letter tile.

   Say: That's the sound of another letter. What is the sound for this letter?

7. Help students if they touch the wrong letter tile after they repeat a sound.

   Say: That letter tile goes with the sound [sound for incorrect letter tile]. We're looking for the letter tile that goes with the sound [target sound].

Sing "Old MacDonald's Farm"

To review digraphs and the letters of the alphabet, have students sing the song "Old MacDonald's Farm." Grab your whiteboard with letters and digraphs.

1. **Say:** Do you remember "Old MacDonald's Farm"? Get ready to sing the song. Think of an animal you want to have on the farm. When you reach that part of the song ("... and on that farm he had a _____ "), point to the beginning letter of that word.

2. Repeat the song until students have named all of the animals they know. When they have finished, you may sing the song and let them point to the first letter of the animals you name.

3. Redirect students if they point to a letter that could be the sound but isn't— such as the letter *k* for *cow*.

   Say: The letter *k* does stand for the sound /k/, but the word *cow* starts with the letter *c*.

Onset and Rime

In a word, the part of the syllable before the first vowel sound is the **onset**. The part of the syllable after the first vowel sound is the **rime**. For example, in *church*, /ch/ is the onset and *urch* is the rime. Help students put together words that are broken down into parts by onset and rime.

1. **Say:** I'm going to break a word into two parts. Your job is to put the parts together and say the word. If the first part of a word is /ch/ and the last part of the word is *urch*, then the whole word is *church*: /ch/ ... *urch* ... *church*.

2. Say the following pairs of word parts. Have students tell you the word that each pair forms.

   ▶ /w/ ... *hile* *while*
   ▶ /ch/ ... *est* *chest*

Word Chains

Have students build words by adding and changing letters to help them recognize and use individual sounds in words.

1. Place the following letters at the top of students' whiteboard: *ch, i, n, p, sh,* and *wh.*

2. **Say:** I am going to build the first word in a chain. The word is *chin.*

   ▶ I will pull down the letters for the sounds /ch/, /ĭ/, and /n/ to spell the word *chin.*

   ▶ I will touch and say *chin.* To change *chin* to *chip,* I will think about which sound is changed from the word *chin* to *chip.* I will need to replace the letter *n* with the letter *p.*

   ▶ Touch and say the word *chip.* Now it's your turn to change *chip* to *whip.* You can spell *whip* by making only one change. Touch and say the new word.

3. Redirect students if they select the incorrect letter for any sound.

   Say: That letter is for the sound [incorrect sound]. We want the letter for the sound [target sound]. What letter makes that sound? Answers will vary.

4. Redirect students if they name the sound incorrectly.

   Say: To change the word [first word] to [target word], we need the letter for the sound [target sound].

   Show students how to make the change. Have them touch and say the new word after they move the letters.

5. Follow this procedure to make the following words: *ship, shin, chin.*

6. For every new word, have students add, replace, or remove only one letter tile.

Try It

"Chad Wants a Pet"

Have students read "Chad Wants a Pet" on page 13 of *K¹² PhonicsWorks Readers Basic 6.*

Students should read the story silently once or twice before reading the story aloud. When students miss a word that can be sounded out, point to it and give them three to six seconds to try the word again. If students still miss the word, tell them the word so the flow of the story isn't interrupted.

After reading the story, make a list of all the words students missed, and go over those words with them. You may use tiles to show students how to read the words.

Objectives

- Read aloud grade-level text with appropriate automaticity, prosody, accuracy, and rate.
- Decode words by applying grade-level word analysis skills.
- Track text from left to right.
- Turn pages sequentially.
- Write words by applying grade-level phonics knowledge.
- Follow three-step directions.

Dictation: Write Words

Have students practice identifying sounds and writing words.

1. Gather a pencil and the dictation notebook. Say the word *chat*. Then give these directions to students:

   ▸ Repeat the word.
   ▸ Write the word in your notebook.
   ▸ Read the word aloud.

2. When students have finished, write the following word on your whiteboard: *chat*.

3. Have them compare their answer to your correct version.

4. Repeat this procedure with the words *chin*, *chop*, *when*, and *whip*.

   ▸ If students make an error and don't see it, help them correct their mistake by having them finger stretch the sounds in the word they missed.
   ▸ If students are having difficulty selecting the correct letters or sounds, review those letters or sounds that are confusing them.
   ▸ If students have difficulty with first, middle, and last sounds, have them finger stretch the sounds in words.

 **20 minutes**

REVIEW: Digraphs *wh* and *ch*

Students will work online independently to

▸ Practice the digraphs *wh* and *ch*.

Help students locate the online activities and provide support as needed.

Offline Alternative

No computer access? Have students point out and name things or words that contain the digraphs *wh* and *ch* (for example, *when* or *chop*). You might also ask students to spell words that contain the digraphs *wh* and *ch*.

 Objectives

- Identify and use the digraph *wh*.
- Identify the sound /w/, given the digraph *wh*.
- Identify the digraph *wh*, given the sound /w/.
- Identify and use the digraph *ch*.
- Identify and use the sound /ch/.
- Identify the letters, given the sound /ch/.
- Identify individual sounds in words.

Unit Checkpoint

Lesson Overview

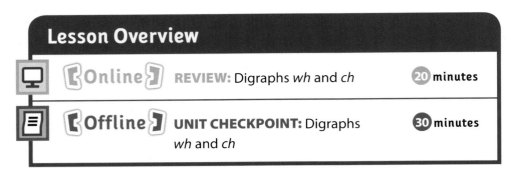

Online — REVIEW: Digraphs *wh* and *ch* — **20** minutes

Offline — UNIT CHECKPOINT: Digraphs *wh* and *ch* — **30** minutes

Materials

Supplied
- *K¹² PhonicsWorks Basic Assessments,* pp. PH 127–132

Objectives

- Identify the digraph *wh*, given the sound /w/.
- Identify the sound /w/, given the digraph *wh*.
- Identify and use the digraph *wh*.
- Identify the letters, given the sound /ch/.
- Identify the sound /ch/, given the digraph *ch*.
- Identify and use the digraph *ch*.
- Identify letters of the alphabet.
- Identify individual sounds in words.
- Given the sound, identify the most common letter or letters.
- Read sight words.
- Read instructional-level text with 90% accuracy.
- Read aloud grade-level text with appropriate automaticity, prosody, accuracy, and rate.
- Write words by applying grade-level phonics knowledge.

 **20** minutes

REVIEW: **Digraphs *wh* and *ch***

Students will review sounds for the digraphs *wh* and *ch* to prepare for the Unit Checkpoint. Help students locate the online activities and provide support as needed.

PH 622   **Language Arts Blue**

[Offline] 30 minutes

UNIT CHECKPOINT: Digraphs *wh* and *ch*

Explain that students are going to show what they have learned about letters, sounds, and words.

1. Give students the Unit Checkpoint pages for the Digraphs *wh* and *ch* unit and print the Unit Checkpoint Answer Key, if you'd like.

2. Use the instructions below to help administer the Checkpoint to students. On the Answer Key or another sheet of paper, note student answers to oral response questions to help with scoring the Checkpoint later.

3. Use the Answer Key to score the Checkpoint, and then enter the results online.

Part 1. Read Word Parts, Nonsense Words, and Words Have students read across the rows from left to right and say the sounds that each word part, nonsense word, or word makes. Note any word or word part they say incorrectly.

Part 2. Word Dissection For each word, say the sound students should identify. Have them read the word aloud and circle the letter or group of letters that spells the requested sound.

19. *beginning sound*

20. *beginning sound*

21. *ending sound*

22. *middle sound*

23. *beginning sound*

Part 3. Finger Stretching Say each word to students. Have them say each word and finger stretch the sounds. Note any words they finger stretch incorrectly.

24. *chin*   27. *such*

25. *which*   28. *whip*

26. *whiz*   29. *much*

Part 4. Dictation Say each word to students. Have them repeat and write the word.

30. *chat*   33. *much*

31. *rich*   34. *what*

32. *chop*   35. *when*

Part 5. Read Aloud Listen to students read the sentences aloud. Count and note the number of words they read correctly.

Part 6. Say Letters Say each sound. Have students say a letter or letters that make that sound. Note any incorrect responses.

37. /ch/
38. /th/
39. /sh/
40. /ĕ/
41. /ks/
42. /w/
43. /ĭ/
44. /ă/
45. /r/

46. /ŏ/
47. /ch/
48. /th/
49. /ŭ/
50. /ks/
51. /w/
52. /kw/
53. /y/
54. /l/

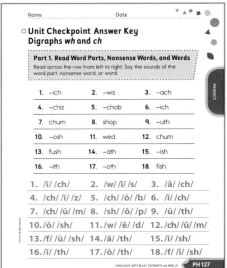

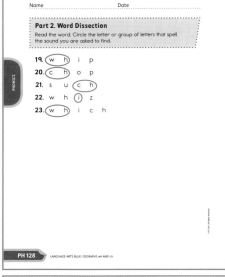

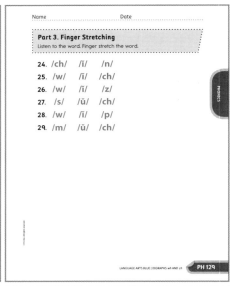

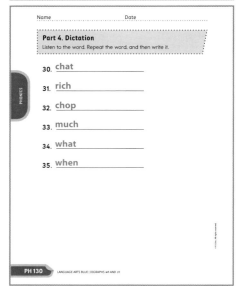

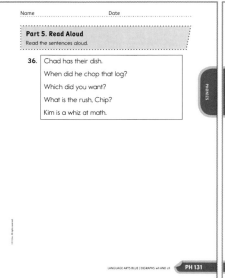

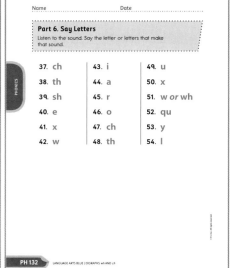

Getting Stronger: Letter Sounds (A)

Unit Overview

In this unit, students will
- ▸ Review sight words.
- ▸ Review the short vowel sounds /ă/, /ě/, /ĭ/, /ŏ/, and /ŭ/ for the letters *a, e, i, o,* and *u.*
- ▸ Review sounds and letters of the alphabet.
- ▸ Review the sound and letters for digraphs.
- ▸ Practice reading and writing.

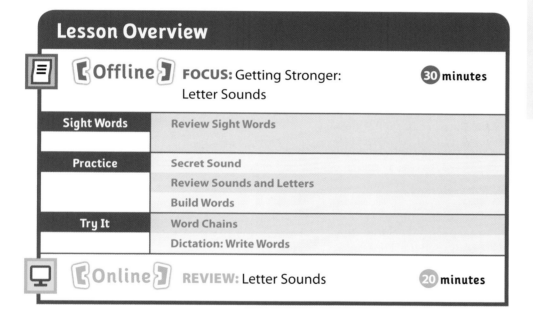

Lesson Overview

📃	**⟦Offline⟧ FOCUS:** Getting Stronger: Letter Sounds	**30** minutes

Sight Words	Review Sight Words
Practice	Secret Sound
	Review Sounds and Letters
	Build Words
Try It	Word Chains
	Dictation: Write Words

🖥	**⟦Online⟧ REVIEW:** Letter Sounds	**20** minutes

Materials

Supplied
- K¹² *PhonicsWorks Basic Activity Book,* p. PH 63
- whiteboard, Learning Coach
- whiteboard, student
- Tile Kit

Also Needed
- sight words box
- dictation notebook
- crayons

 **30 minutes**

FOCUS: Getting Stronger: Letter Sounds

Work **together** with students to complete offline Sight Words, Practice, and Try It activities.

Sight Words

Review Sight Words

Help students learn to recognize sight words.

1. Gather all the sight word cards students have yet to master from their sight words box. Stack the cards on the table face down.

2. Have students pick up a word and read it to you.

3. If they read it quickly and correctly, put the card in one stack. If they hesitate or do not read the word correctly, put it in another stack. The second stack should have words that they will review again.

4. Take the stack of words that students read correctly and dictate each word to them. They may choose to either write the word or spell it aloud.

5. If students spell the word correctly, they have mastered the word. If they misspell the word, add it to the stack of cards to review again.

6. Chart students' progress on the back of each card.

   ▸ Divide the back of the card into two columns.
   ▸ Label the first column "Read" and the second column "Spell."
   ▸ Record the dates that students read or spell the word correctly. When students can read and spell the word correctly three times in a row, they have mastered the word. You may want to put a star or sticker on their card when they have mastered that word.

TIP Even if students can read and spell all the words correctly, it is still beneficial for them to review sight words. Choose as many additional words as you would like for each subsequent activity.

Objectives
- Read sight words.
- Spell sight words.
- Write sight words.

Practice •

Secret Sound

Say groups of words to help students recognize **beginning sounds** in words.

1. **Say:** I am going to say some groups of words. Listen for a secret sound at the beginning of each word. Then tell me what sound you hear at the beginning of each group of words.

2. Say each of the following groups of words. Have students identify the secret sound in each group.

   ▶ *shin, ship, shop* /sh/
   ▶ *mail, milk, myself* /m/
   ▶ *that, then, those* /<u>th</u>/
   ▶ *which, when, why* /w/
   ▶ *dog, dip, deep* /d/

   TIP If students can't identify the secret sound, have them listen while you say each word again and then have them repeat each word. Have students say what sound they hear at the beginning of each word.

Objectives

- Identify beginning sounds in words.
- Given the letter, identify the most common sound.
- Given the sound, identify the most common letter or letters.
- Identify individual sounds in words.
- Blend sounds to create words.
- Write words by applying grade-level phonics knowledge.

Review Sounds and Letters

Help students review sounds for the letters *d, e, i, n, o, p, r, u,* and *z,* plus any letters that are confusing for them.

1. Place the following letter tiles in random order on students' whiteboard: *d, e, i, n, o, p, r, u,* and *z,* plus any letters that are confusing.

2. **Say:** Let's go over some letters and sounds.

3. Point to each letter tile and have students say a sound that letter makes.

   ▶ *i* /ĭ/   ▶ *p* /p/
   ▶ *e* /ĕ/   ▶ *n* /n/
   ▶ *u* /ŭ/   ▶ *d* /d/
   ▶ *o* /ŏ/   ▶ *z* /z/
   ▶ *r* /r/

4. Say each of the following sounds. Have students repeat the sound and touch the corresponding letter tile.

   ▶ /ĭ/ *i*   ▶ /p/ *p*
   ▶ /ĕ/ *e*   ▶ /n/ *n*
   ▶ /ŭ/ *u*   ▶ /d/ *d*
   ▶ /ŏ/ *o*   ▶ /z/ *z*
   ▶ /r/ *r*

5. As you do the activity, point to some letter tiles two or three times so that students don't think they are finished with a sound after they have named it.

6. Redirect students if they say an incorrect sound when you point to a letter tile.

   Say: That's the sound of another letter. What is the sound for this letter?

7. Help students if they touch the wrong letter tile after they repeat a sound.

   Say: That letter tile goes with the sound [sound for incorrect letter tile]. We're looking for the letter tile that goes with the sound [target sound].

Build Words

Help students use letters and sounds to build words.

1. Place the following letter tiles at the top of students' whiteboard: *a, b, c, ch, i, m, n, p, sh, u,* and *w.*

2. Draw three horizontal lines across the middle of students' whiteboard to represent the sounds in a word.

3. **Say:** Let's use letters and sounds to build the word *wish.*

4. Have students finger stretch the sounds in *wish.*

5. Have students
   ▸ Identify the first, next, and last sounds in *wish.*
   ▸ Choose the corresponding letter for each of the sounds.
   ▸ Move the letters to the correct lines on their whiteboard.

6. Guide students with these questions:
   ▸ What is the first sound in *wish*? /w/
     Which line does the letter for that sound go on? the first one
   ▸ What is the next sound in *wish*? /ĭ/
     Which line does the letter for that sound go on? the second one
   ▸ What's the last sound in *wish*? /sh/
     Which line do the letters for that sound go on? the last one

7. Redirect students if they select the incorrect letter.

   Say: That sound is in the word [word], and it is the [first, second, third] sound. We want the sound [target sound].

   Continue until students select the correct letter.

8. Have students touch and say the word.

9. Have them say the word as they use a dry-erase marker to write the word on the whiteboard.

10. Repeat the activity to build the following words:
    ▸ *much* /m/ /ŭ/ /ch/
    ▸ *cub* /k/ /ŭ/ /b/
    ▸ *pan* /p/ /ă/ /n/

Try It

Word Chains

Have students complete page PH 63 in *K¹² PhonicsWorks Basic Activity Book* for more practice with letters and sounds. Have them find and color the box that has one letter changed in the next group of letters.

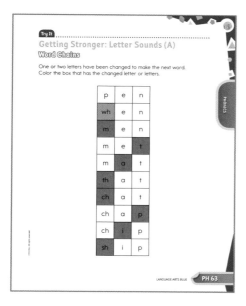

Objectives
- Identify the new word when one sound is changed in a word.
- Write words by applying grade-level phonics knowledge.
- Follow three-step directions.

Dictation: Write Words

Have students practice identifying sounds and writing words.

1. Gather a pencil and the dictation notebook. Say the word *shop*. Then give these directions to students:
   - Repeat the word.
   - Write the word in your notebook.
   - Read the word aloud.

2. When students have finished, write the following word on your whiteboard: *shop*.

3. Have them compare their answer to your correct version.

4. Repeat this procedure with the words *such* and *hash*.
   - If students make an error and don't see it, help them correct their mistake by having them finger stretch the sounds in the word they missed.
   - If students are having difficulty selecting the correct letters or sounds, review those letters or sounds that are confusing them.
   - If students have difficulty with first, middle, and last sounds, have them finger stretch the sounds in words.

 **20 minutes**

REVIEW: Letter Sounds

Students will work online independently to

- ▸ Practice letter sounds.
- ▸ Practice decoding text by reading a story.

Help students locate the online activities and provide support as needed.

Offline Alternative

No computer access? Have students practice the letters and sounds in the alphabet. You might have them spell consonant-vowel-consonant words and state what letter is the vowel, such as *man, a; mop, o; sit, i; get, e;* and *cub, u.*

Objectives

- Given the letter, identify the most common sound.
- Given the sound, identify the most common letter or letters.
- Identify individual sounds in words.
- Identify short vowel sounds.
- Read aloud grade-level text with appropriate automaticity, prosody, accuracy, and rate.
- Decode words by applying grade-level word analysis skills.

Getting Stronger: Letter Sounds (B)

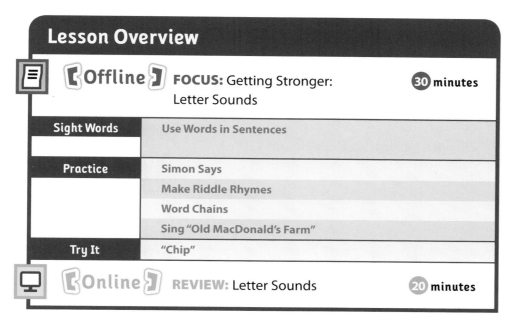

Lesson Overview

Offline FOCUS: Getting Stronger: Letter Sounds — **30** minutes

Sight Words	Use Words in Sentences
Practice	Simon Says
	Make Riddle Rhymes
	Word Chains
	Sing "Old MacDonald's Farm"
Try It	"Chip"

Online REVIEW: Letter Sounds — **20** minutes

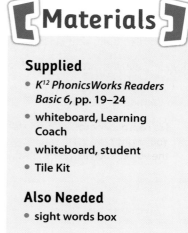

Materials

Supplied

- *K¹² PhonicsWorks Readers Basic 6*, pp. 19–24
- whiteboard, Learning Coach
- whiteboard, student
- Tile Kit

Also Needed

- sight words box

Advance Preparation

Place lowercase letters in alphabetical order and digraphs on your whiteboard.

 **Offline** **30** minutes

FOCUS: Getting Stronger: Letter Sounds

Work **together** with students to complete offline Sight Words, Practice, and Try It activities.

Sight Words

Use Words in Sentences

Help students use sight words in sentences.

1. Gather all the sight word cards students have yet to master from their sight words box. Spread the sight word cards on the table.

2. **Say:** Let's use sight words in sentences.

3. Have students

   ▸ Touch each card and read the word on it.
   ▸ Make up a sentence using the word.
   ▸ Put the card in a pile after using the word in a sentence.
   ▸ Go through the pile of cards and read each sight word again.
   ▸ Spell each word.

 TIP If students have difficulty with any of the sight words, place those cards in a pile to review again.

> **Objectives**
> • Read sight words.
> • Spell sight words.

Practice

Simon Says

Play a game with students to help them recognize words that rhyme.

1. **Say:** We're going to play a Simon Says sound game. Listen carefully for words that rhyme with the Simon Says word. Today the Simon Says word is *pop*. Say *pop*.

   ▸ I'm going to say a word and do something. You will repeat the word.
   ▸ If the word rhymes with *pop*, you will copy the action I made.
   ▸ If the word doesn't rhyme with *pop*, then you will be still. We'll do two together.

2. Touch your nose as you say *top*.

3. **Say:** We both say *top* and touch our noses because *top* rhymes with *pop*.

4. Stomp your foot as you say *seem*.

5. **Say:** The word is *seem*. Repeat the word.

   ▸ We won't stomp our foot when we say *seem* because *seem* doesn't rhyme with *pop*.
   ▸ Let's begin. Remember, the Simon Says word is *pop*. The new word is *mop*.

> **Objectives**
> • Identify words that rhyme.
> • Given the letter, identify the most common sound.
> • Given the sound, identify the most common letter or letters.
> • Identify the new word when one sound is changed in a word.
> • Identify individual sounds in words.
> • Identify letters of the alphabet.

6. Repeat the procedure with each of the following words and actions:

- ▸ *mop* clap your hands
- ▸ *soup* stick out your tongue
- ▸ *pal* touch your nose
- ▸ *cop* stand up
- ▸ *hop* touch your ear
- ▸ *pill* pat your head

(TIP) If students cannot tell which words rhyme, break each word into its onset and rime (for example, /m/ . . . *op* and /s/ . . . *oup*).

Make Riddle Rhymes

Have students identify words that rhyme by playing a riddle game.

1. **Say:** We are going to play a riddle game. I will think of a word and give you some clues. You will guess the word and solve the riddle.

   - ▸ It quacks. It swims. It has wings. It rhymes with *buck*. *duck*

2. Give students clues to words. Have them name each word, and then say and write it. Use these clues and words:

   - ▸ You can sail on it. It rhymes with *dip*. *ship*
   - ▸ It swims in the sea. It rhymes with *dish*. *fish*
   - ▸ You need it for a car to run. It rhymes with *sass*. *gas*
   - ▸ Some people have one as a pet. It rhymes with *bat*. *cat*
   - ▸ It shines in the sky. It rhymes with *bun*. *sun*

Word Chains

Have students build words by adding and changing letters to help them recognize and use individual sounds in words.

1. Place the following letters at the top of students' whiteboard: *a, b, c, ch, d, g, i, m, n, p, r, s, sh,* and *u*.

2. **Say:** I am going to build the first word in a chain. The word is *much*.

   - ▸ I will pull down the letters for the sounds /m/, /ŭ/, and /ch/ to spell the word *much*.
   - ▸ I will touch and say *much*. To change *much* to *such*, I will think about which sound is changed from the word *much* to *such*. I will need to replace the letter *m* with the letter *s*.
   - ▸ Touch and say the word *such*. Now it's your turn to change *such* to *sun*. You can spell *sun* by making only one change. Touch and say the new word.

3. Redirect students if they select the incorrect letter for any sound.

   Say: That letter is for the sound [incorrect sound]. We want the letter for the sound [target sound]. What letter makes that sound? Answers will vary.

4. Redirect students if they name the sound incorrectly.

   Say: To change the word [first word] to [target word], we need the letter for the sound [target sound].

   Show students how to make the change. Have them touch and say the new word after they move the letters.

5. Follow this procedure to make the following words: *run, rush, rash, cash, ash, dash, dish, dip, dig, big, bag.*

6. For every new word, have students add, replace, or remove only one letter tile.

Sing "Old MacDonald's Farm"

To review digraphs and the letters of the alphabet, have students sing the song "Old MacDonald's Farm." Grab your whiteboard with letters and digraphs.

1. **Say:** Do you remember "Old MacDonald's Farm"? Get ready to sing the song. Think of an animal you want to have on the farm. When you reach that part of the song ("... and on that farm he had a _____"), point to the beginning letter of that word.

2. Repeat the song until students have named all of the animals they know. When they have finished, you may sing the song and let them point to the first letter of the animals you name.

3. Redirect students if they point to a letter that could be the sound, but isn't—such as the letter *k* for *cow*.

   Say: The letter *k* does stand for the sound /k/, but the word *cow* starts with the letter *c*.

Try It

"Chip"

Have students read "Chip" on page 19 of *K¹² PhonicsWorks Readers Basic 6.*

Students should read the story silently once or twice before reading the story aloud. When students miss a word that can be sounded out, point to it and give them three to six seconds to try the word again. If students still miss the word, tell them the word so the flow of the story isn't interrupted.

After reading the story, make a list of all the words students missed, and go over those words with them. You may use letter tiles to show students how to read the words.

Objectives

- Read aloud grade-level text with appropriate automaticity, prosody, accuracy, and rate.
- Decode words by applying grade-level word analysis skills.
- Track text from left to right.
- Turn pages sequentially.

 **20 minutes**

REVIEW: Letter Sounds

Students will work online independently to

▶ Practice letter sounds.

Help students locate the online activities and provide support as needed.

Objectives

- Given the letter, identify the most common sound.
- Given the sound, identify the most common letter or letters.
- Identify individual sounds in words.
- Identify and use the digraph *ch*.
- Identify and use the digraph *sh*.
- Identify and use the digraph *wh*.
- Identify and use the digraph *th*.

Offline Alternative

No computer access? Have students point out and name things or words that contain the digraphs *ch*, *sh*, *th*, and *wh* (for example, *chip*, *rash*, *thin*, *that*, or *what*). You might also ask students to spell words that contain the sounds /ch/, /sh/, /th/, /<u>th</u>/, and /w/ for the digraph *wh*.

Getting Stronger: Letter Sounds (C)

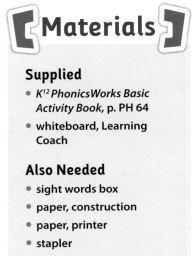

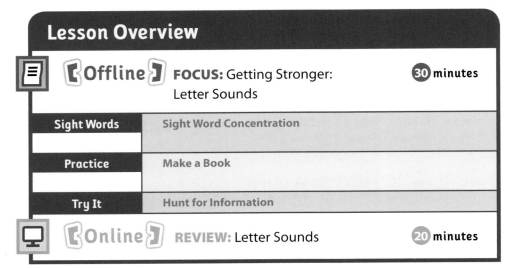

Lesson Overview

Offline	**FOCUS:** Getting Stronger: Letter Sounds	**30** minutes

Sight Words	Sight Word Concentration
Practice	Make a Book
Try It	Hunt for Information

Online	**REVIEW:** Letter Sounds	**20** minutes

Materials

Supplied
- *K¹² PhonicsWorks Basic Activity Book*, p. PH 64
- whiteboard, Learning Coach

Also Needed
- sight words box
- paper, construction
- paper, printer
- stapler

Advance Preparation

Gather two sets of the sight word cards that students have yet to master.

For Make a Book, create a blank book with two sheets of printer paper and a construction paper cover. Fold the pages in half and staple them along the left edge.

 **30 minutes**

FOCUS: Getting Stronger: Letter Sounds

Work **together** with students to complete offline Sight Words, Practice, and Try It activities.

Sight Words

Sight Word Concentration

Help students review sight words.

1. Gather the two sets of sight word cards.

2. Scramble both sets of sight word cards and place them face down on the table or floor.

3. Turn over two cards at a time; take turns with students. If the cards match, the person turning over the matching cards reads the word and uses it in a sentence. If the cards don't match, the person turns them back over.

4. Remove and save the matching cards.

5. Continue the activity until all the cards are paired.

6. Have students read all the words.

7. Take the stack of words that students read correctly and dictate each word to them.

8. Have students write each word or spell it aloud.

TIP If students have difficulty with any sight words, let them work at their own pace to really master these words.

> **Objectives**
> - Read sight words.
> - Spell sight words.
> - Write sight words.

Practice

Make a Book

Have students practice writing words and sentences by having them create a book of their favorite words. Grab your whiteboard and dry-erase marker.

1. **Say:** You are going to make your own book. Let's think of some sentences to write in your book. Name three of your favorite letters. I will write those letters on my whiteboard.

2. Write the letters on the whiteboard.

   Say: Think of a word that starts with the sound for each letter and write it on your paper. Use each word in a sentence and write it on your paper.

> **Objectives**
> - Identify individual sounds in words.
> - Write words by applying grade-level phonics knowledge.
> - Follow three-step directions.

3. Give students the blank book that you prepared before the lesson.

   ▸ Have students write "My Book, by [students' name(s)]" on the cover.
   ▸ Have them copy one sentence each on pages 2, 4, and 6.
   ▸ Have them draw a picture for each sentence on pages 3, 5, and 7.
   ▸ Have students illustrate the cover. When they have finished, read the book with them.

4. Help students if they make a spelling mistake. Write the correct spelling above the word, and have them make the correction.

   Say: That was a good try, but the word is spelled like this.

5. Guide students if they have trouble thinking of or writing sentences. Have them write only a single word on each page and then illustrate it.

 To help students write words that are unfamiliar, tell them the word and help them spell it so that writing becomes a pleasure for them instead of a chore.

Try It

Hunt for Information
Have students complete page PH 64 in *K¹² PhonicsWorks Basic Activity Book* for more practice with reading. Have them read the story aloud, choose a word from the story that best completes each sentence, and write that word.

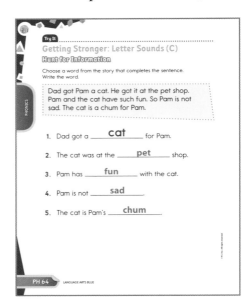

Objectives
- Read aloud grade-level text with appropriate automaticity, prosody, accuracy, and rate.
- Write words by applying grade-level phonics knowledge.

 **20 minutes**

REVIEW: **Letter Sounds**

Students will work online independently to

- ▸ Practice letter sounds.
- ▸ Practice decoding text by reading a story.

Help students locate the online activities and provide support as needed.

Offline Alternative

No computer access? Have students point out and name things or words that contain the digraphs *ch*, *sh*, *th*, and *wh* (for example, *chop*, *hash*, *math*, *than*, or *when*). You might also ask students to spell words that contain the sounds /ch/, /sh/, /th/, /th/, and /w/ for the digraph *wh*.

Objectives

- Given the letter, identify the most common sound.
- Given the sound, identify the most common letter or letters.
- Identify individual sounds in words.
- Identify and use the digraph *ch*.
- Identify and use the digraph *sh*.
- Identify and use the digraph *wh*.
- Identify and use the digraph *th*.
- Read aloud grade-level text with appropriate automaticity, prosody, accuracy, and rate.
- Decode words by applying grade-level word analysis skills.

Getting Stronger: Letter Sounds (D)

Lesson Overview

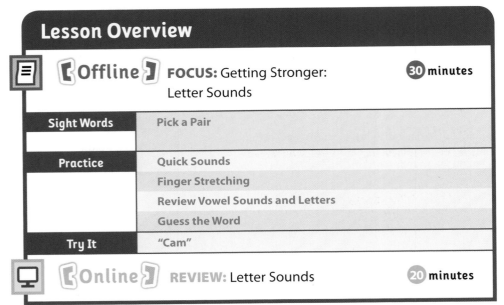

	Offline FOCUS: Getting Stronger: Letter Sounds	**30** minutes
Sight Words	Pick a Pair	
Practice	Quick Sounds	
	Finger Stretching	
	Review Vowel Sounds and Letters	
	Guess the Word	
Try It	"Cam"	

	Online REVIEW: Letter Sounds	**20** minutes

Materials

Supplied
- *K¹² PhonicsWorks Readers Basic 6*, pp. 25–30
- whiteboard, student
- Tile Kit

Also Needed
- sight words box

 **Offline** **30** minutes

FOCUS: Getting Stronger: Letter Sounds

Work **together** with students to complete offline Sight Words, Practice, and Try It activities.

Sight Words ···

Pick a Pair

Play a card game with students for more practice with sight words.

1. Gather the sight word cards that students are reviewing. Choose two words and place the cards on the table.

2. Ask questions to help students identify each word. For example, if the words are *or* and *one*, you could ask, "Which word names a number?" If the words are *on* and *but*, you could ask, "Which word is the opposite of *off*?"

3. Continue the activity until students identify all the words.

4. Take the stack of words that students read correctly and dictate each word to them.

5. Have students write each word or spell it aloud.

 Objectives

- Read sight words.
- Spell sight words.
- Write sight words.

Practice ···

Quick Sounds

Help students name words that have the same **ending sound**.

1. **Say:** I'm going to say some sounds that end a word. Your job is to think of as many words as you can that end with those same sounds. Let's see how many you can name. The first sound is /f/, as in *laugh*. How many words can you say that end with the sound /f/? You might begin with the word *cuff*.

   ▸ If students have trouble thinking of words, have them look around the room and find objects that end with that sound.

2. Continue this procedure with the following sounds:

   ▸ /th/, as in *bath*
   ▸ /sh/, as in *rush*
   ▸ /n/, as in *pan*
   ▸ /b/, as in *cab*

   TIP You can get a book and find pictures of things that end with that sound.

Objectives

- Identify ending sounds in words.
- Identify short vowel sounds.
- Identify and use the sound /ă/.
- Identify and use the sound /ĕ/.
- Identify and use the sound /ĭ/.
- Identify and use the sound /ŏ/.
- Identify and use the sound /ŭ/.
- Given the letter, identify the most common sound.
- Given the sound, identify the most common letter or letters.
- Identify individual sounds in words.
- Identify complete sentences.

Finger Stretching

Use finger stretching to help students identify individual sounds in words.

1. **Say:** Let's review finger stretching. In the word *chip*, the first sound is /ch/, the next sound is /ĭ/, and the last sound is /p/. I will finger stretch each sound as I say it. Then I'll say the word while pulling my fist toward my body.

2. Finger stretch the word *chip* for students.

3. **Say:** I'm going to say words with several sounds in them. You'll say each word and then finger stretch it while you say each sound in the word.

4. Say the following words and have students finger stretch them. After they finger stretch each word, ask them the question for that word.

   ► *with* /w/ /ĭ/ /th/   How many sounds are in the word? three
   ► *pin* /p/ /ĭ/ /n/   How many sounds are in the word? three
   ► *man* /m/ /ă/ /n/   What is the middle sound? /ă/
   ► *chum* /ch/ /ŭ/ /m/   What is the first sound? /ch/
   ► *bad* /b/ /ă/ /d/   What is the last sound? /d/
   ► *wish* /w/ /ĭ/ /sh/   How many sounds are in the word? three
   ► *chop* /ch/ /ŏ/ /p/   What is the first sound? /ch/

 Refer to the *K¹² PhonicsWorks* DVD for a demonstration of finger stretching.

Review Vowel Sounds and Letters

Help students review vowel sounds and letters.

1. Place the following letter tiles on students' whiteboard: *a*, *e*, *i*, *o*, and *u*, plus any letters that are confusing for them.

2. **Say:** I am going to point to each letter. Tell me a sound for that letter.

3. **Say:** I am going to say a sound. Repeat the sound and touch its letter.

4. Point to some letters two or three times, so students don't think that once they have named a sound they are finished with it.

5. Redirect students if they name the letter and not its sound.

   Say: You are right that the name of the letter is [letter]. We want the sound for this letter. What is the sound?

6. Redirect students if they name the sound incorrectly.

   Say: That is the sound of another letter.

7. Provide additional guidance if students touch the wrong letter tile during the review.

   Say: That is the letter tile for the sound [sound for incorrect letter tile]. We are looking for the letter tile for the sound [target sound].

8. If students touch the wrong letter again, point to the correct letter.

   Say: This is the letter tile for the sound [target sound]. Touch this letter tile and say its sound.

Guess the Word

Have students use word meaning and sentence structure to choose a word that best completes a sentence.

1. Write the following words on students' whiteboard: *wish, rich, ship, chin,* and *chat.* Make sure students know the meaning of all the words on their whiteboard before you do this activity.

2. **Say:** We're going to play a guessing game. I'm going to read a sentence with a word missing. Your job is to look at the words on your whiteboard and decide which one is the right word to complete the sentence.

   ▸ Listen to this sentence: "When I blow out the candles on my birthday cake, I make a _____ ."

   ▸ You will tell me what word makes sense in the blank of the sentence. This time the word would be *wish.*

   ▸ The complete sentence would be, "When I blow out the candles on my birthday cake, I make a *wish.*" Now you try it.

3. Continue the procedure with the following sentences:

   ▸ *You have a spot of ice cream on your* _____ . *chin*

   ▸ *If you look far out to sea, you can see the* _____ *sailing. ship*

   ▸ *He has so much money, he must be* _____ . *rich*

   ▸ *When we talked to each other, we had a nice* _____ . *chat*

Try It

"Cam"

Have students read "Cam" on page 25 of *K¹² PhonicsWorks Readers Basic 6.*

Students should read the story silently once or twice before reading the story aloud. When students miss a word that can be sounded out, point to it and give them three to six seconds to try the word again. If students still miss the word, tell them the word so the flow of the story isn't interrupted.

After reading the story, make a list of all the words students missed, and go over those words with them. You may use letter tiles to show students how to read the words.

Objectives

- Read aloud grade-level text with appropriate automaticity, prosody, accuracy, and rate.
- Decode words by applying grade-level word analysis skills.
- Track text from left to right.
- Turn pages sequentially.

 **20 minutes**

REVIEW: Letter Sounds

Students will work online independently to

▸ Practice letters and sounds.

Help students locate the online activities and provide support as needed.

Offline Alternative

No computer access? Have students point out and name things or words that contain the short vowel sounds /ă/, /ĕ/, /ĭ/, /ŏ/, and /ŭ/, such as *cap*, *hen*, *him*, *top*, and *fun*. You might also ask students to spell simple words that contain the sounds /ă/, /ĕ/, /ĭ/, /ŏ/, and /ŭ/ made by the letters *a*, *e*, *i*, *o*, and *u* and other letters students have learned.

 Objectives

- Given the letter, identify the most common sound.
- Given the sound, identify the most common letter or letters.
- Identify individual sounds in words.
- Identify short vowel sounds

Unit Checkpoint

Lesson Overview

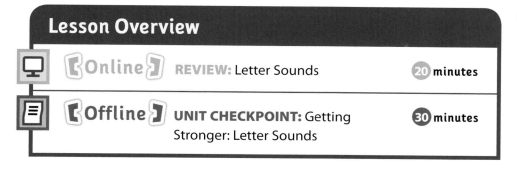

Online REVIEW: Letter Sounds **20** minutes

Offline UNIT CHECKPOINT: Getting Stronger: Letter Sounds **30** minutes

Materials

Supplied

- *K¹² PhonicsWorks Basic Assessments,* pp. PH 133–138

Objectives

- Identify the digraph *wh*, given the sound /w/.
- Identify the sound /w/, given the digraph *wh*.
- Identify and use the digraph *wh*.
- Identify the letters, given the sound /ch/.
- Identify the sound /ch/, given the digraph *ch*.
- Identify and use the digraph *ch*.
- Identify and use the sound /th/.
- Identify and use the sound /th/.
- Identify and use the digraph *th*.
- Identify the letters, given the sound /th/.
- Identify the letters, given the sound /th/.
- Identify and use the sound /sh/.
- Identify the letters, given the sound /sh/.

- Identify and use the digraph *sh*.
- Read, write, and spell words containing short vowel sounds.
- Identify individual sounds in words.
- Given the letter, identify the most common sound.
- Given the sound, identify the most common letter or letters.
- Read instructional-level text with 90% accuracy.
- Read aloud grade-level text with appropriate automaticity, prosody, accuracy, and rate.
- Write words by applying grade-level phonics knowledge.
- Write sight words.
- Read sight words.

 **20** minutes

REVIEW: Letter Sounds

Students will review letter sounds to prepare for the Unit Checkpoint. Help students locate the online activities and provide support as needed.

 **30 minutes**

UNIT CHECKPOINT: Getting Stronger: Letter Sounds

Explain that students are going to show what they have learned about sounds, letters, and words.

1. Give students the Unit Checkpoint pages for the Getting Stronger: Letter Sounds unit and print the Unit Checkpoint Answer Key, if you'd like.

2. Use the instructions below to help administer the Checkpoint to students. On the Answer Key or another sheet of paper, note student answers to oral response questions to help with scoring the Checkpoint later.

3. Use the Answer Key to score the Checkpoint, and then enter the results online.

Part 1. Read Word Parts and Nonsense Words Have students read across the rows from left to right and say the sounds that each word part or nonsense word makes. Note any word parts or words they say incorrectly.

Part 2. Word Dissection For each word, say the sound students should identify. Have them read the word aloud and circle the letter or group of letters that spells the requested sound.

19. *beginning sound*

20. *beginning sound*

21. *ending sound*

22. *middle sound*

23. *beginning sound*

Part 3. Finger Stretching Say each word to students. Have them say each word and finger stretch the sounds. Note any words they finger stretch incorrectly.

24. *chip*	27. *which*
25. *then*	28. *thin*
26. *such*	29. *much*

Part 4. Dictation Say each word to students. Have them repeat and write the word.

30. *much*	32. *then*
31. *chin*	33. *shop*

Part 5. Read Aloud Listen to students read the sentences aloud. Count and note the number of words they read correctly.

Part 6. Say Letters Say each sound. Have students say a letter or letters that make that sound. Note any incorrect responses.

35. /ch/		44. /ĕ/	
36. /sh/		45. /ch/	
37. /ŭ/		46. /th/	
38. /ă/		47. /ŏ/	
39. /ks/		48. /ks/	
40. /w/		49. /w/	
41. /th/		50. /kw/	
42. /y/		51. /y/	
43. /ĭ/		52. /l/	

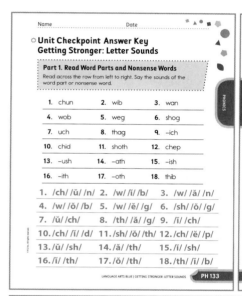

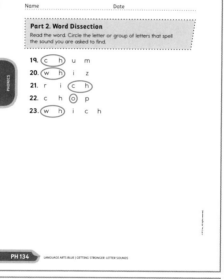

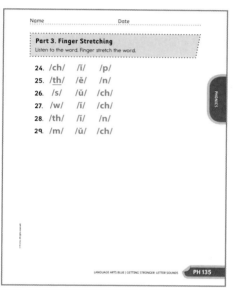

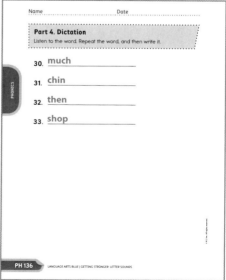

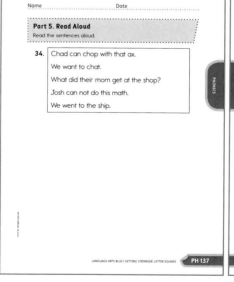

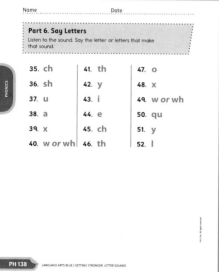

Introduce Trigraph *–tch*

Unit Overview

In this unit, students will

- ► Learn the sight words *said*, *your*, and *so*.
- ► Review letters and digraphs.
- ► Learn the trigraph *–tch* and the ending *–ck*.
- ► Identify beginning and ending sounds in words.
- ► Build words and make rhyming words.
- ► Create sentences.

[Materials]

Supplied

- ● *K¹² PhonicsWorks Basic Activity Book*, p. PH 65
- ● whiteboard, Learning Coach
- ● whiteboard, student
- ● Tile Kit

Also Needed

- ● sight words box
- ● dictation notebook
- ● index cards (5)

Lesson Overview

📄	[Offline] FOCUS: Introduce Trigraph *–tch*		**30** minutes
Sight Words	Introduce Sight Words		
Get Ready	Secret Sound		
	Simon Says		
Learn	Introduce the Trigraph *–tch*		
	Build Words		
	Make Up a Sentence		
Try It	Different Beat		
	Dictation: Write Words		
🖥	[Online] REVIEW: Trigraph *–tch*		**20** minutes

Advance Preparation

For Make Up a Sentence, print each of the following words on index cards, using one card per word: *catch*, *itch*, *patch*, *ditch*, and *hatch*.

 **Offline** **30 minutes**

FOCUS: Introduce Trigraph –*tch*

Work **together** with students to complete offline Sight Words, Get Ready, Learn, and Try It activities.

Sight Words ·

Introduce Sight Words

Help students learn the sight words *said*, *your*, and *so*.

1. Gather the sight word cards *said*, *your*, and *so*.

2. Show students the *said* card.

3. **Say:** This is the word *said*. We see this word so often that we want to be able to read and spell it quickly without thinking about it. Look closely at the word *said*. Spell the word *said* aloud. Take a picture of the word *said* in your mind. When you think you can spell *said* yourself, turn the card over and use your letter tiles to spell the word *said*. Check the card to see if you spelled the *said* correctly. Read aloud the word you spelled with the letter tiles.

4. Repeat the activity with the remaining sight words.

5. Chart students' progress on the back of each card.

   ► Divide the back of the card into two columns.
   ► Label the first column "Read" and the second column "Spell."
   ► Record the dates that students read or spell the word correctly. When students can read and spell the word correctly three times in a row, they have mastered the word. You may want to put a star or sticker on the card when they have mastered that word.

6. Add the cards to students' sight words box.

TIP Sight words can be very difficult for some students. Let students work at their own pace and really master these words, as they occur frequently in reading and writing.

> **Objectives**
> • Read sight words.
> • Spell sight words.

Get Ready

Secret Sound

Say groups of words to help students recognize **ending sounds** in words.

1. **Say:** I am going to say some groups of words. Listen for a secret sound at the end of each word. Then tell me what sound you hear at the end of each group of words.

2. Say each of the following groups of words. Have students identify the secret sound in each group.

   ▸ *Beth, path, cloth, moth* /th/
   ▸ *wish, mash, splash, slush* /sh/
   ▸ *clutch, batch, catch, pitch* /ch/

TIP If students can't identify the secret sound, have them listen while you say each word again and then have them repeat each word. Have students say what sound they hear at the end of each word.

Objectives

- Identify ending sounds in words.
- Identify and use the sound /ch/.
- Identify and use the sound /th/.
- Identify and use the sound /sh/.
- Identify words that rhyme.

Simon Says

Play a game with students to help them recognize words that rhyme.

1. **Say:** We're going to play a Simon Says sound game. Listen carefully for words that rhyme with the Simon Says word. Today the Simon Says word is *pitch*. Say *pitch*.

   ▸ I'm going to say a word and do something. You will repeat the word.
   ▸ If the word rhymes with *pitch*, you will copy the action I make.
   ▸ If the word doesn't rhyme with *pitch*, then you will be still. We'll do two together.

2. Touch your nose as you say *stitch*.

3. **Say:** We both say *stitch* and touch our noses because *stitch* rhymes with *pitch*.

4. Stomp your foot as you say *path*.

5. **Say:** The word is *path*. Repeat the word.

   ▸ We won't stomp our foot when we say *path* because *path* doesn't rhyme with *pitch*.
   ▸ Let's begin. Remember, the Simon Says word is *pitch*. The new word is *ditch*.

6. Repeat the procedure with each of the following words and actions:

   ▸ *ditch*   clap your hands
   ▸ *toss*   pull your ear
   ▸ *hitch*   stomp your foot
   ▸ *itch*   touch your cheek
   ▸ *lunch*   touch your chin

TIP If students cannot tell which words rhyme, break each word into its onset and rime (for example, /p/ . . . *itch* and /st/ . . . *itch*).

Learn

Introduce the Trigraph –tch

The letters *tch* are usually found when the sound /ch/ is the last sound in a word and follows the short vowel in a one-syllable word, as in *pitch*, *etch*, and *catch*. The letters *tch* are not used if there is already another consonant after the vowel, as in *lunch*, *mulch*, and *porch*. Help students learn the trigraph –tch for the sound /ch/.

1. Place the *ch* letter tile on students' whiteboard and point to it.

   Say: You've learned all the letters of the alphabet and the sounds that go with them. Now you're going to learn about a sound that is spelled with three letters. The sound is /ch/, and you already know one way to spell it. Touch the tile that spells /ch/.

2. Place the *tch* letter tile on students' whiteboard and point to it.

   Say: When we see the letters *tch*, we read the sound /ch/. Touch the *tch* tile and say /ch/.

3. **Say:** We call –tch a **trigraph**. In the word trigraph, *tri* means three and *graph* means writing. *Trigraph* means three letters are written together to make one sound.

4. **Say:** Most of the time, –tch comes at the end of a word.

   ▸ Touch the two ways we can spell the sound /ch/.
   ▸ Touch the letter tile for the spelling that almost always comes at the end of a word for the sound /ch/. *tch*

Build Words

Help students use letters and sounds to build words.

1. Place the following letter tiles at the top of students' whiteboard: *a, c, h, i, tch,* and *u*.

2. Draw three horizontal lines across the middle of students' whiteboard to represent the sounds in a word.

3. **Say:** Let's use letters and sounds to build the word *catch*.

4. Have students finger stretch the sounds in *catch*.

5. Have students

   ▸ Identify the first, next, and last sounds in *catch*.
   ▸ Choose the corresponding letter for each of the sounds.
   ▸ Move the letters to the correct lines on their whiteboard.

Objectives

- Identify and use the sound /ch/.
- Identify the trigraph –tch, given the sound /ch/.
- Identify individual sounds in words.
- Blend sounds to create words.
- Write words by applying grade-level phonics knowledge.

6. Guide students with these questions:

   ▶ What is the first sound in *catch*? /k/
     Which line does the letter for that sound go on? the first one
   ▶ What is the next sound in *catch*? /ă/
     Which line does the letter for that sound go on? the second one
   ▶ What's the last sound in *catch*? /ch/
     Which line do the letters for that sound go on? the last one

7. Redirect students if they select the incorrect letter.

   Say: That sound is in the word [word], and it is the [first, second, third] sound. We want the sound [target sound].

   Continue until students select the correct letter.

8. Have students touch and say the word.

9. Have them say the word as they use a dry-erase marker to write the word on the whiteboard.

10. Draw horizontal lines across the middle of students' whiteboard that represent the number of sounds in each word. Repeat the activity to build the following words:

    ▶ *itch* /ĭ/ /ch/
    ▶ *hutch* /h/ /ŭ/ /ch/

Make Up a Sentence

Help students use words to make sentences.

1. Gather the index cards you prepared, and place them face down on the table in one pile.

2. Have students

   ▶ Select a card.
   ▶ Read the word.
   ▶ Use the word in an interesting, fun, or silly sentence.

TIP If students read a word incorrectly, have them finger stretch the sounds in the word, or use letter tiles to spell the word and touch and say.

Try It

Different Beat

Have students complete page PH 65 in *K¹² PhonicsWorks Basic Activity Book* for more practice with the trigraph *–tch*. Have them read each word in the row aloud and circle the word that does not rhyme with the others. Then have students write each word they circled to complete each sentence. Have them read the sentences aloud.

TIP If students read a word incorrectly, have them finger stretch the sounds in the word, or use letter tiles to spell the word and touch and say.

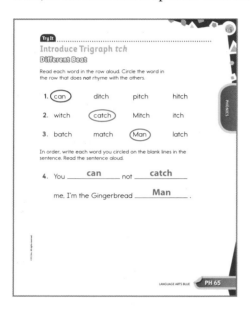

Objectives

- Read aloud grade-level text with appropriate automaticity, prosody, accuracy, and rate.
- Identify and use the sound /ch/.
- Identify the trigraph *–tch*, given the sound /ch/.
- Write words by applying grade-level phonics knowledge.
- Follow three-step directions.

Dictation: Write Words

Have students practice identifying sounds and writing words.

1. Gather a pencil and the dictation notebook. Say the word *patch*. Then give these directions to students:

   ▸ Repeat the word.
   ▸ Write the word in your notebook.
   ▸ Read the word aloud.

2. When students have finished, write the following word on your whiteboard: *patch*.

3. Have them compare their answer to your correct version.

4. Repeat this procedure with the words *blotch* and *snitch*.

   ▶ If students make an error and don't see it, help them correct their mistake by having them finger stretch the sounds in the word they missed.
   ▶ If students are having difficulty selecting the correct letters or sounds, review those letters or sounds that are confusing them.
   ▶ If students have difficulty with first, middle, and last sounds, have them finger stretch the sounds in words.

 **20 minutes**

REVIEW: Trigraph *–tch*

Students will work online independently to

▶ Practice the trigraph *–tch*.
▶ Practice decoding text by reading sentences.

Help students locate the online activities and provide support as needed.

Offline Alternative

No computer access? Have students point out and name things or words that contain the sound /ch/ spelled with the trigraph *–tch* (for example, *etch* or *itch*). You might also ask students to spell words that contain the trigraph *–tch*.

 Objectives

- Identify and use the sound /ch/.
- Identify the trigraph *–tch*, given the sound /ch/.
- Identify individual sounds in words.
- Read aloud grade-level text with appropriate automaticity, prosody, accuracy, and rate.
- Decode words by applying grade-level word analysis skills.

Practice Trigraph *–tch*

Lesson Overview

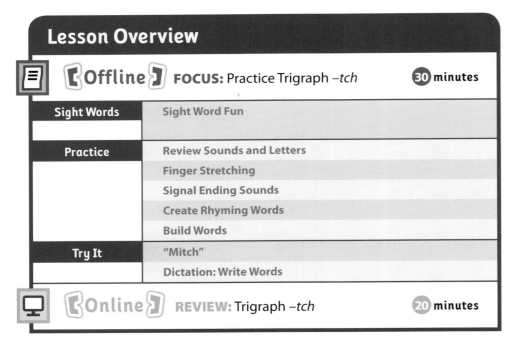

≣ Offline FOCUS: Practice Trigraph *–tch*		**30** minutes
Sight Words	Sight Word Fun	
Practice	Review Sounds and Letters	
	Finger Stretching	
	Signal Ending Sounds	
	Create Rhyming Words	
	Build Words	
Try It	"Mitch"	
	Dictation: Write Words	
💻 Online REVIEW: Trigraph *–tch*		**20** minutes

Materials

Supplied
- *K¹² PhonicsWorks Readers Basic 7*, pp. 1–6
- whiteboard, Learning Coach
- whiteboard, student
- Tile Kit

Also Needed
- sight words box
- dictation notebook

 **30** minutes

FOCUS: Practice Trigraph –*tch*

Work **together** with students to complete offline Sight Words, Practice, and Try It activities.

Sight Words

Sight Word Fun

Help students learn the sight words *said*, *your*, and *so*, and up to two additional sight words they have yet to master.

1. Gather the sight word cards *said*, *your*, and *so*, and up to two additional sight word cards.

2. Choose one sight word card to begin.

   Say: Look at this word and take a picture of it in your mind. When you think you can spell the word yourself, turn the card over and use your letter tiles to spell the word.

3. After students spell the word, have them check the card to see if they spelled the word correctly.

   Say: Read aloud the word you spelled with the letter tiles.

4. Repeat the activity with the remaining sight words.

TIP Sight words can be very difficult for some students. Let them work at their own pace and really master these words.

Objectives
- Read sight words.
- Spell sight words.

Practice

Review Sounds and Letters

Help students review sounds for the letters, digraphs, and trigraph *ch, f, k, o, r, sh,*
–tch, th, w, and *wh,* plus any letters that are confusing for them.

1. Place the following letter tiles in random order on students' whiteboard: *ch, f, k,
o, r, sh, tch, th, w,* and *wh,* plus any letters that are confusing.

2. **Say:** Let's go over some letters and sounds.

3. Point to each letter tile and have students say a sound that letter or
letters make.

   - *ch* /ch/
   - *f* /f/
   - *k* /k/
   - *o* /ŏ/
   - *r* /r/

   - *sh* /sh/
   - *th* /th/ or /th̠/
   - *tch* /ch/
   - *wh* /w/
   - *w* /w/

4. Say each of the following sounds. Have students repeat the sound and touch
the corresponding letter tile:

   - /ch/ *ch* or *tch*
   - /f/ *f*
   - /k/ *k*
   - /ŏ/ *o*

   - /r/ *r*
   - /sh/ *sh*
   - /th/ or /th̠/ *th*
   - /w/ *wh* or *w*

5. As you do the activity, point to some letter tiles two or three times so that
students don't think they are finished with a sound after they have named it.

6. Redirect students if they say an incorrect sound when you point to a letter tile.

   Say: That's the sound of another letter. What is the sound for this letter?

7. Help students if they touch the wrong letter tile after they repeat a sound.

   Say: That letter tile goes with the sound [sound for incorrect letter tile].
   We're looking for the letter tile that goes with the sound [target sound].

Finger Stretching

Use finger stretching to help students identify individual sounds in words.

1. **Say:** Let's review finger stretching. In the word *mash,* the first sound is /m/, the
next sound is /ă/, and the last sound is /sh/. I will finger stretch each sound as
I say it. Then I'll say the word while pulling my fist toward my body.

2. Finger stretch the word *mash* for students.

Objectives

- Given the letter, identify the most common sound.
- Given the sound, identify the most common letter or letters.
- Identify individual sounds in words.
- Identify and use the sound /ch/.
- Identify the trigraph *–tch,* given the sound /ch/.
- Identify ending sounds in words.
- Identify words that rhyme.
- Identify beginning sounds in words.
- Write words by applying grade-level phonics knowledge.
- Blend sounds to create words.

3. **Say:** I'm going to say words with several sounds in them. You'll say each word and then finger stretch it while you say each sound in the word.

4. Say the following words and have students finger stretch them. After they finger stretch each word, ask them the question for that word.

   ▸ *fan* /f/ /ă/ /n/   What is the first sound? /f/
   ▸ *shin* /sh/ /ĭ/ /n/   What is the middle sound? /ĭ/
   ▸ *wish* /w/ /ĭ/ /sh/   What is the last sound? /sh/
   ▸ *itch* /ĭ/ /ch/   What is the last sound? /ch/
   ▸ *batch* /b/ /ă/ /ch/   What is the middle sound? /ă/
   ▸ *botch* /b/ /ŏ/ /ch/   What is the middle sound? /ŏ/
   ▸ *hitch* /h/ /ĭ/ /ch/   What is the last sound? /ch/

 Refer to the *K¹² PhonicsWorks* DVD for a demonstration of finger stretching.

Signal Ending Sounds

Use a special signal to help students identify **ending sounds** in words.

1. **Say:** I'm going to tell you a special sound, and then I'll say some words. Repeat each word I say and make a special signal to tell me where the special sound is. If the special sound is at the end of the word, touch your elbow. If the special sound is **not** at the ending of the word, just smile at me. For example,

   ▸ If I ask you to listen for the sound /sh/ and I say the word *wish*, you'll repeat the word *wish* and touch your elbow because *wish* has the sound /sh/ at the end.
   ▸ If I say the word *which*, you'll repeat the word *which* and smile at me because *which* has the sound /ch/, not /sh/, at the end.

2. Say each sound and group of words. Have students make the special signal to identify the ending sound.

   ▸ /th/: *back, bath, tenth, tent, myth* touch elbow: *bath, tenth, myth*
   ▸ /ch/: *stack, staff, catch, wind, switch, clutch* touch elbow: *catch, switch, clutch*
   ▸ /t/: *ton, plant, land, smart, fit, fib* touch elbow: *plant, smart, fit*
   ▸ /m/: *team, mist, Tim, swim, stop, Jim* touch elbow: *team, Tim, swim, Jim*
   ▸ /k/: *pie, kick, Jack, lip, crack, quack* touch elbow: *kick, Jack, crack, quack*

TIP If students can't identify the ending sound of each word, say the word again and emphasize the ending sound by repeating it three times (for example, *sit* /t/ /t/ /t/). You can also draw out the ending sound when you say the word (for example, *kisssssss*).

Create Rhyming Words

Have students combine word parts and make words that rhyme.

1. **Say:** I'm going to break a word into two parts. Your job is to put the parts back together and say the word.

   ▸ For example, if the first part of the word is /p/ and the last part is /ĭch/, then you'll say *pitch*: /p/ . . . /ĭch/ . . . *pitch*.
   ▸ Next you'll add a new **beginning sound** to make a word that rhymes. For example, you'll use the same last part, /ĭch/, and add a new first sound, like /sw/. The rhyming word is /sw/ . . . /ĭch/ . . . *switch*.

2. **Say:** Now it's your turn: /m/ . . . /ĭch/.

   ▸ What's the word? *Mitch*
   ▸ Now use the same last part, /ĭch/, but add a new sound, /h/, at the beginning. What word did you make? *hitch*

3. Say the two word parts. Have students say the word the parts form. Have them add a new beginning sound to the last part of the following word to make rhyming words: /tw/ . . . /ĭch/ *twitch*   Possible rhyming words: *ditch, witch*

Build Words

Help students use letters and sounds to build words.

1. Place the following letter tiles at the top of students' whiteboard: *a, c, d, i, p, t, tch,* and *w.*

2. Draw three horizontal lines across the middle of students' whiteboard to represent the sounds in a word.

3. **Say:** Let's use letters and sounds to build the word *ditch.*

4. Have students finger stretch the sounds in *ditch.*

5. Have students

   ▸ Identify the first, next, and last sounds in *ditch.*
   ▸ Choose the corresponding letter for each of the sounds.
   ▸ Move the letters to the correct lines on their whiteboard.

6. Guide students with these questions:

   ▸ What is the first sound in *ditch*? /d/
   Which line does the letter for that sound go on? the first one
   ▸ What is the next sound in *ditch*? /ĭ/
   Which line does the letter for that sound go on? the second one
   ▸ What's the last sound in *ditch*? /ch/
   Which line do the letters for that sound go on? the last one

7. Redirect students if they select the incorrect letter.

   Say: That sound is in the word [word], and it is the [first, second, third] sound. We want the sound [target sound].

   Continue until students select the correct letter.

8. Have students touch and say the word.

9. Have them say the word as they use a dry-erase marker to write the word on the whiteboard.

10. Draw horizontal lines across the middle of students' whiteboard to represent the number of sounds in a word. Repeat the activity to build the following words:

    ▸ *patch* /p/ /ă/ /ch/
    ▸ *twitch* /t/ /w/ /ĭ/ /ch/

Try It

"Mitch"

Have students read "Mitch" on page 1 of *K¹² PhonicsWorks Readers Basic 7*.

Students should read the story silently once or twice before reading the story aloud. When students miss a word that can be sounded out, point to it and give them three to six seconds to try the word again. If students still miss the word, tell them the word so the flow of the story isn't interrupted.

After reading the story, make a list of all the words students missed, and go over those words with them. You may use letter tiles to show students how to read the words.

Objectives

- Read aloud grade-level text with appropriate automaticity, prosody, accuracy, and rate.
- Decode words by applying grade-level word analysis skills.
- Track text from left to right.
- Turn pages sequentially.
- Identify the trigraph –*tch*, given the sound /ch/.
- Write words by applying grade-level phonics knowledge.
- Follow three-step directions.

Dictation: Write Words

Have students practice identifying sounds and writing words.

1. Gather a pencil and the dictation notebook. Say the word *fetch*. Then give these directions to students:

   ▸ Repeat the word.
   ▸ Write the word in your notebook.
   ▸ Read the word aloud.

2. When students have finished, write the following word on your whiteboard: *fetch*.

3. Have them compare their answer to your correct version.

4. Repeat this procedure with the words *hutch* and *batch*.

   ▸ If students make an error and don't see it, help them correct their mistake by having them finger stretch the sounds in the word they missed.
   ▸ If students are having difficulty selecting the correct letters or sounds, review those letters or sounds that are confusing them.
   ▸ If students have difficulty with first, middle, and last sounds, have them finger stretch the sounds in words.

 **20** **minutes**

REVIEW: Trigraph *–tch*

Students will work online independently to

▶ Practice the trigraph *–tch*.

Help students locate the online activities and provide support as needed.

Objectives

- Identify the trigraph *–tch*, given the sound /ch/.
- Identify ending sounds in words.

Offline Alternative

No computer access? Have students point out and name things or words that contain the sound /ch/ spelled with the trigraph *–tch* (for example, *patch* or *ditch*). You might also ask students to spell words that contain the trigraph *–tch*.

Introduce Ending –*ck*

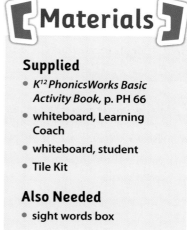

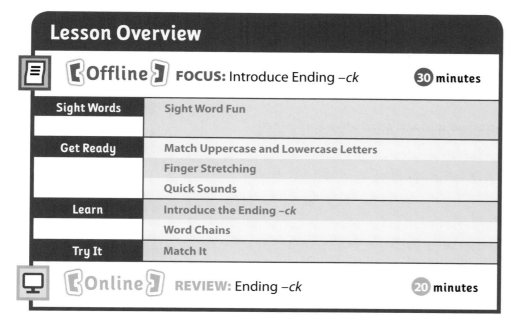

Lesson Overview

Offline FOCUS: Introduce Ending –*ck*   **30** minutes

Sight Words	Sight Word Fun
Get Ready	Match Uppercase and Lowercase Letters
	Finger Stretching
	Quick Sounds
Learn	Introduce the Ending –*ck*
	Word Chains
Try It	Match It

Online REVIEW: Ending –*ck*   **20** minutes

Materials

Supplied
- *K¹² PhonicsWorks Basic Activity Book,* p. PH 66
- whiteboard, Learning Coach
- whiteboard, student
- Tile Kit

Also Needed
- sight words box

Advance Preparation

Place lowercase letter tiles in alphabetical order on your whiteboard.

 **30 minutes**

FOCUS: Introduce Ending –*ck*

Work **together** with students to complete offline Sight Words, Get Ready, Learn, and Try It activities.

Sight Words ....

Sight Word Fun

Help students learn the sight words *said, your,* and *so,* and up to two additional sight words they have yet to master.

1. Gather the sight word cards *said, your,* and *so,* and up to two additional sight word cards.

2. Choose one sight word card to begin.

   Say: Look at this word and take a picture of it in your mind. When you think you can spell the word yourself, turn the card over and use your letter tiles to spell the word.

3. After students spell the word, have them check the card to see if they spelled the word correctly.

   Say: Read aloud the word you spelled with the letter tiles.

4. Repeat the activity with the remaining sight words.

TIP Sight words can be very difficult for some students. Let them work at their own pace and really master these words.

Objectives
- Read sight words.
- Spell sight words.

Get Ready ....

Match Uppercase and Lowercase Letters

To help students learn to recognize the difference between lowercase and uppercase letters of the alphabet, have them practice identifying and naming letters. Grab your whiteboard with letters.

1. Place the following uppercase letters on students' whiteboard in a horizontal row: *A, C, H, K, Q, S,* and *T.*

2. Point to a letter and have students name it.

3. Have students select the matching lowercase letter from your whiteboard.

4. Have students place the lowercase letter under the uppercase letter to make a pair.

TIP If students have difficulty with this activity, have them practice naming the letters in the alphabet. When they can name all the letters in the correct order, have them touch and name the lowercase and uppercase letters for each letter.

Objectives
- Identify letters of the alphabet.
- Match capital letters to lowercase letters.
- Identify individual sounds in words.
- Identify the number of sounds within words.
- Identify beginning sounds in words.

Finger Stretching

Use finger stretching to help students identify individual sounds in words.

1. **Say:** Let's review finger stretching. In the word *sit*, the first sound is /s/, the next sound is /ĭ/, and the last sound is /t/. I will finger stretch each sound as I say it. Then I'll say the word while pulling my fist toward my body.

2. Finger stretch the word *sit* for students.

3. **Say:** I'm going to say words with several sounds in them. You'll say each word and then finger stretch it while you say each sound in the word.

4. Say the following words and have students finger stretch them. After they finger stretch each word, ask them the question for that word.

   ▸ *it* /ĭ/ /t/   How many sounds are in the word? two
   ▸ *cat* /k/ /ă/ /t/   How many sounds are in the word? three
   ▸ *at* /ă/ /t/   What is the last sound? /t/
   ▸ *mash* /m/ /ă/ /sh/   What is the first sound? /m/
   ▸ *ash* /ă/ /sh/   What is the last sound? /sh/
   ▸ *am* /ă/ /m/   What is the first sound? /ă/
   ▸ *Pam* /p/ /ă/ /m/   How many sounds are in the word? three

 Refer to the *K¹² PhonicsWorks* DVD for a demonstration of finger stretching.

Quick Sounds

Help students name words that have the same **beginning sound**.

1. **Say:** I'm going to say some sounds that begin a word. Your job is to think of as many words as you can that begin with those same sounds. Let's see how many you can name. The first sound is /sh/, as in *shop*. How many words can you say that begin with /sh/?

   ▸ If students have trouble thinking of words, have them look around the room and find objects that start with that sound.

2. Continue this procedure with the following sounds:

   ▸ /d/, as in *doll*
   ▸ /ch/, as in *chin*
   ▸ /th/, as in *think*
   ▸ /kw/, as in *queen*

 You can get a book and find pictures of things that begin with that sound.

Learn

Introduce the Ending *–ck*

The sound /k/ is spelled with the letters *ck* when it is the last sound immediately after a short vowel in a one-syllable word, as in *back*, *sock*, and *wick*. To help students learn the ending *–ck*, have them practice identifying and naming the letters for the sound /k/.

1. Place the following letter tiles on students' whiteboard and point to them: *c* and *k*.

2. **Say:** The sound /k/ can be spelled three different ways. You already know two ways to spell the sound /k/.

   ▸ Tell me the letters that spell the sound /k/. *c and k*
   ▸ Touch the tiles that show the two ways to spell /k/. *c and k*

3. Place the *ck* letter tile on students' whiteboard and point to it.

   Say: The sound /k/ can also be spelled with the letters *ck*, with the *c* and *k* together.

4. Touch the *ck* tile and say the sound /k/.

5. Have students touch and say the sound /k/.

6. **Say:** The ending *–ck* is a digraph because it is two letters that spell one sound. The digraph *–ck* almost always spells the sound /k/ at the end of short words.

(TIP) The ending *–ck* is not used if there is already another consonant after the vowel, as in *bank*, *milk*, and *ask*.

Word Chains

Have students build words by adding and changing letters to help them recognize and use individual sounds in words.

1. Place the following letter tiles at the top of students' whiteboard: *a, b, c, ck, d, l, p, r, s, t,* and *tch*.

2. **Say:** I am going to build the first word in a chain. The word is *pad*.

   ▸ I will pull down the letters for the sounds /p/, /ă/, and /d/ to spell the word *pad*.
   ▸ I will touch and say *pad*. To change *pad* to *pack*, I will think about which sound is changed from the word *pad* to *pack*. I will need to replace the letter tile *d* with the letter tile *ck*.
   ▸ Touch and say the word *pack*. Now it's your turn to change *pack* to *patch*. You can spell *patch* by making only one change. Touch and say the new word.

Objectives

- Identify and use the sound /k/.
- Identify the letters, given the sound /k/.
- Identify the sound /k/, given the letters *ck*.
- Identify and use the digraph *–ck*.
- Identify individual sounds in words.
- Identify ending sounds in words.
- Write words by applying grade-level phonics knowledge.

3. Redirect students if they select the incorrect letter for any sound.

   Say: That letter is for the sound [incorrect sound]. We want the letter for the sound [target sound]. What letter makes that sound? Answers will vary.

4. Redirect students if they name the sound incorrectly.

   Say: To change the word [first word] to [target word], we need the letter for the sound [target sound].

   Show students how to make the change. Have them touch and say the new word after they move the letter tiles.

5. Follow this procedure to make the following words: *catch, cap, tap, tack, sack, back, black, lack, latch.*

6. For every new word, have students add, replace, or remove only one letter tile.

TIP If students struggle, review the sounds and letters that are confusing them.

Try It

Match It

Have students complete page PH 66 in *K¹² PhonicsWorks Basic Activity Book* for more practice with the ending *–ck*. Have students read the words in the first column and then the second column aloud. Then have them draw a line to match the words that rhyme.

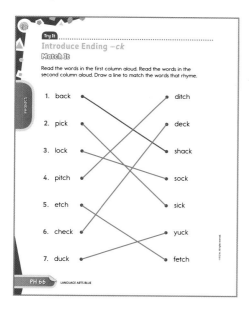

Objectives

- Read aloud grade-level text with appropriate automaticity, prosody, accuracy, and rate.
- Identify words that rhyme.
- Identify and use the digraph *–ck*.
- Identify and use the sound /k/.
- Identify the sound /k/, given the letters *ck*.

 **Online** **20** **minutes**

REVIEW: Ending –*ck*

Students will work online independently to

► Practice the ending –*ck*.

► Practice decoding text by reading a story.

Help students locate the online activities and provide support as needed.

Offline Alternative

No computer access? Have students point out and name things or words that contain the sound /k/ spelled with the ending –*ck* (for example, *rack* or *neck*). You might also ask students to spell words that contain the ending –*ck*.

 Objectives

- Identify and use the sound /k/.
- Identify the letters, given the sound /k/.
- Identify and use the digraph –*ck*.
- Identify the sound /k/, given the letters *ck*.
- Identify individual sounds in words.
- Read aloud grade-level text with appropriate automaticity, prosody, accuracy, and rate.
- Decode words by applying grade-level word analysis skills.

Practice Trigraph –*tch* and Ending –*ck*

Lesson Overview

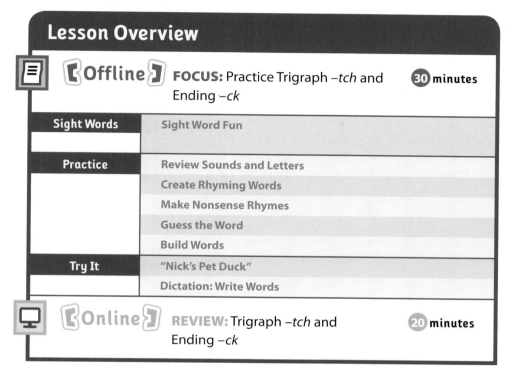

Offline FOCUS: Practice Trigraph –*tch* and Ending –*ck*   **30** minutes

Sight Words	Sight Word Fun
Practice	Review Sounds and Letters
	Create Rhyming Words
	Make Nonsense Rhymes
	Guess the Word
	Build Words
Try It	"Nick's Pet Duck"
	Dictation: Write Words

Online REVIEW: Trigraph –*tch* and Ending –*ck*   **20** minutes

Materials

Supplied
- *K¹² PhonicsWorks Readers Basic 7* , pp. 7–12
- whiteboard, Learning Coach
- whiteboard, student
- Tile Kit

Also Needed
- sight words box
- dictation notebook

 **30 minutes**

FOCUS: Practice Trigraph *–tch* and Ending *–ck*

Work **together** with students to complete offline Sight Words, Practice, and Try It activities.

Sight Words

Sight Word Fun

Help students learn the sight words *said*, *your*, and *so,* and up to two additional sight words they have yet to master.

1. Gather the sight word cards *said*, *your*, and *so,* and up to two additional sight word cards.

2. Choose one sight word card to begin.

   Say: Look at this word and take a picture of it in your mind. When you think you can spell the word yourself, turn the card over and use your letter tiles to spell the word.

3. After students spell the word, have them check the card to see if they spelled the word correctly.

   Say: Read aloud the word you spelled with the letter tiles.

4. Repeat the activity with the remaining sight words.

 Sight words can be very difficult for some students. Let them work at their own pace and really master these words.

> **Objectives**
> - Read sight words.
> - Spell sight words.

Practice

Review Sounds and Letters

Help students review sounds for the letters, digraphs, and trigraph *c*, *ch*, *j*, *qu*, *sh*, *–tch*, *th*, *v*, *wh*, and *x*, plus any letters that are confusing for students.

1. Place the following letter tiles in random order on students' whiteboard: *c*, *ch*, *j*, *qu*, *sh*, *tch*, *th*, *v*, *wh*, and *x*, plus any letters that are confusing.

2. **Say:** Let's go over some letters and sounds.

3. Point to each letter tile and have students say a sound that letter or letters make.

   - ▸ *c* /k/
   - ▸ *j* /j/
   - ▸ *v* /v/
   - ▸ *tch* /ch/
   - ▸ *sh* /sh/

   - ▸ *th* /th/ or /<u>th</u>/
   - ▸ *ch* /ch/
   - ▸ *wh* /w/
   - ▸ *qu* /kw/
   - ▸ *x* /ks/

4. Say each of the following sounds. Have students repeat the sound and touch the corresponding letter tile.

   - ▸ /k/ *c*
   - ▸ /j/ *j*
   - ▸ /v/ *v*
   - ▸ /ch/ *tch* or *ch*
   - ▸ /sh/ *sh*

   - ▸ /th/ or /<u>th</u>/ *th*
   - ▸ /w/ *wh*
   - ▸ /kw/ *qu*
   - ▸ /ks/ *x*

5. As you do the activity, point to some letter tiles two or three times so that students don't think they are finished with a sound after they have named it.

6. Redirect students if they say an incorrect sound when you point to a letter tile.

   Say: That's the sound of another letter. What is the sound for this letter?

7. Help students if they touch the wrong letter tile after they repeat a sound.

   Say: That letter tile goes with the sound [sound for incorrect letter tile]. We're looking for the letter tile that goes with the sound [target sound].

Create Rhyming Words

Have students combine word parts and make words that rhyme.

1. **Say:** I'm going to break a word into two parts. Your job is to put the parts back together and say the word.

   - ▸ For example, if the first part of the word is /r/ and the last part is /ăk/, then you'll say *rack*: /r/ . . . /ăk/ . . . *rack*.
   - ▸ Next you'll add a new **beginning sound** to make a word that rhymes. For example, you'll use the same last part, /ăk/, and add a new first sound, like /s/. The rhyming word is /s/ . . . /ăk/ . . . *sack*.

Objectives

- Given the letter, identify the most common sound.
- Given the sound, identify the most common letter or letters.
- Identify words that rhyme.
- Identify ending sounds in words.
- Identify the letters, given the sound /k/.
- Identify and use the digraph –*ck*.
- Identify the trigraph –*tch*, given the sound /ch/.
- Identify and use the trigraph –*tch*.
- Read aloud grade-level text with appropriate automaticity, prosody, accuracy, and rate.
- Identify complete sentences.
- Blend sounds to create words.
- Identify individual sounds in words.
- Write words by applying grade-level phonics knowledge.

2. **Say:** Now it's your turn: /b/ . . . /ăk/.

   ▸ What's the word? *back*
   ▸ Now use the same last part, /ăk/, but add a new sound, /sh/, at the beginning. What word did you make? *shack*

3. Say the two word parts. Have students say the word the parts form. Have them add a new beginning sound to the last part of the following word to make rhyming words: /p/ . . . /ăk/ *pack*   Possible rhyming words: *tack, jack, lack, whack, quack*

Make Nonsense Rhymes

Help students identify **ending sounds** by having them make nonsense words.

1. **Say:** We're going to use word endings to make up **nonsense words**. First I will give you some ending sounds. Then I'll give you a nonsense word with those ending sounds. Your job is to tell me a nonsense word that rhymes with it. Let's do the first one. Remember, no real words are allowed.

2. **Say:** The first ending sounds are /ĭk/. The nonsense word is *fick*. Can you think of a nonsense word that rhymes with *fick*? How about *zick*?

3. **Say:** Let's do another one. The ending sound is /ŭch/. The nonsense word is *luch*. What is a nonsense word that rhymes with *luch*? Possible rhyming nonsense words: *ruch, nuch*

4. Repeat this procedure with the following sounds and words:

   ▸ /ŏtch/ *jotch*   Possible rhyming nonsense words: *zotch, motch*
   ▸ /ŭsh/ *sush*   Possible rhyming nonsense words: *dush, kush*
   ▸ /ăth/ *dath*   Possible rhyming nonsense words: *gath, sath*

Guess the Word

Have students use word meaning and sentence structure to choose a word that best completes a sentence.

1. Write the following words on students' whiteboard: *back, neck, pack,* and *duck*. Make sure students know the meaning of all the words on their whiteboard before you do this activity.

2. **Say:** We're going to play a guessing game. I'm going to read a sentence with a word missing. Your job is to look at the words on your whiteboard and decide which one is the right word to complete the sentence.

   ▸ Listen to this sentence: "When I finish reading the front side of a sheet, I turn it over and read the _____ ."
   ▸ You will tell me what word makes sense in the blank of the sentence. This time the word would be *back*.
   ▸ The complete sentence would be, "When I finish reading the front side of a sheet, I turn it over and read the *back*." Now you try it.

3. Continue the procedure with the following sentences:

   ▸ *Before I go on a trip, I have to _____ my suitcase.* pack
   ▸ *If it is cold outside, I wrap a scarf around my _____ .* neck
   ▸ *One kind of bird that likes to live by the water is a _____ .* duck

---

Build Words

Help students use letters and sounds to build words.

1. Place the following letter tiles at the top of students' whiteboard: *a, ck, i, l, m, o, p, tch, th,* and *wh*.

2. Draw three horizontal lines across the middle of students' whiteboard to represent the sounds in a word.

3. **Say:** Let's use letters and sounds to build the word *lock*.

4. Have students finger stretch the sounds in *lock*.

5. Have students

   ▸ Identify the first, next, and last sounds in *lock*.
   ▸ Choose the corresponding letter for each of the sounds.
   ▸ Move the letters to the correct lines on their whiteboard.

6. Guide students with these questions:

   ▸ What is the first sound in *lock*? /l/
     Which line does the letter for that sound go on? the first one
   ▸ What is the next sound in *lock*? /ŏ/
     Which line does the letter for that sound go on? the second one
   ▸ What's the last sound in *lock*? /k/
     Which line do the letters for that sound go on? the last one

7. Redirect students if they select the incorrect letter.

   Say: That sound is in the word [word], and it is the [first, second, third] sound. We want the sound [target sound].

   Continue until students select the correct letter.

8. Have students touch and say the word.

9. Have them say the word as they use a dry-erase marker to write the word on the whiteboard.

10. Repeat the activity to build the following words:

    ▸ *match* /m/ /ă/ /ch/
    ▸ *whack* /w/ /ă/ /k/
    ▸ *pitch* /p/ /ĭ/ /ch/
    ▸ *thatch* /th/ /ă/ /ch/

Try It

"Nick's Pet Duck"

Have students read "Nick's Pet Duck" on page 7 of *K¹² PhonicsWorks Readers Basic 7*.

Students should read the story silently once or twice before reading the story aloud. When students miss a word that can be sounded out, point to it and give them three to six seconds to try the word again. If students still miss the word, tell them the word so the flow of the story isn't interrupted.

After reading the story, make a list of all the words students missed, and go over those words with them. You may use letter tiles to show students how to read the words.

Dictation: Write Words

Have students practice identifying sounds and writing words.

1. Gather a pencil and the dictation notebook. Say the word *luck*. Then give these directions to students:

   ▸ Repeat the word.
   ▸ Write the word in your notebook.
   ▸ Read the word aloud.

2. When students have finished, write the following word on your whiteboard: *luck*.

3. Have them compare their answer to your correct version.

4. Repeat this procedure with the words *lock* and *match*.

   ▸ If students make an error and don't see it, help them correct their mistake by having them finger stretch the sounds in the word they missed.
   ▸ If students are having difficulty selecting the correct letters or sounds, review those letters or sounds that are confusing them.
   ▸ If students have difficulty with first, middle, and last sounds, have them finger stretch the sounds in words.

Objectives

- Read aloud grade-level text with appropriate automaticity, prosody, accuracy, and rate.
- Decode words by applying grade-level word analysis skills.
- Track text from left to right.
- Turn pages sequentially.
- Write words by applying grade-level phonics knowledge.
- Follow three-step directions.

 **20 minutes**

REVIEW: Trigraph *–tch* and Ending *–ck*

Students will work online independently to

► Practice the trigraph *–tch* and ending *–ck*.

Help students locate the online activities and provide support as needed.

Offline Alternative

No computer access? Have students point out and name things or words that contain the trigraph *–tch* (for example, *patch* or *notch*) or the ending *–ck* (for example, *back* or *check*). You might also ask students to spell words that contain the trigraph *–tch* or the ending *–ck*.

Objectives

- Identify individual sounds in words.
- Identify ending sounds in words.
- Identify and use the digraph *–ck*.
- Identify the letters, given the sound /k/.
- Identify and use the trigraph *–tch*.
- Identify the trigraph *–tch*, given the sound /ch/.

Unit Checkpoint

Lesson Overview

 [Online] **REVIEW:** Trigraph *–tch* and Ending *–ck* — **20** minutes

[Offline] **UNIT CHECKPOINT:** Trigraph *–tch* and Ending *–ck* — **30** minutes

[Materials]

Supplied

• *K¹² PhonicsWorks Basic Assessments*, PH 139–144

Objectives

- Identify the trigraph *–tch*, given the sound /ch/.
- Identify the letters, given the sound /k/.
- Identify the sound /ch/, given the trigraph *–tch*.
- Identify the sound /k/, given the digraph *–ck*.
- Identify and use the trigraph *–tch*.
- Identify and use the digraph *–ck*.
- Identify individual sounds in words.
- Given the sound, identify the most common letter or letters.
- Read sight words.
- Read instructional-level text with 90% accuracy.
- Read aloud grade-level text with appropriate automaticity, prosody, accuracy, and rate.
- Write words by applying grade-level phonics knowledge.

 **[Online]** **20** minutes

REVIEW: Trigraph *–tch* and Ending *–ck*

Students will review sounds for the trigraph *–tch* and ending *–ck* to prepare for the Unit Checkpoint. Help students locate the online activities and provide support as needed.

[Offline] 🕥 minutes

UNIT CHECKPOINT: Trigraph *–tch* and Ending *–ck*

Explain that students are going to show what they have learned about letters, sounds, and words.

1. Give students the Unit Checkpoint pages for the Trigraph *–tch* and Ending *–ck* unit and print the Unit Checkpoint Answer Key, if you'd like.

2. Use the instructions below to help administer the Checkpoint to students. On the Answer Key or another sheet of paper, note student answers to oral response questions to help with scoring the Checkpoint later.

3. Use the Answer Key to score the Checkpoint, and then enter the results online.

Part 1. Read Word Parts and Nonsense Words Have students read across the rows from left to right and say the sounds that each word part or nonsense word makes. Note any word parts or nonsense words they say incorrectly.

Part 2. Word Dissection For each word, say the sound students should identify. Have them read the word aloud and circle the letter or group of letters that spells the requested sound.

19. *beginning sound*

20. *beginning sound*

21. *ending sound*

22. *middle sound*

23. *ending sound*

Part 3. Finger Stretching Say each word to students. Have them say each word and finger stretch the sounds. Note any words they finger stretch incorrectly.

24. *pitch*

25. *catch*

26. *fetch*

27. *quick*

28. *luck*

29. *sock*

Part 4. Dictation Say each word to students. Have them repeat and write the word.

30. *back*

31. *lock*

32. *catch*

33. *match*

Part 5. Read Aloud Listen to students read the sentences aloud. Count and note the number of words they read correctly.

Part 6. Say Letters Say each sound. Have students say a letter or letters that make that sound. Note any incorrect responses.

35. /ch/

36. /sh/

37. /ĕ/

38. /ĭ/

39. /w/

40. /ă/

41. /k/

42. /ch/

43. /sh/

44. /k/

45. /th/

46. /ŭ/

47. /ŏ/

48. /w/

49. /kw/

50. /ch/

51. /k/

52. /th/

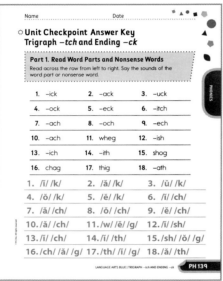

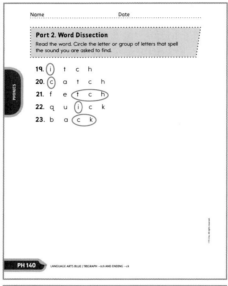

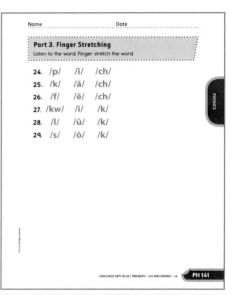

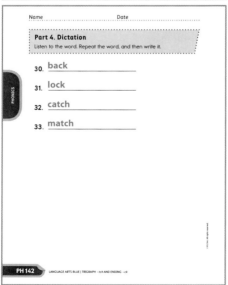

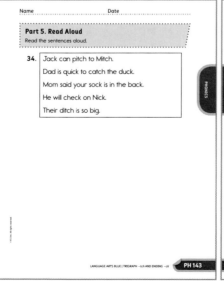

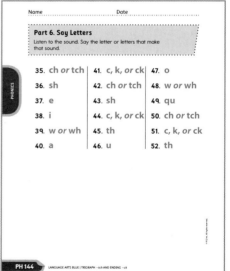

Getting Stronger: Digraphs *ch*, *sh*, and *th*

Unit Overview

In this unit, students will
- ▶ Review sight words.
- ▶ Review digraphs, trigraph *–tch*, and ending *–ck*.
- ▶ Review sounds and letters of the alphabet.
- ▶ Build words and word chains.
- ▶ Practice reading and writing.

[Materials]

Supplied
- *K¹² PhonicsWorks Basic Activity Book,* p. PH 67
- whiteboard, student
- Tile Kit

Also Needed
- sight words box

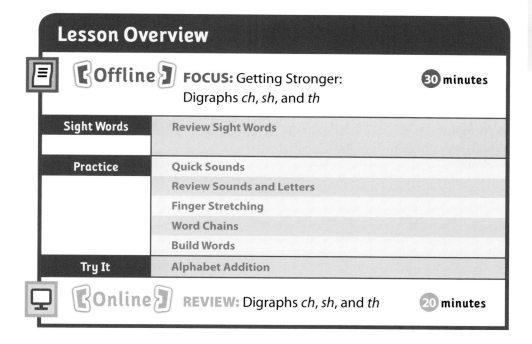

Lesson Overview

[Offline] FOCUS: Getting Stronger: Digraphs *ch*, *sh*, and *th*   **30** minutes

Sight Words	Review Sight Words
Practice	Quick Sounds
	Review Sounds and Letters
	Finger Stretching
	Word Chains
	Build Words
Try It	Alphabet Addition

[Online] REVIEW: Digraphs *ch*, *sh*, and *th*   **20** minutes

 **Offline** **30** minutes

FOCUS: Getting Stronger: Digraphs *ch*, *sh*, and *th*

Work **together** with students to complete offline Sight Words, Practice, and Try It activities.

Sight Words

Review Sight Words

Help students learn to recognize sight words.

1. Gather all the sight word cards students have yet to master from their sight words box. Stack the cards on the table face down.

2. Have students pick up a word and read it to you.

3. If they read it quickly and correctly, put the card in one stack. If they hesitate or do not read the word correctly, put it in another stack. The second stack should have words that they will review again.

4. Take the stack of words that students read correctly and dictate each word to them. They may choose to either write the word or spell it aloud.

5. If students spell the word correctly, put the card in the first stack because they have mastered the word. If they misspell the word, add it to the stack of cards to review again.

6. Chart students' progress on the back of each card.

   ▶ Divide the back of the card into two columns.
   ▶ Label the first column "Read" and the second column "Spell."
   ▶ Record the dates that students read or spell the word correctly. When students can read and spell the word correctly three times in a row, they have mastered the word. You may want to put a star or sticker on their card when they have mastered that word.

TIP Even if students can read and spell all the words correctly, it is still beneficial for them to review sight words. Choose as many additional words as you would like for each subsequent activity.

 Objectives
- Read sight words.
- Spell sight words.
- Write sight words.

Practice ....

Quick Sounds

Help students name words that have the same **beginning sound**.

1. **Say:** I'm going to say some sounds that begin a word. Your job is to think of as many words as you can that begin with those same sounds. Let's see how many you can name. The first sound is /sh/, as in *shop*. How many words can you say that begin with /sh/?

   ▶ If students have trouble thinking of words, have them look around the room and find objects that start with that sound.

2. Continue this procedure with the following sounds:

   ▶ /m/, as in *mat*
   ▶ /ch/, as in *chip*
   ▶ /th/, as in *that*
   ▶ /p/, as in *put*

 TIP You can get a book and find pictures of things that begin with that sound.

Review Sounds and Letters

Help students review sounds for the letters, digraphs, and trigraph *a, b, c, ch, –ck, e, k, sh, –tch, th, w, wh,* and *z,* plus any letters that are confusing for students.

1. Place the following letter tiles in random order on students' whiteboard: *a, b, c, ch, ck, e, k, sh, tch, th, w, wh, wh,* and *z,* plus any letters that are confusing.

2. **Say:** Let's go over some letters and sounds.

3. Point to each letter tile and have students say a sound that letter or letters make.

   ▶ *c* /k/
   ▶ *th* /th/ or /th/
   ▶ *sh* /sh/
   ▶ *a* /ă/
   ▶ *tch* /ch/
   ▶ *e* /ĕ/
   ▶ *ck* /k/

   ▶ *k* /k/
   ▶ *w* /w/
   ▶ *wh* /w/
   ▶ *b* /b/
   ▶ *z* /z/
   ▶ *ch* /ch/

4. Say each of the following sounds. Have students repeat the sound and touch the corresponding letter tile. Students should tell you the three spellings for /k/ as well as the two spellings for the sounds /w/ and /ch/.

   ▶ /k/ *c, ck,* or *k*
   ▶ /th/ or /th/ *th*
   ▶ /sh/ *sh*
   ▶ /ă/ *a*
   ▶ /ch/ *tch* or *ch*

   ▶ /ĕ/ *e*
   ▶ /w/ *w* or *wh*
   ▶ /b/ *b*
   ▶ /z/ *z*

5. As you do the activity, point to some letter tiles two or three times so that students don't think they are finished with a sound after they have named it.

6. Redirect students if they say an incorrect sound when you point to a letter tile.

   Say: That's the sound of another letter. What is the sound for this letter?

7. Help students if they touch the wrong letter tile after they repeat a sound.

   Say: That letter tile goes with the sound [sound for incorrect letter tile]. We're looking for the letter tile that goes with the sound [target sound].

Finger Stretching

Use finger stretching to help students identify individual sounds in words.

1. **Say:** Let's review finger stretching. In the word *shop*, the first sound is /sh/, the next sound is /ŏ/, and the last sound is /p/. I will finger stretch each sound as I say it. Then I'll say the word while pulling my fist toward my body.

2. Finger stretch the word *shop* for students.

3. **Say:** I'm going to say words with several sounds in them. You'll say each word and then finger stretch it while you say each sound in the word.

4. Say the following words and have students finger stretch them. After they finger stretch each word, ask them the question for that word.

   ▸ *fan* /f/ /ă/ /n/   What is the last sound? /n/
   ▸ *choose* /ch/ /o͞o/ /z/   What is the first sound? /ch/
   ▸ *with* /w/ /ĭ/ /th/   What is the middle sound? /ĭ/
   ▸ *ship* /sh/ /ĭ/ /p/   What is the first sound? /sh/
   ▸ *wish* /w/ /ĭ/ /sh/   What is the last sound? /sh/
   ▸ *Sam* /s/ /ă/ /m/   What is the middle sound? /ă/

 Refer to the *K¹² PhonicsWorks* DVD for a demonstration of finger stretching.

Word Chains

Have students build words by adding and changing letters to help them recognize and use individual sounds in words.

1. Place the following letter tiles at the top of students' whiteboard: *ch, g, i, n, p, r, sh, th,* and *w.*

2. **Say:** I am going to build the first word in a chain. The word is *ship.*

   ▸ I will pull down the letters for the sounds /sh/, /ĭ/, and /p/ to spell the word *ship.*
   ▸ I will touch and say *ship.* To change *ship* to *chip,* I will think about which sound is changed from the word *ship* to *chip.* I will need to replace the letter tile *sh* with the letter tile *ch.*
   ▸ Touch and say the word *chip.* Now it's your turn to change *chip* to *chin.* You can spell *chin* by making only one change. Touch and say the new word.

3. Redirect students if they select the incorrect letter for any sound.

   Say: That letter is for the sound [incorrect sound]. We want the letter for the sound [target sound]. What letter makes that sound? Answers will vary.

4. Redirect students if they name the sound incorrectly.

   Say: To change the word [first word] to [target word], we need the letter for the sound [target sound].

   Show students how to make the change. Have them touch and say the new word after they move the letters.

5. Follow this procedure to make the following words: *win, wish, with, wig, rig, rich, rip.*

6. For every new word, have students add, replace, or remove only one letter tile.

TIP If students struggle, review the sounds and letters that are confusing them.

Build Words
Help students use letters and sounds to build words.

1. Place the following letter tiles at the top of students' whiteboard: *a, b, ch, ck, i, p, r, sh, th, u,* and *w.*

2. Draw three horizontal lines across the middle of students' whiteboard to represent the sounds in a word.

3. **Say:** Let's use letters and sounds to build the word *rush.*

4. Have students finger stretch the sounds in *rush.*

5. Have students

   ▸ Identify the first, next, and last sounds in *rush.*
   ▸ Choose the corresponding letter for each sound.
   ▸ Move the letters to the correct lines on their whiteboard.

6. Guide students with these questions:

   ▸ What is the first sound in *rush*? /r/
     Which line does the letter for that sound go on? the first one
   ▸ What is the next sound in *rush*? /ŭ/
     Which line does the letter for that sound go on? the second one
   ▸ What's the last sound in *rush*? /sh/
     Which line do the letters for that sound go on? the last one

7. Redirect students if they select the incorrect letter.

   Say: That sound is in the word [word], and it is the [first, second, third] sound. We want the sound [target sound].

   Continue until students select the correct letter.

8. Have students touch and say the word.

9. Have them say the word as they use a dry-erase marker to write the word on the whiteboard.

10. Repeat the activity to build the following words:

  ▶ *with* /w/ /ĭ/ /th/
  ▶ *chip* /ch/ /ĭ/ /p/
  ▶ *chick* /ch/ /ĭ/ /k/
  ▶ *rash* /r/ /ă/ /sh/
  ▶ *bath* /b/ /ă/ /th/

Try It

Alphabet Addition

Have students complete page PH 67 in *K¹² PhonicsWorks Basic Activity Book* for more practice with the digraphs *sh*, *ch*, and *th*. Have students add the letters together to make a word. Then have them write that word and read it aloud.

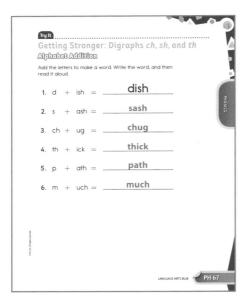

Objectives

- Identify and use the sound /ch/.
- Identify the letters, given the sound /ch/.
- Identify and use the digraph *ch*.
- Identify and use the sound /sh/.
- Identify the letters, given the sound /sh/.
- Identify and use the digraph *sh*.
- Identify and use the sound /th/.
- Identify and use the sound /th/.
- Identify and use the digraph *th*.
- Identify the letters, given the sound /th/.
- Identify the letters, given the sound /th/.

 **20 minutes**

REVIEW: Digraphs *ch*, *sh*, and *th*

Students will work online independently to

- ▶ Practice the digraphs *ch*, *sh*, and *th*.
- ▶ Practice decoding text by reading sentences.

Help students locate the online activities and provide support as needed.

Offline Alternative

No computer access? Have students name words that have the digraphs *ch*, *sh*, and *th*, such as *much*, *cash*, *this*, or *bath*. You might also have them spell words that have the digraphs *ch*, *sh*, and *th*.

Objectives

- Identify individual sounds in words.
- Identify and use the sound /ch/.
- Identify the letters, given the sound /ch/.
- Identify and use the digraph *ch*.
- Identify and use the sound /sh/.
- Identify the letters, given the sound /sh/.
- Identify and use the digraph *sh*.
- Identify and use the sound /th/.
- Identify and use the sound /tẖ/.
- Identify and use the digraph *th*.
- Identify the letters, given the sound /th/.
- Identify the letters, given the sound /tẖ/.
- Read aloud grade-level text with appropriate automaticity, prosody, accuracy, and rate.
- Decode words by applying grade-level word analysis skills.

Getting Stronger: Digraph *wh*, Trigraph *–tch*, and Ending *–ck*

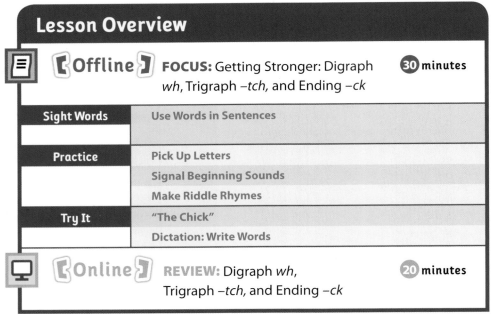

Lesson Overview

Offline **FOCUS:** Getting Stronger: Digraph *wh*, Trigraph *–tch*, and Ending *–ck*   **30** minutes

Sight Words	Use Words in Sentences
Practice	Pick Up Letters
	Signal Beginning Sounds
	Make Riddle Rhymes
Try It	"The Chick"
	Dictation: Write Words

Online **REVIEW:** Digraph *wh*, Trigraph *–tch*, and Ending *–ck*   **20** minutes

Materials

Supplied
- *K¹² PhonicsWorks Readers Basic 7*, pp. 13–18
- whiteboard, Learning Coach
- whiteboard, student
- Tile Kit

Also Needed
- sight words box
- dictation notebook

 **30 minutes**

FOCUS: Getting Stronger: Digraph *wh*, Trigraph *–tch*, and Ending *–ck*

Work **together** with students to complete offline Sight Words, Practice, and Try It activities.

Sight Words

Use Words in Sentences

Help students use sight words in sentences.

1. Gather all the sight word cards students have yet to master from their sight words box. Spread the sight word cards on the table.

2. **Say:** Let's use sight words in sentences.

3. Have students

   ▸ Touch each card and read the word on it.
   ▸ Make up a sentence using the word.
   ▸ Put the card in a pile after using the word in a sentence.
   ▸ Go through the pile of cards and read each sight word again.
   ▸ Spell each word.

TIP If students have difficulty with any of the sight words, place those cards in a pile to review again.

Objectives
- Read sight words.
- Spell sight words.

Practice

Pick Up Letters
Help students use letters and sounds to make words and sentences.

1. Place the following letter tiles on students' whiteboard: *c, d, m, n, p, sh,* and *th.*

2. **Say:** Let's play a game with these letters.

3. Pick up the letter tile for *n.*

4. **Say:** I chose the letter *n.* The sound is /n/. A word that starts with the sound /n/ is *nap.* A sentence using that word is *I take a nap when I'm tired.* Now it's your turn.

5. Continue taking turns until all the letter tiles have been chosen.

6. Have students answer the following questions for each letter or group of letters:

   ▸ What is (are) the letter(s)?
   ▸ Is the tile you chose a digraph that has two letters that make one sound?
   ▸ What is the sound?
   ▸ What is a word that starts with that sound?
   ▸ What sentence can you make with that word?

7. Redirect students if they name a word that starts with the sound, but not the letter (such as *knob*).

   Say: That is a word that doesn't follow the rules that we know for spelling. Try another word.

8. Prompt students if they have trouble matching the sounds with words. For example:

   Say: That's /p/, as in *party.* Can you think of another word that starts with that sound?

Signal Beginning Sounds
Use a special signal to help students identify **beginning sounds** in words.

1. **Say:** I'm going to tell you a special sound, and then I'll say some words. Repeat each word I say and make a special signal to tell me where the special sound is. If the special sound is at the beginning of the word, clap your hands. If the special sound is **not** at the beginning of the word, just smile at me. For example,

   ▸ If I ask you to listen for the sound /ŏ/ and I say the word *odd*, you'll repeat the word *odd* and clap your hands because *odd* has the sound /ŏ/ at the beginning.
   ▸ If I say the word *apple*, you'll repeat the word *apple* and smile at me because *apple* has the sound /ă/, not /ŏ/, at the beginning.

Objectives
- Identify letters of the alphabet.
- Given the letter, identify the most common sound.
- Given the sound, identify the most common letter or letters.
- Identify individual sounds in words.
- Identify beginning sounds in words.
- Identify words that rhyme.
- Identify and use the sound /k/.
- Identify the letters, given the sound /k/.
- Identify the sound /k/, given the letters *ck.*
- Identify and use the digraph *–ck.*
- Identify the trigraph *–tch*, given the sound /ch/.
- Identify the letters, given the sound /ch/.
- Identify and use the sound /ch/.
- Identify the letters, given the sound /w/.
- Identify and use the digraph *wh.*
- Identify the sound /w/, given the digraph *wh.*
- Identify the digraph *wh*, given the sound /w/.

2. Say each sound and group of words. Have students make the special signal to identify the beginning sound.

▶ /ŏ/: *ostrich, action, octopus, under, object* clap hands: *ostrich, octopus, object*
▶ /ĭ/: *on, in, it, at, important* clap hands: *in, it, important*

TIP If students can't identify the beginning sound of each word, say the word again and emphasize the beginning sound by repeating it three times (for example, /t/ /t/ /t/, *taste*). You can also draw out the beginning sound when you say the word (for example, *mmmommy*). If necessary, have students look at your mouth while you repeat the sounds.

Make Riddle Rhymes

Have students identify words that rhyme by playing a riddle game.

1. **Say:** We are going to play a riddle game. I will think of a word and give you some clues. You will guess the word and solve the riddle.

▶ One player on a baseball team does this. It rhymes with *itch*. *pitch*

2. Give students clues to words. Have them name each word and then say and write it. Use these clues and words:

▶ It's the sound a duck makes. It rhymes with *sack*. *quack*
▶ It's what you do to a stamp or lollipop. It rhymes with *pick*. *lick*
▶ It has fins and lives in water. It rhymes with *wish*. *fish*

Try It

"The Chick"

Have students read "The Chick" on page 13 of *K¹² PhonicsWorks Readers Basic 7.*

Students should read the story silently once or twice before reading the story aloud. When students miss a word that can be sounded out, point to it and give them three to six seconds to try the word again. If students still miss the word, tell them the word so the flow of the story isn't interrupted.

After reading the story, make a list of all the words students missed, and go over those words with them. You may use letter tiles to show students how to read the words.

Objectives

- Read aloud grade-level text with appropriate automaticity, prosody, accuracy, and rate.
- Decode words by applying grade-level word analysis skills.
- Track text from left to right.
- Turn pages sequentially.
- Write words by applying grade-level phonics knowledge.
- Follow three-step directions.

Dictation: Write Words

Have students practice identifying sounds and writing words.

1. Gather a pencil and the dictation notebook. Say the word *when*. Then give these directions to students:

   ► Repeat the word.
   ► Write the word in your notebook.
   ► Read the word aloud.

2. When students have finished, write the following word on your whiteboard: *when*.

3. Have them compare their answer to your correct version.

4. Repeat this procedure with the words *catch* and *back*.

   ► If students make an error and don't see it, help them correct their mistake by having them finger stretch the sounds in the word they missed.
   ► If students are having difficulty selecting the correct letters or sounds, review those letters or sounds that are confusing them.
   ► If students have difficulty with first, middle, and last sounds, have them finger stretch the sounds in words.

 **minutes**

REVIEW: **Digraph *wh*, Trigraph *–tch*, and Ending *–ck***

Students will work online independently to

   ► Practice the digraph *wh*, the trigraph *–tch*, and ending *–ck*.

Help students locate the online activities and provide support as needed.

Offline Alternative

No computer access? Have students point out and name things or words that contain the digraph *wh*, trigraph *–tch*, or ending *–ck* (for example, *whiz*, *latch*, or *neck*). You might also ask students to spell words that contain the digraph *wh*, trigraph *–tch*, or ending *–ck*.

 Objectives

- Identify individual sounds in words.
- Identify and use the sound /k/.
- Identify the letters, given the sound /k/.
- Identify the sound /k/, given the letters *ck*.
- Identify and use the digraph *–ck*.
- Identify the trigraph *–tch*, given the sound /ch/.
- Identify the letters, given the sound /w/.
- Identify and use the digraph *wh*.
- Identify the sound /w/, given the digraph *wh*.
- Identify the digraph *wh*, given the sound /w/.

Getting Stronger: Digraphs, Trigraph –*tch*, and Ending –*ck* (A)

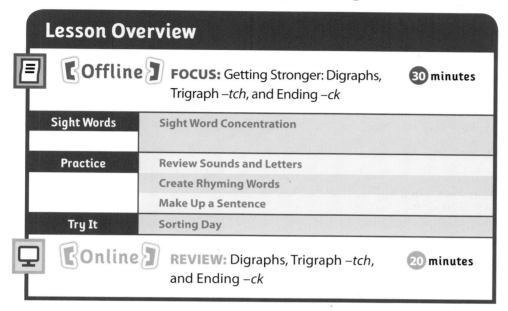

Lesson Overview

[Offline] **FOCUS:** Getting Stronger: Digraphs, Trigraph –*tch*, and Ending –*ck* **30 minutes**

Sight Words	Sight Word Concentration
Practice	Review Sounds and Letters
	Create Rhyming Words
	Make Up a Sentence
Try It	Sorting Day

[Online] **REVIEW:** Digraphs, Trigraph –*tch*, and Ending –*ck* **20 minutes**

Materials

Supplied
- *K¹² PhonicsWorks Basic Activity Book,* p. PH 68
- whiteboard, student
- Tile Kit

Also Needed
- sight words box
- index cards (6)
- crayons

Advance Preparation

Gather two sets of the sight word cards that students have yet to master.

For Make Up a Sentence, print each of the following words on index cards, using one card per word: *duck, fish, lock, which, sack,* and *quick.*

 **30** minutes

FOCUS: Getting Stronger: Digraphs, Trigraph –*tch*, and Ending –*ck*

Work **together** with students to complete offline Sight Words, Practice, and Try It activities.

Sight Words

Sight Word Concentration

Help students review sight words.

1. Gather the two sets of sight word cards.

2. Scramble both sets of sight word cards and place them face down on the table or floor.

3. Turn over two cards at a time; take turns with students. If the cards match, the person turning over the matching cards reads the word and uses it in a sentence. If the cards don't match, the person turns them back over.

4. Remove and save the matching cards.

5. Continue the activity until all the cards are paired.

6. Have students read all the words.

7. Take the stack of words that students read correctly and dictate each word to them.

8. Have students write each word or spell it aloud.

 TIP If students have difficulty with any sight words, let them work at their own pace to really master these words.

Objectives
- Read sight words.
- Spell sight words.
- Write sight words.

Practice •

Review Sounds and Letters

Help students review sounds for the letters, digraphs, and trigraph *ch, –ck, i, m, p, sh, –tch, th, u,* and *wh,* plus any letters that are confusing for students.

1. Place the following letter tiles in random order on students' whiteboard: *ch, ck, i, m, p, sh, tch, th, u,* and *wh,* plus any letters that are confusing.

2. **Say:** Let's go over some letters and sounds.

3. Point to each letter tile and have students say a sound that letter or letters make.

   ► *m* /m/   ► *ch* /ch/
   ► *sh* /sh/   ► *u* /ŭ/
   ► *p* /p/   ► *th* /th/ or /<u>th</u>/
   ► *tch* /ch/   ► *ck* /k/
   ► *i* /ĭ/   ► *wh* /w/

4. Say each of the following sounds. Have students repeat the sound and touch the corresponding letter tile.

   ► /m/ *m*   ► /ŭ/ *u*
   ► /sh/ *sh*   ► /th/ or /<u>th</u>/ *th*
   ► /p/ *p*   ► /k/ *ck*
   ► /ch/ *ch* or *tch*   ► /w/ *wh*
   ► /ĭ/ *i*

5. As you do the activity, point to some letter tiles two or three times so that students don't think they are finished with a sound after they have named it.

6. Redirect students if they say an incorrect sound when you point to a letter tile.

   Say: That's the sound of another letter. What is the sound for this letter?

7. Help students if they touch the wrong letter tile after they repeat a sound.

   Say: That letter tile goes with the sound [sound for incorrect letter tile]. We're looking for the letter tile that goes with the sound [target sound].

Create Rhyming Words

Have students combine word parts and make words that rhyme.

1. **Say:** I'm going to break a word into two parts. Your job is to put the parts back together and say the word.

   ► For example, if the first part of the word is /m/ and the last part is /ăch/, then you'll say *match*: /m/ . . . /ăch/ . . . *match*.
   ► Next you'll add a new **beginning sound** to make a word that rhymes. For example, you'll use the same last part, /ăch/, and add a new first sound, like /b/. The rhyming word is /b/ . . . /ăch/ . . . *batch*.

Objectives

- Identify individual sounds in words.
- Given the letter, identify the most common sound.
- Given the sound, identify the most common letter or letters.
- Identify words that rhyme.
- Identify and use the digraph *ch.*
- Identify and use the digraph *–ck.*
- Identify the trigraph *–tch,* given the sound /ch/.
- Identify and use the digraph *sh.*
- Identify and use the digraph *wh.*
- Identify and use the digraph *th.*
- Read aloud grade-level text with appropriate automaticity, prosody, accuracy, and rate.
- Identify complete sentences.

2. **Say:** Now it's your turn: /l/ . . . /ăch/.

   ▸ What's the word? *latch*
   ▸ Now use the same last part, /ăch/, but add a new sound, /k/, at the beginning. What word did you make? *catch*

3. Say the two word parts. Have students say the word the parts form. Have them add a new beginning sound to the last part of the following word to make rhyming words: /p/ . . . /ăch/ *patch*   Possible rhyming words: *hatch, thatch*

Make Up a Sentence

Help students use words to make sentences.

1. Gather the word cards you prepared, and place them face down on the table in one pile.

2. Have students

   ▸ Select a card.
   ▸ Read the word.
   ▸ Use the word in an interesting, fun, or silly sentence.

TIP If students read a word incorrectly, have them finger stretch the sounds in the word or use letter tiles to spell the word and touch and say.

Try It

Sorting Day

Have students complete page PH 68 in *K¹² PhonicsWorks Basic Activity Book* for more practice reading words that have digraphs and the trigraph *–tch*. Have them read each word aloud and color animal words yellow and other words red.

Objectives
* Read aloud grade-level text with appropriate automaticity, prosody, accuracy, and rate.

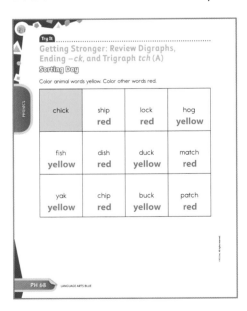

 **minutes**

REVIEW: Digraphs, Trigraph *–tch*, and Ending *–ck*

Students will work online independently to

▸ Practice digraphs, the trigraph *–tch*, and the ending *–ck*.
▸ Practice decoding text by reading a story.

Help students locate the online activities and provide support as needed.

Offline Alternative

No computer access? Have students point out and name things or words that contain digraphs, the trigraph *–tch*, or the ending *–ck* (for example, *fish*, *chop*, *moth*, *that*, *what*, *etch*, or *neck*). You might also ask students to spell words that contain digraphs, the trigraph *–tch*, or the ending *–ck*.

Objectives

- Identify individual sounds in words.
- Identify and use the digraph *ch*.
- Identify and use the digraph *sh*.
- Identify and use the digraph *wh*.
- Identify and use the digraph *th*.
- Identify and use the digraph *–ck*.
- Identify the trigraph *–tch*, given the sound /ch/.
- Read aloud grade-level text with appropriate automaticity, prosody, accuracy, and rate.
- Decode words by applying grade-level word analysis skills.

Getting Stronger: Digraphs, Trigraph –*tch*, and Ending –*ck* (B)

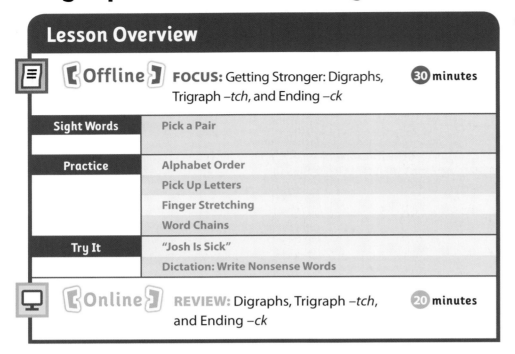

Lesson Overview

Offline **FOCUS:** Getting Stronger: Digraphs, Trigraph –*tch*, and Ending –*ck*   **30** minutes

Sight Words	Pick a Pair
Practice	Alphabet Order
	Pick Up Letters
	Finger Stretching
	Word Chains
Try It	"Josh Is Sick"
	Dictation: Write Nonsense Words

Online **REVIEW:** Digraphs, Trigraph –*tch*, and Ending –*ck*   **20** minutes

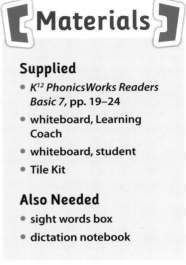

Materials

Supplied
- *K¹² PhonicsWorks Readers Basic 7*, pp. 19–24
- whiteboard, Learning Coach
- whiteboard, student
- Tile Kit

Also Needed
- sight words box
- dictation notebook

Advance Preparation

Place lowercase letters in alphabetical order on your whiteboard.

 **Offline** **30** minutes

FOCUS: Getting Stronger: Digraphs, Trigraph –*tch*, and Ending –*ck*

Work **together** with students to complete offline Sight Words, Practice, and Try It activities.

Sight Words

Pick a Pair

Play a card game with students for more practice with sight words.

1. Gather the sight word cards that students are reviewing. Choose two words and place the cards on the table.

2. Ask questions to help students identify each word. For example, if the words are *or* and *one*, you could ask, "Which word names a number?" If the words are *on* and *but*, you could ask, "Which word is the opposite of *off*?"

3. Continue the activity until students identify all the words.

4. Take the stack of words that students read correctly and dictate each word to them.

5. Have students write each word or spell it aloud.

Objectives
- Read sight words.
- Spell sight words.
- Write sight words.

Practice ∙∙∙

Alphabet Order

Review alphabetic order with students.

1. Place the lowercase letter tiles *a* through *z* on students' whiteboard.

2. **Say:** Let's review the order of some letters in the alphabet.

3. Have students

   ► Name the letter before *l*.
   ► Name the letter after *y*.
   ► Name any letter that comes before *b*.
   ► Name any letter that comes after *j*.
   ► Name any two letters that come before *r*.
   ► Name any two letters that come after *f*.

 TIP If students hesitate, have them check the letters on the whiteboard.

Pick Up Letters

Help students use letters and sounds to make words and sentences.

1. Place the following letter tiles on students' whiteboard: *a*, *b*, *ch*, *g*, *sh*, and *th*.

2. **Say:** Let's play a game with these letters.

3. Pick up the letter tile for *g*.

4. **Say:** I chose the letter *g*. The sound is /g/. A word that starts with the sound /g/ is *girl*. A sentence using that word is *The girl went home.* Now it's your turn.

5. Continue taking turns until all the letter tiles have been chosen.

6. Have students answer the following questions for each letter or group of letters.

   ► What is (are) the letter(s)?
   ► Is the tile you chose a digraph that has two letters that make one sound?
   ► What is the sound?
   ► What is a word that starts with that sound?
   ► What sentence can you make with that word?

7. Redirect students if they name a word that starts with the sound, but not the letter (such as *knob*).

   Say: That is a word that doesn't follow the rules that we know for spelling. Try another word.

8. Prompt students if they have trouble matching the sounds with words. For example:

   Say: That's /j/, as in *jelly*. Can you think of another word that starts with that sound?

Objectives

- Identify letters of the alphabet.
- Given the letter, identify the most common sound.
- Given the sound, identify the most common letter or letters.
- Identify ending sounds in words.
- Identify and use the digraph *ch*.
- Identify and use the digraph *sh*.
- Identify and use the digraph *wh*.
- Identify and use the digraph *th*.
- Identify and use the digraph *–ck*.
- Identify and use the trigraph *–tch*.
- Identify the trigraph *–tch*, given the sound /ch/.
- Identify individual sounds in words.
- Identify the new word when one sound is changed in a word.

Finger Stretching

Use finger stretching to help students identify individual sounds in words.

1. **Say:** Let's review finger stretching. In the word *this*, the first sound is /<u>th</u>/, the next sound is /ĭ/, and the last sound is /s/. I will finger stretch each sound as I say it. Then I'll say the word while pulling my fist toward my body.

2. Finger stretch the word *this* for students.

3. **Say:** I'm going to say words with several sounds in them. You'll say each word and then finger stretch it while you say each sound in the word.

4. Say the following words and have students finger stretch them. After they finger stretch each word, ask them the question for that word.

   ▸ *that* /<u>th</u>/ /ă/ /t/   How many sounds are in the word? three
   ▸ *pitch* /p/ /ĭ/ /ch/   How many sounds are in the word? three
   ▸ *itch* /ĭ/ /ch/   How many sounds are in the word? two
   ▸ *yuck* /y/ /ŭ/ /k/   What is the last sound? /k/
   ▸ *tick* /t/ /ĭ/ /k/   How many sounds are in the word? three
   ▸ *thick* /th/ /ĭ/ /k/   What is the first sound? /th/
   ▸ *ash* /ă/ /sh/   What is the first sound? /ă/

 Refer to the *K¹² PhonicsWorks* DVD for a demonstration of finger stretching.

Word Chains

Have students build words by adding and changing letters to help them recognize and use individual sounds in words.

1. Place the following letter tiles at the top of students' whiteboard: *a, ch, ck, h, i, n, p, tch,* and *th.*

2. **Say:** I am going to build the first word in a chain. The word is *hatch.*

   ▸ I will pull down the letters for the sounds /h/, /ă/, and /ch/ to spell the word *hatch.*
   ▸ I will touch and say *hatch.* To change *hatch* to *patch,* I will think about which sound is changed from the word *hatch* to *patch.* I will need to replace the letter *h* with the letter *p.*
   ▸ Touch and say the word *patch.* Now it's your turn to change *patch* to *pitch.* You can spell *pitch* by making only one change. Touch and say the new word.

3. Redirect students if they select the incorrect letter for any sound.

   Say: That letter is for the sound [incorrect sound]. We want the letter for the sound [target sound]. What letter makes that sound? Answers will vary.

4. Redirect students if they name the sound incorrectly.

   Say: To change the word [first word] to [target word], we need the letter for the sound [target sound].

   Show students how to make the change. Have them touch and say the new word after they move the letters.

5. Follow this procedure to make the following words: *pick, thick, thin, chin, chick.*

6. For every new word, have students add, replace, or remove only one letter tile.

 If students struggle, review the sounds and letters that are confusing them.

Try It

"Josh Is Sick"

Have students read "Josh Is Sick" on page 19 of *K¹² PhonicsWorks Readers Basic 7.*

Students should read the story silently once or twice before reading the story aloud. When students miss a word that can be sounded out, point to it and give them three to six seconds to try the word again. If students still miss the word, tell them the word so the flow of the story isn't interrupted.

After reading the story, make a list of all the words students missed, and go over those words with them. You may use letter tiles to show students how to read the words.

Dictation: Write Nonsense Words

Have students practice identifying sounds and writing nonsense words.

1. Gather a pencil and the dictation notebook.

2. **Say:** Some words don't have any meaning. We call these **nonsense words**. Even though we don't know what a word means, we can still read and write it.

3. Say the nonsense word *ish.* Then give these directions to students:

    ▸ Repeat the word.
    ▸ Write the word in your notebook.
    ▸ Read the word aloud.

4. When students have finished, write the following nonsense word on your whiteboard: *ish.*

5. Have them compare their answer to your correct version.

6. Repeat this procedure with the words *vack, dith,* and *quish.*

    ▸ If students make an error and don't see it, help them correct their mistake by having them finger stretch the sounds in the word they missed.
    ▸ If students are having difficulty selecting the correct letters or sounds, review those letters or sounds that are confusing them.
    ▸ If students have difficulty with first, middle, and last sounds, have them finger stretch the sounds in words.

Objectives

- Read aloud grade-level text with appropriate automaticity, prosody, accuracy, and rate.
- Decode words by applying grade-level word analysis skills.
- Track text from left to right.
- Turn pages sequentially.
- Write words by applying grade-level phonics knowledge.
- Follow three-step directions.

 **20 minutes**

REVIEW: Digraphs, Trigraph *–tch*, and Ending *–ck*

Students will work online independently to

▶ Practice digraphs, the trigraph *–tch*, and the ending *–ck*.

Help students locate the online activities and provide support as needed.

Offline Alternative

No computer access? Have students point out and name things or words that contain digraphs, the trigraph *–tch*, or the ending *–ck* (for example, *mush, chug, math, this, whim, catch,* or *sick*). You might also ask students to spell words that contain digraphs, the trigraph *–tch*, or the ending *–ck*.

Objectives

- Identify individual sounds in words.
- Identify and use the digraph *ch*.
- Identify and use the digraph *sh*.
- Identify and use the digraph *wh*.
- Identify and use the digraph *th*.
- Identify and use the digraph *–ck*.
- Identify the trigraph *–tch*, given the sound /ch/.

Unit Checkpoint

Lesson Overview

 Online   **REVIEW:** Digraphs, Trigraph *–tch*, and Ending *–ck*   **20** minutes

Offline   **UNIT CHECKPOINT:** Getting Stronger: Digraphs, Trigraph *–tch*, and Ending *–ck*   **30** minutes

Materials

Supplied
- *K¹² PhonicsWorks Basic Assessments,* pp. PH 145–150

Objectives

- Identify the digraph *wh*, given the sound /w/.
- Identify the sound /w/, given the digraph *wh*.
- Identify and use the digraph *wh*.
- Identify and use the digraph *ch*.
- Identify the letters, given the sound /ch/.
- Identify the sound /ch/, given the digraph *ch*.
- Identify and use the sound /th/.
- Identify the letters, given the sound /th/.
- Identify and use the digraph *th*.
- Identify the letters, given the sound /th/.
- Identify and use the sound /th/.
- Identify and use the sound /sh/.
- Identify the letters, given the sound /sh/.
- Identify and use the digraph *sh*.
- Identify the sound /k/, given the letters *ck*.
- Identify the letters, given the sound /k/.
- Identify and use the digraph *–ck*.

- Identify and use the sound /tch/.
- Identify the letters, given the sound /tch/.
- Identify the trigraph *–tch*, given the sound /ch/.
- Read, write, and spell words containing short vowel sounds.
- Identify individual sounds in words.
- Given the letter, identify the most common sound.
- Given the sound, identify the most common letter or letters.
- Read instructional-level text with 90% accuracy.
- Read aloud grade-level text with appropriate automaticity, prosody, accuracy, and rate.
- Write words by applying grade-level phonics knowledge.
- Write sight words.
- Read sight words.

 **Online**   **20** minutes

REVIEW: Digraphs, Trigraph *–tch*, and Ending *–ck*

Students will review digraphs, the trigraph *–tch*, and the ending *–ck* to prepare for the Unit Checkpoint. Help students locate the online activities and provide support as needed.

[Offline] 30 minutes

UNIT CHECKPOINT: Getting Stronger: Digraphs, Trigraph –*tch*, and Ending –*ck*

Explain that students are going to show what they have learned about sounds, letters, and words.

1. Give students the Unit Checkpoint pages for the Getting Stronger: Digraphs, Trigraph –*tch*, and Ending –*ck* unit and print the Unit Checkpoint Answer Key, if you'd like.

2. Use the instructions below to help administer the Checkpoint to students. On the Answer Key or another sheet of paper, note student answers to oral response questions to help with scoring the Checkpoint later.

3. Use the Answer Key to score the Checkpoint, and then enter the results online.

Part 1. Read Word Parts, Nonsense Words, and Words Have students read across the rows from left to right and say the sound or sounds that each word part, nonsense word, or word makes. Note any word parts or words they say incorrectly.

Part 2. Word Dissection For each word, say the sound students should identify. Have them read the word aloud and circle the letter or group of letters that spells the requested sound.

19. *beginning sound*

20. *beginning sound*

21. *ending sound*

22. *middle sound*

23. *ending sound*

Part 3. Finger Stretching Say each word to students. Have them say each word and finger stretch the sounds. Note any words they finger stretch incorrectly.

24. *pitch*

25. *which*

26. *shot*

27. *quick*

28. *chin*

29. *math*

Part 4. Dictation Say each word to students. Have them repeat and write the word.

30. *hatch*

31. *shock*

32. *when*

33. *check*

Part 5. Read Aloud Listen to students read the sentences aloud. Count and note the number of words they read correctly.

Part 6. Say Letters Say each sound. Have students say a letter or letters that make that sound. Note any incorrect responses.

35. /ch/

36. /sh/

37. /ĕ/

38. /ĭ/

39. /wh/

40. /ă/

41. /k/

42. /ch/

43. /th/

44. /ŭ/

45. /ŏ/

46. /w/

47. /kw/

48. /ch/

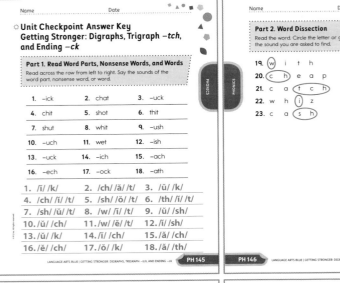

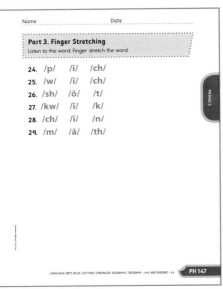

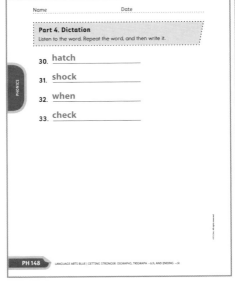

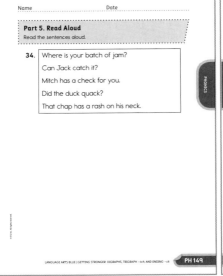

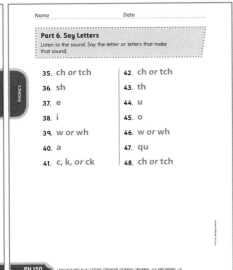

Review Digraphs and the Trigraph *–tch* (A)

Unit Overview

In this unit, students will
- ▸ Learn the sight words *who*, *see*, and *or*.
- ▸ Identify letters and sounds in the alphabet.
- ▸ Review digraphs and the trigraph *–tch*.
- ▸ Identify beginning and ending sounds in words.
- ▸ Build words.

【 Materials 】

Supplied
- *K¹² PhonicsWorks Basic Activity Book*, p. PH 69
- whiteboard, Learning Coach
- whiteboard, student
- Tile Kit

Also Needed
- sight words box
- dictation notebook

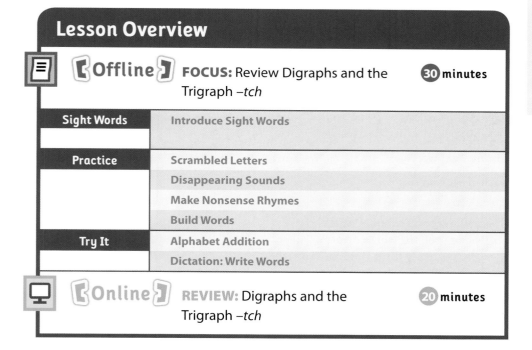

Lesson Overview

≡ 【Offline】 FOCUS: Review Digraphs and the Trigraph *–tch* **30 minutes**

Sight Words	Introduce Sight Words
Practice	Scrambled Letters
	Disappearing Sounds
	Make Nonsense Rhymes
	Build Words
Try It	Alphabet Addition
	Dictation: Write Words

🖥 【Online】 REVIEW: Digraphs and the Trigraph *–tch* **20 minutes**

 **30 minutes**

FOCUS: Review Digraphs and the Trigraph –*tch*

Work **together** with students to complete offline Sight Words, Practice, and Try It activities.

Sight Words ···

Introduce Sight Words

Help students learn the sight words *who, see,* and *or.*

1. Gather the sight word cards *who, see,* and *or.*

2. Show students the *who* card.

3. **Say:** This is the word *who.* We see this word so often that we want to be able to read and spell *who* quickly without thinking about it. Look closely at the word *who.* Spell the word *who* aloud. Take a picture of the word *who* in your mind. When you think you can spell *who* yourself, turn the card over and use your letter tiles to spell the word *who.* Check the card to see if you spelled the word *who* correctly. Read aloud the word you spelled with the letter tiles.

4. Repeat the activity with the remaining sight words.

5. Chart students' progress on the back of each card.

   ▸ Divide the back of the card into two columns.
   ▸ Label the first column "Read" and the second column "Spell."
   ▸ Record the dates that students read or spell the word correctly. When students can read and spell the word correctly three times in a row, they have mastered the word. You may want to put a star or sticker on the card when they have mastered that word.

6. Add the cards to students' sight words box.

TIP Sight words can be very difficult for some students. Let students work at their own pace and really master these words, as they occur frequently in reading and writing.

Objectives
• Read sight words.
• Spell sight words.

Practice

Scrambled Letters

To help students master the alphabet, have them practice identifying and naming letters.

1. Place the following letter tiles in random order on students' whiteboard: *a, c, d, s, v,* and *x.*

2. Have students arrange the letters in alphabetical order.

TIP Students may find this activity easier if they slowly sing "The Alphabet Song" to themselves as they work.

Disappearing Sounds

Help students practice identifying sounds by having them remove ending digraph sounds in words.

1. **Say:** We're going to make parts of words disappear. First I will say a word. Then I will say part of the word that we are going to make disappear. Today the disappearing part of the word is the **ending sound**. To make the ending sound of the word disappear, you will only say the part of the word that is left after you take away the ending sound.

2. **Say:** Let's try one. The word is *catch*. The sound I want you to make disappear is /ch/. What is the sound of the word without the sound /ch/?

3. **Say:** /k/ . . . /ă/ . . . /ch/. The sound /kă/ is left when you take away /ch/.

4. Repeat this procedure with the following sounds and words.

   Say: What are the beginning sounds of the following words without the ending sound /ch/?

   ▸ *batch* /bă/
   ▸ *fetch* /fĕ/
   ▸ *hatch* /hă/

   Say: What are the beginning sounds of the following words without the ending sound /k/?

   ▸ *sick* /sĭ/
   ▸ *luck* /lŭ/
   ▸ *dock* /dŏ/
   ▸ *tuck* /tŭ/

TIP If students cannot figure out the part of the word that is left after taking away the ending sound, use letter tiles to show them what sounds are left when the sounds are taken away. You might also have them finger stretch the word and then finger stretch only the sounds that are left after the ending sound disappears.

Objectives

- Identify letters of the alphabet.
- Identify and use the trigraph *–tch.*
- Identify and use the digraph *–ck.*
- Identify and use the digraph *ch.*
- Identify and use the digraph *sh.*
- Identify and use the digraph *th.*
- Identify and use the digraph *wh.*
- Identify beginning sounds in words.
- Identify ending sounds in words.
- Identify words that rhyme.
- Write words by applying grade-level phonics knowledge.
- Identify individual sounds in words.
- Blend sounds to create words.

Make Nonsense Rhymes
Help students identify **ending sounds** by having them make nonsense words.

1. **Say:** We're going to use word endings to make up nonsense words. First I will give you some ending sounds. Then I'll give you a nonsense word with those ending sounds. Your job is to tell me a nonsense word that rhymes with it. Let's do the first one. Remember, no real words are allowed.

2. **Say:** The first ending sound is /k/. The nonsense word is *gock*. Can you think of a nonsense word that rhymes with *gock*? How about *bock*?

3. **Say:** Let's do another one. The ending sound is /ch/. The nonsense word is *kuch*. What is a nonsense word that rhymes with *kuch*? Possible rhyming words: *ruch, nuch*

4. Repeat this procedure with the following sounds and words:
   - /n/ *zan*   Possible rhyming words: *gan, kan*
   - /th/ *zeth*   Possible rhyming words: *reth, teth*
   - /r/ *ler*   Possible rhyming words: *ser, ner*

Build Words
Help students use letters and sounds to build words.

1. Place the following letter tiles at the top of students' whiteboard: *a, c, ck, i, o, p, r, sh, tch,* and *u.*

2. Draw three horizontal lines across the middle of students' whiteboard to represent the sounds in a word.

3. **Say:** Let's use letters and sounds to build the word *catch*.

4. Have students finger stretch the sounds in *catch*.

5. Have students
   - Identify the first, next, and last sounds in *catch*.
   - Choose the corresponding letter tile for each of the sounds.
   - Move the letters to the correct lines on their whiteboard.

6. Guide students with these questions:
   - What is the first sound in *catch*? /k/
     Which line does the letter for that sound go on? the first one
   - What is the next sound in *catch*? /ă/
     Which line does the letter for that sound go on? the second one
   - What's the last sound in *catch*? /ch/
     Which line do the letters for that sound go on? the last one

7. Redirect students if they select the incorrect letter.

   Say: That sound is in the word [word], and it is the [first, second, third] sound. We want the sound [target sound].

   Continue until students select the correct letter.

8. Have students touch and say the word.

9. Have them say the word as they use a dry-erase marker to write the word on the whiteboard.

10. Repeat the activity to build the following words:

   ▸ *rock* /r/ /ŏ/ /k/
   ▸ *rush* /r/ /ŭ/ /sh/
   ▸ *pick* /p/ /ĭ/ /k/

Try It

Alphabet Addition

Have students complete page PH 69 in *K¹² PhonicsWorks Basic Activity Book* for more practice with digraphs and the trigraph *–tch*. Have students add the letters together to make a word, write the word, and read the word aloud.

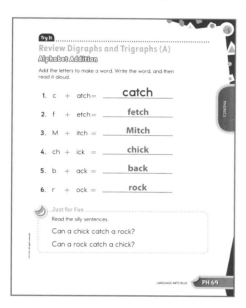

Dictation: Write Words

Have students practice identifying sounds and writing words.

1. Gather a pencil and the dictation notebook. Say the word *hatch*. Then give these directions to students:

   ▸ Repeat the word.
   ▸ Write the word in your notebook.
   ▸ Read the word aloud.

2. When students have finished, write the following word on your whiteboard: *hatch*.

3. Have them compare their answer to your correct version.

4. Repeat this procedure with the words *duck* and *that*.

   ▶ If students make an error and don't see it, help them correct their mistake by having them finger stretch the sounds in the word they missed.
   ▶ If students are having difficulty selecting the correct letters or sounds, review those letters or sounds that are confusing them.
   ▶ If students have difficulty with first, middle, and last sounds, have them finger stretch the sounds in words.

 **20 minutes**

REVIEW: Digraphs and the Trigraph *–tch*

Students will work online independently to

▶ Practice digraphs and the trigraph *–tch*.
▶ Practice decoding text by reading a story.

Help students locate the online activities and provide support as needed.

Offline Alternative

No computer access? Have students spell words that contain the digraphs *ch*, *–ck*, *sh*, *th*, or *wh* (for example, *chin*, *neck*, *shin*, *thin*, or *whim*) or the trigraph *–tch* (for example, *patch* or *catch*).

Objectives
- Identify and use the digraph *ch*.
- Identify and use the digraph *–ck*.
- Identify and use the digraph *sh*.
- Identify and use the digraph *th*.
- Identify and use the digraph *wh*.
- Identify and use the trigraph *–tch*.
- Identify individual sounds in words.
- Read aloud grade-level text with appropriate automaticity, prosody, accuracy, and rate.
- Decode words by applying grade-level word analysis skills.

Review Digraphs and the Trigraph –*tch* (B)

Lesson Overview

[Offline] **FOCUS:** Review Digraphs and the Trigraph –*tch*   **30** minutes

Sight Words	Sight Word Fun
Practice	Review Sounds and Letters
	Search Sentences for Ending Sounds
	Build Words
Try It	"Chad's Pop"
	Dictation: Write Words

[Online] **REVIEW:** Digraphs and the Trigraph –*tch*   **20** minutes

[Materials]

Supplied
- *K¹² PhonicsWorks Readers Basic 7*, pp. 25–30
- whiteboard, Learning Coach
- whiteboard, student
- Tile Kit

Also Needed
- sight words box
- dictation notebook

 **30 minutes**

FOCUS: Review Digraphs and the Trigraph –*tch*

Work **together** with students to complete offline Sight Words, Practice, and Try It activities.

Sight Words

Sight Word Fun

Help students learn the sight words *who*, *see*, and *or*, and up to two additional sight words they have yet to master.

1. Gather the sight word cards *who*, *see*, and *or*, and up to two additional sight words.

2. Choose one sight word card to begin.

   Say: Look at this word and take a picture of it in your mind. When you think you can spell the word yourself, turn the card over and use your letter tiles to spell the word.

3. After students spell the word, have them check the card to see if they spelled the word correctly.

   Say: Read aloud the word you spelled with the letter tiles.

4. Repeat the activity with the remaining sight words.

TIP Sight words can be very difficult for some students. Let them work at their own pace and really master these words.

 Objectives
- Read sight words.
- Spell sight words.

Practice

Review Sounds and Letters

Help students review sounds for the letters, digraphs, and trigraph *c, ch, –ck, sh, –tch, th, w,* and *wh,* plus any letters that are confusing for them.

1. Place the following letter tiles in random order on students' whiteboard: *c, ch, ck, sh, tch, th, w,* and *wh,* plus any letters that are confusing.

2. **Say:** Let's go over some letters and sounds.

3. Point to each letter tile and have students say a sound that letter or letters make:

   - *tch* /ch/
   - *wh* /w/
   - *w* /w/
   - *ch* /ch/
   - *sh* /sh/
   - *ck* /k/
   - *c* /k/
   - *th* /th/ or /<u>th</u>/

4. Say each of the following sounds. Have students repeat the sound and touch the corresponding letter tile:

   - /ch/ *ch* or *tch*
   - /w/ *w* or *wh*
   - /sh/ *sh*
   - /k/ *c* or *ck*
   - /th/ or /<u>th</u>/ *th*

5. As you do the activity, point to some letter tiles two or three times so that students don't think they are finished with a sound after they have named it.

6. Redirect students if they say an incorrect sound when you point to a letter tile.

   Say: That's the sound of another letter. What is the sound for this letter?

7. Help students if they touch the wrong letter tile after they repeat a sound.

   Say: That letter tile goes with the sound [sound for incorrect letter tile]. We're looking for the letter tile that goes with the sound [target sound].

Objectives

- Given the letter, identify the most common sound.
- Given the sound, identify the most common letter or letters.
- Identify and use the trigraph *–tch.*
- Identify and use the digraph *ch.*
- Identify and use the digraph *–ck.*
- Identify and use the digraph *sh.*
- Identify and use the digraph *th.*
- Identify and use the digraph *wh.*
- Identify ending sounds in words.
- Identify individual sounds in words.
- Write words by applying grade-level phonics knowledge.
- Blend sounds to create words.

Search Sentences for Ending Sounds

Have students practice identifying **ending sounds** in words that are in a sentence.

1. **Say:** I'm going to say a special ending sound that is in a word. You will repeat that sound and the word. The first sound is /k/, as in the word *rock.*

2. Have students say the target sound /k/ and the word *rock.*

3. **Say:** Now I will read a sentence. Repeat the sentence and tell me the word that has the same sound. The first sentence is *Pick a cat to pet.* Which word in the sentence has the special ending sound? *pick*

4. Have students repeat the sentence and say the word.

5. Redirect students if they don't name the correct word.

   Say: Let me say the sentence again. Remember, you're listening for the sound [special sound].

6. Guide students if they have difficulty. Say two words from the sentence and have them choose the one with the target ending sound.

7. Use the same procedure with the following words and sentences:

   ▸ /sh/, as in *fish*   *I wish we didn't have to go to the shop.* wish
   ▸ /ch/, as in *which*   *The king was very rich.* rich
   ▸ /th/, as in *bath*   *We ran down the path.* path
   ▸ /ch/, as in *batch*   *The dog can fetch.* fetch

Build Words

Help students use letters and sounds to build words.

1. Place, the following letter tiles at the top of students' whiteboard: *a, b, ck, i, m, o, p, r, s, sh, tch, th, u,* and *wh*.

2. Draw three horizontal lines across the middle of students' whiteboard to represent the sounds in a word.

3. **Say:** Let's use letters and sounds to build the word *puck*.

4. Have students finger stretch the sounds in *puck*.

5. Have students

   ▸ Identify the first, next, and last sounds in *puck*.
   ▸ Choose the corresponding letter for each of the sounds.
   ▸ Move the letters to the correct lines on their whiteboard.

6. Guide students with these questions:

   ▸ What is the first sound in *puck*? /p/
     Which line does the letter for that sound go on? the first one
   ▸ What is the next sound in *puck*? /ŭ/
     Which line does the letter for that sound go on? the second one
   ▸ What's the last sound in *puck*? /k/
     Which line do the letters for that sound go on? the last one

7. Redirect students if they select the incorrect letter.

   Say: That sound is in the word [word], and it is the [first, second, third] sound. We want the sound [target sound].

   Continue until students select the correct letter.

8. Have students touch and say the word.

9. Have them say the word as they use a dry-erase marker to write the word on the whiteboard.

10. Repeat the activity to build the following words:

    ▸ *ship* /sh/ /ĭ/ /p/
    ▸ *bath* /b/ /ă/ /th/
    ▸ *match* /m/ /ă/ /ch/
    ▸ *rock* /r/ /ŏ/ /k/
    ▸ *whip* /w/ /ĭ/ /p/
    ▸ *this* /th/ /ĭ/ /s/

Try It

"Chad's Pop"

Have students read "Chad's Pop" on page 25 of K^{12} *PhonicsWorks Readers Basic 7.*

Students should read the story silently once or twice before reading the story aloud. When students miss a word that can be sounded out, point to it and give them three to six seconds to try the word again. If students still miss the word, tell them the word so the flow of the story isn't interrupted.

After reading the story, make a list of all the words students missed, and go over those words with them. You may use letter tiles to show students how to read the words.

Dictation: Write Words

Have students practice identifying sounds and writing words.

1. Gather a pencil and the dictation notebook. Say the word *pick*. Then give these directions to students:

   ▸ Repeat the word.
   ▸ Write the word in your notebook.
   ▸ Read the word aloud.

2. When students have finished, write the following word on your whiteboard: *pick*.

3. Have them compare their answer to your correct version.

4. Repeat this procedure with the words *batch*, *thin*, and *cash*.

   ▸ If students make an error and don't see it, help them correct their mistake by having them finger stretch the sounds in the word they missed.
   ▸ If students are having difficulty selecting the correct letters or sounds, review those letters or sounds that are confusing them.
   ▸ If students have difficulty with first, middle, and last sounds, have them finger stretch the sounds in words.

Objectives

- Read aloud grade-level text with appropriate automaticity, prosody, accuracy, and rate.
- Decode words by applying grade-level word analysis skills.
- Track text from left to right.
- Turn pages sequentially.
- Write words by applying grade-level phonics knowledge.
- Follow three-step directions.

 **20 minutes**

REVIEW: **Digraphs and the Trigraph** *–tch*

Students will work online independently to

▶ Practice digraphs and the trigraph *–tch*.

Help students locate the online activities and provide support as needed.

Offline Alternative

No computer access? Have students spell words that contain the digraphs *ch*, *–ck*, *sh*, *th*, or *wh* (for example, *chop*, *back*, *sash*, *moth*, or *where*) or the trigraph *–tch* (for example, *itch* or *etch*).

Objectives

- Identify and use the trigraph *–tch*.
- Identify and use the digraph *ch*.
- Identify and use the digraph *–ck*.
- Identify and use the digraph *sh*.
- Identify and use the digraph *th*.
- Identify and use the digraph *wh*.
- Identify individual sounds in words.
- Read aloud grade-level text with appropriate automaticity, prosody, accuracy, and rate.
- Decode words by applying grade-level word analysis skills.

Review Digraphs and the Trigraph *–tch* (C)

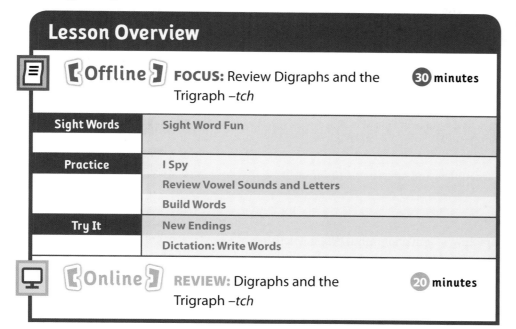

Lesson Overview

Offline FOCUS: Review Digraphs and the Trigraph *–tch*   **30** minutes

Sight Words	Sight Word Fun
Practice	I Spy
	Review Vowel Sounds and Letters
	Build Words
Try It	New Endings
	Dictation: Write Words

Online REVIEW: Digraphs and the Trigraph *–tch*   **20** minutes

Materials

Supplied
- *K¹² PhonicsWorks Basic Activity Book*, p. PH 70
- whiteboard, Learning Coach
- whiteboard, student
- Tile Kit

Also Needed
- sight words box
- dictation notebook

 **30 minutes**

FOCUS: Review Digraphs and the Trigraph –*tch*

Work **together** with students to complete offline Sight Words, Practice, and Try It activities.

Sight Words ••

Sight Word Fun

Help students learn the sight words *who*, *see*, and *or*, and up to two additional sight words they have yet to master.

1. Gather the sight word cards *who*, *see*, and *or*, and up to two additional sight words.

2. Choose one sight word card to begin.

   Say: Look at this word and take a picture of it in your mind. When you think you can spell the word yourself, turn the card over and use your letter tiles to spell the word.

3. After students spell the word, have them check the card to see if they spelled the word correctly.

   Say: Read aloud the word you spelled with the letter tiles.

4. Repeat the activity with the remaining sight words.

 Sight words can be very difficult for some students. Let them work at their own pace and really master these words.

Objectives

- Read sight words.
- Spell sight words.

Review Digraphs and the Trigraph –*tch* (D)

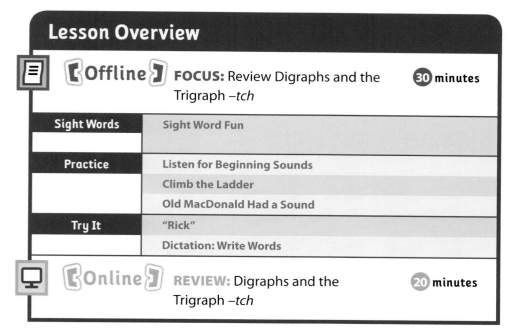

Lesson Overview

Offline **FOCUS:** Review Digraphs and the Trigraph –*tch*   **30** minutes

Sight Words	Sight Word Fun
Practice	Listen for Beginning Sounds
	Climb the Ladder
	Old MacDonald Had a Sound
Try It	"Rick"
	Dictation: Write Words

Online **REVIEW:** Digraphs and the Trigraph –*tch*   **20** minutes

Materials

Supplied
- *K¹² PhonicsWorks Readers Basic 8*, pp. 1–6
- whiteboard, Learning Coach
- whiteboard, student
- Tile Kit

Also Needed
- sight words box
- dictation notebook

 **Offline** **30** minutes

FOCUS: Review Digraphs and the Trigraph –*tch*

Work **together** with students to complete offline Sight Words, Practice, and Try It activities.

Sight Words

Sight Word Fun

Help students learn the sight words *who*, *see*, and *or*, and up to two additional sight words they have yet to master.

1. Gather the sight word cards *who*, *see*, and *or*, and up to two additional sight words.

2. Choose one sight word card to begin.

   Say: Look at this word and take a picture of it in your mind. When you think you can spell the word yourself, turn the card over and use your letter tiles to spell the word.

3. After students spell the word, have them check the card to see if they spelled the word correctly.

   Say: Read aloud the word you spelled with the letter tiles.

4. Repeat the activity with the remaining sight words.

 Sight words can be very difficult for some students. Let them work at their own pace and really master these words.

> **Objectives**
> - Read sight words.
> - Spell sight words.

Practice

Listen for Beginning Sounds

Help students identify beginning sounds in words.

1. **Say:** I'm going to say a word. Listen for the beginning sound. Then tell me the sound.

   ▶ For example, if I say *sap*, you'll say /s/ because the first sound you hear in *sap* is /s/.

   ▶ Now it's your turn. Listen to the word I say. Repeat the word and then tell me the first sound in the word.

2. Repeat the procedure, using the following words to help students recognize beginning sounds:

   ▶ *check* /ch/   ▶ *ship* /sh/
   ▶ *thin* /th/   ▶ *jam* /j/
   ▶ *Edward* /ĕ/   ▶ *that* /th/
   ▶ *what* /w/

Climb the Ladder

Help students use letters to build words.

1. On students' whiteboard or a sheet of paper, draw a ladder with five or more rungs.

2. Write the word *chin* on the bottom rung.

3. Point to the word *chin*.

   Say: I can make the word *chip* by changing one letter in this word.

4. Write the word *chip* on the second rung of the ladder.

   Say: Think of a word that you can make by changing only one letter in *chip*. Tell me the word and write it on the next step on the ladder.

5. If students struggle, coach them to change the first letter in each word.

   Say: Read the word on the bottom rung. What sound do you hear at the beginning of the word? What letter has that sound?

   Say: Name a word that rhymes with the word at the bottom. What sound do you hear at the beginning of the rhyming word? What letter has that sound? Make a new word by using the new letter. Read the new word.

6. Continue the process until students reach the top of the ladder. Remind students that they may change only one sound: the beginning, middle, or last sound.

Objectives

- Identify beginning sounds in words.
- Identify the new word when one sound is changed in a word.
- Identify and use the digraph *ch*.
- Identify and use the digraph *sh*.
- Identify and use the digraph *th*.
- Identify and use the digraph *wh*.
- Identify and use the sound /k/.
- Identify and use the sound /th/.
- Identify and use the sound /sh/.
- Identify and use the sound /ch/.
- Identify and use the sound /m/.
- Identify and use the sound /n/.
- Identify and use the sound /b/.
- Identify and use the sound /w/.

7. Redirect students if they select a word that changes more than one letter.

   Say: How many letters changed from the last word to your new word?
   Try to think of a word that has only one letter change.

8. Redirect students if they spell a word incorrectly, but the sounds they spell are correct (such as *ruf* for *rough*).

   Say: You have the sounds and letters right, but that word doesn't follow our spelling rules. We will learn how to spell it later. Try another word.

   TIP If students have difficulty thinking of real words, have them use nonsense words.

Old MacDonald Had a Sound

To review sounds, sing the song "Old MacDonald's Farm" with students.

1. **Say:** Let's have some fun with "Old MacDonald's Farm." Instead of animals, we'll put sounds on the farm. We'll sing "Old MacDonald had a farm, E-I-E-I-O. And on that farm he had a /ch/, E-I-E-I-O. With a /ch/, /ch/ here and a /ch/, /ch/ there . . . ."

2. Continue singing the song. Alternate singing and having students sing until you have finished all of the following sounds: /sh/, /k/, /m/, /th/, /<u>th</u>/, /n/, /b/, and /w/.

Try It

"Rick"

Have students read "Rick" on page 1 of *K¹² PhonicsWorks Readers Basic 8.*

Students should read the story silently once or twice before reading the story aloud. When students miss a word that can be sounded out, point to it and give them three to six seconds to try the word again. If students still miss the word, tell them the word so the flow of the story isn't interrupted.

After reading the story, make a list of all the words students missed, and go over those words with them. You may use letter tiles to show students how to read the words.

Objectives

- Read aloud grade-level text with appropriate automaticity, prosody, accuracy, and rate.
- Decode words by applying grade-level word analysis skills.
- Track text from left to right.
- Turn pages sequentially.
- Write words by applying grade-level phonics knowledge.
- Follow three-step directions.

Dictation: Write Words

Have students practice identifying sounds and writing words.

1. Gather a pencil and the dictation notebook. Say the word *check*. Then give these directions to students:

   ► Repeat the word.
   ► Write the word in your notebook.
   ► Read the word aloud.

2. When students have finished, write the following word on your whiteboard: *check*.

3. Have them compare their answer to your correct version.

4. Repeat this procedure with the words *match*, *pack*, and *fetch*.

   ► If students make an error and don't see it, help them correct their mistake by having them finger stretch the sounds in the word they missed.
   ► If students are having difficulty selecting the correct letters or sounds, review those letters or sounds that are confusing them.
   ► If students have difficulty with first, middle, and last sounds, have them finger stretch the sounds in words.

 **20 minutes**

REVIEW: Digraphs and the Trigraph *–tch*

Students will work online independently to

► Practice digraphs and the trigraph *–tch*.

Help students locate the online activities and provide support as needed.

___

Offline Alternative

No computer access? Have students spell words that contain the digraphs *ch*, *–ck*, *sh*, *th*, or *wh* (for example, *Chip*, *dock*, *fish*, *bath*, or *whap*) or the trigraph *–tch* (for example, *ditch* or *Dutch*).

Objectives

- Identify and use the trigraph *–tch*.
- Identify and use the digraph *ch*.
- Identify and use the digraph *–ck*.
- Identify and use the digraph *sh*.
- Identify and use the digraph *th*.
- Identify and use the digraph *wh*.
- Identify individual sounds in words.

Unit Checkpoint

Lesson Overview

[Online]	**REVIEW:** Digraphs and the Trigraph –tch	**20** minutes
[Offline]	**UNIT CHECKPOINT:** Review Digraphs and the Trigraph –tch	**30** minutes

[Materials]

Supplied
- *K¹² PhonicsWorks Basic Assessments,* pp. PH 151–156

Objectives

- Identify and use the trigraph –tch.
- Identify and use the digraph ch.
- Identify and use the digraph –ck.
- Identify and use the digraph sh.
- Identify and use the digraph th.
- Identify and use the digraph wh.
- Identify letters of the alphabet.
- Given the sound, identify the most common letter or letters.

- Identify individual sounds in words.
- Read sight words.
- Read instructional-level text with 90% accuracy.
- Read aloud grade-level text with appropriate automaticity, prosody, accuracy, and rate.
- Write words by applying grade-level phonics knowledge.

 **[Online]** **20** minutes

REVIEW: **Digraphs and the Trigraph** *–tch*

Students will review digraphs and the trigraph –tch to prepare for the Unit Checkpoint. Help students locate the online activities and provide support as needed.

[Offline] 30 minutes

UNIT CHECKPOINT: Review Digraphs and the Trigraph –*tch*

Explain that students are going to show what they have learned about letters, sounds, and words.

1. Give students the Unit Checkpoint pages for the Review Digraphs and the Trigraph –*tch* unit and print the Unit Checkpoint Answer Key, if you'd like.

2. Use the instructions below to help administer the Checkpoint to students. On the Answer Key or another sheet of paper, note student answers to oral response questions to help with scoring the Checkpoint later.

3. Use the Answer Key to score the Checkpoint, and then enter the results online.

Part 1. Read Word Parts and Nonsense Words Have students read across the rows from left to right and say the sounds that each word part or nonsense word makes. Note any word parts or nonsense words they say incorrectly.

Part 2. Word Dissection For each word, say the sound students should identify. Have them read the word aloud and circle the letter or group of letters that spells the requested sound.

19. *beginning sound*

20. *beginning sound*

21. *ending sound*

22. *middle sound*

23. *ending sound*

Part 3. Finger Stretching Say each word to students. Have them say each word and finger stretch the sounds. Note any words they finger stretch incorrectly.

24. *witch*

25. *rich*

26. *shop*

27. *quack*

28. *chat*

29. *Beth*

Part 4. Dictation Say each word to students. Have them repeat and write the word.

30. *match*

31. *luck*

32. *catch*

33. *neck*

Part 5. Read Aloud Listen to students read the sentences aloud. Count and note the number of words they read correctly.

Part 6. Say Letters Say each sound. Have students say the letter or letters that make that sound. Note any incorrect responses.

35. /ch/

36. /<u>th</u>/

37. /ă/

38. /ŭ/

39. /w/

40. /ĕ/

41. /k/

42. /ch/

43. /th/

44. /k/

45. /sh/

46. /ĭ/

47. /ŏ/

48. /w/

49. /kw/

50. /ch/

51. /k/

52. /sh/

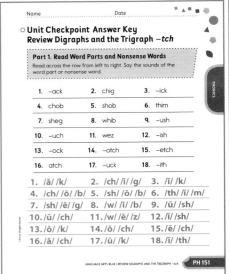

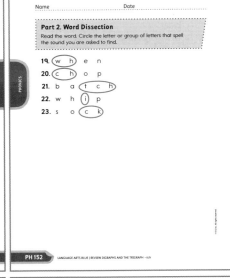

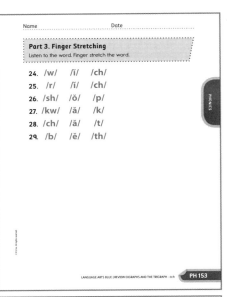

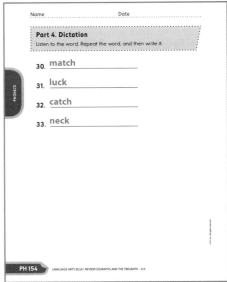

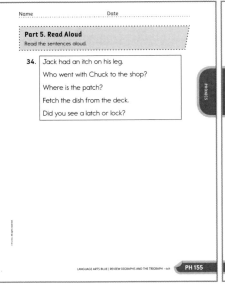

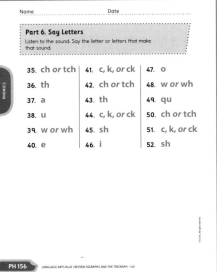

Getting Stronger: Digraphs and the Trigraph –*tch* (A)

Unit Overview

In this unit, students will
- ▸ Review sight words.
- ▸ Review digraphs, the trigraph –*tch*, and the ending –*ck*.
- ▸ Review sounds and letters of the alphabet.
- ▸ Build words and word chains.
- ▸ Practice reading and writing.

[Materials]

Supplied
- K[12] *PhonicsWorks Basic Activity Book,* p. PH 71
- whiteboard, Learning Coach
- whiteboard, student
- Tile Kit

Also Needed
- sight words box
- dictation notebook
- crayons

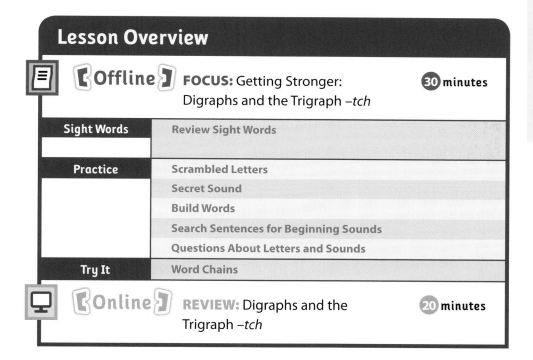

Lesson Overview

[Offline] FOCUS: Getting Stronger: Digraphs and the Trigraph –*tch*	30 minutes
Sight Words	Review Sight Words
Practice	Scrambled Letters
	Secret Sound
	Build Words
	Search Sentences for Beginning Sounds
	Questions About Letters and Sounds
Try It	Word Chains

[Online] REVIEW: Digraphs and the Trigraph –*tch*	20 minutes

Advance Preparation

For Scrambled Letters, place lowercase letter tiles in random order on your whiteboard and place the digraphs and trigraph –*tch* at the bottom of your board.

 **Offline** **30** minutes

FOCUS: Getting Stronger: Digraphs and the Trigraph –*tch*

Work **together** with students to complete offline Sight Words, Practice, and Try It activities.

Sight Words ....

Review Sight Words

Help students learn to recognize sight words.

Objectives
- Read sight words.
- Spell sight words.
- Write sight words.

1. Gather all the sight word cards students have yet to master from their sight words box. Stack the cards on the table face down.

2. Have students pick up a word and read it to you.

3. If they read it quickly and correctly, put the card in one stack because they have mastered the word. If they hesitate or do not read the word correctly, put it in another stack. The second stack should have words that they will review again.

4. Take the stack of words that students read correctly and dictate each word to them. They may choose to either write the word or spell it aloud.

5. If students spell the word correctly, put the card in the first stack because they have mastered the word. If they misspell the word, add it to the stack of cards to review again.

6. Chart students' progress on the back of each card.

    ▸ Divide the back of the card into two columns.
    ▸ Label the first column "Read" and the second column "Spell."
    ▸ Record the dates that students read or spell the word correctly. When students can read and spell the word correctly three times in a row, they have mastered the word. You may want to put a star or sticker on their card when they have mastered that word.

TIP Even if students can read and spell all the words correctly, it is still beneficial for them to review sight words. Choose as many additional words as you would like for each subsequent activity.

Practice

Scrambled Letters

To help students master the alphabet, digraphs, and the trigraph –*tch*, have them practice identifying and naming letters. Grab your whiteboard with letters.

1. Remove the digraphs *ch*, –*ck*, *sh*, *th*, and *wh* and the trigraph –*tch* from your board and set them aside.

2. Have students arrange the letters in alphabetical order.

3. Place the digraphs *ch*, –*ck*, *sh*, *th*, and *wh* and the trigraph –*tch* back on your board.

4. Have students touch and say each of the digraphs and the trigraph.

TIP Students may find this activity easier if they slowly sing "The Alphabet Song" to themselves as they work.

Secret Sound

Say groups of words to help students recognize **ending sounds** in words.

1. **Say:** I am going to say some groups of words. Listen for a secret sound at the end of each word. Then tell me what sound you hear at the end of each group of words.

2. Say each of the following groups of words. Have students identify the secret sound in each group.

   ► *with, bath, path* /th/
   ► *rough, cuff, if* /f/
   ► *sock, rack, quack* /k/
   ► *rush, sash, mush* /sh/
   ► *itch, match, hutch* /ch/

TIP If students can't identify the secret sound, have them listen while you say each word again and then have them repeat each word. Have students say what sound they hear at the end of each word.

Build Words

Help students use letters and sounds to build words.

1. Place the following letter tiles at the top of students' whiteboard: *a, b, ck, h, o, p, sh, tch,* and *u*.

2. Draw three horizontal lines across the middle of students' whiteboard to represent the sounds in a word.

3. **Say:** Let's use letters and sounds to build the word *hush*.

4. Have students finger stretch the sounds in *hush*.

Objectives

- Identify letters of the alphabet.
- Identify and use the trigraph –*tch*.
- Identify and use the digraph *ch*.
- Identify and use the digraph –*ck*.
- Identify and use the digraph *sh*.
- Identify and use the digraph *th*.
- Identify and use the digraph *wh*.
- Identify ending sounds in words.
- Identify beginning sounds in words.
- Blend sounds to create words.
- Identify individual sounds in words.
- Write words by applying grade-level phonics knowledge.
- Given the letter, identify the most common sound.
- Given the sound, identify the most common letter or letters.

5. Have students

  ▸ Identify the first, next, and last sounds in *hush*.
  ▸ Choose the corresponding letter for each sound.
  ▸ Move the letters to the correct lines on their whiteboard.

6. Guide students with these questions:

  ▸ What is the first sound in *hush*? /h/
    Which line does the letter for that sound go on? the first one
  ▸ What is the next sound in *hush*? /ŭ/
    Which line does the letter for that sound go on? the second one
  ▸ What's the last sound in *hush*? /sh/
    Which line do the letters for that sound go on? the last one

7. Redirect students if they select the incorrect letter.

  Say: That sound is in the word [word], and it is the [first, second, third] sound. We want the sound [target sound].

  Continue until students select the correct letter.

8. Have students touch and say the word.

9. Have them say the word as they use a dry-erase marker to write the word on the whiteboard.

10. Repeat the activity to build the following words:

  ▸ *batch* /b/ /ă/ /ch/
  ▸ *pack* /p/ /ă/ /k/
  ▸ *shop* /sh/ /ŏ/ /p/

Search Sentences for Beginning Sounds

Have students practice identifying **beginning sounds** in words that are in a sentence.

1. **Say:** I'm going to say a special beginning sound that is in a word. You will repeat that sound and the word. The first sound is /d/, as in the word *dog*.

2. Have students say the target sound /d/ and the word *dog*.

3. **Say:** Now I will read a sentence. Repeat the sentence and tell me the word that has the same sound. The first sentence is *I have a doll*. Which word in the sentence has the special beginning sound? *doll*

4. Have students repeat the sentence and say the word.

5. Redirect students if they don't name the correct word.

  Say: Let me say the sentence again. Remember, you're listening for the sound [special sound].

6. Guide students if they have difficulty. Say two words from the sentence and have them choose the one with the target beginning sound.

7. Use the same procedure with the following words and sentences:

- /w/, as in *what* *I don't know when he left.* when
- /ch/, as in *chop* *Pass the cheese and crackers, please.* cheese
- /th/, as in *three* *What do you think of this?* think
- /<u>th</u>/, as in *then* *That is a pig.* that
- /sh/, as in *ship* *We go to the shop.* shop

Questions About Letters and Sounds

To help students master the letters and sounds of the alphabet, digraphs, and the trigraph *–tch*, have them practice identifying and naming them. Grab your whiteboard with letters placed in alphabetical order, the digraphs, and trigraph *–tch*.

1. Touch all the digraphs.

   Say: These are tiles that have two letters to spell one sound. Tell me the sounds for each.

2. Touch the trigraph *–tch*.

   Say: What sound do the letters make?

3. **Say:** Touch all the letters that spell the sound /k/. *c, ck,* and *k*

Try It

Word Chains

Have students complete page PH 71 in *K¹² PhonicsWorks Basic Activity Book* for more practice with digraphs and the trigraph *–tch*. Have students find and color the box that has one letter changed in the next group of letters.

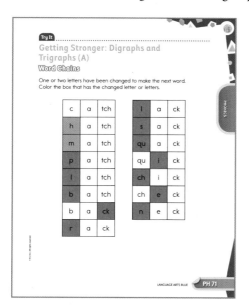

Objectives
- Identify the new word when one sound is changed in a word.

 **Online** 20 **minutes**

REVIEW: **Digraphs and the Trigraph** –*tch*

Students will work online independently to

► Practice digraphs and the trigraph –*tch*.
► Practice decoding text by reading sentences.

Help students locate the online activities and provide support as needed.

Offline Alternative

No computer access? Have students name words that have the digraphs *ch*, –*ck*, *sh*, *th*, and *wh*, such as *chip*, *check*, *ship*, *path*, *that*, and *when*, and the trigraph –*tch*, such as *itch* or *etch*. You might also have them spell words that have the digraphs *ch*, –*ck*, *sh*, *th*, and *wh* and the trigraph –*tch*.

 Objectives

- Identify individual sounds in words.
- Identify the trigraph –*tch*, given the sound /ch/.
- Identify and use the digraph *ch*.
- Identify and use the digraph –*ck*.
- Identify and use the digraph *sh*.
- Identify and use the digraph *th*.
- Identify and use the digraph *wh*.
- Read aloud grade-level text with appropriate automaticity, prosody, accuracy, and rate.
- Decode words by applying grade-level word analysis skills.

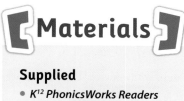

Getting Stronger: Digraphs and the Trigraph –*tch* (B)

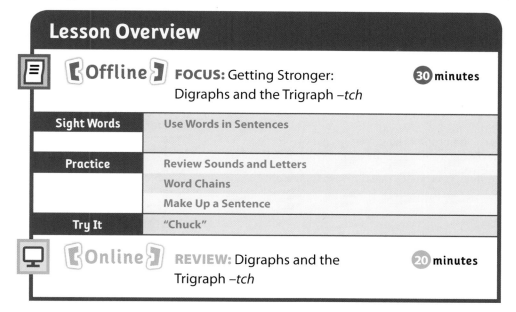

Lesson Overview

📄 【Offline】 **FOCUS:** Getting Stronger: Digraphs and the Trigraph –*tch*   **30** minutes

Sight Words	Use Words in Sentences
Practice	Review Sounds and Letters
	Word Chains
	Make Up a Sentence
Try It	"Chuck"

🖥 【Online】 **REVIEW:** Digraphs and the Trigraph –*tch*   **20** minutes

【Materials】

Supplied
- *K¹² PhonicsWorks Readers Basic 8*, pp. 7–12
- whiteboard, student
- Tile Kit

Also Needed
- sight words box
- dictation notebook
- index cards (3)

Advance Preparation

For Make Up a Sentence, print each of the following groups of words on index cards, using one card per group of words: *that big rock, on the ship,* and *get his wish.*

 **Offline** **30 minutes**

FOCUS: Getting Stronger: Digraphs and the Trigraph –*tch*

Work **together** with students to complete offline Sight Words, Practice, and Try It activities.

Sight Words

Use Words in Sentences

Help students use sight words in sentences.

1. Gather all the sight word cards students have yet to master from their sight words box. Spread the sight word cards on the table.

2. **Say:** Let's use sight words in sentences.

3. Have students
   ▸ Touch each card and read the word on it.
   ▸ Make up a sentence using the word.
   ▸ Put the card in a pile after using the word in a sentence.
   ▸ Go through the pile of cards and read each sight word again.
   ▸ Spell each word.

 TIP If students have difficulty with any of the sight words, place those cards in a pile to review again.

Objectives
- Read sight words.
- Spell sight words.

Practice

Review Sounds and Letters

Help students review sounds for the letters, digraphs, and trigraph *ch, –ck, i, o, sh, –tch, th, u,* and *wh,* plus any letters that are confusing for them.

1. Place the following letter tiles in random order on students' whiteboard: *ch, ck, i, o, sh, tch, th, u,* and *wh,* plus any letters that are confusing.

2. **Say:** Let's go over some letters and sounds.

3. Point to each letter tile and have students say a sound that letter or letters make.

   ▸ *o* /ŏ/   ▸ *tch* /ch/
   ▸ *i* /ĭ/   ▸ *wh* /w/
   ▸ *ch* /ch/   ▸ *sh* /sh/
   ▸ *ck* /k/   ▸ *u* /ŭ/
   ▸ *th* /th/ or /th̲/

4. Say each of the following sounds. Have students repeat the sound and touch the corresponding letter tile.

   ▸ /ŏ/ *o*   ▸ /th/ or /th̲/ *th*
   ▸ /ĭ/ *i*   ▸ /wh/ *w*
   ▸ /ch/ *ch* or *tch*   ▸ /sh/ *sh*
   ▸ /k/ *ck*   ▸ /ŭ/ *u*

5. As you do the activity, point to some letter tiles two or three times so that students don't think they are finished with a sound after they have named it.

6. Redirect students if they say an incorrect sound when you point to a letter tile.

   Say: That's the sound of another letter. What is the sound for this letter?

7. Help students if they touch the wrong letter tile after they repeat a sound.

   Say: That letter tile goes with the sound [sound for incorrect letter tile]. We're looking for the letter tile that goes with the sound [target sound].

Objectives

- Identify letters of the alphabet.
- Given the letter, identify the most common sound.
- Given the sound, identify the most common letter or letters.
- Identify individual sounds in words.
- Identify beginning sounds in words.
- Identify and use the trigraph *–tch.*
- Identify and use the digraph *ch.*
- Identify and use the digraph *–ck.*
- Identify and use the digraph *sh.*
- Identify and use the digraph *th.*
- Identify and use the digraph *wh.*

Word Chains

Have students build words by adding and changing letters to help them recognize and use individual sounds in words.

1. Place the following letter tiles at the top of students' whiteboard: *a, c, ch, ck, i, l, n, o,* and *p.*

2. **Say:** I am going to build the first word in a chain. The word is *chin.*

   ▸ I will pull down the letters for the sounds /ch/, /ĭ/, and /n/ to spell the word *chin.*
   ▸ I will touch and say *chin.* To change *chin* to *chip,* I will think about which sound is changed from the word *chin* to *chip.* I will need to replace the letter *n* with the letter *p.*
   ▸ Touch and say the word *chip.* Now it's your turn to change *chip* to *chap.* You can spell *chap* by making only one change. Touch and say the new word.

3. Redirect students if they select the incorrect letter for any sound.

   Say: That letter is for the sound [incorrect sound]. We want the letter for the sound [target sound]. What letter makes that sound? Answers will vary.

4. Redirect students if they name the sound incorrectly.

   Say: To change the word [first word] to [target word], we need the letter for the sound [target sound].

   Show students how to make the change. Have them touch and say the new word after they move the letters.

5. Follow this procedure to make the following words: *chop, cop, lop, lock.*

6. For every new word, have students add, replace, or remove only one letter tile.

   TIP If students struggle, review the sounds and letters that are confusing them.

Make Up a Sentence

Help students use words to make sentences.

1. Gather the index cards you prepared, and place them face down on the table in one pile.

2. Have students

   ▸ Select a card.
   ▸ Read the group of words.
   ▸ Use the group of words in an interesting, fun, or silly sentence.

   TIP If students read a word incorrectly, have them finger stretch the sounds in the word or use letter tiles to spell the word and touch and say.

Try It ·

"Chuck"

Have students read "Chuck" on page 7 of *K¹² PhonicsWorks Readers Basic 8.*

Students should read the story silently once or twice before reading the story aloud. When students miss a word that can be sounded out, point to it and give them three to six seconds to try the word again. If students still miss the word, tell them the word so the flow of the story isn't interrupted.

After reading the story, make a list of all the words students missed, and go over those words with them. You may use letter tiles to show students how to read the words.

Objectives

- Read aloud grade-level text with appropriate automaticity, prosody, accuracy, and rate.
- Decode words by applying grade-level word analysis skills.
- Track text from left to right.
- Turn pages sequentially.

 **20 minutes**

REVIEW: **Digraphs and the Trigraph** *–tch*

Students will work online independently to

▸ Practice digraphs and the trigraph *–tch.*

Help students locate the online activities and provide support as needed.

Objectives

- Identify individual sounds in words.
- Identify and use the trigraph *–tch.*
- Identify and use the digraph *ch.*
- Identify and use the digraph *–ck.*
- Identify and use the digraph *sh.*
- Identify and use the digraph *th.*
- Identify and use the digraph *wh.*

Offline Alternative

No computer access? Have students name words that have the digraphs *ch, –ck, sh, th,* and *wh,* such as *rich, Rick, wish, bath, that,* and *where,* and the trigraph *–tch,* such as *pitch* or *catch.* You might also have them spell words that have the digraphs *ch, –ck, sh, th,* and *wh* and the trigraph *–tch.*

Getting Stronger: Digraphs and the Trigraph –*tch* (C)

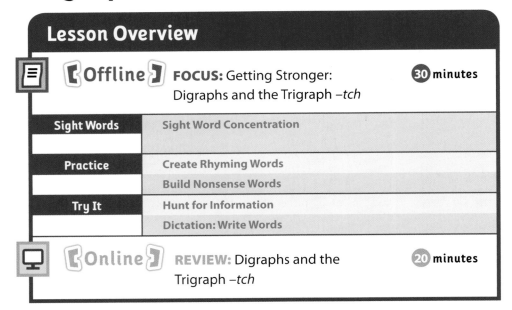

Lesson Overview

Offline **FOCUS:** Getting Stronger: Digraphs and the Trigraph –*tch*   **30** minutes

Sight Words	Sight Word Concentration
Practice	Create Rhyming Words
	Build Nonsense Words
Try It	Hunt for Information
	Dictation: Write Words

Online **REVIEW:** Digraphs and the Trigraph –*tch*   **20** minutes

Materials

Supplied
- *K¹² PhonicsWorks Basic Activity Book,* p. PH 72
- whiteboard, Learning Coach
- whiteboard, student
- Tile Kit

Also Needed
- sight words box
- dictation notebook

Advance Preparation

Gather two sets of the sight word cards that students have yet to master.

 **30 minutes**

FOCUS: Getting Stronger: Digraphs and the Trigraph *–tch*

Work **together** with students to complete offline Sight Words, Practice, and Try It activities.

Sight Words

Sight Word Concentration

Help students review sight words.

1. Gather the two sets of sight word cards.

2. Scramble both sets of sight word cards and place them face down on the table or floor.

3. Turn over two cards at a time; take turns with students. If the cards match, the person turning over the matching cards reads the word and uses it in a sentence. If the cards don't match, the person turns them back over.

4. Remove and save the matching cards.

5. Continue the activity until all the cards are paired.

6. Have students read all the words.

7. Take the stack of words that students read correctly and dictate each word to them.

8. Have students write each word or spell it aloud.

 TIP If students have difficulty with any sight words, let them work at their own pace to really master these words.

> **Objectives**
> - Read sight words.
> - Spell sight words.
> - Write sight words.

Practice

Create Rhyming Words

Have students combine word parts and make words that rhyme.

1. **Say:** I'm going to break a word into two parts. Your job is to put the parts back together and say the word.

   ▸ For example, if the first part of the word is /r/ and the last part is /ŭsh/, then you'll say *rush*: /r/ . . . /ŭsh/ . . . *rush*.

   ▸ Next you'll add a new **beginning sound** to make a word that rhymes. For example, you'll use the same last part, /ŭsh/, and add a new first sound, like /m/. The rhyming word is /m/ . . . /ŭsh/ . . . *mush*.

2. **Say:** Now it's your turn: /h/ . . . /ŭsh/.

   ▸ What's the word? *hush*

   ▸ Now use the same last part, /ŭsh/, but add a new sound, /g/, at the beginning. What word did you make? *gush*

3. Say the two word parts. Have students say the word the parts form. Have them add a new beginning sound to the last part of the following word to make rhyming words: /sh/ . . . /ŭsh/ *shush* Possible rhyming words: *thrush, lush*

Build Nonsense Words

Help students use letters and sounds to build nonsense words.

1. Place the following letter tiles at the top of students' whiteboard: *b, ch, ck, e, g, i, o, s, sh, th, u, wh,* and *z.*

2. Draw three horizontal lines across the middle of students' whiteboard to represent the sounds in a word.

3. **Say:** Some words don't have any meaning. We call these **nonsense words**. Even though we don't know what a word means, we can still read it. Nonsense words will be very important when we read longer words. When we break longer words into parts, sometimes the parts are nonsense words.

4. **Say:** Let's use letters and sounds to build the word *shug.*

5. Have students finger stretch the sounds in *shug.*

6. Have students

   ▸ Identify the first, next, and last sounds in *shug.*

   ▸ Choose the corresponding letter for each sound.

   ▸ Move the letters to the correct lines on their whiteboard.

Objectives

- Identify words that rhyme.
- Identify and use the trigraph *–tch.*
- Identify and use the digraph *ch.*
- Identify and use the digraph *–ck.*
- Identify and use the digraph *sh.*
- Identify and use the digraph *th.*
- Identify and use the digraph *wh.*
- Blend sounds to create words.
- Identify individual sounds in words.
- Write words by applying grade-level phonics knowledge.

7. Guide students with these questions:

   ▶ What is the first sound in *shug*? /sh/
   Which line do the letters for that sound go on? the first one
   ▶ What is the next sound in *shug*? /ŭ/
   Which line does the letter for that sound go on? the second one
   ▶ What's the last sound in *shug*? /g/
   Which line does the letter for that sound go on? the last one

8. Redirect students if they select the incorrect letter.

   Say: That sound is in the word [word], and it is the [first, second, third] sound. We want the sound [target sound].

   Continue until students select the correct letter.

9. Have students touch and say the word.

10. Have them say the word as they use a dry-erase marker to write the word on the whiteboard.

11. Repeat the activity to build the following words:

    ▶ *soth* /s/ /ŏ/ /th/
    ▶ *whez* /w/ /ĕ/ /z/
    ▶ *zick* /z/ /ĭ/ /k/
    ▶ *chib* /ch/ /ĭ/ /b/

Try It

Hunt for Information

Have students complete page PH 72 in *K¹² PhonicsWorks Basic Activity Book* for more practice reading words that have digraphs and the trigraph –*tch*. Have them read the story aloud and choose a word from the story that completes each sentence. Have them write the word and read the sentences aloud.

Objectives

- Read aloud grade-level text with appropriate automaticity, prosody,
- Write words by applying grade-level phonics knowledge.
- Follow three-step directions.

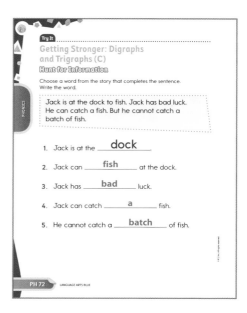

Dictation: Write Words

Have students practice identifying sounds and writing words.

1. Gather a pencil and the dictation notebook. Say the word *chop*. Then give these directions to students:

   ► Repeat the word.
   ► Write the word in your notebook.
   ► Read the word aloud.

2. When students have finished, write the following word on your whiteboard: *chop*.

3. Have them compare their answer to your correct version.

4. Repeat this procedure with the words *hutch*, *sack*, and *tuck*.

   ► If students make an error and don't see it, help them correct their mistake by having them finger stretch the sounds in the word they missed.
   ► If students are having difficulty selecting the correct letters or sounds, review those letters or sounds that are confusing them.
   ► If students have difficulty with first, middle, and last sounds, have them finger stretch the sounds in words.

 **20 minutes**

REVIEW: **Digraphs and the Trigraph** *–tch*

Students will work online independently to

► Practice digraphs and the trigraph *–tch*.
► Practice decoding text by reading sentences.

Help students locate the online activities and provide support as needed.

Offline Alternative

No computer access? Have students name words that have the digraphs *ch*, *–ck*, *sh*, *th*, and *wh*, such as *rich*, *Rick*, *wish*, *bath*, *those*, and *where*, and the trigraph *–tch*, such as *pitch* or *catch*. You might also have them spell words that have the digraphs *ch*, *–ck*, *sh*, *th*, and *wh* and the trigraph *–tch*.

Objectives

- Identify individual sounds in words.
- Identify and use the digraph *ch*.
- Identify and use the digraph *–ck*.
- Identify and use the digraph *sh*.
- Identify and use the digraph *th*.
- Identify and use the digraph *wh*.
- Identify and use the trigraph *–tch*.
- Read aloud grade-level text with appropriate automaticity, prosody, accuracy, and rate.
- Decode words by applying grade-level word analysis skills.

Getting Stronger: Digraphs and the Trigraph –*tch* (D)

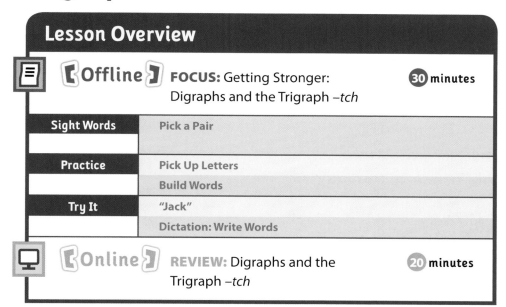

Lesson Overview

Offline FOCUS: Getting Stronger: **30** minutes
Digraphs and the Trigraph –*tch*

Sight Words	Pick a Pair
Practice	Pick Up Letters
	Build Words
Try It	"Jack"
	Dictation: Write Words

Online REVIEW: Digraphs and the **20** minutes
Trigraph –*tch*

Materials

Supplied
- *K¹² PhonicsWorks Readers Basic 8*, pp. 13–18
- whiteboard, Learning Coach
- whiteboard, student
- Tile Kit

Also Needed
- sight words box
- dictation notebook

 **30** minutes

FOCUS: Getting Stronger: Digraphs and the Trigraph *–tch*

Work **together** with students to complete offline Sight Words, Practice, and Try It activities.

Sight Words

Pick a Pair

Play a card game with students for more practice with sight words.

1. Gather the sight word cards that students are reviewing. Choose two words and place the cards on the table.

2. Ask questions to help students identify each word. For example, if the words are *or* and *one*, you could ask, "Which word names a number?" If the words are *on* and *but*, you could ask, "Which word is the opposite of *off*?"

3. Continue the activity until students identify all the words.

4. Take the stack of words that students read correctly and dictate each word to them.

5. Have students write each word or spell it aloud.

Objectives
- Read sight words.
- Spell sight words.
- Write sight words.

Practice ....

Pick Up Letters

Help students use letters and sounds to make words and sentences.

1. Place the following letter tiles on students' whiteboard: *ch, d, f, r, sh, t, tch,* and *th.*

2. **Say:** Let's play a game with these letters.

3. Pick up the letter tile for *sh.*

4. **Say:** I chose the letters *sh.* The sound is /sh/. A word that starts with the sound /sh/ is *ship.* A sentence using that word is *There is a big red ship.* Now it's your turn.

5. Continue taking turns until all the letter tiles have been chosen.

6. Have students answer the following questions for each letter or group of letters.

    ▸ What is (are) the letter(s)?
    ▸ Is the tile you chose a digraph that has two letters that make one sound?
    ▸ What is the sound?
    ▸ What is a word that starts with that sound?
    ▸ What sentence can you make with that word?

7. Redirect students if they name a word that starts with the sound, but not the letter (such as *knob*).

    Say: That is a word that doesn't follow the rules that we know for spelling. Try another word.

8. Prompt students if they have trouble matching the sounds with words. For example:

    Say: That's /j/, as in *jelly.* Can you think of another word that starts with that sound?

Objectives

- Identify letters of the alphabet.
- Given the letter, identify the most common sound.
- Given the sound, identify the most common letter or letters.
- Identify and use the digraph *ch.*
- Identify and use the digraph *–ck.*
- Identify and use the digraph *sh.*
- Identify and use the digraph *th.*
- Identify and use the digraph *wh.*
- Identify and use the trigraph *–tch.*
- Blend sounds to create words.
- Identify individual sounds in words.
- Write words by applying grade-level phonics knowledge.

Build Words

Help students use letters and sounds to build words.

1. Place the following letter tiles at the top of students' whiteboard: *a, ch, ck, d, e, i, sh, tch, th, u,* and *wh.*

2. Draw three horizontal lines across the middle of students' whiteboard to represent the sounds in a word.

3. **Say:** Let's use letters and sounds to build the word *chuck.*

4. Have students finger stretch the sounds in *chuck.*

5. Have students

    ▸ Identify the first, next, and last sounds in *chuck.*
    ▸ Choose the corresponding letter for each sound.
    ▸ Move the letters to the correct lines on their whiteboard.

6. Guide students with these questions:

   ▶ What is the first sound in *chuck*? /ch/
   Which line do the letters for that sound go on? the first one
   ▶ What is the next sound in *chuck*? /ŭ/
   Which line does the letter for that sound go on? the second one
   ▶ What's the last sound in *chuck*? /k/
   Which line do the letters for that sound go on? the last one

7. Redirect students if they select the incorrect letter.

   Say: That sound is in the word [word], and it is the [first, second, third] sound. We want the sound [target sound].

   Continue until students select the correct letter.

8. Have students touch and say the word.

9. Have them say the word as they use a dry-erase marker to write the word on the whiteboard.

10. Draw horizontal lines across the middle of students' whiteboard that represent the number of sounds in each word. Repeat the activity to build the following words:

    ▶ *which* /w/ /ĭ/ /ch/
    ▶ *etch* /ĕ/ /ch/
    ▶ *thud* /th/ /ŭ/ /d/
    ▶ *shack* /sh/ /ă/ /k/

Try It

"Jack"
Have students read "Jack" on page 13 of *K¹² PhonicsWorks Readers Basic 8*.
    Students should read the story silently once or twice before reading the story aloud. When students miss a word that can be sounded out, point to it and give them three to six seconds to try the word again. If students still miss the word, tell them the word so the flow of the story isn't interrupted.
    After reading the story, make a list of all the words students missed, and go over those words with them. You may use letter tiles to show students how to read the words.

Objectives
- Read aloud grade-level text with appropriate automaticity, prosody, accuracy, and rate.
- Decode words by applying grade-level word analysis skills.
- Track text from left to right.
- Turn pages sequentially.
- Write words by applying grade-level phonics knowledge.
- Follow three-step directions.

Dictation: Write Words

Have students practice identifying sounds and writing words.

1. Gather a pencil and the dictation notebook. Say the word *dish.* Then give these directions to students:

   ▶ Repeat the word.
   ▶ Write the word in your notebook.
   ▶ Read the word aloud.

2. When students have finished, write the following word on your whiteboard: *dish.*

3. Have them compare their answer to your correct version.

4. Repeat this procedure with the words *quack, chop,* and *match.*

   ▶ If students make an error and don't see it, help them correct their mistake by having them finger stretch the sounds in the word they missed.
   ▶ If students are having difficulty selecting the correct letters or sounds, review those letters or sounds that are confusing them.
   ▶ If students have difficulty with first, middle, and last sounds, have them finger stretch the sounds in words.

 **minutes**

REVIEW: Digraphs and the Trigraph –*tch*

Students will work online independently to

▶ Practice digraphs and the trigraph –*tch.*

Help students locate the online activities and provide support as needed.

Offline Alternative

No computer access? Have students name words that have the digraphs *ch, –ck, sh, th,* and *wh,* such as *chick, quack, shack, thick, then,* and *which,* and the trigraph –*tch,* such as *hatch* or *patch.* You might also have them spell words that have the digraphs *ch, –ck, sh, th,* and *wh* and the trigraph –*tch.*

Objectives
- Identify individual sounds in words.
- Identify and use the digraph *ch.*
- Identify and use the digraph –*ck.*
- Identify and use the digraph *sh.*
- Identify and use the digraph *th.*
- Identify and use the digraph *wh.*
- Identify the trigraph –*tch,* given the sound /ch/.

Unit Checkpoint

Lesson Overview

🖥	**Online** REVIEW: Digraphs and the Trigraph –*tch*	**20** minutes
▤	**Offline** UNIT CHECKPOINT: Getting Stronger: Digraphs and the Trigraph –*tch*	**30** minutes

Materials

Supplied

- *K¹² PhonicsWorks Basic Assessments* pp. PH 157–162

⭐ Objectives

- Identify and use the digraph *ch*.
- Identify and use the digraph –*ck*.
- Identify and use the digraph *sh*.
- Identify and use the digraph *th*.
- Identify and use the digraph *wh*.
- Identify and use the trigraph –*tch*.
- Read, write, and spell words containing short vowel sounds.
- Identify individual sounds in words.
- Given the letter, identify the most common sound.
- Given the sound, identify the most common letter or letters.
- Read instructional-level text with 90% accuracy.
- Read aloud grade-level text with appropriate automaticity, prosody, accuracy, and rate.
- Write words by applying grade-level phonics knowledge.
- Read sight words.

Online   **20** minutes

REVIEW: Digraphs and the Trigraph –*tch*

Students will review digraphs and the trigraph –*tch* to prepare for the Unit Checkpoint. Help students locate the online activities and provide support as needed.

[Offline] 30 minutes

UNIT CHECKPOINT: Getting Stronger: Digraphs and the Trigraph *–tch*

Explain that students are going to show what they have learned about sounds, letters, and words.

1. Give students the Unit Checkpoint pages for the Getting Stronger: Digraphs and the Trigraph *–tch* unit and print the Unit Checkpoint Answer Key, if you'd like.

2. Use the instructions below to help administer the Checkpoint to students. On the Answer Key or another sheet of paper, note student answers to oral response questions to help with scoring the Checkpoint later.

3. Use the Answer Key to score the Checkpoint, and then enter the results online.

Part 1. Read Word Parts, Nonsense Words, and Words Have students read across the rows from left to right and say the sounds that each word part, nonsense word, or word makes. Note any words or word parts they say incorrectly.

Part 2. Word Dissection For each word, say the sound students should identify. Have them read the word aloud and circle the letter or group of letters that spells the requested sound.

19. *beginning sound*

20. *beginning sound*

21. *ending sound*

22. *middle sound*

23. *ending sound*

Part 3. Finger Stretching Say each word to students. Have them say each word and finger stretch the sounds. Note any words they finger stretch incorrectly.

24. *ditch*

25. *much*

26. *shed*

27. *quick*

28. *chum*

29. *path*

Part 4. Dictation Say each word to students. Have them repeat and write the word.

30. *pitch*

31. *lock*

32. *fetch*

33. *pack*

Part 5. Read Aloud Listen to students read the sentences aloud. Count and note the number of words they read correctly.

Part 6. Say Letters Say each sound. Have students say a letter or letters that make that sound. Note any incorrect responses.

35. /ch/	44. /k/
36. /sh/	45. /th/
37. /ĕ/	46. /ŭ/
38. /ă/	47. /ĭ/
39. /w/	48. /w/
40. /ŏ/	49. /kw/
41. /k/	50. /ch/
42. /ch/	51. /k/
43. /sh/	52. /th/

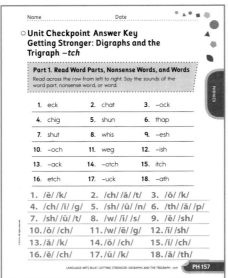

Name ___ Date ___

Unit Checkpoint Answer Key
Getting Stronger: Digraphs and the Trigraph –tch

Part 1. Read Word Parts, Nonsense Words, and Words
Read across the row from left to right. Say the sounds of the word part, nonsense word, or word.

1. eck	2. chat	3. –ock
4. chig	5. shun	6. thap
7. shut	8. whis	9. –esh
10. –och	11. weg	12. –ish
13. –ack	14. –otch	15. itch
16. etch	17. –uck	18. –ath

1. /ĕ/ /k/	2. /ch/ /ă/ /t/	3. /ŏ/ /k/
4. /ch/ /ĭ/ /g/	5. /sh/ /ŭ/ /n/	6. /th/ /ă/ /p/
7. /sh/ /ŭ/ /t/	8. /w/ /ĭ/ /s/	9. /ĕ/ /sh/
10. /ŏ/ /ch/	11. /w/ /ĕ/ /g/	12. /ĭ/ /sh/
13. /ă/ /k/	14. /ŏ/ /ch/	15. /ĭ/ /ch/
16. /ĕ/ /ch/	17. /ŭ/ /k/	18. /ă/ /th/

LANGUAGE ARTS BLUE | GETTING STRONGER: DIGRAPHS AND THE TRIGRAPH –tch   PH 157

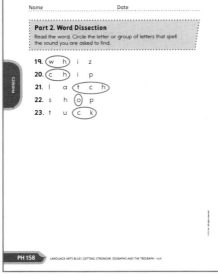

Name ___ Date ___

Part 2. Word Dissection
Read the word. Circle the letter or group of letters that spell the sound you are asked to find.

19. (w h) i z
20. (c h) i p
21. l a (t c h)
22. s h (o) p
23. t u (c k)

PH 158   LANGUAGE ARTS BLUE | GETTING STRONGER: DIGRAPHS AND THE TRIGRAPH –tch

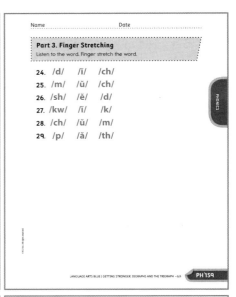

Name ___ Date ___

Part 3. Finger Stretching
Listen to the word. Finger stretch the word.

24. /d/ /ĭ/ /ch/
25. /m/ /ŭ/ /ch/
26. /sh/ /ĕ/ /d/
27. /kw/ /ĭ/ /k/
28. /ch/ /ŭ/ /m/
29. /p/ /ă/ /th/

LANGUAGE ARTS BLUE | GETTING STRONGER: DIGRAPHS AND THE TRIGRAPH –tch   PH 159

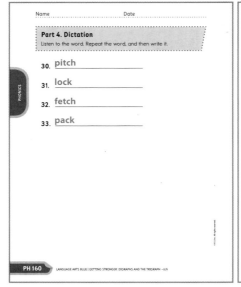

Name ___ Date ___

Part 4. Dictation
Listen to the word. Repeat the word, and then write it.

30. pitch
31. lock
32. fetch
33. pack

PH 160   LANGUAGE ARTS BLUE | GETTING STRONGER: DIGRAPHS AND THE TRIGRAPH –tch

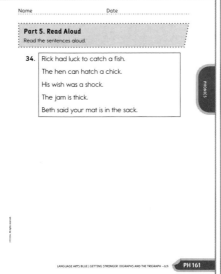

Name ___ Date ___

Part 5. Read Aloud
Read the sentences aloud.

34. Rick had luck to catch a fish.
The hen can hatch a chick.
His wish was a shock.
The jam is thick.
Beth said your mat is in the sack.

LANGUAGE ARTS BLUE | GETTING STRONGER: DIGRAPHS AND THE TRIGRAPH –tch   PH 161

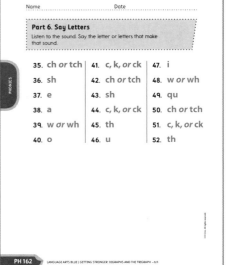

Name ___ Date ___

Part 6. Say Letters
Listen to the sound. Say the letter or letters that make that sound.

35. ch *or* tch	41. c, k, *or* ck	47. i
36. sh	42. ch *or* tch	48. w *or* wh
37. e	43. sh	49. qu
38. a	44. c, k, *or* ck	50. ch *or* tch
39. w *or* wh	45. th	51. c, k, *or* ck
40. o	46. u	52. th

PH 162   LANGUAGE ARTS BLUE | GETTING STRONGER: DIGRAPHS AND THE TRIGRAPH –tch

Capitalize Sentences

Unit Overview

In this unit, students will
- ► Learn the sight words *for*, *she*, and *her*.
- ► Learn how to write complete sentences.
- ► Learn how to use capitalization and punctuation in sentences.
- ► Review lowercase and uppercase letters.
- ► Review short vowel sounds.
- ► Identify individual sounds in words.
- ► Build words and make rhyming words.

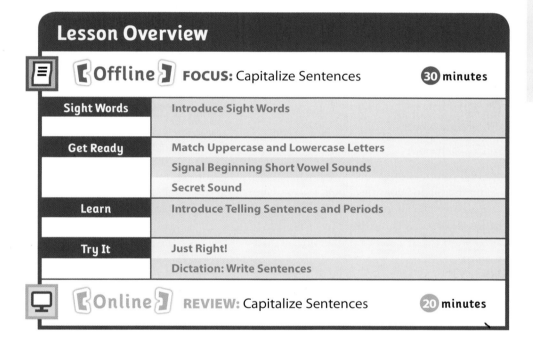

Lesson Overview

[Offline] FOCUS: Capitalize Sentences **30 minutes**

Sight Words	Introduce Sight Words
Get Ready	Match Uppercase and Lowercase Letters
	Signal Beginning Short Vowel Sounds
	Secret Sound
Learn	Introduce Telling Sentences and Periods
Try It	Just Right!
	Dictation: Write Sentences

[Online] REVIEW: Capitalize Sentences **20 minutes**

Materials

Supplied
- *K¹² PhonicsWorks Basic Activity Book,* p. PH 73
- whiteboard, Learning Coach
- whiteboard, student
- Tile Kit

Also Needed
- sight words box
- dictation notebook
- index cards (4)

Advance Preparation

Place lowercase letter tiles in alphabetical order on your whiteboard.

For Introduce Telling Sentences and Periods, print each of the following words on index cards, using one card per word:

- ► *The*
- ► *dog*
- ► *can*
- ► *run.*

 **30 minutes**

FOCUS: Capitalize Sentences

Work **together** with students to complete offline Sight Words, Get Ready, Learn, and Try It activities.

Sight Words ·····································

Introduce Sight Words

Help students learn the sight words *for*, *she*, and *her*.

1. Gather the sight word cards *for*, *she*, and *her*.

2. Show students the *for* card.

3. **Say:** This is the word *for*. We see this word so often that we want to be able to read and spell it quickly without thinking about it. Look closely at the word *for*. Spell the word *for* aloud. Take a picture of the word *for* in your mind. When you think you can spell *for* yourself, turn the card over and use your letter tiles to spell the word *for*. Check the card to see if you spelled *for* correctly. Read aloud the word you spelled with the letter tiles.

4. Repeat the activity with the remaining sight words.

5. Chart students' progress on the back of each card.

   ► Divide the back of the card into two columns.
   ► Label the first column "Read" and the second column "Spell."
   ► Record the dates that students read or spell the word correctly. When students can read and spell the word correctly three times in a row, they have mastered the word. You may want to put a star or sticker on the card when they have mastered that word.

6. Add the cards to students' sight words box.

TIP Sight words can be very difficult for some students. Let students work at their own pace and really master these words, as they occur frequently in reading and writing.

> **Objectives**
> • Read sight words.
> • Spell sight words.

Get Ready ·····································

Match Uppercase and Lowercase Letters

To help students learn to recognize the difference between lowercase and uppercase letters of the alphabet, have them practice identifying and naming letters. Grab your whiteboard with letters.

1. Place the following uppercase letters on students' whiteboard in a horizontal row: *B*, *E*, *S*, *T*, and *W*.

2. Point to a letter and have students name it.

> **Objectives**
> • Identify letters of the alphabet.
> • Match capital letters to lowercase letters.
> • Identify beginning sounds in words.
> • Identify short vowel sounds.

3. Have students select the matching lowercase letter from your whiteboard.

4. Have students place the lowercase letter under the uppercase letter to make a pair.

TIP If students have difficulty with this activity, have them practice naming the letters in the alphabet. When they can name all the letters in the correct order, have them touch and name the lowercase and uppercase letters for each letter.

Signal Beginning Short Vowel Sounds

Use a special signal to help students identify **beginning short vowel sounds** in words.

1. **Say:** I'm going to tell you a special vowel sound, and then I'll say some words. Repeat each word I say and make a special signal to tell me where the special sound is.

   ► If the special vowel sound is at the beginning of the word, clap your hands.
   ► If the special vowel sound is **not** at the beginning of the word, just smile at me.
   ► For example, if I ask you to listen for the sound /ă/ and I say the word *add*, you'll repeat the word *add* and clap your hands because *add* has the short vowel sound /ă/ at the beginning.
   ► If I say the word *on*, you'll repeat the word *on* and smile at me because *on* has the sound /ŏ/, not /ă/, at the beginning.

2. Say each sound and group of words. Have students make the special signal to identify the beginning sound.

   ► /ă/: *add, on, as, under, act* clap: *add, as, act*
   ► /ĕ/: *Ed, elf, milk, edge, open* clap: *Ed, elf, edge*
   ► /ĭ/: *is, tell, if, play, inside* clap: *is, if, inside*
   ► /ŏ/: *it, on, cup, ox, olive* clap: *on, ox, olive*
   ► /ŭ/: *up, ask, under, us, car* clap: *up, under, us*

TIP If students can't identify the beginning sound of each word, say the word again and emphasize the beginning sound by repeating it three times (for example, /t/ /t/ /t/, *taste*). You can also draw out the beginning sound when you say the word (for example, *mmmommy*). If necessary, have students look at your mouth while you repeat the sounds.

Secret Sound

Say groups of words to help students recognize **middle sounds** in words.

1. **Say:** I am going to say some groups of words. Listen for a secret sound in the middle of each word. Then tell me what sound you hear in the middle of each group of words.

2. Say each of the following groups of words. Have students identify the secret sound in each group.

   ▸ *hat, map, last* /ă/
   ▸ *fell, wet, desk* /ĕ/
   ▸ *fish, slip, wig* /ĭ/
   ▸ *drop, jog, lock* /ŏ/
   ▸ *cut, just, rush* /ŭ/

(TIP) If students can't identify the secret sound, have them listen while you say each word again and then have them repeat each word. Have students say what sound they hear in the middle of each word.

Learn

Introduce Telling Sentences and Periods

Help students learn telling sentences and the use of capital letters and periods.

1. Gather the index cards you prepared, and place them in front of students to make the sentence *The dog can run.*

2. Point to the capital letter at the beginning of the sentence.

   Say: We use a capital letter to make the first word in this sentence so that we know we are starting a new sentence.

3. **Say:** *The dog can run.* is a telling sentence. It tells us that the dog can run. A sentence that tells us something always ends with a period.

4. Point to the period at the end of the sentence.

   Say: This dot is called a period. The period tells us to stop for a moment between words.

5. **Say:** There are two rules we must follow when we write telling sentences:

   ▸ At the beginning of any sentence, the first word starts with a capital letter.
   ▸ At the end of a telling sentence, we always put a period to mark the end of the sentence.

6. Talk like a robot when saying the first sentence below; use no inflection and don't pause between words.

   Say: If-we-didn't-have-capital-letters-or-periods-our-words-would-run-together-we-wouldn't-know-when-to-stop. That's why it is important when we write words in telling sentences to always begin with a capital letter and end with a period.

Objectives
- Capitalize the first word in a sentence.
- Use periods to end telling sentences.
- Identify complete sentences.
- Write words by applying grade-level phonics knowledge.

7. Scramble the index cards when you feel confident that students understand what a sentence is. Have students

- ▶ Rearrange the words to make a sentence.
- ▶ Touch each word in the sentence as they read it aloud.
- ▶ Touch the capital letter that signals the beginning of the sentence.
- ▶ Touch the period that signals the end of the sentence.
- ▶ Write the sentence on their whiteboard.

8. Help students if they have difficulty arranging the words correctly.

   Say: Read the sentence aloud. Does it make sense?

9. Point to any word that seems out of place and guide students with the following prompts:

- ▶ What is this word?
- ▶ Find a word that would make better sense.
- ▶ Switch the words. Now read the sentence.
- ▶ Does it make sense now?

10. Ask students the following questions if they continue to have difficulty:

- ▶ What is special about the first word in a sentence? It begins with a capital letter.
- ▶ What is special about the end of a telling sentence? It ends with a period.

Try It

Just Right!

Have students complete page PH 73 in *K¹² PhonicsWorks Basic Activity Book* for more practice capitalizing sentences. Have students capitalize the first word, write it, and place a period at the end of each sentence. Then have them read each completed sentence aloud.

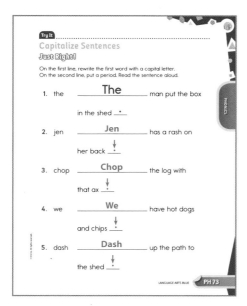

Objectives

- Read aloud grade-level text with appropriate automaticity, prosody, accuracy, and rate.
- Identify complete sentences.
- Capitalize the first word in a sentence.
- Use periods to end telling sentences.
- Write words by applying grade-level phonics knowledge.
- Follow three-step directions.

Dictation: Write Sentences
Use sentences to help students identify individual sounds in words.

1. Gather a pencil and the dictation notebook. Say the sentence, *We can run.*
   Then give these directions to students:

   ▸ Repeat the sentence.
   ▸ Write the sentence in your notebook.
   ▸ Read the sentence aloud.

2. When students have finished, write the following sentence on your
   whiteboard: *We can run.*

3. Have them compare their answer to your correct version.

4. Repeat this procedure with the sentence, *That cat ran.*

   ▸ If students make an error and don't see it, help them correct their mistake
     by having them finger stretch the sounds in the word they missed.
   ▸ If students are having difficulty selecting the correct letters or sounds,
     review those letters or sounds that are confusing them.
   ▸ If students have difficulty with first, middle, and last sounds, have them
     finger stretch the sounds in words.

TIP Remind students that a telling sentence starts with a capital letter and ends
with a period.

 ⓜ **minutes**

REVIEW: Capitalize Sentences
Students will work online independently to

▸ Practice capitalizing sentences.
▸ Practice decoding text by reading a story.

Help students locate the online activities and provide support as needed.

Offline Alternative

No computer access? Say telling sentences to students, such as *He got a dog.* and *She
ran fast.* Have students tell you which word in each sentence should begin with a capital
letter. Have them say where the period should go. You might also have students write
short telling sentences in their dictation notebook, on their whiteboard, or on a sheet of
paper. Make sure students begin each sentence with a capital letter and place a period
at the end.

 Objectives

- Identify complete sentences.
- Capitalize the first word in
  a sentence.
- Use periods to end
  telling sentences.
- Identify individual sounds
  in words.
- Read aloud grade-level
  text with appropriate
  automaticity, prosody,
  accuracy, and rate.
- Decode words by
  applying grade-level
  word analysis skills.

Punctuate Sentences

Lesson Overview

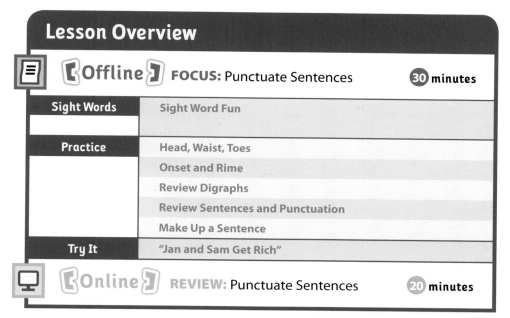

Offline	FOCUS: Punctuate Sentences	30 minutes

Sight Words	Sight Word Fun	
Practice	Head, Waist, Toes	
	Onset and Rime	
	Review Digraphs	
	Review Sentences and Punctuation	
	Make Up a Sentence	
Try It	"Jan and Sam Get Rich"	

Online	REVIEW: Punctuate Sentences	20 minutes

Materials

Supplied
- *K¹² PhonicsWorks Readers Basic 8*, pp. 19–24
- whiteboard, Learning Coach
- whiteboard, student
- Tile Kit

Also Needed
- sight words box
- dictation notebook
- index cards (11)

Advance Preparation

Place the digraphs *ch, –ck, sh, th,* and *wh* and trigraph *–tch* in alphabetical order on your whiteboard.

For Review Sentences and Punctuation, print each of the following words on index cards, using one card per word:

- *the*
- *bag*
- *is*
- *red*
- *The*
- *bag*
- *is*
- *red.*

For Make Up a Sentence, print each of the following words on index cards, using one card per word: *hatch, sock,* and *chip.*

 **30 minutes**

FOCUS: Punctuate Sentences

Work **together** with students to complete offline Sight Words, Practice, and Try It activities.

Sight Words

Sight Word Fun

Help students learn the sight words *for, she,* and *her,* and up to two additional sight words they have yet to master.

1. Gather the sight word cards *for, she,* and *her,* and up to two additional sight word cards.

2. Choose one sight word card to begin.

   Say: Look at this word and take a picture of it in your mind. When you think you can spell the word yourself, turn the card over and use your letter tiles to spell the word.

3. After students spell the word, have them check the card to see if they spelled the word correctly.

   Say: Read aloud the word you spelled with the letter tiles.

4. Repeat the activity with the remaining sight words.

 Sight words can be very difficult for some students. Let them work at their own pace and really master these words.

> **Objectives**
> - Read sight words.
> - Spell sight words.

Practice •

Head, Waist, Toes

Help students practice identifying the sounds in words.

1. **Say:** Let's identify sounds in words by touching parts of our body as we say each sound. For example, I'll say *shape*, which has three sounds, and you'll repeat the word. Do these steps with me:

   ▶ The first sound in *shape* is /sh/, so I touch my head as I say /sh/.
   ▶ The middle sound is /ā/, so I touch my waist as I say /ā/.
   ▶ The last sound is /p/, so I touch my toes as I say /p/.

2. Say the words below. Have students repeat each word and then touch their head, waist, and toes as they say each sound in the word. After they say the sounds in each word, ask them the question for that word.

   ▶ dish /d/ /ĭ/ /sh/   What is the last sound? /sh/
   ▶ thick /th/ /ĭ/ /k/   What is the first sound? /th/
   ▶ bath /b/ /ă/ /th/   What is the middle sound? /ă/
   ▶ chop /ch/ /ŏ/ /p/   What is the first sound? /ch/
   ▶ beach /b/ /ē/ /ch/   What is the last sound? /ch/

   TIP If students have difficulty with this activity, be sure they can identify beginning, middle, and end. If students still have difficulty with this activity, try finger stretching the words instead.

Onset and Rime

In a word, the part of the syllable before the first vowel sound is the **onset**. The part of the syllable after the first vowel sound is the **rime**. For example, in *shut*, /sh/ is the onset and *ut* is the rime. Help students put together words that are broken down into parts by onset and rime.

1. **Say:** I'm going to break a word into two parts. Your job is to put the parts together and say the word. If the first part of a word is /sh/ and the last part of the word is *ut*, then the whole word is *shut*: /sh/ . . . *ut* . . . *shut*.

2. Say the following pairs of word parts. Have students tell you the word that each pair forms.

   ▶ /d/ . . . *ash dash*
   ▶ /th/ . . . *umb thumb*
   ▶ /p/ . . . *ath path*
   ▶ /ch/ . . . *ip chip*
   ▶ /f/ . . . *ish fish*

Objectives

• Identify individual sounds in words.
• Identify a word when given the onset and rime.
• Given the letter, identify the most common sound.
• Given the sound, identify the most common letter or letters.
• Identify complete sentences.
• Capitalize the first word in a sentence.
• Use periods to end telling sentences.
• Write words by applying grade-level phonics knowledge.

Review Digraphs

To help students master digraphs and the trigraph –*tch*, have them practice identifying and naming them. Grab your whiteboard with the digraphs and trigraph.

1. Remind students that the letter tiles with two letters that make only one sound are called **digraphs**. The tile that has three letters that make only one sound is called a **trigraph**.

2. Have students

   ▸ Touch and say the sound for each of the digraphs and the trigraph –*tch*.
   ▸ Touch and say the letters that make up each digraph and the trigraph –*tch*.

TIP Remind students that the digraph *th* makes two different sounds: the quiet sound /th/, as in *thin*, and the noisy sound /<u>th</u>/, as in *this*. The sound /<u>th</u>/ is called a noisy sound because we use our voice.

Review Sentences and Punctuation

Help students practice telling sentences and the use of capital letters and periods.

1. Gather the index cards you prepared, and place them in front of students so that they make two sentences: *the bag is red* and *The bag is red.*

2. Point to each group of words and ask students the following questions:

   ▸ How are these groups of words alike? Both have the same words in the same order.
   ▸ How are these groups of words different? One group is missing the capital letter and the period.
   ▸ What are the rules a telling sentence must follow? To begin any sentence, use a capital letter in the first word. To end a telling sentence, add a period to mark the end of the sentence.
   ▸ Point to the group of words that is not written correctly. What is needed to make the sentence correct? Capitalize the letter *t* in the first word. Add a period after *red*.

3. Read the second group of words aloud to students. Have students

   ▸ Read the sentence along with you.
   ▸ Touch the capital letter that signals the beginning of the sentence.
   ▸ Touch the period that signals the end of the sentence.

4. Take apart the sentence *The bag is red.* and scramble the words. Have students

   ▸ Rearrange the words to make a sentence.
   ▸ Touch each word in the sentence as they read it aloud.
   ▸ Point to the capital letter at the beginning of the sentence.
   ▸ Point to the period at the end of the sentence.
   ▸ Write the sentence on their whiteboard.

5. Help students if they have difficulty arranging the words correctly to make a sentence.

   Say: Read the sentence aloud. Does it make sense?

6. Point to any word that seems out of place and state the following:

   ▸ What is this word?
   ▸ Find a word that would make better sense.
   ▸ Switch the words. Now read the sentence.
   ▸ Does it make sense now?

7. Ask students the following questions if they continue to have difficulty:

   ▸ What is special about the first word in a sentence? It begins with a capital letter.
   ▸ What is special about the end of a telling sentence? It ends with a period.

Make Up a Sentence

Help students use words to make sentences.

1. Gather the index cards you prepared, and place them face down on the table in one pile.

2. Have students

   ▸ Select a card.
   ▸ Read the word.
   ▸ Use the word in an interesting, fun, or silly sentence.

TIP If students read a word incorrectly, have them finger stretch the sounds in the word or use letter tiles to spell the word and touch and say.

Try It

"Jan and Sam Get Rich"

Have students read "Jan and Sam Get Rich" on page 19 of *K¹² PhonicsWorks Readers Basic 8.*

Students should read the story silently once or twice before reading the story aloud. When students miss a word that can be sounded out, point to it and give them three to six seconds to try the word again. If students still miss the word, tell them the word so the flow of the story isn't interrupted.

After reading the story, make a list of all the words students missed, and go over those words with them. You may use letter tiles to show students how to read the words.

Objectives
- Read aloud grade-level text with appropriate automaticity, prosody, accuracy, and rate.
- Decode words by applying grade-level word analysis skills.
- Track text from left to right.
- Turn pages sequentially.

 **20 minutes**

REVIEW: **Punctuate Sentences**

Students will work online independently to

► Practice capitalizing and punctuating telling sentences.

Help students locate the online activities and provide support as needed.

Offline Alternative

No computer access? Say telling sentences to students, such as *Tad is mad.* and *Deb has a pet fish.* Have students tell you which word in each sentence should begin with a capital letter. Have them say where the period should go. You might also have students write short telling sentences in their dictation notebook, on their whiteboard, or on a sheet of paper. Make sure students begin each sentence with a capital letter and place a period at the end.

Create Sentences

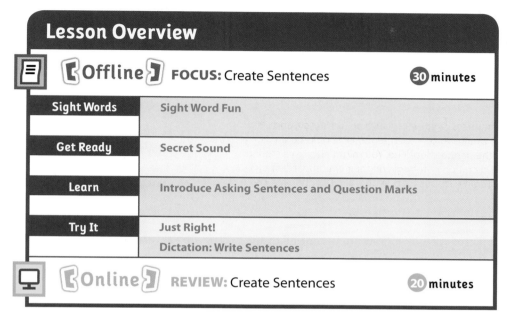

Lesson Overview

Offline FOCUS: Create Sentences — **30** minutes

Sight Words	Sight Word Fun
Get Ready	Secret Sound
Learn	Introduce Asking Sentences and Question Marks
Try It	Just Right!
	Dictation: Write Sentences

Online REVIEW: Create Sentences — **20** minutes

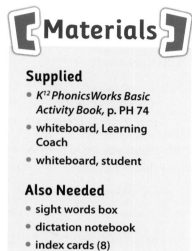

Materials

Supplied
- *K¹² PhonicsWorks Basic Activity Book*, p. PH 74
- whiteboard, Learning Coach
- whiteboard, student

Also Needed
- sight words box
- dictation notebook
- index cards (8)

Advance Preparation

For Introduce Asking Sentences and Question Marks, print each of the following words on index cards, using one card per word:

- ► *It*
- ► *is*
- ► *a*
- ► *cat.*
- ► *Is*
- ► *it*
- ► *a*
- ► *cat?*

 **30 minutes**

FOCUS: Create Sentences

Work **together** with students to complete offline Sight Words, Get Ready, Learn, and Try It activities.

Sight Words

Sight Word Fun

Help students learn the sight words *for*, *she*, and *her*, and up to two additional sight words they have yet to master.

1. Gather the sight word cards *for*, *she*, and *her*, and up to two additional sight word cards.

2. Choose one sight word card to begin.

   Say: Look at this word and take a picture of it in your mind. When you think you can spell the word yourself, turn the card over and use your letter tiles to spell the word.

3. After students spell the word, have them check the card to see if they spelled the word correctly.

   Say: Read aloud the word you spelled with the letter tiles.

4. Repeat the activity with the remaining sight words.

TIP Sight words can be very difficult for some students. Let them work at their own pace and really master these words.

> **Objectives**
> - Read sight words.
> - Spell sight words.

Get Ready

Secret Sound

Say groups of words to help students recognize **ending sounds** in words.

1. **Say:** I am going to say some groups of words. Listen for a secret sound at the end of each word. Then tell me what sound you hear at the end of each group of words.

2. Say each of the following groups of words. Have students identify the secret sound in each group.

   ▶ *batch, notch, pitch* /ch/
   ▶ *pack, quick, duck* /k/
   ▶ *clock, Zack, luck* /k/
   ▶ *latch, botch, hitch* /ch/

 Sight words can be very difficult for some students. Let them work at their own pace and really master these words.

> **Objectives**
> - Identify ending sounds in words.

Learn ••

Introduce Asking Sentences and Question Marks
Help students learn asking sentences and question marks.

1. Gather the index cards you prepared, and place them in front of students to make the sentences *It is a cat.* and *Is it a cat?*

2. Point to the telling sentence *It is a cat.* and read it aloud. Encourage students to read the sentence aloud with you.

3. Have students

   ▸ Touch each word in the telling sentence as they read it aloud.
   ▸ Touch the capital letter that signals the beginning of the sentence.
   ▸ Touch the period that signals the end of the sentence.
   ▸ Write the sentence on their whiteboard.

4. Point to the asking sentence *Is it a cat?* and read it aloud. Encourage students to read the sentence aloud with you.

5. Touch the question mark that signals the end of the question.

   Say: This sentence is an asking sentence. It is asking about the cat. We put a special mark at the end of asking sentences. It is called a question mark.

6. Have students

   ▸ Touch each word in the asking sentence as they read it aloud.
   ▸ Touch the capital letter that signals the beginning of the sentence.
   ▸ Touch the question mark that signals the end of the sentence.
   ▸ Write the sentence on their whiteboard.

7. **Say:** There are two rules we must follow when we write asking sentences:

   ▸ At the beginning of any sentence, the first word starts with a capital letter.
   ▸ At the end of an asking sentence, we always put a question mark after the last word.

8. Scramble the index cards in each of the sentences when you feel confident that students understand what an asking sentence is. Have students

   ▸ Rearrange the words to make a sentence.
   ▸ Touch each word in the sentence as they read it aloud.
   ▸ Touch the capital letter that signals the beginning of the sentence.
   ▸ Touch the punctuation that signals the end of the sentence. period or question mark
   ▸ Write the sentence on their whiteboard.

9. Help students if they have difficulty arranging the words correctly.

   Say: Read the sentence aloud. Does it make sense?

Objectives

- Identify complete sentences.
- Capitalize the first word in a sentence.
- Use question marks to end asking sentences.
- Use periods to end telling sentences.
- Identify individual sounds in words.
- Identify ending sounds in words.
- Write words by applying grade-level phonics knowledge.

10. Point to any word that seems out of place and state the following:

   ▸ What is this word?
   ▸ Find a word that would make better sense.
   ▸ Switch the words. Now read the sentence.
   ▸ Does it make sense now?

11. Ask students the following questions if they continue to have difficulty:

   ▸ What is special about the first word in a sentence? It begins with a capital letter.
   ▸ What is special about the end of an asking sentence? It ends with a question mark.

Try It

Just Right!

Have students complete page PH 74 in *K¹² PhonicsWorks Basic Activity Book* for more practice creating sentences. Have students read the sentences aloud and put a question mark at the end of each sentence.

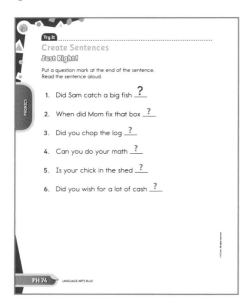

Objectives
- Read aloud grade-level text with appropriate automaticity, prosody, accuracy, and rate.
- Use question marks to end asking sentences.
- Write words by applying grade-level phonics knowledge.
- Follow three-step directions.

Dictation: Write Sentences

Use sentences to help students identify individual sounds in words.

1. Gather a pencil and the dictation notebook. Say the sentence, *Can Jim go?* Then give these directions to students:

   ▸ Repeat the sentence.
   ▸ Write the sentence in your notebook.
   ▸ Read the sentence aloud.

2. When students have finished, write the following sentence on your whiteboard: *Can Jim go?*

3. Have them compare their answer to your correct version.

4. Repeat this procedure with the following sentences: *Jim can go. Is the dog big? The dog is big.*

   ▸ If students make an error and don't see it, help them correct their mistake by having them finger stretch the sounds in the word they missed.
   ▸ If students are having difficulty selecting the correct letters or sounds, review those letters or sounds that are confusing them.
   ▸ If students have difficulty with first, middle, and last sounds, have them finger stretch the sounds in words.

 **20 minutes**

REVIEW: **Create Sentences**

Students will work online independently to

▸ Practice asking sentences.
▸ Practice decoding text by reading sentences.

Help students locate the online activities and provide support as needed.

___

Offline Alternative

No computer access? Say asking sentences to students, such as *Does a fish have a fin?* and *Can she run fast?* Have students tell you which word in each sentence should begin with a capital letter. Have them say where the question mark should go. You might also have students write short asking sentences in their dictation notebook, on their whiteboard, or on a sheet of paper. Make sure students begin each sentence with a capital letter and place a question mark at the end.

Objectives

- Identify complete sentences.
- Capitalize the first word in a sentence.
- Use question marks to end asking sentences.
- Use periods to end telling sentences.
- Identify individual sounds in words.
- Read aloud grade-level text with appropriate automaticity, prosody, accuracy, and rate.
- Decode words by applying grade-level word analysis skills.

Write Sentences

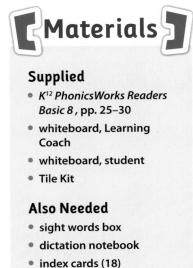

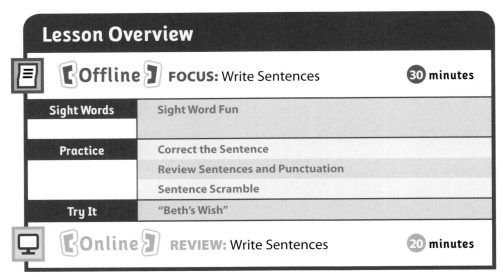

Lesson Overview

Offline FOCUS: Write Sentences — **30** minutes

Sight Words	Sight Word Fun
Practice	Correct the Sentence
	Review Sentences and Punctuation
	Sentence Scramble
Try It	"Beth's Wish"

Online REVIEW: Write Sentences — **20** minutes

Materials

Supplied
- *K¹² PhonicsWorks Readers Basic 8*, pp. 25–30
- whiteboard, Learning Coach
- whiteboard, student
- Tile Kit

Also Needed
- sight words box
- dictation notebook
- index cards (18)

Advance Preparation

For Review Sentences and Punctuation, print each of the following words on index cards, using one card per word:

- *Can*
- *the*
- *dog*
- *run?*
- *The*
- *dog*
- *can*
- *run.*

For Sentence Scramble, print each of the following words on index cards, using one card per word: *can, where, she, go, in, run, dash, up, the,* and *hill*.

 **30 minutes**

FOCUS: Write Sentences

Work **together** with students to complete offline Sight Words, Practice, and Try It activities.

Sight Words

Sight Word Fun

Help students learn the sight words *for*, *she*, and *her*, and up to two additional sight words they have yet to master.

1. Gather the sight word cards *for*, *she*, and *her*, and up to two additional sight word cards.

2. Choose one sight word card to begin.

   Say: Look at this word and take a picture of it in your mind. When you think you can spell the word yourself, turn the card over and use your letter tiles to spell the word.

3. After students spell the word, have them check the card to see if they spelled the word correctly.

   Say: Read aloud the word you spelled with the letter tiles.

4. Repeat the activity with the remaining sight words.

   TIP Sight words can be very difficult for some students. Let them work at their own pace and really master these words.

> **Objectives**
> - Read sight words.
> - Spell sight words.

Practice

Correct the Sentence

Have students practice correcting capitalization and punctuation in sentences. Grab your whiteboard and dry-erase marker.

1. Write the following sentence on your whiteboard: *the hat is red*. Don't use any capitalization or punctuation.

2. Have students read the sentence aloud. Have them

   ▸ Cross out the lowercase letter at the beginning of the first word and write the capital letter.
   ▸ Add punctuation to the end of the sentence.

3. **Say:** Read the sentence again. How do you know this sentence is correct?
   The sentence is correct if it follows the rules. To begin any sentence, use a capital letter in the first word. To end a telling sentence, add a period to mark the end of the sentence. To end an asking sentence, add a question mark to the end of the sentence.

> **Objectives**
> - Identify complete sentences.
> - Capitalize the first word in a sentence.
> - Use question marks to end asking sentences.
> - Use periods to end telling sentences.
> - Read aloud grade-level text with appropriate automaticity, prosody, accuracy, and rate.
> - Identify individual sounds in words.
> - Write words by applying grade-level phonics knowledge.

4. Repeat the procedure for each of the following sentences:

   ▸ *can you go in* Can you go in?
   ▸ *his dad is big* His dad is big.
   ▸ *who can go up* Who can go up?

5. Help students if they have difficulty identifying what is wrong with the sentence. Ask the following questions:

   ▸ What is special about the first word in a sentence?
   ▸ Does the first word in this sentence start with a capital letter?
   ▸ How can you change the sentence so it begins with a capital letter?
   ▸ What is special about the mark at the end of a sentence?

6. Guide students by asking one of the following questions if they continue having difficulty:

   ▸ Is this sentence a telling or asking sentence?
   ▸ Is the last word in the sentence followed by a period or a question mark?
   ▸ What mark do you put at the end of [a telling or an asking] sentence?

Review Sentences and Punctuation

Help students practice telling and asking sentences.

1. Gather the index cards you prepared, and place them in front of students so that they make two sentences: *The dog can run.* and *Can the dog run?*

2. Point to each group of words and ask students the following questions:

   ▸ How are these groups of words alike? Both have the same words.
   ▸ How are these groups of words different? The words are in a different order and have different ending punctuation.
   ▸ What are the rules a telling and an asking sentence must follow? To begin a sentence, use a capital letter in the first word. To end a telling sentence, add a period to mark the end of the sentence. To end an asking sentence, add a question mark to the end of the sentence.

3. Read the following telling sentence aloud to students: *The dog can run.* Have students

   ▸ Read the sentence aloud to you.
   ▸ Touch the capital letter that signals the beginning of the sentence.
   ▸ Touch the period that signals the end of the sentence.

4. Read the following asking sentence aloud to students: *Can the dog run?* Have students

   ▸ Read the sentence along with you.
   ▸ Touch the capital letter that signals the beginning of the sentence.
   ▸ Touch the question mark that signals the end of the sentence.

5. Scramble the index cards in the sentence *The dog can run.* Have students

   ▸ Rearrange the words to make a sentence.
   ▸ Touch each word in the sentence as they read it aloud.
   ▸ Point to the capital letter at the beginning of the sentence.
   ▸ Point to the period at the end of the sentence.
   ▸ Write the sentence on their whiteboard.

6. Follow the same procedure with the asking sentence *Can the dog run?*

7. Help students if they have difficulty arranging the words correctly to make a sentence.

   Say: Read the sentence aloud. Does it make sense?

8. Point to any word that seems out of place and state the following:

   ▸ What is this word?
   ▸ Find a word that would make better sense.
   ▸ Switch the words. Now read the sentence.
   ▸ Does it make sense now?

9. Ask students the following questions if they continue to have difficulty:

   ▸ What is special about the first word in a sentence? It begins with a capital letter.
   ▸ What is special about the end of a telling sentence? It ends with a period.
   ▸ What is special about the end of an asking sentence? It ends with a question mark.

Sentence Scramble

Have students build sentences by rearranging words to help them learn the meaning of words and phrases.

1. Gather the index cards you prepared, a pencil, and the dictation notebook.

2. Place the index cards in front of students.

3. Point to each word and have students read it aloud with you.

4. Arrange three of the cards as follows: *can she go.*

5. Have students say if the words make sense. Tell them that the words make an asking sentence.

6. Write the words as a sentence on students' whiteboard. Be sure to capitalize the first letter in *can* and insert the proper punctuation at the end of the sentence.

7. Point out the capital letter and the question mark in the sentence.

8. Read the sentence with students.

   Say: I am going to put these words back with the others. Choose some word cards and put them together to make a different sentence. Read the words in the order you put them.

   ▸ Does your sentence make sense? Is it an asking or a telling sentence?
   ▸ Now write the sentence. Be sure to start with a capital letter. Remember to put a period or a question mark at the end.

9. Return the words to the original group, and repeat the steps so that students can create and write one or more sentences.

10. Help students if they have difficulty arranging the words correctly to make a sentence.

    Say: Read the sentence aloud. Does it make sense?

11. Point to any word that seems out of place and state the following:

    ▶ What is this word?
    ▶ Find a word that would make better sense.
    ▶ Switch the words. Now read the sentence.
    ▶ Does it make sense now?

Try It

"Beth's Wish"

Have students read "Beth's Wish" on page 25 of *K¹² PhonicsWorks Readers Basic 8.*

Students should read the story silently once or twice before reading the story aloud. When students miss a word that can be sounded out, point to it and give them three to six seconds to try the word again. If students still miss the word, tell them the word so the flow of the story isn't interrupted.

After reading the story, make a list of all the words students missed, and go over those words with them. You may use letter tiles to show students how to read the words.

Objectives

- Read aloud grade-level text with appropriate automaticity, prosody, accuracy, and rate.
- Decode words by applying grade-level word analysis skills.
- Track text from left to right.
- Turn pages sequentially.

 **20 minutes**

REVIEW: Write Sentences

Students will work online independently to

▶ Practice telling and asking sentences.

Help students locate the online activities and provide support as needed.

Offline Alternative

No computer access? Say telling and asking sentences to students, such as *It was a pig.* and *Was it a pig?* Have students tell you which word in each sentence should begin with a capital letter. Have them say where the period or question mark should go. You might also have students write short telling and asking sentences in their dictation notebook, on their whiteboard, or on a sheet of paper. Make sure students begin each sentence with a capital letter and place a period or question mark at the end.

Objectives

- Identify complete sentences.
- Capitalize the first word in a sentence.
- Use question marks to end asking sentences.
- Use periods to end telling sentences.

Unit Checkpoint

Lesson Overview

 Online REVIEW: Telling and Asking Sentences — **20** minutes

Offline UNIT CHECKPOINT: Telling and Asking Sentences — **30** minutes

Materials

Supplied
- *K¹² PhonicsWorks Basic Assessments,* pp. PH 163–168

Objectives
- Identify complete sentences.
- Capitalize the first word in a sentence.
- Use question marks to end asking sentences.
- Use periods to end telling sentences.
- Identify individual sounds in words.
- Given the letter, identify the most common sound.
- Given the sound, identify the most common letter or letters.
- Read sight words.
- Read instructional-level text with 90% accuracy.
- Read aloud grade-level text with appropriate automaticity, prosody, accuracy, and rate.

 **Online** **20** minutes

REVIEW: **Telling and Asking Sentences**

Students will review telling and asking sentences to prepare for the Unit Checkpoint. Help students locate the online activities and provide support as needed.

 **30 minutes**

UNIT CHECKPOINT: Telling and Asking Sentences

Explain that students are going to show what they have learned about letters, sounds, and words.

1. Give students the Unit Checkpoint pages for the Telling and Asking Sentences unit and print the Unit Checkpoint Answer Key, if you'd like.

2. Use the instructions below to help administer the Checkpoint to students. On the Answer Key or another sheet of paper, note student answers to oral response questions to help with scoring the Checkpoint later.

3. Use the Answer Key to score the Checkpoint, and then enter the results online.

Part 1. Say Sounds Have students read across the rows from left to right and say a sound that the letter, letters, or digraph makes. Note any sounds they say incorrectly.

Part 2. Word Dissection For each word, say the sound students should identify. Have them read the word aloud and circle the letter or group of letters that spells the requested sound.

21. *beginning sound*

22. *beginning sound*

23. *ending sound*

24. *beginning sound*

25. *middle sound*

Part 3. Finger Stretching Say each word to students. Have them say each word and finger stretch the sounds. Note any words they finger stretch incorrectly.

26. *ship*

27. *quack*

28. *whip*

29. *thick*

30. *thin*

31. *chop*

Part 4. Writing: Periods and Question Marks Have students read each sentence aloud and write a period or question mark to complete the sentence.

Part 5. Read Aloud Listen to students read the sentences aloud. Count and note the number of words they read correctly.

Part 6. Say Letters Say each sound. Have students say a letter or letters that make that sound. Note any incorrect responses.

39. /ă/

40. /ĕ/

41. /ĭ/

42. /ŏ/

43. /ŭ/

44. /sh/

45. /w/

46. /th/

47. /ch/

48. /r/

49. /w/

50. /y/

51. /v/

52. /g/

53. /h/

54. /j/

55. /kw/

56. /ks/

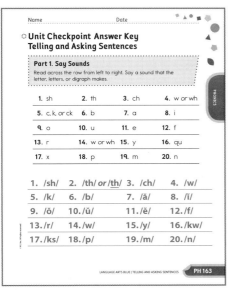

Name _____ Date _____

Unit Checkpoint Answer Key
Telling and Asking Sentences

Part 1. Say Sounds
Read across the row from left to right. Say a sound that the letter, letters, or digraph makes.

1. sh	2. th	3. ch	4. w or wh
5. c, k, or ck	6. b	7. a	8. i
9. o	10. u	11. e	12. f
13. r	14. w or wh	15. y	16. qu
17. x	18. p	19. m	20. n

1. /sh/	2. /th/ or /th/	3. /ch/	4. /w/
5. /k/	6. /b/	7. /ă/	8. /ĭ/
9. /ŏ/	10. /ŭ/	11. /ĕ/	12. /f/
13. /r/	14. /w/	15. /y/	16. /kw/
17. /ks/	18. /p/	19. /m/	20. /n/

PH 163

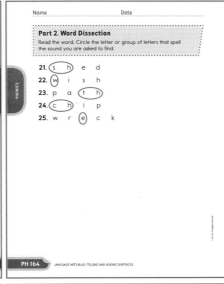

Name _____ Date _____

Part 2. Word Dissection
Read the word. Circle the letter or group of letters that spell the sound you are asked to find.

21. s h e d
22. w i s h
23. p a t h
24. c h i p
25. w r e c k

PH 164 LANGUAGE ARTS BLUE | TELLING AND ASKING SENTENCES

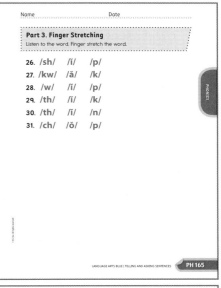

Name _____ Date _____

Part 3. Finger Stretching
Listen to the word. Finger stretch the word.

26. /sh/ /ĭ/ /p/
27. /kw/ /ă/ /k/
28. /w/ /ĭ/ /p/
29. /th/ /ĭ/ /k/
30. /th/ /ĭ/ /n/
31. /ch/ /ŏ/ /p/

PH 165

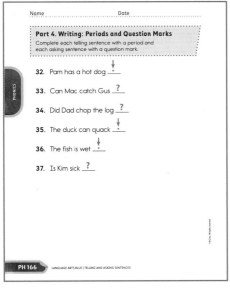

Name _____ Date _____

Part 4. Writing: Periods and Question Marks
Complete each telling sentence with a period and each asking sentence with a question mark.

32. Pam has a hot dog __.
33. Can Mac catch Gus __?
34. Did Dad chop the log __?
35. The duck can quack __.
36. The fish is wet __.
37. Is Kim sick __?

PH 166 LANGUAGE ARTS BLUE | TELLING AND ASKING SENTENCES

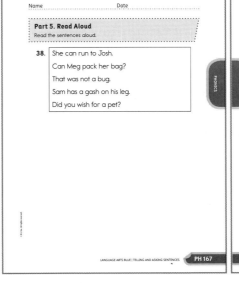

Name _____ Date _____

Part 5. Read Aloud
Read the sentences aloud.

38. She can run to Josh.
Can Meg pack her bag?
That was not a bug.
Sam has a gash on his leg.
Did you wish for a pet?

PH 167

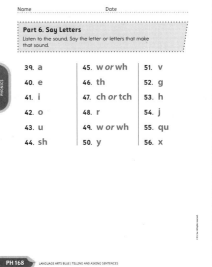

Name _____ Date _____

Part 6. Say Letters
Listen to the sound. Say the letter or letters that make that sound.

39. a	45. w or wh	51. v
40. e	46. th	52. g
41. i	47. ch or tch	53. h
42. o	48. r	54. j
43. u	49. w or wh	55. qu
44. sh	50. y	56. x

PH 168 LANGUAGE ARTS BLUE | TELLING AND ASKING SENTENCES

Getting Stronger: Short Vowels

Unit Overview

In this unit, students will
- ► Review sight words.
- ► Review the short vowel sounds /ă/, /ĕ/, /ĭ/, /ŏ/, and /ŭ/ for the letters *a, e, i, o,* and *u.*
- ► Review the digraphs *ch, –ck, sh, th,* and *wh.*
- ► Capitalize and punctuate sentences.
- ► Build words.
- ► Practice reading and writing.

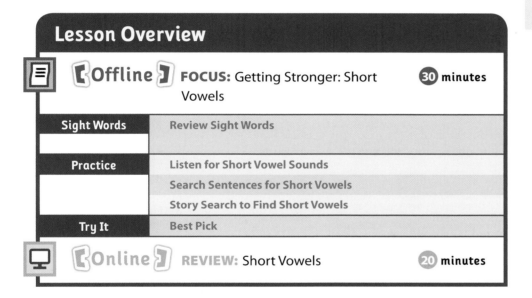

Lesson Overview

【Offline】 FOCUS: Getting Stronger: Short Vowels — **30 minutes**

Sight Words	Review Sight Words
Practice	Listen for Short Vowel Sounds
	Search Sentences for Short Vowels
	Story Search to Find Short Vowels
Try It	Best Pick

【Online】 REVIEW: Short Vowels — **20 minutes**

Advance Preparation

For Story Search to Find Short Vowels, select students' favorite story from one of the following Readers: *K¹² PhonicsWorks Readers Basic 5, 6,* or *7.*

Materials

Supplied
- *K¹² PhonicsWorks Basic Activity Book,* p. PH 75
- *K¹² PhonicsWorks Readers Basic 5, 6,* or *7*

Also Needed
- sight words box

 **Offline** **30** minutes

FOCUS: Getting Stronger: Short Vowels

Work **together** with students to complete offline Sight Words, Practice, and
Try It activities.

Sight Words

Review Sight Words

Help students learn to recognize sight words.

> **Objectives**
> • Read sight words.
> • Spell sight words.
> • Write sight words.

1. Gather all the sight word cards students have yet to master from their sight
   words box. Stack the cards on the table face down.

2. Have students pick up a word and read it to you.

3. If they read it quickly and correctly, put the card in one stack. If they hesitate or
   do not read the word correctly, put it in another stack. The second stack should
   have words that they will review again.

4. Take the stack of words that students read correctly and dictate each word to
   them. They may choose to either write the word or spell it aloud.

5. If students spell the word correctly, put the card in the first stack because they
   have mastered the word. If they misspell the word, add it to the stack of cards
   to review again.

6. Chart students' progress on the back of each card.

   ▸ Divide the back of the card into two columns.
   ▸ Label the first column "Read" and the second column "Spell."
   ▸ Record the dates that students read or spell the word correctly.
     When students can read and spell the word correctly three times in a row,
     they have mastered the word. You may want to put a star or sticker on
     their card when they have mastered that word.

TIP Even if students can read and spell all the words correctly, it is still beneficial for
them to review sight words. Choose as many additional words as you would like for
each subsequent activity.

Practice

Listen for Short Vowel Sounds

Say words with the sounds /ă/, /ĕ/, /ĭ/, /ŏ/, and /ŭ/ to help students identify the difference between short vowels sounds in words.

1. **Say:** I'm going to say a word. You'll listen for the **vowel sounds /ă/, /ĕ/, /ĭ/, /ŏ/, or /ŭ/** in the word. Tell me the vowel sound that you hear. For example, if I say *sat*, you'll say /ă/ because the vowel sound you hear in *sat* is /ă/.

2. Guide students with these questions if they have difficulty identifying the vowel sound:

   ▸ What is the sound you hear in the middle of the word? Answers will vary.
   ▸ Do you hear the sound [target sound] in the word? Listen to the word [target word] again.
   ▸ Can you think of another word that has the sound [target sound]? Answers will vary.

3. Say each word. Have students identify the vowel sound in the word.

   ▸ *dog* /ŏ/   ▸ *quiz* /ĭ/
   ▸ *him* /ĭ/   ▸ *clap* /ă/
   ▸ *pet* /ĕ/   ▸ *stop* /ŏ/
   ▸ *cup* /ŭ/   ▸ *rug* /ŭ/
   ▸ *yes* /ĕ/

Objectives

- Identify short vowel sounds.
- Identify and use the sound /ă/.
- Identify and use the sound /ĕ/.
- Identify and use the sound /ĭ/.
- Identify and use the sound /ŏ/.
- Identify and use the sound /ŭ/.
- Given the sound, identify the most common letter or letters.

Search Sentences for Short Vowels

Have students practice identifying **vowel sounds** in words that are in a sentence.

1. **Say:** I'm going to say a special sound that is in a word. You will repeat that sound and the word. The first sound is /ŏ/, as in the word *dog*.

2. Have students say the target sound /ŏ/ and the word *dog*.

3. **Say:** Now I will read a sentence. Repeat the sentence and tell me the word that has the same sound. The first sentence is *The fish is in the pot.* Which word in the sentence has the special sound? *pot*

4. Have students repeat the sentence and say the word.

5. Redirect students if they don't name the correct word.

   Say: Let me say the sentence again. Remember, you're listening for the sound [special sound].

6. Guide students if they have difficulty. Say two words from the sentence and have them choose the one with the target vowel sound.

7. Follow the same procedure with the following words and sentences:

   ▸ /ĕ/, as in *hen*   *Liz has a pet dog.* pet
   ▸ /ŭ/, as in *jump*   *Can I ride the bus?* bus
   ▸ /ĭ/, as in *hit*   *I hope our team wins.* wins
   ▸ /ă/, as in *jam*   *The cat is on the bed.* cat

Story Search to Find Short Vowels

Have students identify words with the short vowel sounds /ă/, /ĕ/, /ĭ/, /ŏ/, and /ŭ/ for the letters *a, e, i, o,* and *u*.

1. Gather the *K¹² PhonicsWorks Reader* and turn to students' favorite story.

2. **Say:** Find a word that has the sound /ă/, as in *bat*. Read the word to me.

3. Have students continue the activity until they have found at least two words for each short vowel sound.

   ▸ /ă/, as in *bat*
   ▸ /ĕ/, as in *bed*
   ▸ /ĭ/, as in *hit*
   ▸ /ŏ/, as in *cot*
   ▸ /ŭ/, as in *cup*

Try It

Best Pick

Have students complete page PH 75 in *K¹² PhonicsWorks Basic Activity Book* for more practice with short vowel sounds. Have students read each sentence aloud. Have them circle the word that best completes each sentence, write that word in the sentence, and read the sentence aloud again.

Objectives
- Identify short vowel sounds.
- Identify complete sentences.

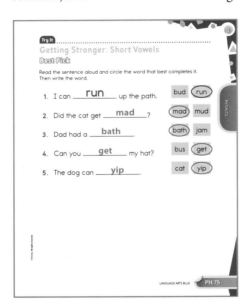

 **20** **minutes**

REVIEW: **Short Vowels**

Students will work online independently to

▶ Practice the short vowel sounds /ă/, /ĕ/, /ĭ/, /ŏ/, and /ŭ/ for the letters *a, e, i, o,* and *u.*

▶ Practice decoding text by reading sentences.

Help students locate the online activities and provide support as needed.

Offline Alternative

No computer access? Have students name words that contain the short vowel sounds /ă/, /ĕ/, /ĭ/, /ŏ/, and /ŭ/, such as *rag, met, hip, pot,* and *cup.* You might also ask students to spell simple words that contain the sounds /ă/, /ĕ/, /ĭ/, /ŏ/, and /ŭ/ made by the letters *a, e, i, o,* and *u* and other letters they have learned.

Objectives

- Identify short vowel sounds.
- Given the letter, identify the most common sound.
- Given the sound, identify the most common letter or letters.
- Identify and use the sound /ă/.
- Identify and use the sound /ĕ/.
- Identify and use the sound /ĭ/.
- Identify and use the sound /ŏ/.
- Identify and use the sound /ŭ/.
- Identify individual sounds in words.
- Read aloud grade-level text with appropriate automaticity, prosody, accuracy, and rate.
- Decode words by applying grade-level word analysis skills.

Getting Stronger: Digraphs

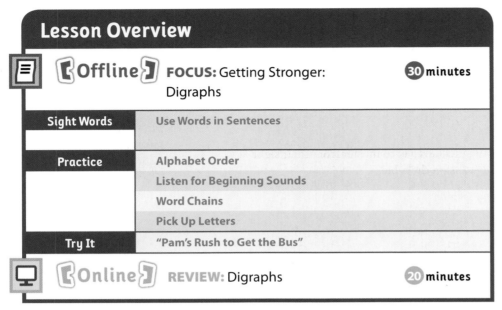

Lesson Overview

Offline FOCUS: Getting Stronger: Digraphs   **30** minutes

Sight Words	Use Words in Sentences
Practice	**Alphabet Order**
	Listen for Beginning Sounds
	Word Chains
	Pick Up Letters
Try It	"Pam's Rush to Get the Bus"

Online REVIEW: Digraphs   **20** minutes

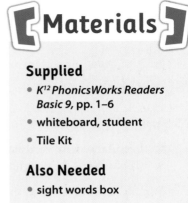

Materials

Supplied
- *K¹² PhonicsWorks Readers Basic 9*, pp. 1–6
- whiteboard, student
- Tile Kit

Also Needed
- sight words box

 **30 minutes**

FOCUS: Getting Stronger: Digraphs

Work **together** with students to complete offline Sight Words, Practice, and Try It activities.

Sight Words

Use Words in Sentences

Help students use sight words in sentences.

1. Gather all the sight word cards students have yet to master from their sight words box. Spread the sight word cards on the table.

2. **Say:** Let's use sight words in sentences.

3. Have students

   ▶ Touch each card and read the word on it.
   ▶ Make up a sentence using the word.
   ▶ Put the card in a pile after using the word in a sentence.
   ▶ Go through the pile of cards and read each sight word again.
   ▶ Spell each word.

 TIP If students have difficulty with any of the sight words, place those cards in a pile to review again.

Practice

Alphabet Order

Review alphabetic order with students.

1. Place the lowercase letter tiles *a* through *z* on students' whiteboard.

2. **Say:** Let's review the order of some letters in the alphabet.

3. Have students

   ► Name the letter after *d*.
   ► Name the letter after *p*.
   ► Name any letter that comes after *m*.
   ► Name any letter that comes after *t*.
   ► Name any two letters that come before *s*.
   ► Name any two letters that come after *l*.

 If students hesitate, have them check the letters on the whiteboard.

Listen for Beginning Sounds

Help students identify beginning sounds in words.

1. **Say:** I'm going to say a group of words. Listen for the beginning sound in all the words in the group. Then tell me the sound.

   ► For example, if I say *shop, shed, shut, ship*, you'll say /sh/ because the first sound you hear in all of the words in the group is /sh/.
   ► Now it's your turn. Listen to the words I say. You repeat the words and then tell me the first sound in the group of words.

2. Repeat the procedure, using the following words to help students recognize beginning sounds:

   ► *this, that, there, then* /th/
   ► *when, which, where, whack* /w/
   ► *chair, chin, chop, cheese* /ch/
   ► *the, those, these, they* /th/
   ► *check, chew, chum, chick* /ch/
   ► *shark, shirt, sheep, shin* /sh/
   ► *whale, while, whip, whistle* /w/

Objectives

- Identify letters of the alphabet.
- Given the letter, identify the most common sound.
- Given the sound, identify the most common letter or letters.
- Identify beginning sounds in words.
- Identify individual sounds in words.
- Identify the new word when one sound is changed in a word.
- Identify and use the digraph *ch*.
- Identify and use the digraph *–ck*.
- Identify and use the digraph *sh*.
- Identify and use the digraph *th*.
- Identify and use the digraph *wh*.

Word Chains

Have students build words by adding and changing letters to help them recognize and use individual sounds in words.

1. Place the following letter tiles at the top of students' whiteboard: *a, c, e, h, l, m, n, sh, tch,* and *th.*

2. **Say:** I am going to build the first word in a chain. The word is *hem.*

   ▸ I will pull down the letters for the sounds /h/, /ĕ/, and /m/ to spell the word *hem.*

   ▸ I will touch and say *hem.* To change *hem* to *them,* I will think about which sound is changed from the word *hem* to *them.* I will need to replace the letter tile *h* with the letter tile *th.*

   ▸ Touch and say the word *them.* Now it's your turn to change *them* to *then.* You can spell *then* by making only one change. Touch and say the new word.

3. Redirect students if they select the incorrect letter for any sound.

   Say: That letter is for the sound [incorrect sound]. We want the letter for the sound [target sound]. What letter makes that sound? Answers will vary.

4. Redirect students if they name the sound incorrectly.

   Say: To change the word [first word] to [target word], we need the letter for the sound [target sound].

   Show students how to make the change. Have them touch and say the new word after they move the letters.

5. Follow this procedure to make the following words: *than, man, mash, cash, catch, latch.*

6. For every new word, have students add, replace, or remove only one letter tile.

(TIP) If students struggle, review the sounds and letters that are confusing them.

Pick Up Letters

Help students use letters and sounds to make words and sentences.

1. Place the following letter tiles on students' whiteboard: *ch, d, m, sh, th,* and *wh.*

2. **Say:** Let's play a game with these letters and digraphs. Remember, two letters that make one sound are called a digraph. Tiles with digraphs have two letters.

3. Pick up the letter tile for *d.*

4. **Say:** I chose the letter *d.* The sound is /d/. This tile has only one letter, so it is not a digraph. A word that starts with the sound /d/ is *dance.* A sentence using that word is *Do you know how to dance?* Now it's your turn.

5. Continue taking turns until all the letter tiles have been chosen.

6. Have students answer the following questions for each letter or group of letters.

   ► What is (are) the letter(s)?
   ► Is it a digraph or a single letter?
   ► What is the sound?
   ► What is a word that starts with that sound?
   ► What sentence can you make with that word?

7. Redirect students if they name a word that starts with the sound, but not the letter (such as *knob*).

   Say: That is a word that doesn't follow the rules that we know for spelling. Try another word.

8. Prompt students if they have trouble matching the sounds with words. For example:

   Say: That's /j/, as in *jelly*. Can you think of another word that starts with that sound?

Try It •

"Pam's Rush to Get the Bus"
Have students read "Pam's Rush to Get the Bus" on page 1 of *K¹² PhonicsWorks Readers Basic 9*.

Students should read the story silently once or twice before reading the story aloud. When students miss a word that can be sounded out, point to it and give them three to six seconds to try the word again. If students still miss the word, tell them the word so the flow of the story isn't interrupted.

After reading the story, make a list of all the words students missed, and go over those words with them. You may use letter tiles to show students how to read the words.

Objectives
- Read aloud grade-level text with appropriate automaticity, prosody, accuracy, and rate.
- Decode words by applying grade-level word analysis skills.
- Track text from left to right.
- Turn pages sequentially.

 **20** minutes

REVIEW: Digraphs
Students will work online independently to

   ► Practice the digraphs *ch*, *–ck*, *sh*, *th*, and *wh*.

Help students locate the online activities and provide support as needed.

Objectives
- Identify individual sounds in words.
- Identify and use the digraph *ch*.
- Identify and use the digraph *–ck*.
- Identify and use the digraph *sh*.
- Identify and use the digraph *th*.
- Identify and use the digraph *wh*.

Offline Alternative

No computer access? Have students name words that have the digraphs *ch*, *–ck*, *sh*, *th*, and *wh*, such as *chum*, *neck*, *shop*, *thin*, *that*, and *when*. You might also have them spell words that have the digraphs *ch*, *–ck*, *sh*, *th*, and *wh*.

Getting Stronger: Capitalize and Punctuate Sentences

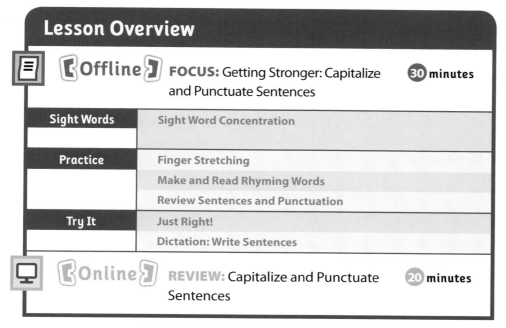

Lesson Overview

Offline — **FOCUS:** Getting Stronger: Capitalize and Punctuate Sentences — **30** minutes

Sight Words	Sight Word Concentration
Practice	Finger Stretching
	Make and Read Rhyming Words
	Review Sentences and Punctuation
Try It	Just Right!
	Dictation: Write Sentences

Online — **REVIEW:** Capitalize and Punctuate Sentences — **20** minutes

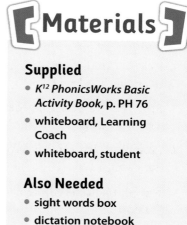

Materials

Supplied

- *K¹² PhonicsWorks Basic Activity Book,* p. PH 76
- whiteboard, Learning Coach
- whiteboard, student

Also Needed

- sight words box
- dictation notebook
- index cards (8)

Advance Preparation

Gather two sets of the sight word cards that students have yet to master.

For Review Sentences and Punctuation, print each of the following words on index cards, using one card per word:

- ▶ *The*
- ▶ *duck*
- ▶ *can*
- ▶ *quack.*
- ▶ *the*
- ▶ *duck*
- ▶ *can*
- ▶ *quack*

 **30 minutes**

FOCUS: Getting Stronger: Capitalize and Punctuate Sentences

Work **together** with students to complete offline Sight Words, Practice, and Try It activities.

Sight Words

Sight Word Concentration

Help students review sight words.

Objectives
- Read sight words.
- Spell sight words.
- Write sight words.

1. Gather the two sets of sight word cards.

2. Scramble both sets of sight word cards and place them face down on the table or floor.

3. Turn over two cards at a time; take turns with students. If the cards match, the person turning over the matching cards reads the word and uses it in a sentence. If the cards don't match, the person turns them back over.

4. Remove and save the matching cards.

5. Continue the activity until all the cards are paired.

6. Have students read all the words.

7. Take the stack of words that students read correctly and dictate each word to them.

8. Have students write each word or spell it aloud.

TIP If students have difficulty with any sight words, let them work at their own pace to really master these words.

Practice

Finger Stretching

Use finger stretching to help students identify individual sounds in words.

Objectives
- Identify individual sounds in words.
- Produce rhyming words.
- Identify complete sentences.
- Capitalize the first word in a sentence.
- Use periods to end telling sentences.

1. **Say:** Let's review finger stretching. In the word *than*, the first sound is /th/, the next sound is /ă/, and the last sound is /n/. I will finger stretch each sound as I say it. Then I'll say the word while pulling my fist toward my body.

2. Finger stretch the word *than* for students.

3. **Say:** I'm going to say words with several sounds in them. You'll say each word and then finger stretch it while you say each sound in the word.

4. Say the following words and have students finger stretch them. After they finger stretch each word, ask them the question for that word.

   ▸ *shop* /sh/ /ŏ/ /p/   What is the middle sound? /ŏ/
   ▸ *dish* /d/ /ĭ/ /sh/   What is the last sound? /sh/
   ▸ *witch* /w/ /ĭ/ /ch/   What is the last sound? /ch/
   ▸ *match* /m/ /ă/ /ch/   What is the middle sound? /ă/
   ▸ *catch* /k/ /ă/ /ch/   What is the middle sound? /ă/
   ▸ *sock* /s/ /ŏ/ /k/   What is the last sound? /k/

 Refer to the *K¹² PhonicsWorks* DVD for a demonstration of finger stretching.

Make and Read Rhyming Words

Have students make and read words that rhyme.

1. Gather students' whiteboard and dry-erase marker.

2. Say the following words to students: *batch* and *patch*.

   Say: How are these two words alike? The words have the same last sound /ch/.

3. Write the word *batch* on students' whiteboard and have them read it.

4. Replace the letter *b* with the letter *p,* and have students read the new word *patch.*

5. Repeat this procedure with the letters *m, c, l,* and *th* to make the words *match, catch, latch,* and *thatch.*

6. Say the following words to students: *sack* and *pack.*

   Say: How are these two words alike? The words have the same last sound /k/.

7. Write the word *sack* on students' whiteboard and have them read it.

8. Replace the letter *s* with the letter *p,* and have students read the new word *pack.*

9. Have students write the new word *pack* under *sack.*

10. Repeat this procedure with the letters *t, b, l, J, h, qu,* and *wh* to make the words *tack, back, lack, Jack, hack, quack,* and *whack.*

Review Sentences and Punctuation

Help students review sentences and the use of punctuation.

1. Gather the index cards you prepared, and place them in front of students so that they make two sentences: *the duck can quack* and *The duck can quack.*

2. **Say:** Let's review the rules telling and asking sentences must follow.

   ▸ To begin a sentence, use a capital letter in the first word.
   ▸ To end a telling sentence, add a period to mark the end of the sentence.
   ▸ To end an asking sentence, add a question mark to the end of the sentence.

3. Point to each group of words and ask students the following questions:

   ▸ How are these groups of words alike? Both have the same words in the same order.
   ▸ How are these groups of words different? One group is missing the capital letter and the period.
   ▸ Point to the group of words that is not written correctly. What is needed to make the sentence correct? Capitalize the letter *t* in the first word. Add a period after *quack*.

4. Read the sentence *The duck can quack.* aloud to students. Have students

   ▸ Read the sentence along with you.
   ▸ Touch the capital letter that signals the beginning of the sentence.
   ▸ Touch the period that signals the end of the sentence.

5. Scramble the index cards in the sentence *The duck can quack.* Have students

   ▸ Rearrange the words to make a sentence.
   ▸ Touch each word in the sentence as they read it aloud.
   ▸ Point to the capital letter at the beginning of the sentence.
   ▸ Point to the period at the end of the sentence.
   ▸ Write the sentence on their whiteboard.

6. Help students if they have difficulty arranging the index cards correctly to make a sentence.

   Say: Read the sentence aloud. Does it make sense?

7. Point to any word that seems out of place and state the following:

   ▸ What is this word?
   ▸ Find a word that would make better sense.
   ▸ Switch the words. Now read the sentence.
   ▸ Does it make sense now?

8. Ask students the following questions if they continue to have difficulty:

   ▸ What is special about the first word in a sentence? It begins with a capital letter.
   ▸ What is special about the end of a telling sentence? It ends with a period.
   ▸ What is special about the end of an asking sentence? It ends with a question mark.

Try It

Just Right!

Have students complete page PH 76 in *K¹² PhonicsWorks Basic Activity Book* for more practice punctuating sentences. Have students read the sentences aloud, rewrite the first word in each sentence using a capital letter, and put a period at the end of the sentence.

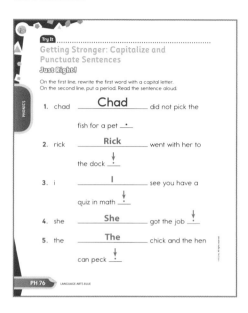

Dictation: Write Sentences

Use sentences to help students identify individual sounds in words.

1. Gather a pencil and the dictation notebook. Say the sentence, *Seth had one sock.* Then give these directions to students:

   ▸ Repeat the sentence.
   ▸ Write the sentence in your notebook.
   ▸ Read the sentence aloud.

2. When students have finished, write the following sentence on your whiteboard: *Seth had one sock.*

3. Have them compare their answer to your correct version.

4. Repeat this procedure with the sentence, *Mitch had such a big sack.*

   ▸ If students make an error and don't see it, help them correct their mistake by having them finger stretch the sounds in the word they missed.
   ▸ If students are having difficulty selecting the correct letters or sounds, review those letters or sounds that are confusing them.
   ▸ If students have difficulty with first, middle, and last sounds, have them finger stretch the sounds in words.

 **20 minutes**

REVIEW: Capitalize and Punctuate Sentences

Students will work online independently to

▶ Practice capitalizing and punctuating sentences.
▶ Practice decoding text by reading sentences.

Help students locate the online activities and provide support as needed.

Offline Alternative

No computer access? Say telling and asking sentences to students, such as *It was ham and hash.* and *Was it ham and hash?* Have students tell you which word in each sentence should begin with a capital letter. Have them say where the period or question mark should go. You might also have students write short telling and asking sentences in their dictation notebook, on their whiteboard, or on a sheet of paper. Make sure students begin each sentence with a capital letter and place a period or question mark at the end.

 Objectives
- Identify complete sentences.
- Capitalize the first word in a sentence.
- Use question marks to end asking sentences.
- Use periods to end telling sentences.
- Identify individual sounds in words.
- Read aloud grade-level text with appropriate automaticity, prosody, accuracy, and rate.
- Decode words by applying grade-level word analysis skills.

Getting Stronger: Write Sentences

Lesson Overview

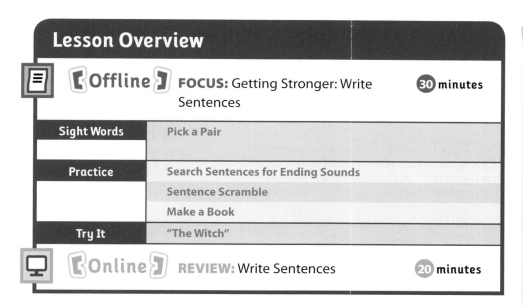

	Offline FOCUS: Getting Stronger: Write Sentences	**30** minutes
Sight Words	Pick a Pair	
Practice	Search Sentences for Ending Sounds	
	Sentence Scramble	
	Make a Book	
Try It	"The Witch"	
	Online REVIEW: Write Sentences	**20** minutes

Materials

Supplied
- *K¹² PhonicsWorks Readers Basic 9*, pp. 7–12
- whiteboard, Learning Coach
- whiteboard, student
- Tile Kit

Also Needed
- sight words box
- index cards (10)
- paper, construction
- paper, printer
- stapler

Advance Preparation

For Sentence Scramble, print each of the following words on index cards, using one card per word: *what, is, which, this, a, dish, big, cat, the,* and *rock.*

For Make a Book, create a blank book with two sheets of printer paper and a construction paper cover. Fold the pages in half and staple them along the left edge.

 **30** minutes

FOCUS: Getting Stronger: Write Sentences

Work **together** with students to complete offline Sight Words, Practice, and Try It activities.

Sight Words

Pick a Pair

Play a card game with students for more practice with sight words.

1. Gather the sight word cards that students are reviewing. Choose two words and place the cards on the table.

2. Ask questions to help students identify each word. For example, if the words are *or* and *one*, you could ask, "Which word names a number?" If the words are *on* and *but*, you could ask, "Which word is the opposite of *off*?"

3. Continue the activity until students identify all the words.

4. Take the stack of words that students read correctly and dictate each word to them.

5. Have students write each word or spell it aloud.

 Objectives
- Read sight words.
- Spell sight words.
- Write sight words.

Practice

Search Sentences for Ending Sounds

Have students practice identifying **ending sounds** in words that are in a sentence.

1. **Say:** I'm going to say a special ending sound that is in a word. You will repeat that sound and the word. The first sound is /m/, as in the word *Sam*.

2. Have students say the target ending sound /m/ and the word *Sam*.

   Say: Now I will read a sentence. Repeat the sentence and tell me the word that has the same sound. The first sentence is *The light is dim.* Which word in the sentence has the special sound? *dim*

3. Have students repeat the sentence and say the word.

4. Redirect students if they don't name the correct word.

   Say: Let me say the sentence again. Remember, you're listening for the ending sound [special sound].

5. Guide students if they have difficulty. Say two words from the sentence and have them choose the one with the target ending sound.

6. Follow the same procedure with the following words and sentences:

   ▶ /sh/, as in *sash*   *Dad got a fish.* *fish*
   ▶ /k/, as in *duck*   *I will pick one.* *pick*
   ▶ /ch/, as in *fetch*   *Can you catch?* *catch*
   ▶ /th/, as in *math*   *A rock is on the path.* *path*
   ▶ /p/, as in *ship*   *Can you chop this?* *chop*

 Objectives
- Identify ending sounds in words.
- Identify complete sentences.
- Capitalize the first word in a sentence.
- Use question marks to end asking sentences.
- Use periods to end telling sentences.
- Read aloud grade-level text with appropriate automaticity, prosody, accuracy, and rate.
- Decode words by applying grade-level word analysis skills.
- Use context and sentence structure to determine meaning of words, phrases, and/or sentences.
- Write words by applying grade-level phonics knowledge.
- Follow three-step directions.

Sentence Scramble

Have students build sentences by rearranging words to help them learn the meaning of words and phrases.

1. Gather the index cards you prepared, a pencil, and the dictation notebook.

2. Place the index cards in front of students.

3. Point to each word and have students read it aloud with you.

4. Arrange three of the cards as follows: *what is this*.

5. Have students say if the words make sense. Tell them that the words make an asking sentence.

6. Write the words as a sentence on students' whiteboard. Be sure to capitalize the first letter in *what* and insert the proper punctuation at the end of the sentence.

7. Point out the capital letter and the question mark in the sentence.

8. Read the sentence with students.

9. **Say:** I am going to put these words back with the others. Choose some word cards and put them together to make a different sentence. Read the words in the order you put them.

   ‣ Does your sentence make sense? Is it an asking or a telling sentence?
   ‣ Now write the sentence. Be sure to start with a capital letter. Remember to put a period or a question mark at the end.

10. Return the words to the original group and repeat the steps so that students can create and write one or more sentences.

11. Help students if they have difficulty arranging the words correctly to make a sentence.

    Say: Read the sentence aloud. Does it make sense?

12. Point to any word that seems out of place and state the following:

    ‣ What is this word?
    ‣ Find a word that would make better sense.
    ‣ Switch the words. Now read the sentence.
    ‣ Does it make sense now?

Make a Book

Have students practice writing words and sentences by having them create a book of their favorite words. Grab your whiteboard, dry-erase marker, and a pencil.

1. **Say:** You are going to make your own book. Let's think of some sentences to write in your book. Name three of your favorite letters. I will write those letters on my whiteboard.

2. Write the letters on the whiteboard.

   Say: Think of a word that starts with the sound for each letter and write it on your paper. Use each word in a sentence and write it on your paper.

3. Give students the blank book.

   ▸ Have students write "My Book, by [students' name(s)]" on the cover.
   ▸ Have students copy one sentence each on pages 2, 4, and 6.
   ▸ Have students draw a picture for each sentence on pages 3, 5, and 7.
   ▸ Have students illustrate the cover. When they have finished, read the book with them.

4. Help students if they make a spelling mistake. Write the correct spelling above the word and have them make the correction.

   Say: That was a good try, but the word is spelled like this.

5. Guide students if they have trouble thinking of or writing sentences: Have them write only a single word on each page and then illustrate it.

TIP To help students write words that are unfamiliar, tell them the word and help them spell it so that writing becomes a pleasure for them instead of a chore.

TIP Depending upon the amount of time students have for this activity, you may want to have them finish the illustrations later.

Try It

"The Witch"
Have students read "The Witch" on page 7 of *K¹² PhonicsWorks Readers Basic 9.*

Students should read the story silently once or twice before reading the story aloud. When students miss a word that can be sounded out, point to it and give them three to six seconds to try the word again. If students still miss the word, tell them the word so the flow of the story isn't interrupted.

After reading the story, make a list of all the words students missed, and go over those words with them. You may use letter tiles to show students how to read the words.

Objectives
- Read aloud grade-level text with appropriate automaticity, prosody, accuracy, and rate.
- Decode words by applying grade-level word analysis skills.
- Track text from left to right.
- Turn pages sequentially.

 **20 minutes**

REVIEW: **Write Sentences**

Students will work online independently to

▶ Practice making sentences.

Help students locate the online activities and provide support as needed.

Offline Alternative

No computer access? Say telling and asking sentences to students, such as *It is a pet rat.* and *Is it a pet rat?* Have students tell you which word in each sentence should begin with a capital letter. Have them say where the period or question mark should go. You might also have students write short telling and asking sentences in their dictation notebook, on their whiteboard, or on a sheet of paper. Make sure students begin each sentence with a capital letter and place a period or question mark at the end.

 Objectives

- Identify complete sentences.
- Capitalize the first word in a sentence.
- Use question marks to end asking sentences.
- Use periods to end telling sentences.
- Identify individual sounds in words.

Unit Checkpoint

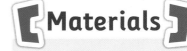

Lesson Overview

[Online] **REVIEW:** Short Vowels, Digraphs, and Sentences — **20** minutes

[Offline] **UNIT CHECKPOINT:** Getting Stronger: Short Vowels, Digraphs, and Sentences — **30** minutes

[Materials]

Supplied
- *K¹² PhonicsWorks Basic Assessments,* pp. PH 169–174

Objectives

- Identify and use the sound /ă/.
- Identify and use the sound /ĕ/.
- Identify and use the sound /ĭ/.
- Identify and use the sound /ŏ/.
- Identify and use the sound /ŭ/.
- Identify short vowel sounds.
- Identify and use the digraph *ch*.
- Identify and use the digraph *–ck*.
- Identify and use the digraph *sh*.
- Identify and use the digraph *th*.
- Identify and use the digraph *wh*.
- Identify complete sentences.
- Capitalize the first word in a sentence.
- Use question marks to end asking sentences.
- Use periods to end telling sentences.

- Read, write, and spell words containing short vowel sounds.
- Identify individual sounds in words.
- Given the letter, identify the most common sound.
- Given the sound, identify the most common letter or letters.
- Read instructional-level text with 90% accuracy.
- Read aloud grade-level text with appropriate automaticity, prosody, accuracy, and rate.
- Write words by applying grade-level phonics knowledge.
- Write sight words.
- Read sight words.

[Online] **20** minutes

REVIEW: Short Vowels, Digraphs, and Sentences

Students will review the short vowel sounds /ă/, /ĕ/, /ĭ/, /ŏ/, and /ŭ/ for the letters *a, e, i, o,* and *u*; the digraphs *ch, –ck, sh, th,* and *wh*; and sentences to prepare for the Unit Checkpoint. Help students locate the online activities and provide support as needed.

 **30 minutes**

UNIT CHECKPOINT: Getting Stronger: Short Vowels, Digraphs, and Sentences

Explain that students are going to show what they have learned about sounds, letters, and words.

1. Give students the Unit Checkpoint pages for the Getting Stronger: Short Vowels, Digraphs, and Sentences unit and print the Unit Checkpoint Answer Key, if you'd like.

2. Use the instructions below to help administer the Checkpoint to students. On the Answer Key or another sheet of paper, note student answers to oral response questions to help with scoring the Checkpoint later.

3. Use the Answer Key to score the Checkpoint, and then enter the results online.

Part 1. Say Sounds Have students read across the rows from left to right and say a sound that the letter, letters, or digraph makes. Note any sounds they say incorrectly.

Part 2. Word Dissection For each word, say the sound students should identify. Have them read the word aloud and circle the letter or group of letters that spells the requested sound.

21. *beginning sound*

22. *ending sound*

23. *ending sound*

24. *beginning sound*

25. *middle sound*

Part 3. Finger Stretching Say each word to students. Have them say each word and finger stretch the sounds. Note any words they finger stretch incorrectly.

26. *shop*

27. *quick*

28. *whiz*

29. *shock*

30. *thin*

31. *chat*

Part 4. Writing: Periods and Question Marks Have students read each sentence aloud and write a period or question mark to complete the sentence.

Part 5. Read Aloud Listen to students read the sentences aloud. Count and note the number of words they read correctly.

Part 6. Say Letters
Say each sound. Have students say the letter or letters that make that sound. Note any incorrect responses.

39. /r/	**48.** /ă/
40. /ĕ/	**49.** /ĭ/
41. /w/	**50.** /ŏ/
42. /ŏ/	**51.** /h/
43. /y/	**52.** /kw/
44. /th/	**53.** /v/
45. /w/	**54.** /j/
46. /sh/	**55.** /g/
47. /ch/	**56.** /ks/

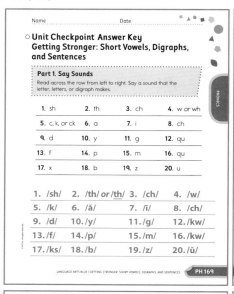

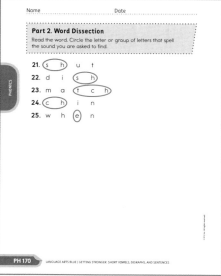

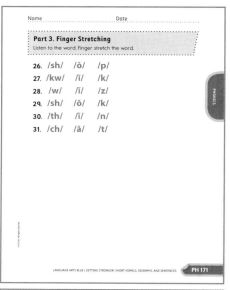

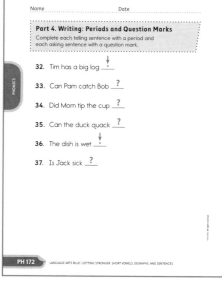

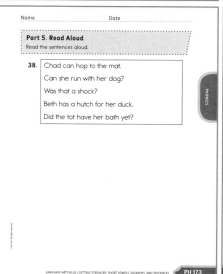

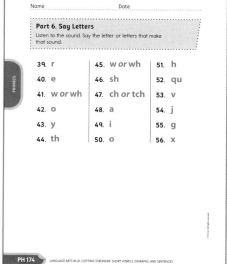

Introduce Ending –*s*

Unit Overview

In this unit, students will
- ► Learn the sight words *does*, *why*, and *one*.
- ► Review lowercase and uppercase letters.
- ► Learn base words and the endings –*s* and –*es*.
- ► Identify individual sounds in words.
- ► Build words and make rhyming words.

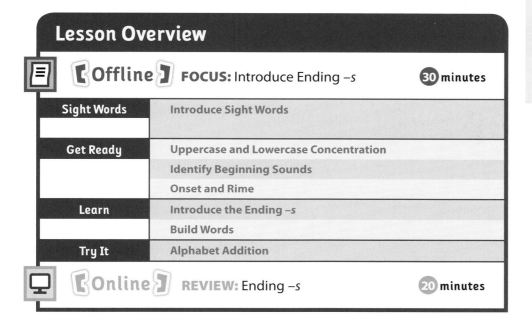

Lesson Overview

Offline FOCUS: Introduce Ending –*s*   **30** minutes

Sight Words	Introduce Sight Words
Get Ready	Uppercase and Lowercase Concentration
	Identify Beginning Sounds
	Onset and Rime
Learn	Introduce the Ending –*s*
	Build Words
Try It	Alphabet Addition

Online REVIEW: Ending –*s*   **20** minutes

Materials

Supplied
- *K¹² PhonicsWorks Basic Activity Book*, p. PH 77
- whiteboard, student
- Tile Kit

Also Needed
- sight words box
- dictation notebook
- index cards (12)

Advance Preparation

For Uppercase and Lowercase Letter Concentration, print matching pairs of 6 uppercase and lowercase letters on 12 individual index cards, using one card per letter. Select letters that students need to review or use these 6 pairs of letters: *K, k; U, u; W, w; I, i; S, s;* and *Z, z.*

 Offline 🕙 minutes

FOCUS: Introduce Ending –*s*

Work **together** with students to complete offline Sight Words, Get Ready, Learn, and Try It activities.

Sight Words ....

Introduce Sight Words

Help students learn the sight words *does*, *why*, and *one*.

1. Gather the sight word cards *does*, *why*, and *one*.

2. Show students the *does* card.

3. **Say:** This is the word *does*. We see this word so often that we want to be able to read and spell it quickly without thinking about it. Look closely at the word *does*. Spell the word *does* aloud. Take a picture of the word *does* in your mind. When you think you can spell *does* yourself, turn the card over and use your letter tiles to spell the word *does*. Check the card to see if you spelled the *does* correctly. Read aloud the word you spelled with the letter tiles.

4. Repeat the activity with the remaining sight words.

5. Chart students' progress on the back of each card.

   ▸ Divide the back of the card into two columns.
   ▸ Label the first column "Read" and the second column "Spell."
   ▸ Record the dates that students read or spell the word correctly. When students can read and spell the word correctly three times in a row, they have mastered the word. You may want to put a star or sticker on the card when they have mastered that word.

6. Add the cards to students' sight words box.

TIP Sight words can be very difficult for some students. Let students work at their own pace and really master these words, as they occur frequently in reading and writing.

> **Objectives**
> * Read sight words.
> * Spell sight words.

Get Ready

Uppercase and Lowercase Concentration
Help students practice pairing uppercase and lowercase letters.

1. Gather the uppercase and lowercase letter pairs of index cards you prepared.

2. Mix up the index cards and place them face down on the table or floor.

3. **Say:** Let's practice matching uppercase and lowercase letters. We can also call these letters big letters and small letters.

4. **Say:** You'll turn over the cards two at a time. If you turn over a card that has a lowercase letter and a card that has the uppercase form of the same letter, the cards match and you can keep them. If the cards don't match, turn them back over.

5. Continue the activity until all the cards are paired.

Objectives
- Identify letters of the alphabet.
- Match capital letters to lowercase letters.
- Identify beginning sounds in words.
- Identify a word when given the onset and rime.
- Identify short vowel sounds.

Identify Beginning Sounds
Help students identify beginning sounds in words.

1. **Say:** I'm going to say a word. Listen for the beginning sound. Then tell me the sound.

   ▶ For example, if I say *mom*, you will say /m/ because the first sound you hear in *mom* is /m/.
   ▶ Now it's your turn. Listen to the word I say. You repeat the word and then tell me the first sound in the word.

2. **Say:** The word is *mop*.

3. If students incorrectly identify the beginning sound, say the word again and present the following:

   ▶ What sound do you hear at the beginning of *mop*?
   ▶ Say the word *man*.
   ▶ Do you hear the sound /m/ at the beginning of this word?
   ▶ Say the word *mat*.
   ▶ Do you hear the sound /m/ at the beginning of *mat*?
   ▶ Can you think of another word that starts with the sound /m/?

4. Suggest a clue word if students need prompting. For example,

   Say: I am thinking of a word that starts with the sound /m/. It is another name we use for *cash*. Can you guess the word? *money*

5. Repeat the procedure, using the following words to help students recognize beginning sounds:

   ▶ *boy* /b/   ▶ *which* /w/
   ▶ *see* /s/   ▶ *olive* /ŏ/
   ▶ *third* /th/   ▶ *chain* /ch/
   ▶ *apple* /ă/   ▶ *shape* /sh/

TIP If students struggle, encourage them to name another word that begins with the same sound.

Onset and Rime

Help students put together words that are broken down into parts by onset and rime.

1. **Say:** I'm going to break a word into two parts. Your job is to put the parts together and say the words. If the first part of a word is /sh/ and the last part of the word is *ape*, then the whole word is *shape*: /sh/ . . . *ape* . . . *shape*.

2. Say the following pairs of word parts. Have students tell you the word that each pair forms.

   ▸ /ch/ . . . *air* chair
   ▸ /th/ . . . *ick* thick
   ▸ /s/ . . . *it* sit
   ▸ /r/ . . . *oad* road

Learn

Introduce the Ending –*s*

Have students make plural words by adding the letter *s* to the end of base words.

1. Place the following letter tiles at the top of students' whiteboard: *a, c, d, e, g, i, o, p,* and *t*.

2. Place two *s* letter tiles at the bottom of students' whiteboard.

3. Make the word *cat* and point to it.

   Say: This is the word *cat*.

   ▸ When I say the word *cat*, I am talking about one *cat*.
   ▸ When I say the word *cats*, I am talking about more than one *cat*.

4. Make the word *cats* and point to it.

   Say: To make the word *cats*, I put the letter *s* at the end of the word *cat*.

5. Have students touch and say the word *cats*.

   Say: The word we start with before we add an ending is called the **base word**. We changed the base word *cat* to *cats*. Adding the ending –*s* tells us there is more than one *cat*.

6. Make the word *pig* and point to it.

   Say: This is the word *pig*. Touch and say the word *pig*.

   ▸ When we say the word *pig*, how many pigs do you think we mean? *one*
   ▸ What do we need to add to the word *pig* to make it mean more than one pig? *We need to add the letter s to the end of the word.*

7. Have students add the letter *s* to the end of the word *pig* to make the word *pigs*. Have them draw a line under the base word *pig*.

8. Continue the procedure to make the words *dogs* and *pets*.

Objectives
- Identify ending sounds in words.
- Read, write, and spell words containing the ending –*s*.
- Blend sounds to create words.
- Identify individual sounds in words.
- Write words by applying grade-level phonics knowledge.

Build Words

Help students use letters and sounds to build words.

1. Place the following letter tiles at the top of students' whiteboard: *a, m, o, p, s,* and *t.*

2. Draw four horizontal lines across the middle of students' whiteboard to represent the sounds in a word.

3. **Say:** Let's use letters and sounds to build the word *mats.*

4. Have students finger stretch the sounds in *mats.*

5. Have students

   ► Identify the first, next, and last sounds in *mats.*
   ► Choose the corresponding letter for each of the sounds.
   ► Move the letters to the correct lines on their whiteboard.

6. Guide students with these questions:

   ► What is the first sound in *mats?* /m/
   Which line does the letter for that sound go on? the first one
   ► What is the next sound in *mats?* /ă/
   Which line does the letter for that sound go on? the second one
   ► What is the next sound in *mats?* /t/
   Which line does the letter for that sound go on? the third one
   ► What's the last sound in *mats?* /s/
   Which line does the letter for that sound go on? the last one

7. Redirect students if they select the incorrect letter.

   Say: That sound is in the word [word], and it is the [first, second, third, fourth] sound. We want the sound [target sound].

   Continue until students select the correct letter.

8. Have students touch and say the word.

9. Have them say the word as they use a dry-erase marker to write the word on the whiteboard.

10. Repeat the activity to build the following word: *pots.* /p/ /ŏ/ /t/ /s/

Try It •

Alphabet Addition

Have students complete page PH 77 in *K¹² PhonicsWorks Basic Activity Book* for more practice with the ending –s. Have students add the letters together to make a word, write it, and read the complete word aloud.

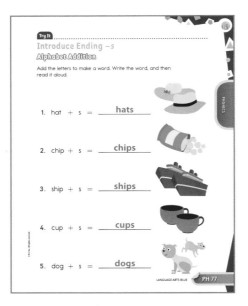

Try It ....
Introduce Ending –s
Alphabet Addition

Add the letters to make a word. Write the word, and then read it aloud.

1. hat + s = _____ hats
2. chip + s = _____ chips
3. ship + s = _____ ships
4. cup + s = _____ cups
5. dog + s = _____ dogs

LANGUAGE ARTS BLUE   PH 77

> ### Objectives
> - Read, write, and spell words containing the ending –s.

 **Online** **20** minutes

REVIEW: Ending –s

Students will work online independently to

▸ Practice the ending –s.
▸ Practice decoding text by reading sentences.

Help students locate the online activities and provide support as needed.

___

Offline Alternative

No computer access? Read the following words to students: *bat*, *ball*, *hat*, and *slug*. Have students add the ending –s to each word, and say and spell the new word aloud: *bats*, *balls*, *hats*, and *slugs*.

> ### Objectives
> - Identify individual sounds in words.
> - Identify ending sounds in words.
> - Read, write, and spell words containing the ending –s.
> - Read aloud grade-level text with appropriate automaticity, prosody, accuracy, and rate.
> - Decode words by applying grade-level word analysis skills.

Practice Ending –s

Lesson Overview

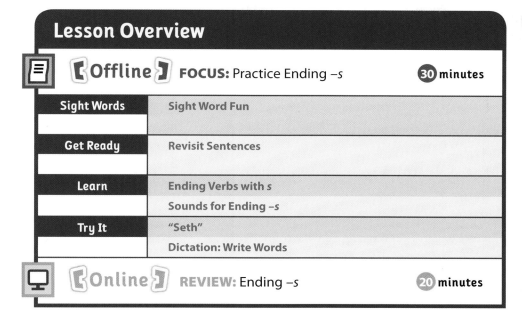

[Offline] **FOCUS:** Practice Ending –s   **30** minutes

Sight Words	Sight Word Fun
Get Ready	Revisit Sentences
Learn	Ending Verbs with *s*
	Sounds for Ending –s
Try It	"Seth"
	Dictation: Write Words

[Online]   **REVIEW:** Ending –s   **20** minutes

[Materials]

Supplied
- *K¹² PhonicsWorks Readers Basic 9,* pp. 13–18
- *K¹² PhonicsWorks Readers Basic,* any volume
- whiteboard, Learning Coach
- whiteboard, student
- Tile Kit

Also Needed
- sight words box
- dictation notebook

Offline **30** minutes

FOCUS: Practice Ending –s

Work **together** with students to complete offline Sight Words, Get Ready, Learn, and Try It activities.

Sight Words ....

Sight Word Fun

Help students learn the sight words *does*, *why*, and *one*, and up to two additional sight words they have yet to master.

1. Gather the sight word cards *does*, *why*, and *one*, and up to two additional sight word cards.

2. Choose one sight word card to begin.

3. **Say:** Look at this word and take a picture of it in your mind. When you think you can spell the word yourself, turn the card over and use your letter tiles to spell the word.

4. After students spell the word, have them check the card to see if they spelled the word correctly.

   Say: Read aloud the word you spelled with the letter tiles.

5. Repeat the activity with the remaining sight words.

TIP Sight words can be very difficult for some students. Let them work at their own pace and really master these words.

> **Objectives**
> - Read sight words.
> - Spell sight words.

Get Ready ....

Revisit Sentences

Have students practice identifying telling and asking sentences in a story.

1. Have students choose one of their favorite stories from any volume of the *K¹² PhonicsWorks Readers Basic* and read that story aloud.

2. After students have read the story, turn to any page and underline a telling sentence.

   Say: I've drawn a line under a telling sentence on this page. I know that this sentence is a telling sentence because it begins with a capital letter and ends with a period.

   ▸ The first word in the sentence is [point to word and name it.].
   ▸ The sentence starts with the capital letter [point to letter and name it].
   ▸ The last word in the sentence is [point to word and name it], and it is followed by a period.

> **Objectives**
> - Identify complete sentences.
> - Capitalize the first word in a sentence.
> - Use periods to end telling sentences.

3. Have students choose telling sentences and do the following steps:

   ▸ Draw a line under a telling sentence.
   ▸ Touch and say the capital letter that signals the beginning of the sentence, and draw a circle around it.
   ▸ Touch and say the punctuation that signals the end of the sentence, and draw a circle around the period.

4. Redirect students if they identify a capital letter that begins a name rather than a sentence.

   Say: You are right. All names start with capital letters, but they do not always begin the sentence. Let's look for another capital letter that is at the beginning of the sentence.

Learn

Ending Verbs with *s*
Have students practice identifying verbs ending with the letter *s*. Grab students' whiteboard and the dry-erase marker.

1. **Say:** I'm going to write a sentence that includes the word *sit*. You will read the sentence to me and point to the word *sit*.

2. Write the following sentence on the whiteboard: *I sit on the mat.*

3. Have students point to the word *sit*.

4. **Say:** I'm going to write another sentence for you to read.

5. Write the following sentence on the whiteboard: *Ben sits on the mat.*

6. **Say:** When the letter *s* is added to some words, it makes the word mean more than one. This happens when the ending –*s* is added to a person, place, or thing, as in *boys*, *stores*, and *toys*. When the letter *s* is added to an action word, such as *sits*, *plays*, or *runs*, the letter *s* helps show what the person, place, or thing is doing.

7. **Say:** What happened to the word *sit* in this second sentence? The letter *s* was added to the end of the word.

8. **Say:** In this sentence, the word *sits* doesn't mean "more than one person sits." It just means the way we say that a person does something.

9. Have students do the following:

   ▸ Write the base word *sit*.
   ▸ Add the ending –*s* to the base word
   ▸ Underline the base word.
   ▸ Circle the ending –*s*.

10. Erase the board and repeat the activity with the following sentence pairs:

    ▸ *run*   We run to the shop.
      runs   Pat runs to the shop.
    ▸ *hit*   I hit the ball.
      hits   Pam hits the ball.
    ▸ *get*   You get to go.
      gets   Lee gets to go.

Objectives
- Identify individual sounds in words.
- Identify ending sounds in words.
- Read, write, and spell words containing the ending –*s*.

Sounds for Ending –s

Have students read words in which the ending –s makes the sounds /s/ and /z/.

1. Place the following letter tiles at the top of students' whiteboard: *a, b, c, e, g, h, i, n, p, t, u,* and *w.*

2. Place the following letter tile at the bottom of students' whiteboard: *s.*

3. Make the word *cat* and point to it.

4. Have students touch and say the word *cat.*

5. Make the word *cats* and point to it.

   Say: We make some sounds with a whisper and some sounds with our voice. Let's figure out whether the sound /s/ in *cats* is whispered or voiced. Say /s/ and put your fingers on the lump in your throat called your voice box. Do you feel your voice box vibrate? No, /s/ is a whispered sound because we don't use our voice box when we make the sound.

6. Have students
   - ▸ Touch and say the word. *cats*
   - ▸ Say the base word. *cat*
   - ▸ Touch the ending letter and say its sound. *s, /s/*

7. Make the word *bug* and point to it.

8. Have students touch and say the word *bug.*

9. Make the word *bugs* and point to it.

   Say: The letter *s* in *bugs* makes the sound /z/. Let's figure out whether the sound /z/ in *bugs* is whispered or voiced. Say the sound /z/ and put your fingers on the lump in your throat called your voice box. Do you feel your voice box vibrate? Yes, /z/ is a noisy sound because we use our voice box when we make the sound.

10. Have students
    - ▸ Touch and say the word. *bugs*
    - ▸ Say the base word. *bug*
    - ▸ Touch the ending letter and say its sound. *s, /z/*

11. Repeat the procedure with the following words:
    - ▸ *hats* hat, s, /s/
    - ▸ *wins* win, s, /z/
    - ▸ *pens* pen, s, /z/
    - ▸ *cups* cup, s, /s/

12. If students have difficulty distinguishing between the sound /s/ and the sound /z/, say the word pairs in the list below.

    Say: I will say two words. Your job is to listen for the **ending sound** in each word. After I say the words, repeat them. Then tell me which word ends in the sound /s/ and which word ends with the sound /z/.

    ► *hats* and *bugs* *hats, /s/; bugs, /z/*
    ► *pins* and *walks* *walks, /s/; pins, /z/*
    ► *sings* and *hops* *hops, /s/; sings, /z/*
    ► *mitts* and *swims* *mitts, /s/; swims, /z/*
    ► *books* and *plays* *books, /s/; plays, /z/*

Try It

"Seth"

Have students read "Seth" on page 13 of *K¹² PhonicsWorks Readers Basic 9.*

Students should read the story silently once or twice before reading the story aloud. When students miss a word that can be sounded out, point to it and give them three to six seconds to try the word again. If students still miss the word, tell them the word so the flow of the story isn't interrupted.

After reading the story, make a list of all the words students missed, and go over those words with them. You may use letter tiles to show students how to read the words.

Objectives
- Read aloud grade-level text with appropriate automaticity, prosody, accuracy, and rate.
- Decode words by applying grade-level word analysis skills.
- Track text from left to right.
- Turn pages sequentially.
- Write words by applying grade-level phonics knowledge.
- Follow three-step directions.

Dictation: Write Words

Have students practice identifying sounds and writing words.

1. Gather a pencil and the dictation notebook. Say the word *hats*. Then give these directions to students:

    ► Repeat the word.
    ► Write the word in your notebook.
    ► Read the word aloud.

2. When students have finished, write the following word on your whiteboard: *hats*.

3. Have them compare their answer to your correct version.

4. Repeat this procedure with the words *chins*, *runs*, and *shops*.

    ► If students make an error and don't see it, help them correct their mistake by having them finger stretch the sounds in the word they missed.
    ► If students are having difficulty selecting the correct letters or sounds, review those letters or sounds that are confusing them.
    ► If students have difficulty with first, middle, and last sounds, have them finger stretch the sounds in words.

 **minutes**

REVIEW: Ending –s

Students will work online independently to

► Practice the ending –s.

Help students locate the online activities and provide support as needed.

Offline Alternative

No computer access? Read the following words to students: *rat*, *nut*, *hen*, and *moth*. Have students add the ending –s to each word, and say and spell the new word aloud: *rats*, *nuts*, *hens*, and *moths*.

Introduce Ending –es

Lesson Overview

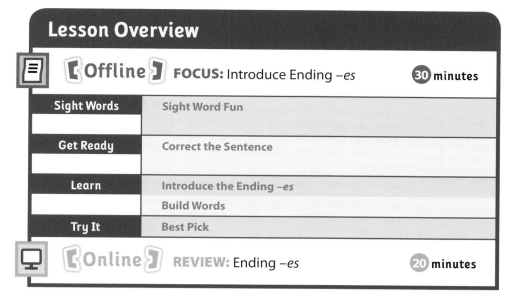

Offline FOCUS: Introduce Ending –es — **30** minutes

Sight Words	Sight Word Fun
Get Ready	Correct the Sentence
Learn	Introduce the Ending –es
	Build Words
Try It	Best Pick

Online REVIEW: Ending –es — **20** minutes

Materials

Supplied
- *K¹² PhonicsWorks Basic Activity Book,* p. PH 78
- whiteboard, Learning Coach
- whiteboard, student
- Tile Kit

Also Needed
- sight words box

 **Offline** **30** minutes

FOCUS: Introduce Ending –*es*

Work **together** with students to complete offline Sight Words, Get Ready, Learn, and Try It activities.

Sight Words

Sight Word Fun

Help students learn the sight words *does, why,* and *one,* and up to two additional sight words they have yet to master.

1. Gather the sight word cards *does, why,* and *one,* and up to two additional sight word cards.

2. Choose one sight word card to begin.

   Say: Look at this word and take a picture of it in your mind. When you think you can spell the word yourself, turn the card over and use your letter tiles to spell the word.

3. After students spell the word, have them check the card to see if they spelled the word correctly.

   Say: Read aloud the word you spelled with the letter tiles.

4. Repeat the activity with the remaining sight words.

TIP Sight words can be very difficult for some students. Let them work at their own pace and really master these words.

Objectives
- Read sight words.
- Spell sight words.

Get Ready

Correct the Sentence

Have students practice correcting capitalization and punctuation in sentences. Grab your whiteboard and dry-erase marker.

1. Write the following sentence without any capitalization or punctuation on your whiteboard: *the dog is big.*

2. Have students read the sentence aloud. Have them

   ▸ Cross out the lowercase letter at the beginning of the first word and write the capital letter.
   ▸ Add punctuation to the end of the sentence.

3. **Say:** Read the sentence again. How do you know this sentence is correct?
   The sentence is correct if it follows the rules. To begin any sentence, use a capital letter in the first word. To end a telling sentence, add a period to mark the end of the sentence. To end an asking sentence, add a question mark to the end of the sentence.

Objectives
- Identify complete sentences.
- Capitalize the first word in a sentence.
- Use question marks to end asking sentences.
- Use periods to end telling sentences.

4. Repeat the procedure for each of the sentences.

 ▸ *where did Tim go* Where did Tim go?
 ▸ *we can shop* We can shop.
 ▸ *is it the bus* Is it the bus?

5. Help students if they have difficulty identifying what is wrong with the sentence. Ask the following questions:

 ▸ What is special about the first word in a sentence?
 ▸ Does the first word in this sentence start with a capital letter?
 ▸ How can you change the sentence so it begins with a capital letter?
 ▸ What is special about the mark at the end of a sentence?

6. Guide students by asking one of the following questions if they continue having difficulty:

 ▸ Is this sentence a telling sentence or an asking sentence?
 ▸ Is the last word in the sentence followed by a period or a question mark?
 ▸ What mark do you put at the end of [a telling or an asking] sentence?

Learn

Introduce the Ending –es

Have students make words that end in the letters *es*.

1. Place the following letter tiles at the top of students' whiteboard: *b, ch, f, i, k, o, r, sh, ss, u, w, x*, and *zz*.

2. Place the *es* letter tile at the bottom of students' whiteboard.

3. Make the word *wish* and point to it.

 Say: This is the word *wish*.

 ▸ What sound do you hear at the end of *wish*? /sh/

4. **Say:** When a word ends with a double *z*, double *s, x, ch,* or *sh*, we need to add the ending *–es*. The ending *–es* makes the sound /iz/.

5. Put the *es* tile at the end of *wish* to make the word *wishes* and point to it.

 Say: This is the word *wishes*.

 ▸ Read the word. *wishes*
 ▸ What is the base word? *wish*
 ▸ What sound do you hear at the end of the base word? /sh/
 ▸ Touch and say the ending letters in the word. *es*
 ▸ What is the ending sound in the word? /iz/

6. Repeat the activity to build the following words:

 ▸ *fox* foxes, fox, /ks/, es, /iz/
 ▸ *kiss* kisses, kiss, /s/, es, /iz/
 ▸ *buzz* buzzes, buzz, /z/, es, /iz/
 ▸ *rich* riches, rich, /ch/, es, /iz/

Objectives
- Identify ending sounds in words.
- Read, write, and spell words containing the ending *–es*.
- Blend sounds to create words.
- Identify individual sounds in words.
- Write words by applying grade-level phonics knowledge.

Build Words

Help students use letters and sounds to build words.

1. Place the following letter tiles at the top of students' whiteboard: *a, d, es, i, sh, t,* and *x.*

2. Draw four horizontal lines across the middle of students' whiteboard to represent the sounds in a word.

3. **Say:** Let's use letters and sounds to build the word *dishes.*

4. Have students finger stretch the sounds in *dishes.*

5. Have students

   ▸ Identify the first, next, and last sounds in *dishes.*
   ▸ Choose the corresponding letter for each of the sounds.
   ▸ Move the letters to the correct lines on their whiteboard.

6. Guide students with these questions:

   ▸ What is the first sound in *dishes?* /d/
     Which line does the letter for that sound go on? the first one
   ▸ What is the next sound in *dishes?* /ĭ/
     Which line does the letter for that sound go on? the second one
   ▸ What is the next sound in *dishes?* /sh/
     Which line do the letters for that sound go on? the third one
   ▸ What's the last sound in *dishes?* /iz/
     Which line do the letters for that sound go on? the last one

7. Redirect students if they select the incorrect letter.

   Say: That sound is in the word [word], and it is the [first, second, third, fourth] sound. We want the sound [target sound].

   Continue until students select the correct letter.

8. Have students touch and say the word.

9. Have them say the word as they use a dry-erase marker to write the word on the whiteboard.

10. Repeat the activity to build the following word: *taxes.* /t/ /ă/ /ks/ /iz/

Try It ••

Best Pick

Have students complete page PH 78 in *K¹² PhonicsWorks Basic Activity Book* for more practice with the ending –*es*. Have students read the sentences aloud, circle the word that best completes the sentence, and write that word. Have them read the completed sentence aloud.

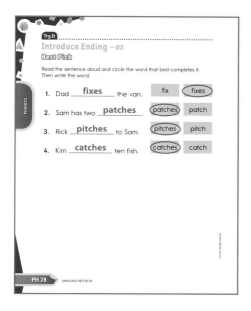

[Online] 20 minutes

REVIEW: Ending –*es*

Students will work online independently to

- ▸ Practice the ending –*es*.
- ▸ Practice decoding text by reading a story.

Help students locate the online activities and provide support as needed.

_____

Offline Alternative

No computer access? Read the following words to students: *buzz*, *ax*, *fox*, and *catch*. Have students add the ending –*es* to each word, spell the new word aloud, and say the ending sound in each word: *buzzes*, /iz/; *axes*, /iz/; *foxes*, /iz/; and *catches*, /iz/.

Objectives
- Identify individual sounds in words.
- Identify ending sounds in words.
- Read, write, and spell words containing the ending –*es*.
- Read aloud grade-level text with appropriate automaticity, prosody, accuracy, and rate.
- Decode words by applying grade-level word analysis skills.

Practice Ending –es

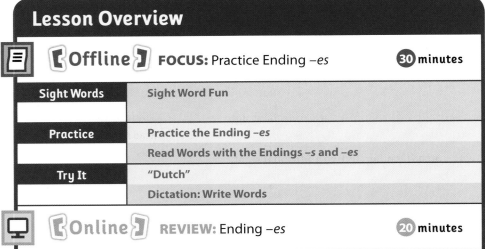

Lesson Overview

Offline FOCUS: Practice Ending –es — **30** minutes

Sight Words	Sight Word Fun
Practice	Practice the Ending –es
	Read Words with the Endings –s and –es
Try It	"Dutch"
	Dictation: Write Words

Online REVIEW: Ending –es — **20** minutes

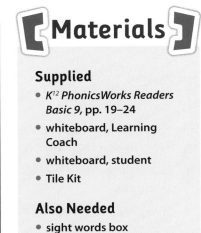

Materials

Supplied
- *K¹² PhonicsWorks Readers Basic 9,* pp. 19–24
- whiteboard, Learning Coach
- whiteboard, student
- Tile Kit

Also Needed
- sight words box
- dictation notebook

 **Offline** **30** minutes

FOCUS: Practice Ending –*es*

Work **together** with students to complete offline Sight Words, Practice, and Try It activities.

Sight Words

· ·

Sight Word Fun

Help students learn the sight words *does, why,* and *one,* and up to two additional sight words they have yet to master.

1. Gather the sight word cards *does, why,* and *one,* and up to two additional sight word cards.

2. Choose one sight word card to begin.

   Say: Look at this word and take a picture of it in your mind. When you think you can spell the word yourself, turn the card over and use your letter tiles to spell the word.

3. After students spell the word, have them check the card to see if they spelled the word correctly.

   Say: Read aloud the word you spelled with the letter tiles.

4. Repeat the activity with the remaining sight words.

   (TIP) Sight words can be very difficult for some students. Let them work at their own pace and really master these words.

> **Objectives**
> * Read sight words.
> * Spell sight words.

Practice

· ·

Practice the Ending –*es*

Have students make words that end in the letters *es*.

1. Place the following letter tiles at the top of students' whiteboard: *a, b, c, d, f, h, i, m, sh, ss, tch, u, w, x,* and *zz*.

2. Place the *es* letter tile at the bottom of students' whiteboard.

3. Make the word *buzz* and point to it.

   Say: This is the word *buzz*. What sound do you hear at the end of buzz? /z/

4. Put the *es* tile at the end of *buzz* to make the word *buzzes* and point to it.

   Say: This is the word *buzzes*.

   ▸ Read the word. *buzzes*
   ▸ What is the base word? *buzz*
   ▸ Touch and say the ending letters in the word. *es*
   ▸ What is the ending sound in the word? /iz/

> **Objectives**
> * Identify ending sounds in words.
> * Read, write, and spell words containing the ending –*s*.
> * Read, write, and spell words containing the ending –*es*.

5. **Say:** Remember, words that end with double *z*, double *s*, *x*, *ch*, or *sh* need the ending –*es*.

6. Have students repeat the procedure, adding the ending –*es* to the following words:

   ▶ *match* matches, match, /ch/, es, /iz/
   ▶ *dish* dishes, dish, /sh/, es, /iz/
   ▶ *ax* axes, ax, /ks/, es, /iz/
   ▶ *catch* catches, catch, /ch/, es, /iz/
   ▶ *hitch* hitches, hitch, /ch/, es, /iz/
   ▶ *miss* misses, miss, /s/, es, /iz/
   ▶ *wish* wishes, wish, /sh/, es, /iz/
   ▶ *fix* fixes, fix, /ks/, es, /iz/

Read Words Ending in –s and –es

Have students practice reading words with the endings –*s* and –*es*. Grab students' whiteboard and the dry-erase marker.

1. Write the word *bugs* on the whiteboard. Have students

   ▶ Read the word. bugs
   ▶ Say the base word. bug
   ▶ Touch and say the ending letter or letters in the word. s
   ▶ Say the ending sound in the word. /z/

2. Repeat the procedure with the following words:

   ▶ *rats* rat, s, /s/
   ▶ *foxes* fox, es, /iz/
   ▶ *runs* run, s, /z/
   ▶ *picks* pick, s, /s/
   ▶ *pitches* pitch, es, /iz/
   ▶ *boxes* box, es, /iz/
   ▶ *paths* path, s, /s/

3. Point to the word if students struggle because they can't identify the base word.

   Say: What sound do you hear at the end of the word? What letter makes the ending sound [sound] in the [word]? Answers will vary.

4. Take away the ending –*s* or –*es* from the word if students continue to have difficulty.

   Say: Now you are left with the base word. Read the base word.

5. Put the ending –*s* or –*es* back on the base word.

Say: Read the new word.

> ▶ What is the base word?
> ▶ What is the ending?
> ▶ What sound does the ending make?

TIP If students struggle because they cannot see the difference between a base word and the word with the ending –*s* or –*es*, align the base word and the word with the ending directly above each other so students can see that both words contain the same letters. Point to each word and have students read it. Have them say how the words are alike and different.

Try It ··

"Dutch"

Have students read "Dutch" on page 19 of *K¹² PhonicsWorks Readers Basic 9.*

Students should read the story silently once or twice before reading the story aloud. When students miss a word that can be sounded out, point to it and give them three to six seconds to try the word again. If students still miss the word, tell them the word so the flow of the story isn't interrupted.

After reading the story, make a list of all the words students missed, and go over those words with them. You may use letter tiles to show students how to read the words.

Objectives

- Read aloud grade-level text with appropriate automaticity, prosody, accuracy, and rate.
- Decode words by applying grade-level word analysis skills.
- Track text from left to right.
- Turn pages sequentially.
- Write words by applying grade-level phonics knowledge.
- Follow three-step directions.

Dictation: Write Words

Have students practice identifying sounds and writing words.

1. Gather a pencil and the dictation notebook. Say the word *bats.* Then give these directions to students:

> ▶ Repeat the word.
> ▶ Write the word in your notebook.
> ▶ Read the word aloud.

2. When students have finished, write the following word on your whiteboard: *bats.*

3. Have them compare their answer to your correct version.

4. Repeat this procedure with the words *dishes, hens,* and *boxes.*

> ▶ If students make an error and don't see it, help them correct their mistake by having them finger stretch the sounds in the word they missed.
> ▶ If students are having difficulty selecting the correct letters or sounds, review those letters or sounds that are confusing them.
> ▶ If students have difficulty with first, middle, and last sounds, have them finger stretch the sounds in words.

 ⏱ **20 minutes**

REVIEW: Ending –es

Students will work online independently to

▶ Practice the ending –es.

Help students locate the online activities and provide support as needed.

Offline Alternative

No computer access? Read the following words to students: *cup, mat, pen, rich,* and *miss.* Have students add the ending –s or –es to each word, spell the word aloud, and say the ending sound in the new word: *cups,* /s/; *mats,* /s/; *pens,* /z/; *riches,* /iz/; and *misses,* /iz/.

Objectives

- Identify ending sounds in words.
- Read, write, and spell words containing the ending –s.
- Read, write, and spell words containing the ending –es.

Unit Checkpoint

Lesson Overview

Materials

Supplied
- *K¹² PhonicsWorks Basic Assessments,* pp. PH 175–180

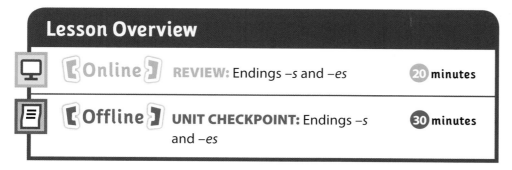 **Online** REVIEW: Endings –s and –es	**20** minutes
Offline UNIT CHECKPOINT: Endings –s and –es	**30** minutes

Objectives

- Identify complete sentences.
- Capitalize the first word in a sentence.
- Use question marks to end asking sentences.
- Use periods to end telling sentences.
- Identify ending sounds in words.
- Read, write, and spell words containing the ending –s.
- Read, write, and spell words containing the ending –es.
- Given the letter, identify the most common sound.
- Given the sound, identify the most common letter or letters.
- Identify individual sounds in words.
- Read instructional-level text with 90% accuracy.
- Read aloud grade-level text with appropriate automaticity, prosody, accuracy, and rate.
- Read sight words.
- Write words by applying grade-level phonics knowledge.

 **Online** **20** minutes

REVIEW: Endings –s and –es

Students will review the endings –s and –es to prepare for the Unit Checkpoint.
Help students locate the online activities and provide support as needed.

 **30 minutes**

UNIT CHECKPOINT: Endings –s and –es

Explain that students are going to show what they have learned about letters, sounds, and words.

1. Give students the Unit Checkpoint pages for the Endings –s and –es unit and print the Unit Checkpoint Answer Key, if you'd like.

2. Use the instructions below to help administer the Checkpoint to students. On the Answer Key or another sheet of paper, note student answers to oral response questions to help with scoring the Checkpoint later.

3. Use the Answer Key to score the Checkpoint, and then enter the results online.

Part 1. Say Sounds Have students read across the rows from left to right and say a sound that the letter, letters, or digraph makes. Note any sounds they say incorrectly.

Part 2. Find the Base Word For each word, have students read the word aloud and underline the base word.

Part 3. Finger Stretching Say each word to students. Have them say each word and finger stretch the sounds. Note any words they finger stretch incorrectly.

27. *ships*

28. *fishes*

29. *lads*

30. *chins*

31. *buzzes*

32. *rocks*

Part 4. Correct the Sentence Have students read each sentence aloud, write the first word with a capital letter, and add a period or question mark to the end of the sentence.

Part 5. Read Aloud Listen to students read the sentences aloud. Count and note the number of words they read correctly.

Part 6. Say Letters
Say each sound. Have students tell you a letter or letters that make that sound. Note any incorrect responses.

39. /ă/
40. /ĕ/
41. /ĭ/
42. /ŏ/
43. /ŭ/
44. /sh/
45. /w/
46. /th/
47. /ch/

48. /r/
49. /w/
50. /y/
51. /v/
52. /g/
53. /h/
54. /l/
55. /kw/
56. /ks/

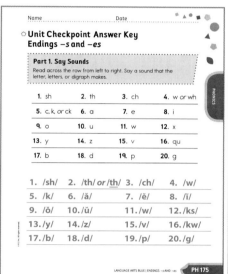

Name _____ Date _____

○ **Unit Checkpoint Answer Key**
Endings −s and −es

Part 1. Say Sounds
Read across the row from left to right. Say a sound that the letter, letters, or digraph makes.

1. sh	2. th	3. ch	4. w or wh
5. c, k, or ck	6. a	7. e	8. i
9. o	10. u	11. w	12. x
13. y	14. z	15. v	16. qu
17. b	18. d	19. p	20. g

1. /sh/	2. /th/ or /th/	3. /ch/	4. /w/
5. /k/	6. /ă/	7. /ĕ/	8. /ĭ/
9. /ŏ/	10. /ŭ/	11. /w/	12. /ks/
13. /y/	14. /z/	15. /v/	16. /kw/
17. /b/	18. /d/	19. /p/	20. /g/

LANGUAGE ARTS BLUE | ENDINGS −s AND −es   PH 175

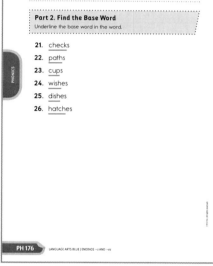

Name _____ Date _____

PH 176   LANGUAGE ARTS BLUE | ENDINGS −s AND −es

Part 2. Find the Base Word
Underline the base word in the word.

21. checks
22. paths
23. cups
24. wishes
25. dishes
26. hatches

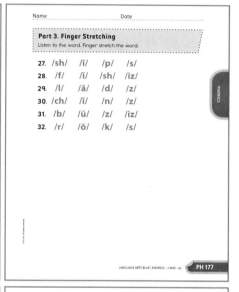

Name _____ Date _____

Part 3. Finger Stretching
Listen to the word. Finger stretch the word.

27. /sh/	/ĭ/	/p/	/s/
28. /f/	/ĭ/	/sh/	/iz/
29. /l/	/ă/	/d/	/z/
30. /ch/	/ĭ/	/n/	/z/
31. /b/	/ŭ/	/z/	/iz/
32. /r/	/ŏ/	/k/	/s/

LANGUAGE ARTS BLUE | ENDINGS −s AND −es   PH 177

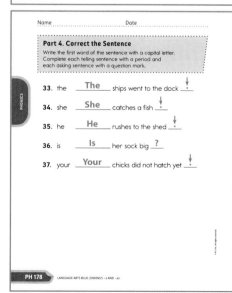

Name _____ Date _____

Part 4. Correct the Sentence
Write the first word of the sentence with a capital letter. Complete each telling sentence with a period and each asking sentence with a question mark.

33. the _The_ ships went to the dock __.__
34. she _She_ catches a fish __.__
35. he _He_ rushes to the shed __.__
36. is _Is_ her sock big _?_
37. your _Your_ chicks did not hatch yet __.__

PH 178   LANGUAGE ARTS BLUE | ENDINGS −s AND −es

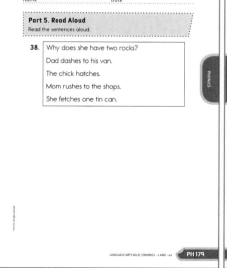

Name _____ Date _____

Part 5. Read Aloud
Read the sentences aloud.

38. | Why does she have two rocks? |
| Dad dashes to his van. |
| The chick hatches. |
| Mom rushes to the shops. |
| She fetches one tin can. |

LANGUAGE ARTS BLUE | ENDINGS −s AND −es   PH 179

Name _____ Date _____

PH 180   LANGUAGE ARTS BLUE | ENDINGS −s AND −es

Part 6. Say Letters
Listen to the sound. Say the letter or letters that make that sound.

39. a	45. w or wh	51. v
40. e	46. th	52. g
41. i	47. ch or tch	53. h
42. o	48. r	54. l
43. u	49. w or wh	55. qu
44. sh	50. y	56. x

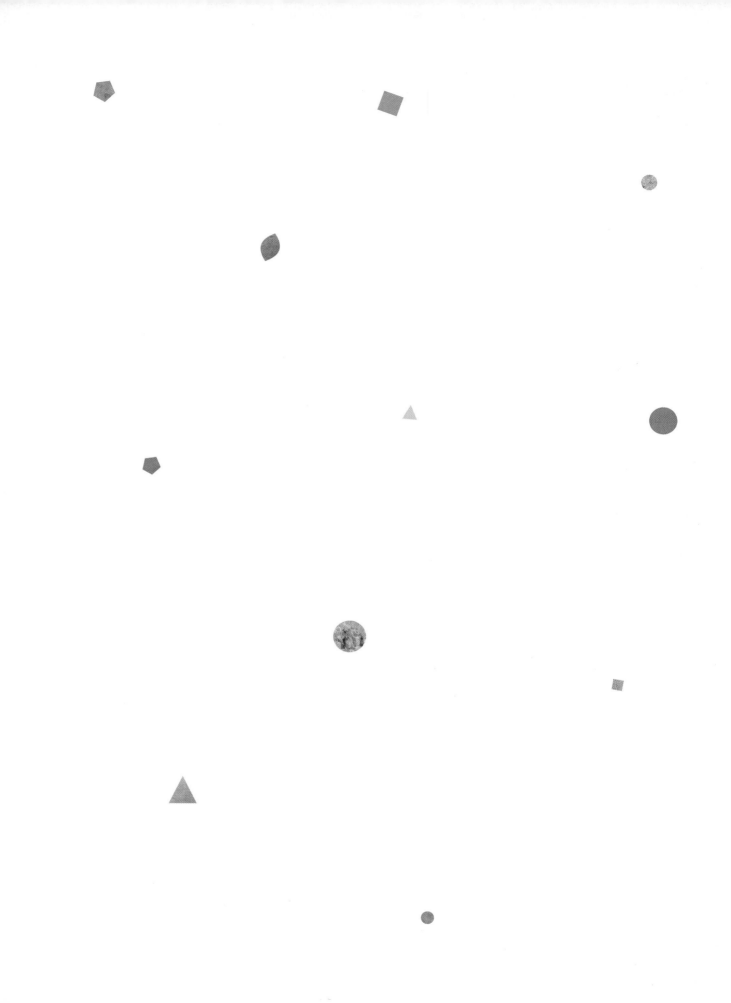

Getting Stronger: Vowels (A)

Unit Overview

In this unit, students will
- Review sight words.
- Review the short vowel sounds /ă/, /ĕ/, /ĭ/, /ŏ/, and /ŭ/ for the letters *a*, *e*, *i*, *o*, and *u*.
- Review the digraphs *ch*, *–ck*, *sh*, *th*, and *wh*.
- Capitalize and punctuate sentences.
- Build words.
- Practice reading and writing.

Lesson Overview

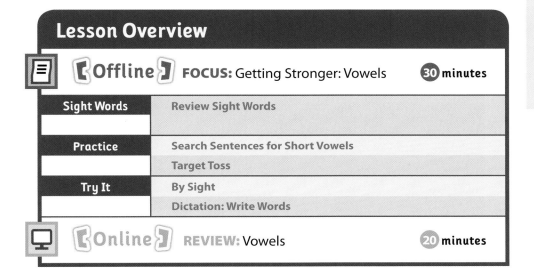

〔Offline〕 FOCUS: Getting Stronger: Vowels	**30** minutes
Sight Words	Review Sight Words
Practice	Search Sentences for Short Vowels
	Target Toss
Try It	By Sight
	Dictation: Write Words

〔Online〕 REVIEW: Vowels	**20** minutes

Advance Preparation

Go to Target Toss for the lists of words with short vowel sounds. Print the words in each word list on index cards, using one index card per word.

 **30 minutes**

FOCUS: Getting Stronger: Vowels

Work **together** with students to complete offline Sight Words, Practice, and Try It activities.

Sight Words

Review Sight Words

Help students learn to recognize sight words.

1. Gather all the sight word cards students have yet to master from their sight words box. Stack the cards on the table face down.

2. Have students pick up a word and read it to you.

3. If they read it quickly and correctly, put the card in one stack. If they hesitate or do not read the word correctly, put it in another stack. The second stack should have words that they will review again.

4. Take the stack of words that students read correctly and dictate each word to them. They may choose to either write the word or spell it aloud.

5. If students spell the word correctly, put the card in the first stack because they have mastered the word. If they misspell the word, add it to the stack of cards to review again.

6. Chart students' progress on the back of each card.

   ▸ Divide the back of the card into two columns.
   ▸ Label the first column "Read" and the second column "Spell."
   ▸ Record the dates that students read or spell the word correctly. When students can read and spell the word correctly three times in a row, they have mastered the word. You may want to put a star or sticker on their card when they have mastered that word.

 Even if students can read and spell all the words correctly, it is still beneficial for them to review sight words. Choose as many additional words as you would like for each subsequent activity.

Practice ....

Search Sentences for Short Vowels

Have students practice identifying **vowel sounds** in words that are in a sentence.

1. **Say:** I'm going to say a special vowel sound that is in a word. You will repeat that sound and the word. The first sound is /ŏ/, as in the word *hot*.

2. Have students say the target sound /ŏ/ and the word *hot*.

3. **Say:** Now I will read a sentence. Repeat the sentence and tell me the word that has the same sound. The first sentence is *The mop is wet*. Which word in the sentence has the special sound? *mop*

4. Have students repeat the sentence and say the word.

5. Redirect students if they don't name the correct word.

   Say: Let me say the sentence again. Remember, you're listening for the sound [special sound].

6. Guide students if they have difficulty. Say two words from the sentence and have them choose the one with the target vowel sound.

7. Follow the same procedure with the following words and sentences:

   ▸ /ă/, as in *sat*   *We chat on the bed.* *chat*
   ▸ /ĕ/, as in *let*   *Tell me your name.* *tell*
   ▸ /ĭ/, as in *pin*   *What do you wish for?* *wish*
   ▸ /ŭ/, as in *hum*   *The car is stuck.* *stuck*

Objectives

- Identify short vowel sounds.
- Identify and use the sound /ă/.
- Identify and use the sound /ĕ/.
- Identify and use the sound /ĭ/.
- Identify and use the sound /ŏ/.
- Identify and use the sound /ŭ/.
- Read, write, and spell words containing short vowel sounds.
- Given the sound, identify the most common letter or letters.

Target Toss

Play a game with students to help them review vowel sounds. The following word lists will be used in this game:

▸ **List 1** (/ă/): *bag, bath, bet, dash, ran, ship, sat, math, rap*
▸ **List 2** (/ĕ/): *bet, yes, tub, deck, wish, ten, vet, peg, mesh*
▸ **List 3** (/ĭ/): *lip, them, lid, tick, bus, this, fish, fit, Rick*
▸ **List 4** (/ŏ/): *bat, box, rock, lot, got, pen, hog, chop, sock*
▸ **List 5** (/ŭ/): *bun, cap, nut, batch, sit, up, tub, mop, fun*

1. Gather the word cards you created for list 1 and organize the cards face up in a rectangular grid that measures approximately 1½ feet on one side and 1 foot on the other side. Make the grid on a tabletop or on the floor.

2. Gather a small household object, such as a key, button, or bean bag.

3. **Say:** I am going to say a special vowel sound. The first sound is /ă/, as in *rap*. Try to toss this object onto a card that shows a word with the sound /ă/, as in *rap*.

4. Have students toss the small object onto a card on the grid and read the word on the card where it lands.

5. Give students one point for each word that the object lands on and that they can read that contains the target vowel sound.

6. Keep track of students' points. When they score five points, replace the cards in the grid with the cards from list 2.

7. Repeat the activity using the cards from lists 2 through 5.

TIP This game can be played outdoors. Just use chalk to make the grid on the sidewalk or driveway and write the words inside the boxes.

Try It

By Sight

Have students complete page PH 79 in *K¹² PhonicsWorks Basic Activity Book* for more practice with reading words. Have students read the words aloud, moving across the rows from left to right. Have them read as many words as they can correctly in one minute.

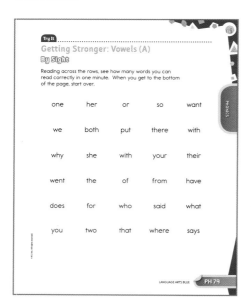

Objectives

- Read aloud grade-level text with appropriate automaticity, prosody, accuracy, and rate.
- Read, write, and spell words containing short vowel sounds.
- Write words by applying grade-level phonics knowledge.
- Follow three-step directions.

Dictation: Write Words

Have students practice identifying sounds and writing words.

1. Gather a pencil and the dictation notebook. Say the word *than*. Then give these directions to students:
   - ▶ Repeat the word.
   - ▶ Write the word in your notebook.
   - ▶ Read the word aloud.

2. When students have finished, write the following word on your whiteboard: *than*.

3. Have them compare their answer to your correct version.

4. Repeat this procedure with the words *with*, *but*, *sock* and *web*.

> ► If students make an error and don't see it, help them correct their mistake by having them finger stretch the sounds in the word they missed.
> ► If students are having difficulty selecting the correct letters or sounds, review those letters or sounds that are confusing them.
> ► If students have difficulty with first, middle, and last sounds, have them finger stretch the sounds in words.

 **20 minutes**

REVIEW: **Vowels**

Students will work online independently to

> ► Practice the vowel sounds /ă/, /ĕ/, /ĭ/, /ŏ/, and /ŭ/ for the letters *a*, *e*, *i*, *o*, and *u*.
> ► Practice decoding text by reading sentences.

Help students locate the online activities and provide support as needed.

Offline Alternative

No computer access? Have students say words that contain the short vowel sounds /ă/, /ĕ/, /ĭ/, /ŏ/, and /ŭ/, such as *cash*, *yes*, *fish*, *chop*, and *rush*. You might also ask students to write simple words that contain the sounds /ă/, /ĕ/, /ĭ/, /ŏ/, and /ŭ/ made by the letters *a*, *e*, *i*, *o*, and *u* and other letters they have learned.

Objectives
- Identify short vowel sounds.
- Given the letter, identify the most common sound.
- Given the sound, identify the most common letter or letters.
- Read, write, and spell words containing short vowel sounds.
- Identify and use the sound /ă/.
- Identify and use the sound /ĕ/.
- Identify and use the sound /ĭ/.
- Identify and use the sound /ŏ/.
- Identify and use the sound /ŭ/.
- Identify individual sounds in words.
- Read aloud grade-level text with appropriate automaticity, prosody, accuracy, and rate.
- Decode words by applying grade-level word analysis skills.

Getting Stronger: Vowels (B)

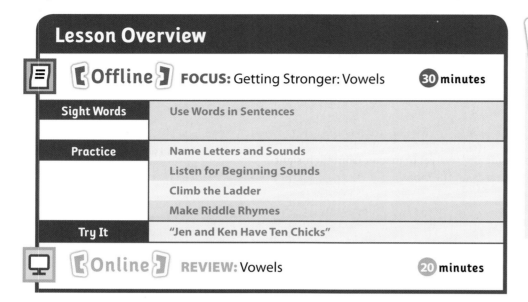

Lesson Overview

[Offline] **FOCUS:** Getting Stronger: Vowels — **30** minutes

Sight Words	Use Words in Sentences
Practice	Name Letters and Sounds
	Listen for Beginning Sounds
	Climb the Ladder
	Make Riddle Rhymes
Try It	"Jen and Ken Have Ten Chicks"

[Online] **REVIEW:** Vowels — **20** minutes

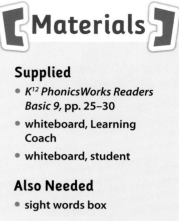

Materials

Supplied
- *K¹² PhonicsWorks Readers Basic 9*, pp. 25–30
- whiteboard, Learning Coach
- whiteboard, student

Also Needed
- sight words box

Advance Preparation

For Name Letters and Sounds, scramble all lowercase letter tiles on your whiteboard, and put the digraphs *ch, –ck, sh, th,* and *wh* and the trigraph *–tch* on the bottom of your whiteboard.

 **30 minutes**

FOCUS: Getting Stronger: Vowels

Work **together** with students to complete offline Sight Words, Practice, and Try It activities.

Sight Words

Use Words in Sentences

Help students use sight words in sentences.

Objectives
- Read sight words.
- Spell sight words.

1. Gather all the sight word cards students have yet to master from their sight words box. Spread the sight word cards on the table.

2. **Say:** Let's use sight words in sentences.

3. Have students

   ▸ Touch each card and read the word on it.
   ▸ Make up a sentence using the word.
   ▸ Put the card in a pile after using the word in a sentence.
   ▸ Go through the pile of cards and read each sight word again.
   ▸ Spell each word.

TIP If students have difficulty with any of the sight words, place those cards in a pile to review again.

Practice

Name Letters and Sounds

Have students play a game to master the letters of the alphabet and digraphs. Grab your whiteboard with the scrambled letters; digraphs *ch*, *–ck*, *sh*, *th*, and *wh*; and the trigraph *–tch*.

1. **Say:** We're going to play a game. All of the letters of the alphabet, the digraphs, and the trigraph *–tch* are on my whiteboard. We will put the letters in alphabetical order and then do the same with the digraphs and the trigraph. We will touch the tile, say the name of the letter or letters, say the sound the letter or letters make, and then say the name of something that begins with that sound.

2. Help students put the letters in alphabetical order and then touch the letter *a*.

3. Have students answer these questions:
   - ▸ What is the name of this letter? *a*
   - ▸ What sound does the letter make? /ă/
   - ▸ What is a word that begins with /ă/? Answers will vary; an example is *apple.*

4. Take turns with students until you have touched all the letters, the digraphs, and the trigraph.

TIP If students have trouble remembering what letter comes next in the alphabet, have them sing "The Alphabet Song."

Listen for Beginning Sounds

Help students identify beginning sounds in words.

1. **Say:** I'm going to say a word. Listen for the beginning sound in the word. Then tell me the sound.
   - ▸ For example, if I say *ship*, you'll say /sh/ because the first sound you hear in *ship* is /sh/.
   - ▸ Now it's your turn. Listen to the word I say. Repeat the word and then tell me the first sound in the word.

2. Repeat the procedure, using the following words to help students recognize beginning sounds:
   - ▸ *cheese* /ch/
   - ▸ *thank* /th/
   - ▸ *wheel* /w/
   - ▸ *edge* /ĕ/
   - ▸ *itch* /ĭ/
   - ▸ *apple* /ă/
   - ▸ *October* /ŏ/
   - ▸ *under* /ŭ/

TIP If students have difficulty, give them multiple words that have the same beginning sound and emphasize that sound in each word.

Objectives

- Identify letters of the alphabet.
- Given the letter, identify the most common sound.
- Given the sound, identify the most common letter or letters.
- Identify and use the digraph *ch*.
- Identify and use the digraph *–ck*.
- Identify and use the digraph *sh*.
- Identify and use the digraph *th*.
- Identify and use the digraph *wh*.
- Identify the trigraph *–tch*, given the sound /ch/.
- Identify beginning sounds in words
- Identify short vowel sounds.
- Identify and use the sound /ă/.
- Identify and use the sound /ĕ/.
- Identify and use the sound /ĭ/.
- Identify and use the sound /ŏ/.
- Identify and use the sound /ŭ/.

Climb the Ladder

Help students use letters to build words.

1. On students' whiteboard or a sheet of paper, draw a ladder with five or more rungs.

2. Write the word *fish* on the bottom rung.

3. Point to the word *fish*.

   Say: I can make the word *wish* by changing one letter in this word.

4. Write the word *wish* on the second rung of the ladder.

   Say: Think of a word that you can make by changing only one letter in *wish*. Tell me the word and write it on the next step on the ladder.

5. If students struggle, coach them to change the first letter in each word.

   Say: Read the word on the bottom rung. What sound do you hear at the beginning of the word? What letter has that sound?

   Say: Name a word that rhymes with the word at the bottom. What sound do you hear at the beginning of the rhyming word? What letter has that sound? Make a new word by using the new letter. Read the new word.

6. Continue the process until students reach the top of the ladder. Remind students that they may change only one sound: the beginning, middle, or last sound.

7. Redirect students if they select a word that changes more than one letter.

   Say: How many letters changed from the last word to your new word? Try to think of a word that has only one letter change.

8. Redirect students if they spell a word incorrectly, but the sounds they spell are correct (such as *ruf* for *rough*).

   Say: You have the sounds and letters right, but that word doesn't follow our spelling rules. We will learn how to spell it later. Try another word.

TIP If students have difficulty thinking of real words, have them use nonsense words.

Make Riddle Rhymes

Have students identify words that rhyme by playing a riddle game.

1. **Say:** We are going to play a riddle game. I will think of a word and give you some clues. You will guess the word and solve the riddle.

   ▸ It is a little talk. It rhymes with *bat*. *chat*

2. Give students clues to words. Have them name each word, and then say and write it. Use these clues and words:

   ▸ It is the opposite of thin. It rhymes with *Rick*. *thick*
   ▸ You can eat your dinner on it. It rhymes with *wish*. *dish*
   ▸ You take this to get clean. It rhymes with *math*. *bath*

Try It •

"Jen and Ken Have Ten Chicks"
Have students read "Jen and Ken Have Ten Chicks" on page 25 of *K¹² PhonicsWorks Readers Basic 9*.

Students should read the story silently once or twice before reading the story aloud. When students miss a word that can be sounded out, point to it and give them three to six seconds to try the word again. If students still miss the word, tell them the word so the flow of the story isn't interrupted.

After reading the story, make a list of all the words students missed, and go over those words with them. You may use letter tiles to show students how to read the words.

Objectives
- Read aloud grade-level text with appropriate automaticity, prosody, accuracy, and rate.
- Decode words by applying grade-level word analysis skills.
- Track text from left to right.
- Turn pages sequentially.

 **20 minutes**

REVIEW: Vowels

Students will work online independently to

▶ Practice the vowel sounds /ă/, /ĕ/, /ĭ/, /ŏ/, and /ŭ/ for the letters *a*, *e*, *i*, *o*, and *u*.

Help students locate the online activities and provide support as needed.

Objectives
- Identify short vowel sounds.
- Read, write, and spell words containing short vowel sounds.
- Given the letter, identify the most common sound.
- Given the sound, identify the most common letter or letters.
- Identify and use the sound /ă/.
- Identify and use the sound /ĕ/.
- Identify and use the sound /ĭ/.
- Identify and use the sound /ŏ/.
- Identify and use the sound /ŭ/.

Offline Alternative

No computer access? Have students say words that contain the short vowel sounds /ă/, /ĕ/, /ĭ/, /ŏ/, and /ŭ/, such as *gash*, *went*, *dish*, *shop*, and *shut*. You might also ask students to write simple words that contain the sounds /ă/, /ĕ/, /ĭ/, /ŏ/, and /ŭ/ made by the letters *a*, *e*, *i*, *o*, and *u* and other letters they have learned.

Getting Stronger: Vowels (C)

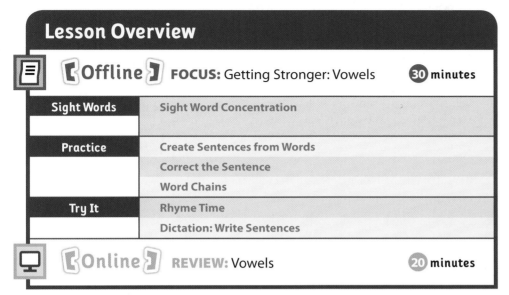

Lesson Overview

Offline FOCUS: Getting Stronger: Vowels   30 minutes

Sight Words	Sight Word Concentration
Practice	Create Sentences from Words
	Correct the Sentence
	Word Chains
Try It	Rhyme Time
	Dictation: Write Sentences

Online REVIEW: Vowels   20 minutes

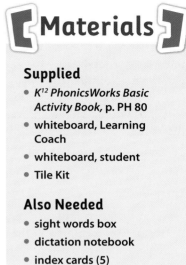

Materials

Supplied
- *K¹² PhonicsWorks Basic Activity Book,* p. PH 80
- whiteboard, Learning Coach
- whiteboard, student
- Tile Kit

Also Needed
- sight words box
- dictation notebook
- index cards (5)

Advance Preparation

Gather two sets of the sight word cards that students have yet to master.

For Create Sentences from Words, print each of the following words on index cards, using one card per word: *catch, fish, run, shop,* and *men.*

 **Offline** **30** minutes

FOCUS: Getting Stronger: Vowels

Work **together** with students to complete offline Sight Words, Practice, and Try It activities.

Sight Words ....

Sight Word Concentration

Help students review sight words.

1. Gather the two sets of sight word cards.

2. Scramble both sets of sight word cards and place them face down on the table or floor.

3. Turn over two cards at a time; take turns with students. If the cards match, the person turning over the matching cards reads the word and uses it in a sentence. If the cards don't match, the person turns them back over.

4. Remove and save the matching cards.

5. Continue the activity until all the cards are paired.

6. Have students read all the words.

7. Take the stack of words that students read correctly and dictate each word to them.

8. Have students write each word or spell it aloud.

TIP If students have difficulty with any sight words, let them work at their own pace to really master these words.

Objectives
- Read sight words.
- Spell sight words.
- Write sight words.

Practice ••

Create Sentences from Words

Help students practice writing sentences using familiar words.

1. Gather the index cards you prepared and the dictation notebook.

2. Have students read all the words.

3. Have students choose a word and write it in a sentence in their dictation notebook. Help them with any words that are difficult for them; tell them the word so that the flow of the sentence is not interrupted.

4. Repeat the procedure until students have selected all the words.

5. Have students read the sentences aloud.

Correct the Sentence

Have students practice correcting capitalization and punctuation in sentences. Grab your whiteboard and dry-erase marker.

1. Write the following sentence without any capitalization or punctuation on your whiteboard: *your van is red*.

2. Have students read the sentence aloud. Have them
   ► Cross out the lowercase letter at the beginning of the first word and write the capital letter.
   ► Add punctuation to the end of the sentence.

3. **Say:** Read the sentence again. How do you know this sentence is correct? The sentence is correct if it follows the rules. To begin any sentence, use a capital letter in the first word. To end a telling sentence, add a period to mark the end of the sentence. To end an asking sentence, add a question mark to the end of the sentence.

4. Repeat the procedure for each of the sentences.
   ► *can Zach run fast* Can Zach run fast?
   ► *that ship is big* That ship is big.
   ► *who had bad luck* Who had bad luck?

5. Help students if they have difficulty identifying what is wrong with the sentence. Ask the following questions:
   ► What is special about the first word in a sentence?
   ► Does the first word in this sentence start with a capital letter?
   ► How can you change the sentence so it begins with a capital letter?
   ► What is special about the mark at the end of a sentence?

6. Guide students by asking one of the following questions if they continue having difficulty:
   ► Is this sentence a telling sentence or an asking sentence?
   ► Is the last word in the sentence followed by a period or a question mark?
   ► What mark do you put at the end of [a telling or an asking] sentence?

Objectives

- Read aloud grade-level text with appropriate automaticity, prosody, accuracy, and rate.
- Write words by applying grade-level phonics knowledge.
- Decode words by applying grade-level word analysis skills.
- Identify complete sentences.
- Capitalize the first word in a sentence.
- Use periods to end telling sentences.
- Use question marks to end asking sentences.
- Read, write, and spell words containing short vowel sounds.
- Identify short vowel sounds.
- Identify individual sounds in words.
- Identify the new word when one sound is changed in a word.

Word Chains

Have students build words by adding and changing letters to help them recognize and use individual sounds in words.

1. Place the following letter tiles at the top of students' whiteboard: *a, c, e, h, i, l, o, p, t, tch,* and *u.*

2. **Say:** I am going to build the first word in a chain. The word is *latch.*

   ▸ I will pull down the letters for the sounds /l/, /ă/, and /ch/ to spell the word *latch.*

   ▸ I will touch and say *latch.* To change *latch* to *lap,* I will think about which sound is changed from the word *latch* to *lap.* I will need to replace the letter tile for *tch* with the letter *p.*

   ▸ Touch and say the word *lap.* Now it's your turn to change *lap* to *cap.* You can spell *cap* by making only one change. Touch and say the new word.

3. Redirect students if they select the incorrect letter for any sound.

   Say: That letter is for the sound [incorrect sound]. We want the letter for the sound [target sound]. What letter makes that sound? Answers will vary.

4. Redirect students if they name the sound incorrectly.

   Say: To change the word [first word] to [target word], we need the letter for the sound [target sound].

   Show students how to make the change. Have them touch and say the new word after they move the letters.

5. Follow this procedure to make the following words: *cup, cut, cot, cat, pat, pet, pit, hit, hut, hutch, hatch.*

6. For every new word, have students add, replace, or remove only one letter tile.

TIP If students struggle, review the sounds and letters that are confusing them.

Try It

Rhyme Time

Have students complete page PH 80 in *K¹² PhonicsWorks Basic Activity Book* for more practice with identifying words that rhyme. Have students choose a word that rhymes with the underlined word in the sentence and write that word in the sentence to complete it. Have them read the completed sentences aloud.

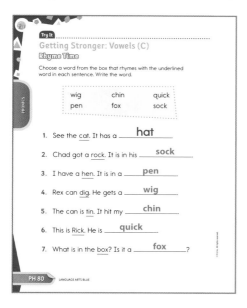

Objectives

- Identify words that rhyme.
- Read aloud grade-level text with appropriate automaticity, prosody, accuracy, and rate.
- Write words by applying grade-level phonics knowledge.
- Follow three-step directions.

Dictation: Write Sentences

Use sentences to help students identify individual sounds in words.

1. Gather a pencil and the dictation notebook. Say the sentence, *Jack had a quick nap.* Then give these directions to students:

   ▸ Repeat the sentence.
   ▸ Write the sentence in your notebook.
   ▸ Read the sentence aloud.

2. When students have finished, write the following sentence on your whiteboard: *Jack had a quick nap.*

3. Have them compare their answer to your correct version.

4. Repeat this procedure with the following sentence: *Can Pam chat with us?*

   ▸ If students make an error and don't see it, help them correct their mistake by having them finger stretch the sounds in the word they missed.
   ▸ If students are having difficulty selecting the correct letters or sounds, review those letters or sounds that are confusing them.
   ▸ If students have difficulty with first, middle, and last sounds, have them finger stretch the sounds in words.

 **minutes**

REVIEW: **Vowels**

Students will work online independently to

▶ Practice the vowel sounds /ă/, /ĕ/, /ĭ/, /ŏ/, and /ŭ/ for the letters *a*, *e*, *i*, *o*, and *u*.

▶ Practice decoding text by reading sentences.

Help students locate the online activities and provide support as needed.

Offline Alternative

No computer access? Have students say words that contain the short vowel sounds /ă/, /ĕ/, /ĭ/, /ŏ/, and /ŭ/, such as *gag*, *ten*, *quiz*, *Tom*, and *bud*. You might also ask students to write simple words that contain the sounds /ă/, /ĕ/, /ĭ/, /ŏ/, and /ŭ/ made by the letters *a*, *e*, *i*, *o*, and *u* and other letters they have learned.

Objectives

- Identify short vowel sounds.
- Given the letter, identify the most common sound.
- Given the sound, identify the most common letter or letters.
- Read, write, and spell words containing short vowel sounds.
- Identify and use the sound /ă/.
- Identify and use the sound /ĕ/.
- Identify and use the sound /ĭ/.
- Identify and use the sound /ŏ/.
- Identify and use the sound /ŭ/.
- Read aloud grade-level text with appropriate automaticity, prosody, accuracy, and rate.
- Decode words by applying grade-level word analysis skills.

Getting Stronger: Vowels (D)

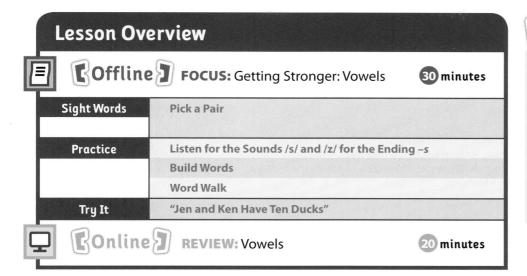

Lesson Overview

≡ [Offline] FOCUS: Getting Stronger: Vowels **30** minutes

Sight Words	Pick a Pair
Practice	Listen for the Sounds /s/ and /z/ for the Ending –s
	Build Words
	Word Walk
Try It	"Jen and Ken Have Ten Ducks"

💻 [Online] REVIEW: Vowels **20** minutes

[Materials]

Supplied
- *K¹² PhonicsWorks Readers Basic 10*, pp. 1–6
- whiteboard, student
- Tile Kit

Also Needed
- sight words box

 **Offline** **30** minutes

FOCUS: Getting Stronger: Vowels

Work **together** with students to complete offline Sight Words, Practice, and Try It activities.

Sight Words

Pick a Pair

Play a card game with students for more practice with sight words.

1. Gather the sight word cards that students are reviewing. Choose two words and place the cards on the table.

2. Ask questions to help students identify each word. For example, if the words are *or* and *one*, you could ask, "Which word names a number?" If the words are *on* and *but*, you could ask, "Which word is the opposite of *off*?"

3. Continue the activity until students identify all the words.

4. Take the stack of words that students read correctly and dictate each word to them.

5. Have students write each word or spell it aloud.

 Objectives
- Read sight words.
- Spell sight words.
- Write sight words.

Practice

Listen for the Sounds /s/ and /z/ for the Ending –s

Have students read words with the ending –s for sounds /s/ and /z/.

1. Place the following letter tiles at the top of students' whiteboard: *a, b, c, ch, d, g, i, m, o, p, sh,* and *u.*

2. Place the following letter tile at the bottom of students' whiteboard: *s.*

3. Make the word *cap* and point to it.

4. Have students touch and say the word *cap.*

5. Have students add the letter *s* to *cap* to make the word *caps.*

   Say: What sound do you hear at the end of the word *caps*? /s/

6. Make the word *bug* and point to it.

7. Have students touch and say the word *bug.*

8. Have students add the letter *s* to *bug* to make the word *bugs.* Ask students the following questions:

   ▶ What sound do you hear at the end of the word *bugs*? /z/
   ▶ What two sounds can the letter *s* make at the end of words? /s/ and /z/

9. Repeat the procedure with the following words:

   ▶ *chum* chums, /z/
   ▶ *dog* dogs, /z/
   ▶ *ship* ships, /s/

10. If students have difficulty distinguishing between the sound /s/ and the sound /z/, say the word pairs in the list below.

    Say: I will say two words. Listen for the **ending sound** in each word. After I say the words, repeat them. Then tell me which word ends with the sound /s/ and which word ends with the sound /z/.

    ▶ *cats* and *dogs* cats, /s/; dogs, /z/
    ▶ *colors* and *eggs* colors, /s/; eggs, /z/
    ▶ *books* and *rooms* books, /s/; rooms, /z/

Build Words

Help students use letters and sounds to build words.

1. Place the following letter tiles at the top of students' whiteboard: *a, b, ch, ck, e, h, i, m, o, s, sh, th, tch, u,* and *w.*

2. Draw three horizontal lines across the middle of students' whiteboard to represent the sounds in a word.

3. **Say:** Let's use letters and sounds to build the word *bath.*

4. Have students finger stretch the sounds in *bath.*

Objectives

- Identify ending sounds in words.
- Read, write, and spell words containing the ending –s.
- Read, write, and spell words containing the ending –es.
- Identify letters of the alphabet.
- Given the sound, identify the most common letter or letters.
- Given the letter, identify the most common sound.
- Read aloud grade-level text with appropriate automaticity, prosody, accuracy, and rate.
- Identify individual sounds in words.
- Blend sounds to create words.
- Read, write, and spell words containing short vowel sounds.
- Write words by applying grade-level phonics knowledge.

5. Have students

  ▸ Identify the first, next, and last sounds in *bath*.
  ▸ Choose the corresponding letter tile for each of the sounds.
  ▸ Move the letters to the correct lines on their whiteboard.

6. Guide students with these questions:

  ▸ What is the first sound in *bath*? /b/
    Which line does the letter for that sound go on? the first one
  ▸ What is the next sound in *bath*? /ă/
    Which line does the letter for that sound go on? the second one
  ▸ What's the last sound in *bath*? /th/
    Which line do the letters for that sound go on? the last one

7. Redirect students if they select the incorrect letter.

   Say: That sound is in the word [word], and it is the [first, second, third] sound. We want the sound [target sound].

   Continue until students select the correct letter tile.

8. Have students touch and say the word.

9. Have them say the word as they use a dry-erase marker to write the word on the whiteboard.

10. Draw horizontal lines across the middle of students' whiteboard that represent the number of sounds in each word. Repeat the activity to build the following words:

   ▸ *etch* /ĕ/ /ch/
   ▸ *which* /w/ /ĭ/ /ch/
   ▸ *sock* /s/ /ŏ/ /k/
   ▸ *mush* /m/ /ŭ/ /sh/

Word Walk
Help students recognize words that have the short vowel sounds /ă/, /ĕ/, /ĭ/, /ŏ/, and /ŭ/.

1. **Say:** We're going to take a walk outside to see what we can find. We will make a list of things that we may find.

2. Help students write down at least five words that contain the short vowel sounds /ă/, /ĕ/, /ĭ/, /ŏ/, and /ŭ/ for the letters *a, e, i, o,* and *u*. These words are things that might be seen outdoors, such as *cat, rocks, bugs, buds, kids, van, shops, bus, pups, web,* and *pet.*

   Say: If you think we will see something, write it on your list. Remember, when we take our walk, check off each thing you see.

   (TIP) If the weather is bad, create a list of words that students are likely to see indoors, and add those words to the list before you do a word walk inside. Here are some examples of words with short vowel sounds: *socks, ham, pen, dish, pot,* and *cup.*

Try It •

"Jen and Ken Have Ten Ducks"
Have students read "Jen and Ken Have Ten Ducks" on page 1 of *K¹² PhonicsWorks Readers Basic 10*.

Students should read the story silently once or twice before reading the story aloud. When students miss a word that can be sounded out, point to it and give them three to six seconds to try the word again. If students still miss the word, tell them the word so the flow of the story isn't interrupted.

After reading the story, make a list of all the words students missed, and go over those words with them. You may use letter tiles to show students how to read the words.

Objectives
- Read aloud grade-level text with appropriate automaticity, prosody, accuracy, and rate.
- Decode words by applying grade-level word analysis skills.
- Track text from left to right.
- Turn pages sequentially.

 **20 minutes**

REVIEW: Vowels
Students will work online independently to

▸ Practice the vowel sounds /ă/, /ĕ/, /ĭ/, /ŏ/, and /ŭ/ for the letters *a, e, i, o,* and *u*.

Help students locate the online activities and provide support as needed.

___

Offline Alternative

No computer access? Have students say words that contain the short vowel sounds /ă/, /ĕ/, /ĭ/, /ŏ/, and /ŭ/, such as *sap, wet, kit, lot,* and *tub.* You might also ask students to write simple words that contain the sounds /ă/, /ĕ/, /ĭ/, /ŏ/, and /ŭ/ made by the letters *a, e, i, o,* and *u* and other letters they have learned.

Objectives
- Identify short vowel sounds.
- Given the letter, identify the most common sound.
- Given the sound, identify the most common letter or letters.
- Read, write, and spell words containing short vowel sounds.
- Identify and use the sound /ă/.
- Identify and use the sound /ĕ/.
- Identify and use the sound /ĭ/.
- Identify and use the sound /ŏ/.
- Identify and use the sound /ŭ/.
- Identify individual sounds in words.

Unit Checkpoint

Lesson Overview

 **Online** REVIEW: Vowels **20** minutes

Offline UNIT CHECKPOINT: Getting Stronger: Vowels **30** minutes

Materials

Supplied

- *K¹² PhonicsWorks Basic Assessments*, pp. PH 181–186

Objectives

- Identify and use the sound /ă/.
- Identify and use the sound /ĕ/.
- Identify and use the sound /ĭ/.
- Identify and use the sound /ŏ/.
- Identify and use the sound /ŭ/.
- Identify and use the digraph *ch*.
- Identify and use the digraph *–ck*.
- Identify and use the digraph *sh*.
- Identify and use the digraph *th*.
- Identify and use the digraph *wh*.
- Identify the trigraph *–tch*, given the sound /ch/.
- Read, write, and spell words containing the ending *–s*.
- Read, write, and spell words containing the ending *–es*.
- Identify short vowel sounds.
- Identify complete sentences.
- Capitalize the first word in a sentence.
- Use question marks to end asking sentences.
- Use periods to end telling sentences.
- Read, write, and spell words containing short vowel sounds.
- Identify individual sounds in words.
- Given the letter, identify the most common sound.
- Given the sound, identify the most common letter or letters.
- Read instructional-level text with 90% accuracy.
- Read aloud grade-level text with appropriate automaticity, prosody, accuracy, and rate.
- Write words by applying grade-level phonics knowledge.
- Write sight words.
- Read sight words.

 **Online** **20** minutes

REVIEW: **Vowels**

Students will review the short vowel sounds /ă/, /ĕ/, /ĭ/, /ŏ/, and /ŭ/ for the letters *a*, *e*, *i*, *o*, and *u* to prepare for the Unit Checkpoint. Help students locate the online activities and provide support as needed.

[Offline] 30 minutes

UNIT CHECKPOINT: Getting Stronger: Vowels

Explain that students are going to show what they have learned about sounds, letters, and words.

1. Give students the Unit Checkpoint pages for the Getting Stronger: Vowels unit and print the Unit Checkpoint Answer Key, if you'd like.

2. Use the instructions below to help administer the Checkpoint to students. On the Answer Key or another sheet of paper, note student answers to oral response questions to help with scoring the Checkpoint later.

3. Use the Answer Key to score the Checkpoint, and then enter the results online.

Part 1. Say Sounds Have students read across the rows from left to right and say a sound that the letter, letters, or digraph makes. Note any sounds they say incorrectly.

Part 2. Find the Vowel For each word, have students read the word aloud and underline the vowel in each word.

Part 3. Finger Stretching Say each word to students. Have them say each word, finger stretch the sounds, and write *s* or *es*, depending on what the word ends with. Note any words they finger stretch incorrectly.

27. *chins*

28. *wishes*

29. *shops*

30. *chaps*

31. *sacks*

32. *catches*

Part 4. Correct the Sentence Have students read each sentence aloud, write the first word with a capital letter, and add a period or question mark to the end.

Part 5. Read Aloud Listen to students read the sentences aloud. Count and note the number of words they read correctly.

Part 6. Say Letters Say each sound. Have students tell you the letter or letters that make that sound. Note any incorrect responses.

39. /ă/	48. /y/
40. /ĕ/	49. /w/
41. /ĭ/	50. /r/
42. /ŏ/	51. /v/
43. /ŭ/	52. /h/
44. /th/	53. /g/
45. /w/	54. /m/
46. /sh/	55. /kw/
47. /ch/	56. /ks/

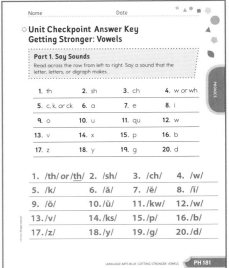

Name _____ Date _____

Unit Checkpoint Answer Key
Getting Stronger: Vowels

Part 1. Say Sounds
Read across the row from left to right. Say a sound that the letter, letters, or digraph makes.

1. th	2. sh	3. ch	4. w or wh
5. c, k, or ck	6. a	7. e	8. i
9. o	10. u	11. qu	12. w
13. v	14. x	15. p	16. b
17. z	18. y	19. g	20. d

1. /th/ or /th/	2. /sh/	3. /ch/	4. /w/
5. /k/	6. /ă/	7. /ĕ/	8. /ĭ/
9. /ŏ/	10. /ŭ/	11. /kw/	12. /w/
13. /v/	14. /ks/	15. /p/	16. /b/
17. /z/	18. /y/	19. /g/	20. /d/

LANGUAGE ARTS BLUE | GETTING STRONGER: VOWELS **PH 181**

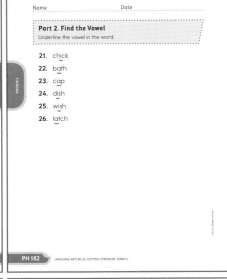

Name _____ Date _____

Part 2. Find the Vowel
Underline the vowel in the word.

21. chick
22. bath
23. cap
24. dish
25. wish
26. latch

PH 182 LANGUAGE ARTS BLUE | GETTING STRONGER: VOWELS

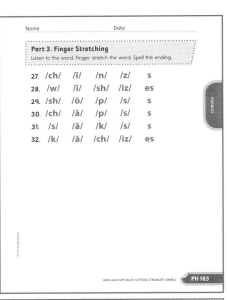

Name _____ Date _____

Part 3. Finger Stretching
Listen to the word. Finger stretch the word. Spell the ending.

27. /ch/	/ĭ/	/n/	/z/	s
28. /w/	/ĭ/	/sh/	/iz/	es
29. /sh/	/ŏ/	/p/	/s/	s
30. /ch/	/ă/	/p/	/s/	s
31. /s/	/ă/	/k/	/s/	s
32. /k/	/ă/	/ch/	/iz/	es

LANGUAGE ARTS BLUE | GETTING STRONGER: VOWELS **PH 183**

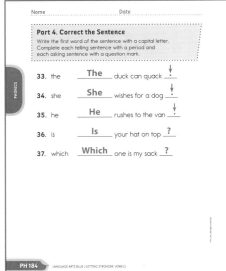

Name _____ Date _____

Part 4. Correct the Sentence
Write the first word of the sentence with a capital letter. Complete each telling sentence with a period and each asking sentence with a question mark.

33. the **The** duck can quack ↓ .
34. she **She** wishes for a dog ↓ .
35. he **He** rushes to the van ↓ .
36. is **Is** your hat on top ?
37. which **Which** one is my sack ?

PH 184 LANGUAGE ARTS BLUE | GETTING STRONGER: VOWELS

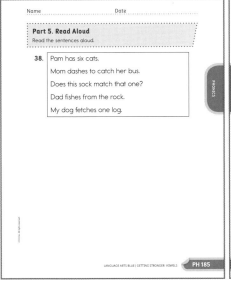

Name _____ Date _____

Part 5. Read Aloud
Read the sentences aloud.

38. Pam has six cats.
Mom dashes to catch her bus.
Does this sock match that one?
Dad fishes from the rock.
My dog fetches one log.

LANGUAGE ARTS BLUE | GETTING STRONGER: VOWELS **PH 185**

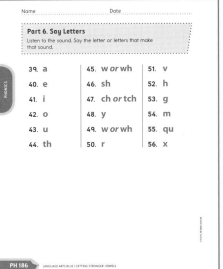

Name _____ Date _____

Part 6. Say Letters
Listen to the sound. Say the letter or letters that make that sound.

39. a	45. w or wh	51. v
40. e	46. sh	52. h
41. i	47. ch or tch	53. g
42. o	48. y	54. m
43. u	49. w or wh	55. qu
44. th	50. r	56. x

PH 186 LANGUAGE ARTS BLUE | GETTING STRONGER: VOWELS

Introduce Endings –ff, –ll, –ss, and –zz

Unit Overview

In this unit, students will
- Learn the sight words *were*, *my*, and *are*.
- Learn the double-letter endings –ff, –ll, –ss, –zz, and –all.
- Review words with digraphs.
- Identify individual sounds in words.

[Materials]

Supplied
- *K¹² PhonicsWorks Basic Activity Book*, p. PH 81
- whiteboard, student
- Tile Kit

Also Needed
- sight words box
- crayons

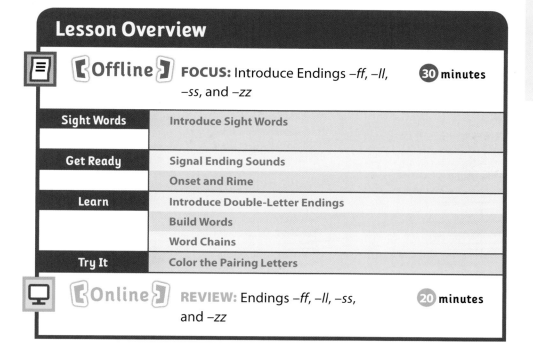

Lesson Overview

[Offline] FOCUS: Introduce Endings –ff, –ll, –ss, and –zz   **30** minutes

Sight Words	Introduce Sight Words
Get Ready	Signal Ending Sounds
	Onset and Rime
Learn	Introduce Double-Letter Endings
	Build Words
	Word Chains
Try It	Color the Pairing Letters

[Online] REVIEW: Endings –ff, –ll, –ss, and –zz   **20** minutes

 **30 minutes**

FOCUS: Introduce Endings *–ff*, *–ll*, *–ss*, and *–zz*

Work **together** with students to complete offline Sight Words, Get Ready, Learn, and Try It activities.

Sight Words

Introduce Sight Words

Help students learn the sight words *were*, *my*, and *are*.

1. Gather the sight word cards *were*, *my*, and *are*.

2. Show students the *were* card.

3. **Say:** This is the word *were*. We see this word so often that we want to be able to read and spell it quickly without thinking about it. Look closely at the word *were*. Spell the word *were* aloud. Take a picture of the word *were* in your mind. When you think you can spell *were* yourself, turn the card over and use your letter tiles to spell the word *were*. Check the card to see if you spelled *were* correctly. Read aloud the word you spelled with the letter tiles.

4. Repeat the activity with the remaining sight words.

5. Chart students' progress on the back of each card.

   ▸ Divide the back of the card into two columns.
   ▸ Label the first column "Read" and the second column "Spell."
   ▸ Record the dates that students read or spell the word correctly. When students can read and spell the word correctly three times in a row, they have mastered the word. You may want to put a star or sticker on the card when they have mastered that word.

6. Add the cards to students' sight words box.

 Sight words can be very difficult for some students. Let students work at their own pace and really master these words, as they occur frequently in reading and writing.

> **Objectives**
> • Read sight words.
> • Spell sight words.

Get Ready

Signal Ending Sounds

Use a special signal to help students identify **ending sounds** in words.

1. **Say:** I'm going to tell you a special sound, and then I'll say some words. Repeat each word I say and make a special signal to tell me where the special sound is. If the special sound is at the end of the word, touch your nose. If the special sound is **not** at the end of the word, just smile at me. For example,

   ▸ If I ask you to listen for the sound /l/ and I say the word *call*, you'll repeat the word *call* and touch your nose because *call* has the sound /l/ at the end.
   ▸ If I say the word *flip*, you'll repeat the word *flip* and smile at me because *flip* has the sound /p/, not /l/, at the end.

> **Objectives**
> • Identify ending sounds in words.
> • Identify a word when given the onset and rime.

2. Say each sound and group of words. Have students make the special signal to identify the ending sound.

- ► /l/: *pull, cab, fill, well, brush* touch nose: *pull, fill, well*
- ► /f/: *stuff, laugh, plate, crack, puff* touch nose: *stuff, laugh, puff*
- ► /k/: *black, sell, pick, knock, bug, fib* touch nose: *black, pick, knock*
- ► /ch/: *hat, much, reach, bus, peach, Jim* touch nose: *much, reach, peach*

TIP If students can't identify the ending sound of each word, say the word again and emphasize the ending sound by repeating it three times (for example, *sit* /t/ /t/ /t/). You can also draw out the ending sound when you say the word (for example, *kissssssss*).

Onset and Rime

Help students put together words that are broken down into parts by onset and rime.

1. **Say:** I'm going to break a word into two parts. Your job is to put the parts together and say the word. If the first part of a word is /sh/ and the last part of the word is *ut*, then the whole word is *shut*: /sh/ . . . *ut* . . . *shut*.

2. Say the following pairs of word parts. Have students tell you the word that each pair forms.

- ► /p/ . . . *art part*
- ► /g/ . . . *one gone*
- ► /w/ . . . *ich which*
- ► /ch/ . . . *est chest*

Learn

Introduce Double-Letter Endings

Use letter tiles and finger stretching to help students spell words that have double-letter endings.

1. Place the following letter tiles at the top of students' whiteboard: *b, f, ff, i, k, ll, p, ss, u,* and *zz*.

2. Draw three horizontal lines across the middle of students' whiteboard to represent the sounds in a word.

3. **Say:** You are going to spell the words I say. Some of the letters on your whiteboard are the **double-letter endings**. The letters *f, l, s,* and *z* are often doubled at the end of words. I'll say a word that ends with a double-letter ending. The first word is *kiss*.

4. Have students finger stretch the sounds in *kiss*.

5. Have students

- ► Identify the first, next, and last sounds in *kiss*.
- ► Choose the corresponding letter tile for each of the sounds.
- ► Move the letters to the correct lines on their whiteboard.

Objectives
- Identify ending sounds in words.
- Identify and use the ending *–ff*.
- Identify and use the ending *–ll*.
- Identify and use the ending *–ss*.
- Identify and use the ending *–zz*.
- Identify individual sounds in words.
- Blend sounds to create words.
- Write words by applying grade-level phonics knowledge.
- Identify the new word when one sound is changed in a word.

6. Guide students with these questions:

   ▸ What is the first sound in *kiss*? /k/
     Which line does the letter for that sound go on? the first one
   ▸ What is the next sound in *kiss*? /ĭ/
     Which line does the letter for that sound go on? the second one
   ▸ What's the last sound in *kiss*? /s/
     Which line do the letters for that sound go on? the last one

7. Redirect students if they select the incorrect letter.

   Say: That sound is in the word [word], and it is the [first, second, third] sound. We want the sound [target sound].

   Continue until students select the correct letter.

8. Have students touch and say the word.

9. Have them say the word as they use a dry-erase marker to write the word on the whiteboard.

10. Repeat the procedure with the following words:

    ▸ *puff* /p/ /ŭ/ /f/
    ▸ *bill* /b/ /ĭ/ /l/
    ▸ *fuzz* /f/ /ŭ/ /z/

Build Words

Help students use letters and sounds to build words.

1. Place the following letter tiles at the top of students' whiteboard: *b, c, ff, h, i, k, ll, ss, u, w,* and *zz*.

2. Draw three horizontal lines across the middle of students' whiteboard to represent the sounds in a word.

3. **Say:** Let's use letters and sounds to build the word *cuff*.

4. Have students finger stretch the sounds in *cuff*.

5. Have students

   ▸ Identify the first, next, and last sounds in *cuff*.
   ▸ Choose the corresponding letter tile for each of the sounds.
   ▸ Move the letters to the correct lines on their whiteboard.

6. Guide students with these questions:

   ▸ What is the first sound in *cuff*? /k/
     Which line does the letter for that sound go on? the first one
   ▸ What is the next sound in *cuff*? /ŭ/
     Which line does the letter for that sound go on? the second one
   ▸ What's the last sound in *cuff*? /f/
     Which line do the letters for that sound go on? the last one

7. Redirect students if they select the incorrect letter.

   Say: That sound is in the word [word], and it is the [first, second, third] sound. We want the sound [target sound].

   Continue until students select the correct letter.

8. Have students touch and say the word.

9. Have them say the word as they use a dry-erase marker to write the word on the whiteboard.

10. Repeat the activity to build the following words:

    ▸ *huff* /h/ /ŭ/ /f/
    ▸ *buzz* /b/ /ŭ/ /z/
    ▸ *will* /w/ /ĭ/ /l/
    ▸ *kiss* /k/ /ĭ/ /s/

    TIP Remind students to place two fingers on the double letters when they touch and say them because the letters make one sound.

Word Chains

Have students build words by adding and changing letters to help them recognize and use individual sounds in words.

1. Place the following letter tiles at the top of students' whiteboard: *e, f, g, h, i, ll, m, ss, u, w,* and *zz*.

2. **Say:** I am going to build the first word in a chain. The word is *fill*.

   ▸ I will pull down the letters for the sounds /f/, /ĭ/, and /l/ to spell the word *fill*.
   ▸ I will touch and say *fill*. To change *fill* to *gill*, I will think about what sound is changed from the word *fill* to *gill*. I will need to replace the letter *f* with the letter *g*.
   ▸ Touch and say the word *gill*. Now it's your turn to change *gill* to *hill*. You can spell *hill* by making only one change. Touch and say the new word.

3. Redirect students if they select the incorrect letter for any sound.

   Say: That letter is for the sound [incorrect sound]. We want the letter for the sound [target sound]. What letter makes that sound? Answers will vary.

4. Redirect students if they name the sound incorrectly.

   Say: To change the word [first word] to [target word], we need the letter for the sound [target sound].

   Show students how to make the change. Have them touch and say the new word after they move the letters.

5. Follow this procedure to make the following words: *mill, will, well, fell, fill, fizz, fuzz, fuss, muss, miss.*

6. For every new word, have students add, replace, or remove only one letter tile.

   TIP If students struggle, review the sounds and letters that are confusing them.

Try It

Color the Pairing Letters

Have students complete page PH 81 in *K¹² PhonicsWorks Basic Activity Book* for more practice with double-letter endings. Have students touch and say each word, and draw a square around the double-letter endings.

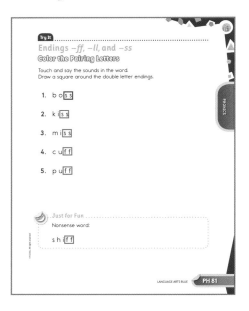

Online ⏱ 20 minutes

REVIEW: Endings *–ff*, *–ll*, *–ss*, and *–zz*

Students will work online independently to

▸ Practice the double-letter endings *–ff*, *–ll*, *–ss*, and *–zz*.
▸ Practice decoding text by reading a story.

Help students locate the online activities and provide support as needed.

Offline Alternative

No computer access? Have students spell words that have the double-letter endings *–ff*, *–ll*, *–ss*, and *–zz* (for example, *off*, *ill*, *lass*, and *fizz*).

Objectives

- Identify and use the ending *–ff*.
- Identify and use the ending *–ll*.
- Identify and use the ending *–ss*.
- Identify and use the ending *–zz*.
- Identify ending sounds in words.
- Read aloud grade-level text with appropriate automaticity, prosody, accuracy, and rate.
- Decode words by applying grade-level word analysis skills.

Practice Endings –*ff*, –*ll*, –*ss*, and –*zz*

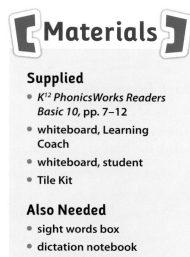

Materials

Supplied

- *K¹² PhonicsWorks Readers Basic 10*, pp. 7–12
- whiteboard, Learning Coach
- whiteboard, student
- Tile Kit

Also Needed

- sight words box
- dictation notebook
- index cards (16)

Lesson Overview

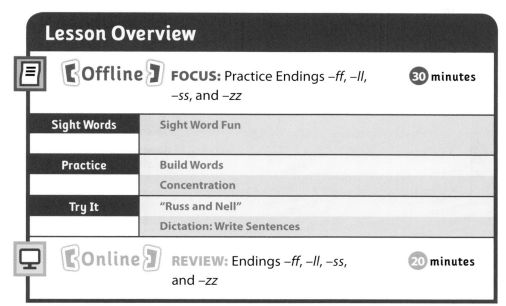

☰	**〔Offline〕 FOCUS:** Practice Endings –*ff*, –*ll*, –*ss*, and –*zz*	**30** minutes

Sight Words	Sight Word Fun
Practice	Build Words
	Concentration
Try It	"Russ and Nell"
	Dictation: Write Sentences

🖥	**〔Online〕 REVIEW:** Endings –*ff*, –*ll*, –*ss*, and –*zz*	**20** minutes

Advance Preparation

For Concentration, print each of the following words on index cards, using one card per word: *Russ, Bess, moss, hiss, jazz, fizz, fuzz, buzz, Bill, sell, dull, will, Jeff, off, huff,* and *puff*.

 **Offline** **30** minutes

FOCUS: Practice Endings *–ff*, *–ll*, *–ss*, and *–zz*

Work **together** with students to complete offline Sight Words, Practice, and Try It activities.

Sight Words

Sight Word Fun

Help students learn the sight words *were*, *my*, and *are,* and up to two additional sight words they have yet to master.

1. Gather the sight word cards *were*, *my*, and *are,* and up to two additional sight word cards.

2. Choose one sight word card to begin.

   Say: Look at this word and take a picture of it in your mind. When you think you can spell the word yourself, turn the card over and use your letter tiles to spell the word.

3. After students spell the word, have them check the card to see if they spelled the word correctly.

   Say: Read aloud the word you spelled with the letter tiles.

4. Repeat the activity with the remaining sight words.

TIP Sight words can be very difficult for some students. Let them work at their own pace and really master these words.

> **Objectives**
> - Read sight words.
> - Spell sight words.

Practice

Build Words

Help students use letters and sounds to build words.

1. Place the following letter tiles at the top of students' whiteboard: *b, e, f, ff, h, i, k, m, p, ll, ss, u, w,* and *zz*.

2. Draw three horizontal lines across the middle of students' whiteboard to represent the sounds in a word.

3. **Say:** Let's use letters and sounds to build the word *will*.

4. Have students finger stretch the sounds in *will*.

5. Have students
   - ▸ Identify the first, next, and last sounds in *will*.
   - ▸ Choose the corresponding letter tile for each of the sounds.
   - ▸ Move the letters to the correct lines on their whiteboard.

> **Objectives**
> - Blend sounds to create words.
> - Identify individual sounds in words.
> - Identify ending sounds in words.
> - Write words by applying grade-level phonics knowledge.
> - Identify and use the ending *–ff.*
> - Identify and use the ending *–ll.*
> - Identify and use the ending *–ss.*
> - Identify and use the ending *–zz.*

6. Guide students with these questions:
   ▶ What is the first sound in *will*? /w/
   Which line does the letter for that sound go on? the first one
   ▶ What is the next sound in *will*? /ĭ/
   Which line does the letter for that sound go on? the second one
   ▶ What's the last sound in *will*? /l/
   Which line do the letters for that sound go on? the last one

7. Redirect students if they select the incorrect letter.

   Say: That sound is in the word [word], and it is the [first, second, third] sound. We want the sound [target sound].

   Continue until students select the correct letter.

8. Have students touch and say the word.

9. Have them say the word as they use a dry-erase marker to write the word on the whiteboard.

10. Repeat the activity to build the following words:
    ▶ *huff* /h/ /ŭ/ /f/
    ▶ *bell* /b/ /ĕ/ /l/
    ▶ *pill* /p/ /ĭ/ /l/
    ▶ *fizz* /f/ /ĭ/ /z/
    ▶ *buzz* /b/ /ŭ/ /z/
    ▶ *kiss* /k/ /ĭ/ /s/
    ▶ *well* /w/ /ĕ/ /l/
    ▶ *miss* /m/ /ĭ/ /s/

TIP Remind students to place two fingers on the double letters when they touch and say them because the letters make one sound.

Concentration
Help students review words with double-letter endings.

1. Gather the cards you prepared.

2. Scramble the cards and place them face down on the table or floor.

3. Turn over two cards at a time; take turns with students. If the two words have the same double-letter ending (*–ff, –ll, –ss,* or *–zz*), it's a match. The person turning over the matching cards reads the words and uses them in a sentence. If the cards don't match, the person turns them back over.

4. Remove and save the matching cards.

5. Continue the activity until all the cards are paired.

6. Have students read all the words.

7. Take the stack of words that students read correctly and dictate each word to them.

8. Have students write each word or spell it aloud.

Try It ••

"Russ and Nell"

Have students read "Russ and Nell" on page 7 of *K¹² PhonicsWorks Readers Basic 10.*

Students should read the story silently once or twice before reading the story aloud. When students miss a word that can be sounded out, point to it and give them three to six seconds to try the word again. If students still miss the word, tell them the word so the flow of the story isn't interrupted.

After reading the story, make a list of all the words students missed, and go over those words with them. You may use letter tiles to show students how to read the words.

Objectives

- Read aloud grade-level text with appropriate automaticity, prosody, accuracy, and rate.
- Decode words by applying grade-level word analysis skills.
- Track text from left to right.
- Turn pages sequentially.
- Write words by applying grade-level phonics knowledge.
- Follow three-step directions.

Dictation: Write Sentences

Use sentences to help students identify individual sounds in words.

1. Gather a pencil and the dictation notebook. Say the sentence, *The dresses are red.* Then give these directions to students:

   ▸ Repeat the sentence.
   ▸ Write the sentence in your notebook.
   ▸ Read the sentence aloud.

2. When students have finished, write the following sentence on your whiteboard: *The dresses are red.*

3. Have them compare their answer to your correct version.

4. Repeat this procedure with the following sentence: *I will miss jazz.*

   ▸ If students make an error and don't see it, help them correct their mistake by having them finger stretch the sounds in the word they missed.
   ▸ If students are having difficulty selecting the correct letters or sounds, review those letters or sounds that are confusing them.
   ▸ If students have difficulty with first, middle, and last sounds, have them finger stretch the sounds in words.

TIP Remind students that a telling sentence starts with a capital letter and ends with a period.

 **20 minutes**

REVIEW: Endings *–ff*, *–ll*, *–ss*, and *–zz*

Students will work online independently to

▶ Practice the double-letter endings *–ff*, *–ll*, *–ss*, and *–zz*.

Help students locate the online activities and provide support as needed.

Offline Alternative

No computer access? Have students spell words that have the double-letter endings *–ff*, *–ll*, *–ss*, and *–zz* (for example, *tuff*, *Bill*, *grass*, and *jazz*).

> **Objectives**
> - Identify ending sounds in words.
> - Identify and use the ending *–ff*.
> - Identify and use the ending *–ll*.
> - Identify and use the ending *–ss*.
> - Identify and use the ending *–zz*.

Ending –all

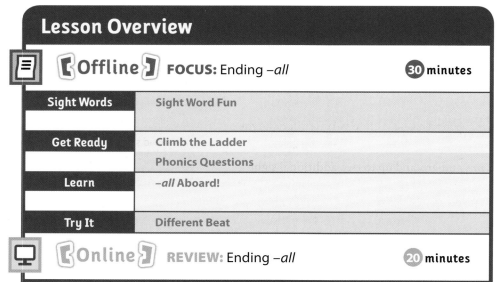

Lesson Overview

⟨Offline⟩ FOCUS: Ending –all   **30** minutes

Sight Words	Sight Word Fun
Get Ready	Climb the Ladder
	Phonics Questions
Learn	–all Aboard!
Try It	Different Beat

⟨Online⟩ REVIEW: Ending –all   **20** minutes

Materials

Supplied
- *K¹² PhonicsWorks Basic Activity Book*, p. PH 82
- whiteboard, Learning Coach
- whiteboard, student
- Tile Kit

Also Needed
- sight words box

Advance Preparation

Place lowercase letter tiles in alphabetical order and the double-letter ending tiles *ff*, *ll*, *ss*, and *zz* on your whiteboard.

 **Offline** **30** minutes

FOCUS: Ending –all

Work **together** with students to complete offline Sight Words, Get Ready, Learn, and Try It activities.

Sight Words

Sight Word Fun

Help students learn the sight words *were, my,* and *are,* and up to two additional sight words they have yet to master.

1. Gather the sight word cards *were, my,* and *are,* and up to two additional sight word cards.

2. Choose one sight word card to begin.

   Say: Look at this word and take a picture of it in your mind. When you think you can spell the word yourself, turn the card over and use your letter tiles to spell the word.

3. After students spell the word, have them check the card to see if they spelled the word correctly.

   Say: Read aloud the word you spelled with the letter tiles.

4. Repeat the activity with the remaining sight words.

   TIP Sight words can be very difficult for some students. Let them work at their own pace and really master these words.

 Objectives
- Read sight words.
- Spell sight words.

Get Ready

Climb the Ladder

Help students use letters to build words.

1. On students' whiteboard or a sheet of paper, draw a ladder with five or more rungs.

2. Write the word *tell* on the bottom rung.

3. Point to the word *tell*.

   Say: I can make the word *bell* by changing one letter in this word.

4. Write the word *bell* on the second rung of the ladder.

   Say: Think of a word that you can make by changing only one letter in *bell.* Tell me the word and write it on the next step on the ladder.

 Objectives
- Identify the new word when one sound is changed in a word.
- Identify and use the ending –ll.
- Identify ending sounds in words.
- Given the letter, identify the most common sound.
- Given the sound, identify the most common letter or letters.
- Identify letters of the alphabet.
- Identify short vowel sounds.

5. If students struggle, coach them to change the first letter in each word.

   Say: Read the word on the bottom rung. What sound do you hear at the beginning of the word? What letter has that sound?

   Say: Name a word that rhymes with the word at the bottom. What sound do you hear at the beginning of the rhyming word? What letter has that sound? Make a new word by using the new letter. Read the new word.

6. Continue the process until students reach the top of the ladder. Remind students that they may change only one sound: the beginning, middle, or last sound.

7. Redirect students if they select a word that changes more than one letter.

   Say: How many letters changed from the last word to your new word? Try to think of a word that has only one letter change.

8. Redirect students if they spell a word incorrectly, but the sounds they spell are correct (such as *ruf* for *rough*).

   Say: You have the sounds and letters right, but that word doesn't follow our spelling rules. We will learn how to spell it later. Try another word.

   TIP If students have difficulty thinking of real words, have them use nonsense words.

Phonics Questions

To help students master the letters and the sounds of the alphabet, have them review and practice identifying and naming letters and the double-letter endings.

1. Grab your whiteboard with letters placed in alphabetical order and the double-letter ending tiles *ff, ll, ss,* and *zz.*

2. Ask students the following questions:

   ► What letter is always followed by the letter *u*? *q*
   ► Touch and say the short sound for each vowel. /ă/, /ĕ/, /ĭ/, /ŏ/, /ŭ/
   ► Touch all the letters that have the sound /k/. *c, ck, k*
   ► What letters are almost always doubled at the end of a one-syllable word if they follow a short vowel? the double letters *ff, ll, ss,* and *zz*
   ► Touch the double-letter tiles on the whiteboard.

Learn

--*all* Aboard!

Help students practice identifying and making double-letter ending words that contain the base word *all.*

1. Place the following letter tiles on students' whiteboard: *a, all, b, c, f, h, l, m, p, t,* and *w.*

2. Put the *all* letter tile in the middle of the whiteboard and point to it.

   Say: The letters on this tile spell the word *all.* Touch and say the word *all.*

Objectives
- Identify ending sounds in words.
- Identify and use the ending –*all.*

3. Make the word *pal* and point to it.

   Say: When we have one *l* after the letter *a*, we say *a* as in *pal*. But when we have two *l*s after the letter *a*, we say *all*.

4. Make the word *ball* and point to it.

   Say: This is the word *ball*. To spell the word *ball*, we only need two tiles: the letter *b* and the *all* tile. When we touch and say *ball*, we say /b/ and /all/.

5. Follow this procedure with the following words: *fall, mall, tall, wall, call,* and *hall*.

TIP If students have difficulty understanding that the letters *all* make the sound /all/ and not the sound /al/, use the letter tiles to make the word *pal*. Remind them that that when a word has an *a* followed by only one *l*, it is pronounced /al/, as in *pal*. The words *gal, Al,* and *Sal* may also be used as examples.

Try It

Different Beat

Have students complete page PH 82 in *K¹² PhonicsWorks Basic Activity Book* for more practice with the ending *–all*. Have students read each word aloud and circle the words that do not rhyme. After they circle all the words, have them write the circled words to complete the sentence.

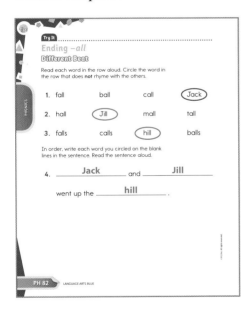

Objectives

- Read aloud grade-level text with appropriate automaticity, prosody, accuracy, and rate.
- Identify words that rhyme.
- Identify complete sentences.
- Identify and use the ending *–all*.

 **minutes**

REVIEW: Ending *–all*

Students will work online independently to

- ▶ Practice the ending *–all*.
- ▶ Practice decoding text by reading a story.

Help students locate the online activities and provide support as needed.

Offline Alternative

No computer access? Have students spell words that have the ending *–all* (for example, *all*, *call*, and *ball*).

> **Objectives**
> - Identify and use the ending *–all*.
> - Identify ending sounds in words.
> - Read aloud grade-level text with appropriate automaticity, prosody, accuracy, and rate.
> - Decode words by applying grade-level word analysis skills.

Practice Endings –*ff*, –*ll*, –*ss*, –*zz*, and –*all*

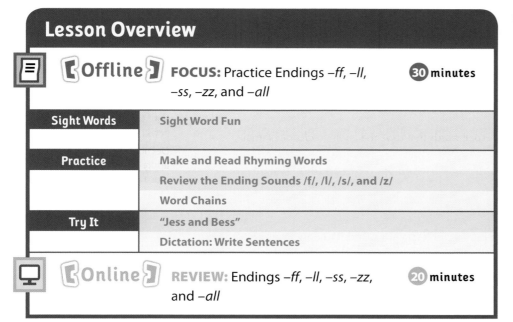

Lesson Overview

Offline **FOCUS:** Practice Endings –*ff*, –*ll*, –*ss*, –*zz*, and –*all*   **30** minutes

Sight Words	Sight Word Fun
Practice	Make and Read Rhyming Words
	Review the Ending Sounds /f/, /l/, /s/, and /z/
	Word Chains
Try It	"Jess and Bess"
	Dictation: Write Sentences

Online **REVIEW:** Endings –*ff*, –*ll*, –*ss*, –*zz*, and –*all*   **20** minutes

Materials

Supplied
- *K¹² PhonicsWorks Readers Basic 10,* pp. 13–18
- whiteboard, Learning Coach
- whiteboard, student
- Tile Kit

Also Needed
- sight words box
- dictation notebook

【 Offline 】 ⏰ 30 minutes

FOCUS: Practice Endings –*ff*, –*ll*, –*ss*, –*zz*, and –*all*

Work **together** with students to complete offline Sight Words, Practice, and Try It activities.

Sight Words ·

Sight Word Fun

Help students learn the sight words *were, my,* and *are,* and up to two additional sight words they have yet to master.

1. Gather the sight word cards *were, my,* and *are,* and up to two additional sight word cards.

2. Choose one sight word card to begin.

   Say: Look at this word and take a picture of it in your mind. When you think you can spell the word yourself, turn the card over and use your letter tiles to spell the word.

3. After students spell the word, have them check the card to see if they spelled the word correctly.

   Say: Read aloud the word you spelled with the letter tiles.

4. Repeat the activity with the remaining sight words.

TIP) Sight words can be very difficult for some students. Let them work at their own pace and really master these words.

Objectives
- Read sight words.
- Spell sight words.

Practice ·

Make and Read Rhyming Words

Have students make and read words that rhyme.

1. Gather students' whiteboard and dry-erase marker.

2. Read the following words aloud: *ball* and *fall*.

   Say: How are these two words alike? The words have the same last sound, /all/; the same last letters, *all;* and they rhyme.

   Say: How are these two words different? They start with a different letter.

3. Write the word *ball* on students' whiteboard and have them read it.

4. Replace the letter *b* with the letter *f* and have students read the new word, *fall*.

5. Repeat this procedure with the letters *m, h, c,* and *t* to make the words *mall, hall, call,* and *tall*.

Objectives
- Produce rhyming words.
- Identify ending sounds in words.
- Identify and use the ending –*all*.
- Identify and use the ending –*ff*.
- Identify and use the ending –*ll*.
- Identify and use the ending –*ss*.
- Identify and use the ending –*zz*.
- Identify the new word when one sound is changed in a word.

Review the Ending Sounds /f/, /l/, /s/, and /z/

Have students practice words with the ending sounds /f/, /l/, /s/, and /z/.

1. Write the following words on students' whiteboard: *puff, sell, miss, and fuzz*.

2. For each word, have students do the following:

   ‣ Touch and say the word.
   ‣ Say the ending sound in the word. /f/, /l/, /s/, /z/
   ‣ Draw a line under the letters that make the ending sound. *puff, sell, miss, fuzz*

Word Chains

Have students build words by adding and changing letters to help them recognize and use individual sounds in words.

1. Place the following letter tiles at the top of students' whiteboard: *a, all, b, e, f, h, i, ll, m, ss, u,* and *zz*.

2. **Say:** I am going to build the first word in a chain. The word is *buzz*.

   ‣ I will pull down the letters for the sounds /b/, /ŭ/, and /z/ to spell the word *buzz*.
   ‣ I will touch and say *buzz*. To change *buzz* to *fuzz*, I will think about what sound is changed from the word *buzz* to *fuzz*. I will need to replace the letter *b* with the letter *f*.
   ‣ Touch and say the word *fuzz*. Now it's your turn to change *fuzz* to *fizz*. You can spell *fizz* by making only one change. Touch and say the new word.

3. Redirect students if they select the incorrect letter for any sound.

   Say: That letter is for the sound [incorrect sound]. We want the letter for the sound [target sound]. What letter makes that sound? Answers will vary.

4. Redirect students if they name the sound incorrectly.

   Say: To change the word [first word] to [target word], we need the letter for the sound [target sound].

   Show students how to make the change. Have them touch and say the new word after they move the letters.

5. Follow this procedure to make the following words: *fill, bill, hill, hiss, miss, mess, mass, mall, ball, hall, fall, fell, bell*.

6. For every new word, have students add, replace, or remove only one letter tile. Exception: Sometimes students will need to change two tiles (for example, changing the word *fall* to *fell* involves exchanging the letter tile *all* for the *e* and *ll* letter tiles).

Try It •

"Jess and Bess"

Have students read "Jess and Bess" on page 13 of *K¹² PhonicsWorks Readers Basic 10*.

Students should read the story silently once or twice before reading the story aloud. When students miss a word that can be sounded out, point to it and give them three to six seconds to try the word again. If students still miss the word, tell them the word so the flow of the story isn't interrupted.

After reading the story, make a list of all the words students missed, and go over those words with them. You may use letter tiles to show students how to read the words.

Dictation: Write Sentences

Use sentences to help students identify individual sounds in words.

1. Gather a pencil and the dictation notebook. Say the sentence, *I will fix the mess.* Then give these directions to students:

   ▸ Repeat the sentence.
   ▸ Write the sentence in your notebook.
   ▸ Read the sentence aloud.

2. When students have finished, write the following sentence on your whiteboard: *I will fix the mess.*

3. Have them compare their answer to your correct version.

4. Repeat this procedure with the following sentence: *There is fuzz on the ball.*

   ▸ If students make an error and don't see it, help them correct their mistake by having them finger stretch the sounds in the word they missed.
   ▸ If students are having difficulty selecting the correct letters or sounds, review those letters or sounds that are confusing them.
   ▸ If students have difficulty with first, middle, and last sounds, have them finger stretch the sounds in words.

TIP Remind students that a telling sentence starts with a capital letter and ends with a period.

Objectives

- Read aloud grade-level text with appropriate automaticity, prosody, accuracy, and rate.
- Decode words by applying grade-level word analysis skills.
- Track text from left to right.
- Turn pages sequentially.
- Write words by applying grade-level phonics knowledge.
- Follow three-step directions.

 **20 minutes**

REVIEW: Endings –ff, –ll, –ss, –zz, and –all

Students will work online independently to

▶ Practice the endings –ff, –ll, –ss, –zz, and –all.

Help students locate the online activities and provide support as needed.

___

Offline Alternative

No computer access? Have students spell words that have the endings –ff, –ll, –ss, –zz, and –all (for example, *puff, pull, pass, fuzz,* and *wall*).

Objectives
- Identify ending sounds in words.
- Identify and use the ending –all.
- Identify and use the ending –ff.
- Identify and use the ending –ll.
- Identify and use the ending –ss.
- Identify and use the ending –zz.

Unit Checkpoint

Lesson Overview

  **REVIEW:** Endings *–ff, –ll, –ss, –zz,* and *–all* **20** minutes

 **UNIT CHECKPOINT:** Endings *–ff, –ll, –ss, –zz,* and *–all* **30** minutes

 Materials

Supplied
- *K¹² PhonicsWorks Basic Assessments,* pp. PH 187–192

Objectives
- Identify complete sentences.
- Capitalize the first word in a sentence.
- Use question marks to end asking sentences.
- Use periods to end telling sentences.
- Identify ending sounds in words.
- Identify and use the ending *–all.*
- Identify and use the ending *–ff.*
- Identify and use the ending *–ll.*
- Identify and use the ending *–ss.*
- Identify and use the ending *–zz.*
- Identify individual sounds in words.
- Given the letter, identify the most common sound.
- Given the sound, identify the most common letter or letters.
- Read sight words.
- Read instructional-level text with 90% accuracy.
- Read aloud grade-level text with appropriate automaticity, prosody, accuracy, and rate.
- Write words by applying grade-level phonics knowledge.

 **20** minutes

REVIEW: **Endings *–ff, –ll, –ss, –zz,* and *–all***

Students will review the endings *–ff, –ll, –ss, –zz,* and *–all* to prepare for the Unit Checkpoint. Help students locate the online activities and provide support as needed.

 **30 minutes**

UNIT CHECKPOINT: Endings *–ff*, *–ll*, *–ss*, *–zz*, and *–all*

Explain that students are going to show what they have learned about letters, sounds, and words.

1. Give students the Unit Checkpoint pages for the Endings *–ff*, *–ll*, *–ss*, *–zz*, and *–all* unit and print the Unit Checkpoint Answer Key, if you'd like.

2. Use the instructions below to help administer the Checkpoint to students. On the Answer Key or another sheet of paper, note student answers to oral response questions to help with scoring the Checkpoint later.

3. Use the Answer Key to score the Checkpoint, and then enter the results online.

Part 1. Read Words and Words Parts Have students read across the rows from left to right and say the sound or sounds of each word or word part. Note any words or word parts they say incorrectly.

Part 2. Finger Stretching Say each word to students. Have them say each word and finger stretch the sounds. Note any words they finger stretch incorrectly.

19. *fizz*

20. *miss*

21. *off*

22. *fill*

23. *pass*

24. *puff*

Part 3. Dictation Say each word to students. Have them repeat and write the word.

25. *ball*

26. *fill*

27. *buzz*

28. *miss*

29. *off*

30. *boss*

Part 4. Read Aloud Listen to students read the sentences aloud. Count and note the number of words they read correctly.

Part 5. Say Letters Say each sound. Have students tell you a letter or letters that make that sound. Note any incorrect responses.

32. /ă/

33. /sh/

34. /kw/

35. /ĕ/

36. /ks/

37. /k/

38. /ĭ/

39. /ŏ/

40. /ŭ/

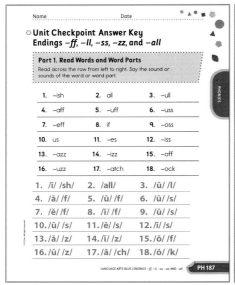

Name _____ Date _____

⚙ Unit Checkpoint Answer Key
Endings –*ff*, –*ll*, –*ss*, –*zz*, and –*all*

Part 1. Read Words and Word Parts
Read across the row from left to right. Say the sound or sounds of the word or word part.

1. –ish	2. all	3. –ull
4. –aff	5. –uff	6. –uss
7. –eff	8. if	9. –oss
10. us	11. –es	12. –iss
13. –azz	14. –izz	15. –off
16. –uzz	17. –atch	18. –ock

1. /ĭ/ /sh/	2. /all/	3. /ŭ/ /l/
4. /ă/ /f/	5. /ŭ/ /f/	6. /ŭ/ /s/
7. /ĕ/ /f/	8. /ĭ/ /f/	9. /ŭ/ /s/
10. /ŭ/ /s/	11. /ĕ/ /s/	12. /ĭ/ /s/
13. /ă/ /z/	14. /ĭ/ /z/	15. /ŏ/ /f/
16. /ŭ/ /z/	17. /ă/ /ch/	18. /ŏ/ /k/

Name _____ Date _____

Part 2. Finger Stretching
Listen to the word. Finger stretch the word.

19. /f/ /ĭ/ /z/
20. /m/ /ĭ/ /s/
21. /ŏ/ /f/
22. /f/ /ĭ/ /l/
23. /p/ /ă/ /s/
24. /p/ /ŭ/ /f/

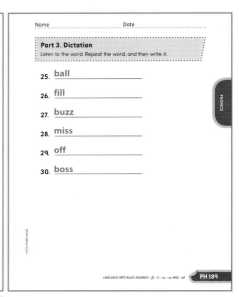

Name _____ Date _____

Part 3. Dictation
Listen to the word. Repeat the word, and then write it.

25. ball
26. fill
27. buzz
28. miss
29. off
30. boss

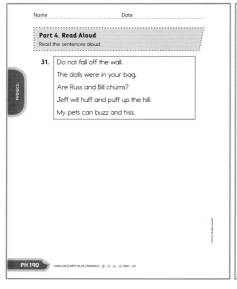

Name _____ Date _____

Part 4. Read Aloud
Read the sentences aloud.

31.
> Do not fall off the wall.
> The dolls were in your bag.
> Are Russ and Bill chums?
> Jeff will huff and puff up the hill.
> My pets can buzz and hiss.

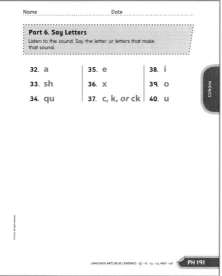

Name _____ Date _____

Part 6. Say Letters
Listen to the sound. Say the letter or letters that make that sound.

32. a	35. e	38. i
33. sh	36. x	39. o
34. qu	37. c, k, *or* ck	40. u

Introduce Compound Words

Unit Overview

In this unit, students will
- ▶ Learn the sight words *Mr.*, *Mrs.*, and *Dr.*
- ▶ Learn compound words.
- ▶ Review letters of the alphabet.
- ▶ Identify individual sounds in words.

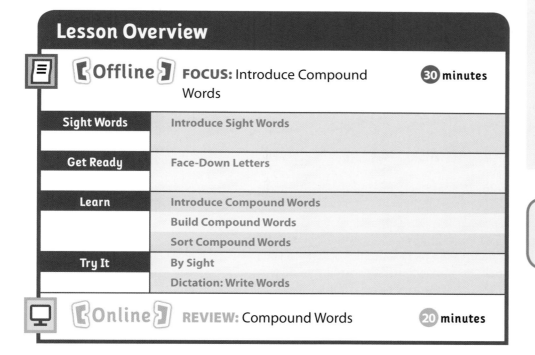

Lesson Overview

〖Offline〗 FOCUS: Introduce Compound Words	30 minutes
Sight Words	Introduce Sight Words
Get Ready	Face-Down Letters
Learn	Introduce Compound Words
	Build Compound Words
	Sort Compound Words
Try It	By Sight
	Dictation: Write Words

〖Online〗 REVIEW: Compound Words	20 minutes

〖Materials〗

Supplied
- K¹² *PhonicsWorks Basic Activity Book,* p. PH 83
- whiteboard, Learning Coach
- whiteboard, student
- small whiteboards (2)
- Tile Kit

Also Needed
- sight words box
- dictation notebook
- index cards (10)

Keywords

compound word – a word made from two smaller words

Advance Preparation

Place lowercase letter tiles in alphabetical order on your whiteboard.

For Sort Compound Words, print each of the following words on index cards, using one card per word: *suntan, backpack, hatbox, sunfish, cobweb, buzz, ship, hatch, mush,* and *tack.*

Big Ideas

- ▶ The word *backpack* is a compound word made from the two smaller words *back* and *pack.*
- ▶ The ability to break compound words into two smaller words is a demonstration of phonological awareness.
- ▶ The ability to put two small words together to form a compound word is a demonstration of phonological awareness.

 **30 minutes**

FOCUS: Introduce Compound Words

Work **together** with students to complete offline Sight Words, Get Ready, Learn, and Try It activities.

Sight Words

Introduce Sight Words

Help students learn the sight words *Mr.*, *Mrs.*, and *Dr.*

 Objectives
- Read sight words.
- Spell sight words.

1. Gather the sight word cards *Mr.*, *Mrs.*, and *Dr.*

2. Gather the tile for the period.

3. Show students the *Mr.* card.

   Say: This is the abbreviation for the word *mister*. An abbreviation is a shorter, faster way of writing something.

4. Point to the period.

   Say: This is a period. When we spell abbreviations, we always put a period at the end of the abbreviation.

5. Point to the word *Mr.*

   Say: The abbreviation for the word *mister* is used so often that we want to be able to read and spell it quickly without thinking about it. Look closely at the word *Mr.* Spell the word *Mr.* aloud. Take a picture of the word *Mr.* in your mind. When you think you can spell *Mr.* yourself, turn the card over and use your letter tiles to spell the word *Mr.* Check the card to see if you spelled *Mr.* correctly. Read aloud the abbreviation you spelled with the letter tiles.

6. Repeat the activity with the remaining sight words.

7. Chart students' progress on the back of each card.

   ► Divide the back of the card into two columns.
   ► Label the first column "Read" and the second column "Spell."
   ► Record the dates that students read or spell the word correctly. When students can read and spell the word correctly three times in a row, they have mastered the word. You may want to put a star or sticker on the card when they have mastered that word.

8. Add the cards to students' sight words box.

TIP Sight words can be very difficult for some students. Let students work at their own pace and really master these words, as they occur frequently in reading and writing.

Get Ready

Face-Down Letters

To help students master the ability to recognize the letters of the alphabet, have them practice identifying and naming letters. Grab your whiteboard with letters placed in alphabetical order.

1. Lay your whiteboard down on a flat surface and flip over the following letter tiles so they are face down on the whiteboard: *a, c, g, h, n, p, r, w, x,* and *z*.

2. **Say:** These letters are face down. We are looking at the back of them. Name each letter and then turn it over to see if you were right.

(TIP) If students miss any of the letters, have them turn over the missed ones and try again.

Objectives
- Identify letters of the alphabet.
- Given the letter, identify the most common sound.
- Given the sound, identify the most common letter or letters.

Learn

Introduce Compound Words

Introduce compound words to students.

1. Place the following letter tiles on students' whiteboard: *a, b, b, t, th,* and *u*.

2. Make the following words on students' whiteboard: *bath* and *tub*.

3. **Say:** Today we are going to learn how to put words together to make other words.
   - You know how to read the first word. What's this word? bath
   - You know how to read the second word, too. What's this word? tub
   - Now we're going to put these two words together to make one word, which is called a compound word. We always make a compound word by putting two small words together.

4. Slide the two words together to make one word.

   Say: I'll read the new word: *bathtub*.
   - How many syllables are in the compound word *bathtub*? two
   - Underline each word in the compound and read the word aloud.

Objectives
- Identify and use compound words.
- Identify individual sounds in words.
- Blend sounds to create words.
- Write words by applying grade-level phonics knowledge.

Build Compound Words

Help students practice identifying and making compound words. Grab two small whiteboards and a dry-erase marker.

1. **Say:** Now we are going to build some **compound words**. Say the word *uphill*.
   - How many syllables do you hear? two

2. **Say:** Each syllable in the word *uphill* is also a small word: *up, hill*. Together they make the compound word *uphill*.

3. **Say:** When we spell compound words, we will first spell each syllable on the small whiteboards. To build the word, I will write the first syllable, *up*, on one whiteboard. Next I will write the second syllable, *hill*, on the other whiteboard. I'll push the two whiteboards together and read *uphill*.

4. **Say:** Now it's your turn. Build the word *cannot*.

   ▸ Fist tap the syllables on the table.
   ▸ Spell the first syllable on one whiteboard.
   ▸ Spell the second syllable on the other whiteboard.
   ▸ Put the boards together and read the word.

5. Repeat the procedure with the words *suntan* and *hatbox*.

Sort Compound Words

Have students read words and decide if each word is a compound or noncompound word.

1. Gather the index cards you prepared. Mix the cards well and place them in a stack face down on the table.

2. **Say:** You are going to sort some words. You will take a card from the pile and read it to me. Some of the words are compound words and some are not. You will think about the word and decide if it is a compound word or not.

3. **Say:** You will place compound words in one pile and noncompound words in another pile. I'll do the first one for you.

4. Demonstrate the following for students:

   ▸ Draw a card from the pile.
   ▸ Read the word aloud.
   ▸ Say if the word is a compound or noncompound word and place the card in that pile.

5. Have students continue the procedure with the remaining words:

   ▸ **Compound Words:** *suntan, backpack, hatbox, sunfish, cobweb*
   ▸ **Noncompound Words:** *buzz, ship, hatch, mush, tack*

Try It

By Sight

Have students complete page PH 83 in *K¹² PhonicsWorks Basic Activity Book* for more practice with reading sight words. Have students read as many words as they can in one minute.

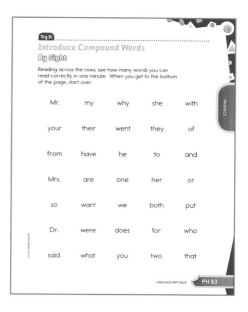

Dictation: Write Words

Have students practice identifying sounds and writing words.

1. Gather a pencil and the dictation notebook. Say the word *cobweb*. Then give these directions to students:

   ▸ Repeat the word.
   ▸ Write the word in your notebook.
   ▸ Read the word aloud.

2. When students have finished, write the following word on your whiteboard: *cobweb*.

3. Have them compare their answer to your correct version.

4. Repeat this procedure with the words *suntan* and *backpack*.

   ▸ If students make an error and don't see it, help them correct their mistake by having them finger stretch the sounds in the word they missed.
   ▸ If students are having difficulty selecting the correct letters or sounds, review those letters or sounds that are confusing them.
   ▸ If students have difficulty with first, middle, and last sounds, have them finger stretch the sounds in words.

 **20 minutes**

REVIEW: **Compound Words**

Students will work online independently to

- ► Practice compound words.
- ► Practice decoding text by reading a story.

Help students locate the online activities and provide support as needed.

Offline Alternative

No computer access? Have students spell compounds words, say the two separate words that make the compound word, and use the compound word in a sentence (for example, *suntan*, *sun* and *tan*, *Jill got a suntan* or *backpack*, *back* and *pack*, *John used a backpack on his hike*).

Objectives

- Identify and use compound words.
- Identify individual sounds in words.
- Read aloud grade-level text with appropriate automaticity, prosody, accuracy, and rate.
- Decode words by applying grade-level word analysis skills.

Practice Compound Words (A)

Lesson Overview

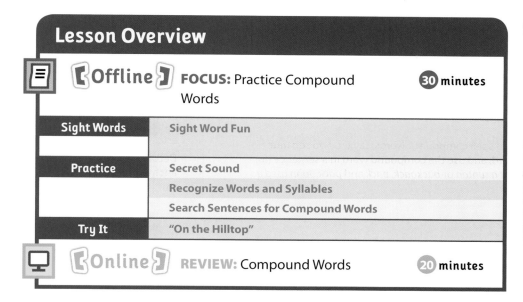

Offline **FOCUS:** Practice Compound Words — **30** minutes

Sight Words	Sight Word Fun
Practice	Secret Sound
	Recognize Words and Syllables
	Search Sentences for Compound Words
Try It	"On the Hilltop"

Online **REVIEW:** Compound Words — **20** minutes

 **Offline** **30** minutes

FOCUS: Practice Compound Words

Work **together** with students to complete offline Sight Words, Practice, and
Try It activities.

Sight Words

Sight Word Fun

Help students learn the sight words *Mr., Mrs.,* and *Dr.,* and up to two additional sight
words they have yet to master.

1. Gather the sight word *Mr., Mrs.,* and *Dr.,* and up to two additional sight word
   cards.

2. Choose one sight word card to begin.

   Say: Look at this word and take a picture of it in your mind. When you think
   you can spell the word yourself, turn the card over and use your letter tiles to
   spell the word.

3. After students spell the word, have them check the card to see if they spelled
   the word correctly.

   Say: Read aloud the word you spelled with the letter tiles.

4. Repeat the activity with the remaining sight words.

 Sight words can be very difficult for some students. Let them work at their own
pace and really master these words.

> **Objectives**
> - Read sight words.
> - Spell sight words.

Practice

Secret Sound

Say groups of words to help students recognize **beginning sounds** in words.

1. **Say:** I am going to say some groups of words. Listen for a secret sound in at the
   beginning of each word. Then tell me what sound you hear at the beginning of
   each group of words.

2. Say each of the following groups of words. Have students identify the secret
   sound in each group.

   ▸ *shop, shine, short* /sh/
   ▸ *top, tame, tiny* /t/
   ▸ *chase, chop, chin* /ch/
   ▸ *boy, baby, bin* /b/
   ▸ *very, van, village* /v/

 If students can't identify the secret sound, have them listen while you say each
word again and then have them repeat each word. Have students say what sound they
hear at the beginning of each word.

> **Objectives**
> - Identify beginning sounds in words.
> - Identify individual sounds in words.
> - Identify syllables in words.
> - Identify the number of sounds within words.
> - Write words by applying grade-level phonics knowledge.
> - Identify complete sentences.
> - Identify and use compound words.

Recognize Words and Syllables

Review the concept of syllables with students.

1. **Say:** When we talk, we make words by pushing air out of our mouths. Each push of air in a word is called a **syllable**. Each word has one or more syllables. You can think of syllables as chunks of words.

2. **Say:** Let's break some words into syllables.

   - ▸ I'll say a word. I'll repeat the word.
   - ▸ You'll say the word after me, and you'll break it into syllables by saying the separate chunks of the word and tapping your fist on the table as you say each chunk.
   - ▸ For example, I'll say *morning* and then I'll say it again.
   - ▸ You'll say *morn / ing* and tap your fist on the table as you say each syllable.

3. Say each word and repeat it. Have students fist tap on the table as they say the syllables in each word.

   - ▸ *mistake* mis / take
   - ▸ *gallop* gal / lop
   - ▸ *elephant* el / e / phant
   - ▸ *chick* chick
   - ▸ *traffic* traf / fic
   - ▸ *establish* es / tab / lish
   - ▸ *tonsil* ton / sil
   - ▸ *bird* bird
   - ▸ *Pacific* Pa / cif / ic

   TIP Have students name items in a category, such as foods, furniture, or animals, and fist tap the syllables with you. For example, have them name and fist tap words such as *ta / ble* and *win / dow*. Challenge students to name and fist tap something with several syllables (for example, *tel / e / vi / sion*).

Search Sentences for Compound Words

Help students recognize **compound words** in sentences.

1. Gather a pencil and the dictation notebook.

2. **Say:** I'm going to read some sentences. Listen for the compound word in the sentence. First repeat the sentence and then tell me the compound word.

   - ▸ For example, if I say the sentence, *My cat loves catnip*, you will repeat the sentence and then say the word *catnip*, which is a compound word.
   - ▸ Then you will write the compound word in your notebook, spelling one syllable at a time.

3. Read this sentence aloud: *The pig is in the pigpen.*

   - ▸ What word in the sentence is a compound word? *pigpen*
   - ▸ Write the compound word, spelling one syllable at a time.

4. Follow the procedure with the following words and sentences:

   - ▸ *We cannot go to the shop. cannot*
   - ▸ *Stuff the mess in my backpack. backpack*
   - ▸ *Put the hat in the hatbox. hatbox*

Try It ●

"On the Hilltop"

Have students read "On the Hilltop" on page 19 of *K¹² PhonicsWorks Readers Basic 10.*

Students should read the story silently once or twice before reading the story aloud. When students miss a word that can be sounded out, point to it and give them three to six seconds to try the word again. If students still miss the word, tell them the word so the flow of the story isn't interrupted.

After reading the story, make a list of all the words students missed, and go over those words with them. You may use letter tiles to show students how to read the words.

Objectives

- Read aloud grade-level text with appropriate automaticity, prosody, accuracy, and rate.
- Decode words by applying grade-level word analysis skills.
- Track text from left to right.
- Turn pages sequentially.

 **20 minutes**

REVIEW: Compound Words

Students will work online independently to

▶ Practice compound words.

Help students locate the online activities and provide support as needed.

Objectives

- Identify and use compound words.
- Identify individual sounds in words.

Offline Alternative

No computer access? Have students think of compound words, say the two separate words that make the compound word, and use the compound word in a sentence (for example, *catnap*, *cat* and *nap*, *He took a catnap* or *cobweb*, *cob* and *web*, *See the cobweb*).

Practice Compound Words (B)

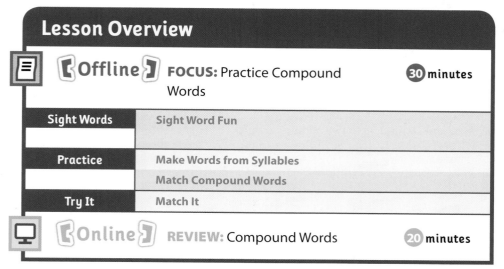

Lesson Overview

Offline FOCUS: Practice Compound Words		**30** minutes

Sight Words	Sight Word Fun	
Practice	Make Words from Syllables	
	Match Compound Words	
Try It	Match It	

Online REVIEW: Compound Words		**20** minutes

Materials

Supplied
- *K¹² PhonicsWorks Basic Activity Book*, p. PH 84
- whiteboard, student
- Tile Kit

Also Needed
- sight words box
- index cards (14)

Advance Preparation

For Match Compound Words, print each of the following words on index cards, using one card per word: *cat, nap, in, to, back, pack, up, hill, sun, tan, nut, shell, sun,* and *set*.

 **30 minutes**

FOCUS: Practice Compound Words

Work **together** with students to complete offline Sight Words, Practice, and Try It activities.

Sight Words

Sight Word Fun

Help students learn the sight words *Mr.*, *Mrs.*, and *Dr.*, and up to two additional sight words they have yet to master.

1. Gather the sight word *Mr.*, *Mrs.*, and *Dr.*, and up to two additional sight word cards.

2. Choose one sight word card to begin.

   Say: Look at this word and take a picture of it in your mind. When you think you can spell the word yourself, turn the card over and use your letter tiles to spell the word.

3. After students spell the word, have them check the card to see if they spelled the word correctly.

   Say: Read aloud the word you spelled with the letter tiles.

4. Repeat the activity with the remaining sight words.

TIP Sight words can be very difficult for some students. Let them work at their own pace and really master these words.

> **Objectives**
> - Read sight words.
> - Spell sight words.

Practice

Make Words from Syllables

Have students fist tap syllables and put them together to make words.

1. **Say:** I'm going to say some syllables. Your job is to repeat the syllables while fist tapping them. Then tell me the word the syllables make when we put them together.

2. **Say:** The syllables are *ti* and *ger*.

   ▸ Repeat the syllables while fist tapping each one.
   ▸ What word do you get when you put the syllables together? *tiger*

3. Repeat the procedure with the following syllables:

   ▸ *can / yon* canyon
   ▸ *Fri / day* Friday
   ▸ *bas / ket / ball* basketball
   ▸ *mo / vie* movie
   ▸ *mu / sic* music

   ▸ *sam / ple* sample
   ▸ *fan / tas / tic* fantastic
   ▸ *ex / pert* expert
   ▸ *pen / man / ship* penmanship

> **Objectives**
> - Identify individual sounds in words.
> - Identify syllables in words.
> - Identify the number of sounds within words.
> - Identify and use compound words.

Match Compound Words

Help students practice making compound words.

1. Gather the index cards that you prepared.

   ▶ Place the following words face up in one row: *cat, in, back, up, sun, nut,* and *sun*.
   ▶ Place the following words face up in another row under the first row: *nap, to, pack, hill, tan, shell,* and *set*.

2. **Say:** I'm going to make a compound word by matching a word from the top row with a word from the bottom row. The first word is [word from top row]. Now I'll find a word from the bottom row that makes this a compound word.

3. **Say:** Now it's your turn. Choose a word from the top row. Next find a word in the bottom row that you can put with the first word to make a compound word.

   If students do not understand the concept of compound words, give them the word *sun*. Then have them choose between the words *tan* and *hill*. Have them tell you which word goes with the word *sun* to make a word they know.

4. Guide students who put together two words that do not make a compound word. Have them read the word aloud.

   Say: Does that word make sense, or is it a nonsense word?

5. Continue with the activity until students have used all the cards to make compound words.

Try It

Match It

Have students complete page PH 84 in *K¹² PhonicsWorks Basic Activity Book* for more practice with compound words. Have students read each sentence aloud and draw a line to the matching picture for the compound word.

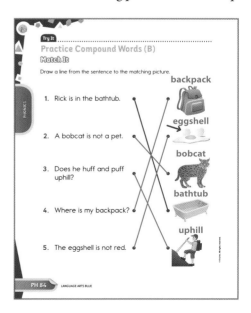

Objectives

• Read aloud grade-level text with appropriate automaticity, prosody, accuracy, and rate.

• Identify and use compound words.

20 minutes

REVIEW: **Compound Words**

Students will work online independently to

- ▶ Practice compound words.
- ▶ Practice decoding text by reading a story.

Help students locate the online activities and provide support as needed.

Offline Alternative

No computer access? Have students think of compound words, say the two separate word that make the compound word, and use the compound word in a sentence (for example, *eggshell*, *egg* and *shell*, *Break the eggshell* or *uphill*, *up* and *hill*, *Walking uphill is fun*).

 Objectives

- Identify and use compound words.
- Identify individual sounds in words.
- Read aloud grade-level text with appropriate automaticity, prosody, accuracy, and rate.
- Decode words by applying grade-level word analysis skills.

Practice Compound Words (C)

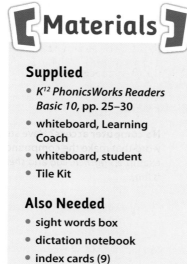

Lesson Overview

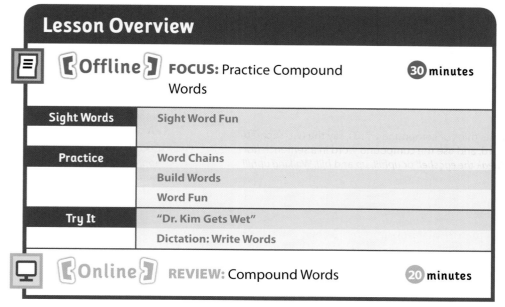

Offline	**FOCUS:** Practice Compound Words	**30** minutes

Sight Words	Sight Word Fun
Practice	Word Chains
	Build Words
	Word Fun
Try It	"Dr. Kim Gets Wet"
	Dictation: Write Words

Online	**REVIEW:** Compound Words	**20** minutes

Materials

Supplied
- *K¹² PhonicsWorks Readers Basic 10*, pp. 25–30
- whiteboard, Learning Coach
- whiteboard, student
- Tile Kit

Also Needed
- sight words box
- dictation notebook
- index cards (9)

Advance Preparation

For Word Fun, print the following words on index cards, using one card per word: *sunset, pigpen, bathtub, cobweb, zigzag, hatbox, bobcat, eggshell,* and *suntan.*

Offline 30 minutes

FOCUS: Practice Compound Words

Work **together** with students to complete offline Sight Words, Practice, and Try It activities.

Sight Words

Sight Word Fun

Help students learn the sight words *Mr., Mrs.,* and *Dr.,* and up to two additional sight words they have yet to master.

1. Gather the sight word *Mr., Mrs.,* and *Dr.,* and up to two additional sight word cards.

2. Choose one sight word card to begin.

   Say: Look at this word and take a picture of it in your mind. When you think you can spell the word yourself, turn the card over and use your letter tiles to spell the word.

3. After students spell the word, have them check the card to see if they spelled the word correctly.

   Say: Read aloud the word you spelled with the letter tiles.

4. Repeat the activity with the remaining sight words.

TIP Sight words can be very difficult for some students. Let them work at their own pace and really master these words.

Objectives
- Read sight words.
- Spell sight words.

Practice

Word Chains

Have students build words by adding and changing letters to help them recognize and use individual sounds in words.

1. Place the following letter tiles at the top of students' whiteboard: *a, b, ck, e, g, h, i, l, m, sh, sh, t,* and *u.*

2. **Say:** I am going to build the first word in a chain. The word is *back.*

   ▸ I will pull down the letters for the sounds /b/, /ă/, and /k/ to spell the word *back.*
   ▸ I will touch and say *back.* To change *back* to *bat,* I will think about what sound is changed from the word *back* to *bat.* I will need to replace the letter tile *ck* with the letter *t.*
   ▸ Touch and say the word *bat.* Now it's your turn to change *bat* to *bash.* You can spell *bash* by making only one change. Touch and say the new word.

3. Redirect students if they select the incorrect letter for any sound.

   Say: That letter is for the sound [incorrect sound]. We want the letter for the sound [target sound]. What letter makes that sound? Answers will vary.

Objectives
- Identify the new word when one sound is changed in a word.
- Identify individual sounds in words.
- Produce rhyming words.
- Identify individual sounds in words.
- Blend sounds to create words.
- Write words by applying grade-level phonics knowledge.
- Read aloud grade-level text with appropriate automaticity, prosody, accuracy, and rate.

4. Redirect students if they name the sound incorrectly.

   Say: To change the word [first word] to [target word], we need the letter for the sound [target sound].

   Show students how to make the change. Have them touch and say the new word after they move the letters.

5. Follow this procedure to make the following words: *hash, mash, mush, shush, hush, hash, ham, him, hit, bit, bet, let, met, get.*

6. For every new word, have students add, replace, or remove only one letter tile.

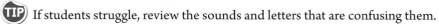 If students struggle, review the sounds and letters that are confusing them.

Build Words

Help students use letters and sounds to build words.

1. Place the following letter tiles at the top of students' whiteboard: *a, a, all, b, c, e, g, h, i, ll, m, n, o, p, s, s, t,* and *u.*

2. Draw six horizontal lines across the middle of students' whiteboard to represent the sounds in a word.

3. **Say:** Let's use letters and sounds to build the word *hilltop.*

4. Have students finger stretch the sounds in *hilltop.*

5. Have students

   ► Fist tap the syllables in the word.
   ► Identify the first, next, and last sounds in *hilltop.*
   ► Choose the corresponding letter tile for each of the sounds.
   ► Move the letters to the correct lines on their whiteboard.

6. Guide students with these questions:

   ► What is the first sound in *hilltop*? /h/
     Which line does the letter for that sound go on? the first one
   ► What is the next sound in *hilltop*? /ĭ/
     Which line does the letter for that sound go on? the second one
   ► What's the next sound in *hilltop*? /l/
     Which line do the letters for that sound go on? the third one
   ► What's the next sound in *hilltop*? /t/
     Which line does the letter for that sound go on? the fourth one
   ► What's the next sound in *hilltop*? /ŏ/
     Which line does the letter for that sound go on? the fifth one
   ► What's the last sound in *hilltop*? /p/
     Which line does the letter for that sound go on? the last one

7. Redirect students if they select the incorrect letter.

   Say: That sound is in the word [word], and it is the [first, second, third] sound. We want the sound [target sound].

   Continue until students select the correct letter.

8. Have students touch and say the word.

9. Have them say the word as they use a dry-erase marker to write the word on the whiteboard.

10. Draw horizontal lines across the middle of students' whiteboard that represent the number of sounds in each word. Repeat the activity to build the following words:

▸ *catnap* /k/ /ă/ /t/ /n/ /ă/ /p/
▸ *gumball* /g/ /ŭ/ /m/ /b/ /all/
▸ *subset* /s/ /ŭ/ /b/ /s/ /ĕ/ /t/

Word Fun
Have students practice reading compound words.

1. Gather the index cards you prepared and place them face down in one pile.

2. **Say:** You are going to practice reading and writing some words.

   ▸ You will choose a card from the pile and read the word on it.
   ▸ Then you are going to flip the card over and write the word on the backside of the card.
   ▸ I'll try first.

3. Choose a card from the pile and say and write the word.

   Say: Now it's your turn. Choose a card and read it to me.

4. If time permits, have students choose two words and draw a picture of those words on the back of the card.

TIP If students stumble over any words, have them touch and say the words. Touch and say these words along with them.

Try It •

"Dr. Kim Gets Wet"
Have students read "Dr. Kim Gets Wet" on page 25 of *K¹² PhonicsWorks Readers Basic 10.*

 Students should read the story silently once or twice before reading the story aloud. When students miss a word that can be sounded out, point to it and give them three to six seconds to try the word again. If students still miss the word, tell them the word so the flow of the story isn't interrupted.

 After reading the story, make a list of all the words students missed, and go over those words with them. You may use letter tiles to show students how to read the words.

Objectives
• Read aloud grade-level text with appropriate automaticity, prosody, accuracy, and rate.
• Decode words by applying grade-level word analysis skills.
• Track text from left to right.
• Turn pages sequentially.
• Write words by applying grade-level phonics knowledge.
• Follow three-step directions.

Dictation: Write Words

Have students practice identifying sounds and writing words.

1. Gather a pencil and the dictation notebook. Say the word *uphill*. Then give these directions to students:

   ▸ Repeat the word.
   ▸ Write the word in your notebook.
   ▸ Read the word aloud.

2. When students have finished, write the following word on your whiteboard: *uphill*.

3. Have them compare their answer to your correct version.

4. Repeat this procedure with the words *cannot* and *upset*.

   ▸ If students make an error and don't see it, help them correct their mistake by having them finger stretch the sounds in the word they missed.
   ▸ If students are having difficulty selecting the correct letters or sounds, review those letters or sounds that are confusing them.
   ▸ If students have difficulty with first, middle, and last sounds, have them finger stretch the sounds in words.

 **20 minutes**

REVIEW: **Compound Words**

Students will work online independently to

▸ Practice compound words.

Help students locate the online activities and provide support as needed.

Objectives
- Identify and use compound words.
- Identify individual sounds in words.

Offline Alternative

No computer access? Have students think of compound words, say the two separate words that make the compound word, and use the compound word in a sentence (for example, *into, in* and *to, Go into the house* or *sunset, sun* and *set, That's a pretty sunset*).

Unit Checkpoint

Lesson Overview

	[Online] REVIEW: Compound Words	**20** minutes	
	[Offline] UNIT CHECKPOINT: Compound Words	**30** minutes	

Materials

Supplied
- *K¹² PhonicsWorks Basic Assessments,* pp. PH 193–198

Objectives
- Identify complete sentences.
- Identify individual sounds in words.
- Identify and use compound words.
- Given the sound, identify the most common letter or letters.
- Read instructional-level text with 90% accuracy.
- Read sight words.
- Read aloud grade-level text with appropriate automaticity, prosody, accuracy, and rate.
- Write words by applying grade-level phonics knowledge.

 **20** minutes

REVIEW: Compound Words

Students will review compound words to prepare for the Unit Checkpoint. Help students locate the online activities and provide support as needed.

[Offline] 30 minutes

UNIT CHECKPOINT: Compound Words

Explain that students are going to show what they have learned about letters, sounds, and words.

1. Give students the Unit Checkpoint pages for the Compound Words unit and print the Unit Checkpoint Answer Key, if you'd like.

2. Use the instructions below to help administer the Checkpoint to students. On the Answer Key or another sheet of paper, note student answers to oral response questions to help with scoring the Checkpoint later.

3. Use the Answer Key to score the Checkpoint, and then enter the results online.

Part 1. Read Word Parts Have students read across the rows from left to right and say the sound or sounds of each word part. Note any word parts they say incorrectly.

Part 2. Finger Stretching Say each word to students. Have them say each word and finger stretch the sounds. Note any words they finger stretch incorrectly.

19. *buzz*	**23.** *bill*
20. *cuff*	**24.** *mess*
21. *hatch*	**25.** *puff*
22. *whiff*	**26.** *doll*

Part 3. Dictation Say each word to students. Have them repeat and write the word.

27. *bathtub*	**30.** *suntan*
28. *uphill*	**31.** *hotrod*
29. *cobweb*	**32.** *cannot*

Part 4. Writing Read each sentence to students. Have them repeat and write the sentence.

33. *Can I have a hotdog?*

34. *Ross has a red backpack.*

Part 5. Read Aloud Listen to students read the sentences aloud. Count and note the number of words they read correctly.

Part 6. Say Letters Say each sound. Have students tell you a letter or letters that make that sound. Note any incorrect responses.

36. /ĕ/

37. /kw/

38. /sh/

39. /ŏ/

40. /ks/

41. /k/

42. /ŭ/

43. /ă/

44. /l/

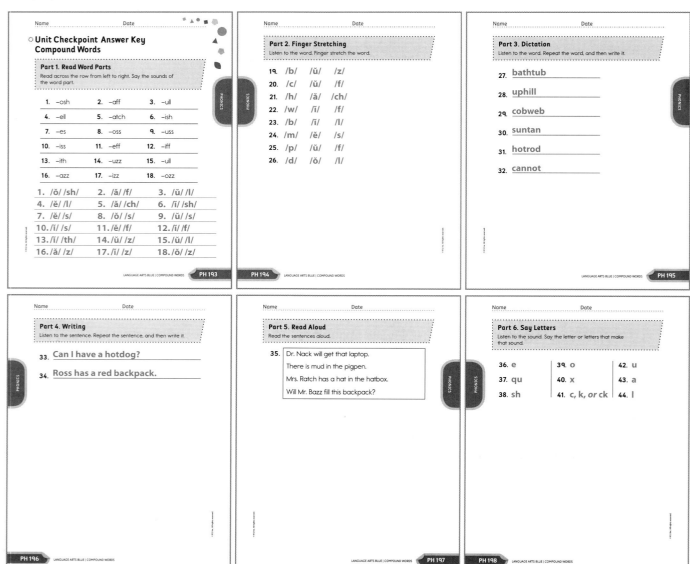

Name _____ Date _____

Unit Checkpoint Answer Key
Compound Words

Part 1. Read Word Parts
Read across the row from left to right. Say the sounds of the word part.

1. –osh	2. –aff	3. –ull
4. –ell	5. –atch	6. –ish
7. –es	8. –oss	9. –uss
10. –iss	11. –eff	12. –iff
13. –ith	14. –uzz	15. –ull
16. –azz	17. –izz	18. –ozz

1. /ŏ/ /sh/	2. /ă/ /f/	3. /ŭ/ /l/
4. /ĕ/ /l/	5. /ă/ /ch/	6. /ĭ/ /sh/
7. /ĕ/ /s/	8. /ŏ/ /s/	9. /ŭ/ /s/
10. /ĭ/ /s/	11. /ĕ/ /f/	12. /ĭ/ /f/
13. /ĭ/ /th/	14. /ŭ/ /z/	15. /ŭ/ /l/
16. /ă/ /z/	17. /ĭ/ /z/	18. /ŏ/ /z/

Name _____ Date _____

Part 2. Finger Stretching
Listen to the word. Finger stretch the word.

19. /b/ /ŭ/ /z/
20. /c/ /ŭ/ /f/
21. /h/ /ă/ /ch/
22. /w/ /ĭ/ /f/
23. /b/ /ĭ/ /l/
24. /m/ /ĕ/ /s/
25. /p/ /ŭ/ /f/
26. /d/ /ŏ/ /l/

Name _____ Date _____

Part 3. Dictation
Listen to the word. Repeat the word, and then write it.

27. bathtub _____

28. uphill _____

29. cobweb _____

30. suntan _____

31. hotrod _____

32. cannot _____

Name _____ Date _____

Part 4. Writing
Listen to the sentence. Repeat the sentence, and then write it.

33. Can I have a hotdog? _____

34. Ross has a red backpack. _____

Name _____ Date _____

Part 5. Read Aloud
Read the sentences aloud.

35. Dr. Nack will get that laptop.
There is mud in the pigpen.
Mrs. Ratch has a hat in the hatbox.
Will Mr. Bazz fill this backpack?

Name _____ Date _____

Part 6. Say Letters
Listen to the sound. Say the letter or letters that make that sound.

36. e	39. o	42. u
37. qu	40. x	43. a
38. sh	41. c, k, or ck	44. l

Getting Stronger: Punctuation and Capitalization

Unit Overview

In this unit, students will
- ▶ Review sight words.
- ▶ Create sentences using correct capitalization and punctuation.
- ▶ Review the endings –s and –es.
- ▶ Review the endings –ff, –ll, –ss, –zz, and –all.
- ▶ Review compound words.
- ▶ Practice reading and writing.

Materials

Supplied
- *K¹² PhonicsWorks Basic Activity Book*, p. PH 85
- whiteboard, Learning Coach
- whiteboard, student

Also Needed
- sight words box
- dictation notebook
- index cards (13)

Lesson Overview

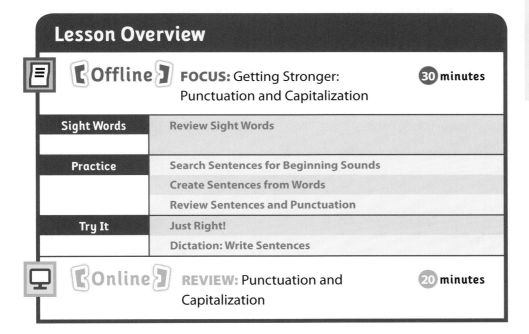

[Offline] FOCUS: Getting Stronger: Punctuation and Capitalization — **30** minutes

Sight Words	Review Sight Words
Practice	Search Sentences for Beginning Sounds
	Create Sentences from Words
	Review Sentences and Punctuation
Try It	Just Right!
	Dictation: Write Sentences

[Online] REVIEW: Punctuation and Capitalization — **20** minutes

Advance Preparation

For Create Sentences from Words, print each of the following words on index cards, using one card per word: *there, shell, toss, pack,* and *are.*

For Review Sentences and Punctuation, print each of the following words on index cards, using one card per word:

- ▶ *Can*
- ▶ *a*
- ▶ *duck*
- ▶ *quack?*
- ▶ *A*
- ▶ *duck*
- ▶ *can*
- ▶ *quack.*

 **30 minutes**

FOCUS: Getting Stronger: Punctuation and Capitalization

Work **together** with students to complete offline Sight Words, Practice, and Try It activities.

Sight Words

Review Sight Words

Help students learn to recognize sight words.

Objectives
- Read sight words.
- Spell sight words.
- Write sight words.

1. Gather all the sight word cards students have yet to master from their sight words box. Stack the cards on the table face down.

2. Have students pick up a word and read it to you.

3. If they read it quickly and correctly, put the card in one stack. If they hesitate or do not read the word correctly, put it in another stack. The second stack should have words that they will review again.

4. Take the stack of words that students read correctly and dictate each word to them. They may choose to either write the word or spell it aloud.

5. If students spell the word correctly, put the card in the first stack because they have mastered the word. If they misspell the word, add it to the stack of cards to review again.

6. Chart students' progress on the back of each card.

   ▶ Divide the back of the card into two columns.
   ▶ Label the first column "Read" and the second column "Spell."
   ▶ Record the dates that students read or spell the word correctly. When students can read and spell the word correctly three times in a row, they have mastered the word. You may want to put a star or sticker on their card when they have mastered that word.

TIP Even if students can read and spell all the words correctly, it is still beneficial for them to review sight words. Choose as many additional words as you would like for each subsequent activity.

Practice

Search Sentences for Beginning Sounds

Have students practice identifying **beginning sounds** in words that are in a sentence.

1. **Say:** I'm going to say a special beginning sound that is in a word. You will repeat that sound and the word. The first sound is /d/, as in the word *dog*.

2. Have students say the target sound /d/ and the word *dog*.

3. **Say:** Now I will read a sentence. Repeat the sentence and tell me the word that has the same sound. The first sentence is *I have a doll.* Which word in the sentence has the special beginning sound? *doll*

4. Have students repeat the sentence and say the word.

5. Redirect students if they don't name the correct word.

   Say: Let me say the sentence again. Remember, you're listening for the sound [special sound].

6. Guide students if they have difficulty. Say two words from the sentence and have them choose the one with the target beginning sound.

7. Use the same procedure with the following words and sentences:

   ▸ /m/, as in *map*   *The toy belongs to me.* me
   ▸ /f/, as in *foot*   *Lisa filled the glass.* filled
   ▸ /s/, as in *sit*   *Take a seat.* seat
   ▸ /g/, as in *go*   *This gift is for you.* gift

Objectives

- Identify beginning sounds in words.
- Identify individual sounds in words.
- Write words by applying grade-level phonics knowledge.
- Capitalize the first word in a sentence.
- Identify complete sentences.
- Use periods to end telling sentences.
- Use question marks to end asking sentences.

Create Sentences from Words

Help students practice writing sentences using familiar words.

1. Gather the index cards you prepared and the dictation notebook.

2. Have students read all the words.

3. Have students choose a word and write it in a sentence in their dictation notebook. Help them with any words that are difficult for them; tell them the word so that the flow of the sentence is not interrupted.

4. Repeat the procedure until students have selected all the words.

5. Have students read the sentences aloud.

Review Sentences and Punctuation

Help students practice telling and asking sentences.

1. Gather the index cards you prepared and place them in front of students so that they make two sentences: *A duck can quack.* and *Can a duck quack?*

2. Point to each group of words and ask students the following questions:

   ▸ How are these groups of words alike? Both have the same words.
   ▸ How are these groups of words different? The words are in a different order and have different ending punctuation.
   ▸ What are the rules a telling sentence and an asking sentence must follow? To begin a sentence, use a capital letter in the first word. To end a telling sentence, add a period to mark the end of the sentence. To end an asking sentence, add a question mark to the end of the sentence.

3. Read aloud the telling sentence *A duck can quack.* Have students

   ▸ Read the sentence aloud to you.
   ▸ Touch the capital letter that signals the beginning of the sentence.
   ▸ Touch the period that signals the end of the sentence.

4. Read aloud the asking sentence *Can a duck quack?* Have students

   ▸ Read the sentence aloud to you.
   ▸ Touch the capital letter that signals the beginning of the sentence.
   ▸ Touch the question mark that signals the end of the sentence.

5. Scramble the words in the telling sentence *A duck can quack.* Have students

   ▸ Rearrange the words to make a sentence.
   ▸ Touch each word in the sentence as they read it aloud.
   ▸ Point to the capital letter at the beginning of the sentence.
   ▸ Point to the punctuation mark at the end of the sentence.
   ▸ Write the sentence on their whiteboard.

6. Follow the same procedure with the asking sentence *Can a duck quack?*

7. Help students if they have difficulty arranging the words correctly to make a sentence.

   Say: Read the sentence aloud. Does it make sense?

8. Point to any word that seems out of place and state the following:

   ▸ What is this word?
   ▸ Find a word that would make better sense.
   ▸ Switch the words. Now read the sentence.
   ▸ Does it make sense now?

9. Ask students the following questions if they continue to have difficulty:

   ▸ What is special about the first word in a sentence? It begins with a capital letter.
   ▸ What is special about the end of a telling sentence? It ends with a period.
   ▸ What is special about the end of an asking sentence? It ends with a question mark.

Try It

Just Right!

Have students complete page PH 85 in *K¹² PhonicsWorks Basic Activity Book* for more practice with punctuation and capitalization. Have students put a period or a question mark at the end of the sentence and read the sentence aloud.

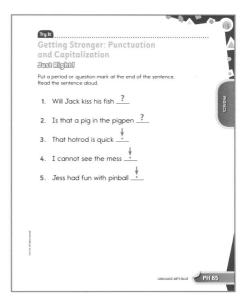

Dictation: Write Sentences

Use sentences to help students identify individual sounds in words.

1. Gather a pencil and the dictation notebook. Say the sentence, *Get off the mat.* Then give these directions to students:

   ▶ Repeat the sentence.
   ▶ Write the sentence in your notebook.
   ▶ Read the sentence aloud.

2. When students have finished, write the following sentence on your whiteboard: *Get off the mat.*

3. Have them compare their answer to your correct version.

4. Repeat this procedure with the following sentence: *Can Bess hug the dog?*

   ▶ If students make an error and don't see it, help them correct their mistake by having them finger stretch the sounds in the word they missed.
   ▶ If students are having difficulty selecting the correct letters or sounds, review those letters or sounds that are confusing them.
   ▶ If students have difficulty with first, middle, and last sounds, have them finger stretch the sounds in words.

 **20 minutes**

REVIEW: Punctuation and Capitalization

Students will work online independently to

► Practice punctuation and capitalization.

► Practice decoding text by reading a story.

Help students locate the online activities and provide support as needed.

Offline Alternative

No computer access? Say telling and asking sentences to students, such as *It was a jumping frog.* and *Was it a jumping frog?* Have students tell you which word in each sentence should begin with a capital letter. Have them say where the period or question mark should go. You might also have students write short telling and asking sentences in their dictation notebook, on the whiteboard, or on a sheet of paper. Make sure students begin each sentence with a capital letter and place a period or question mark at the end.

 Objectives

- Identify individual sounds in words.
- Capitalize the first word in a sentence.
- Identify complete sentences.
- Use periods to end telling sentences.
- Use question marks to end asking sentences.
- Read aloud grade-level text with appropriate automaticity, prosody, accuracy, and rate.
- Decode words by applying grade-level word analysis skills.

Getting Stronger: Endings –s and –es

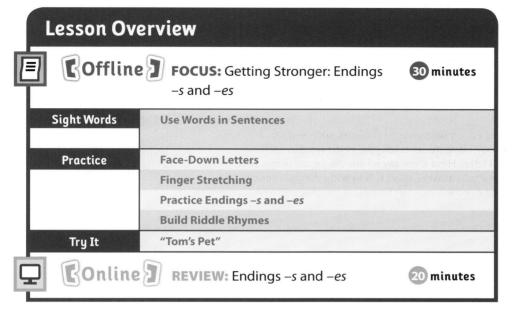

Lesson Overview

Offline FOCUS: Getting Stronger: Endings –s and –es **30 minutes**

Sight Words	Use Words in Sentences
Practice	Face-Down Letters
	Finger Stretching
	Practice Endings –s and –es
	Build Riddle Rhymes
Try It	"Tom's Pet"

Online REVIEW: Endings –s and –es **20 minutes**

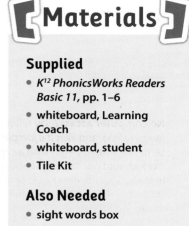

Materials

Supplied
- *K¹² PhonicsWorks Readers Basic 11*, pp. 1–6
- whiteboard, Learning Coach
- whiteboard, student
- Tile Kit

Also Needed
- sight words box

Advance Preparation

Place lowercase letter tiles in alphabetical order on your whiteboard.

Offline · 30 minutes

FOCUS: Getting Stronger: Endings –s and –es

Work **together** with students to complete offline Sight Words, Practice, and Try It activities.

Sight Words

Use Words in Sentences

Help students use sight words in sentences.

1. Gather all the sight word cards students have yet to master from their sight words box. Spread the sight word cards on the table.

2. **Say:** Let's use sight words in sentences.

3. Have students

   ▸ Touch each card and read the word on it.
   ▸ Make up a sentence using the word.
   ▸ Put the card in a pile after using the word in a sentence.
   ▸ Go through the pile of cards and read each sight word again.
   ▸ Spell each word.

 TIP If students have difficulty with any of the sight words, place those cards in a pile to review again.

> **Objectives**
> - Read sight words.
> - Spell sight words.

Practice

Face-Down Letters

To help students master the ability to recognize the letters of the alphabet, have them practice identifying and naming letters. Grab your whiteboard with letters placed in alphabetical order.

1. Lay your whiteboard down on a flat surface and flip over the following letter tiles so they are face down on the whiteboard: *a, d, f, h, m, qu, s, t,* and *y.*

2. **Say:** These letters are face down. We are looking at the back of them. Name each letter and then turn it over to see if you were right.

 TIP If students miss any of the letters, have them turn over the missed ones and try again.

Finger Stretching

Use finger stretching to help students identify individual sounds in words.

1. **Say:** Let's review finger stretching. In the word *risk,* the first sound is /r/, the next sound is /ĭ/, the next sound is /s/, and the last sound is /k/. I will finger stretch each sound as I say it. Then I'll say the word while pulling my fist toward my body.

> **Objectives**
> - Identify letters of the alphabet.
> - Given the letter, identify the most common sound.
> - Given the sound, identify the most common letter or letters.
> - Identify individual sounds in words.
> - Identify ending sounds in words.
> - Read, write, and spell words containing the ending –s.
> - Read, write, and spell words containing the ending –es.
> - Identify words that rhyme.
> - Blend sounds to create words.

2. Finger stretch the word *risk* for students.

3. **Say:** I'm going to say words with several sounds in them. You'll say each word and then finger stretch it while you say each sound in the word.

4. Say the following words and have students finger stretch them. After they finger stretch each word, ask them the question for that word.

   ► *sifts* /s/ /ĭ/ /f/ /t/ /s/   How many sounds are in the word? five
   ► *misses* /m/ /ĭ/ /s/ /iz/   How many sounds are in the word? four
   ► *bases* /b/ /ā/ /s/ /iz/   What is the last sound? /iz/
   ► *laughs* /l/ /ă/ /f/ /s/   What is the last sound? /s/
   ► *dances* /d/ /ă/ /n/ /s/ /iz/   What is the last sound? /iz/

 Refer to the *K¹² PhonicsWorks* DVD for a demonstration of finger stretching.

Practice Endings –s and –es

Have students practice identifying verbs that end with the letter *s*. Grab students' whiteboard and the dry-erase marker.

1. **Say:** I'm going to write a sentence that includes the word *hop*. You will read the sentence to me and point to the word *hop*.

2. Write the following sentence on the whiteboard: *I can hop on the mat.*

3. Have students read the sentence aloud and point to the word *hop*.

4. **Say:** I'm going to write another sentence for you to read.

5. Write the following sentence on the whiteboard: *Jack hops on the mat.* Have students read the sentence aloud.

   Say: What happened to the word *hop* in this second sentence? The letter *s* was added to the end of the word.

6. Have students do the following:

   ► Write the base word *hop*.
   ► Add the ending –s to the base word.
   ► Underline the base word.
   ► Circle the ending –s.
   ► Say the ending sound in the new word. /s/

7. Erase the board and repeat the activity with the following sentence pair:

   ► *chat*   We chat with Pam.
   ► *chats*   Dan chats with Pam. /s/

8. **Say:** I'm going to write a sentence that includes the word *wish*. You will read the sentence to me and point to the word *wish*.

9. Write the following sentence on the whiteboard: *I wish it was fall.*

10. Have students do the following:

    ► Read the sentence aloud.
    ► Point to the word *wish*.

11. **Say:** I'm going to write another sentence for you to read.

12. Write the following sentence on the whiteboard: *Kim wishes it was fall.* Have students read the sentence aloud.

    Say: What happened to the word *wish* in this second sentence? The letters *es* were added to the end of the word.

13. Have students do the following

    ▸ Write the base word *wish*.
    ▸ Add the ending –*es* to the base word.
    ▸ Underline the base word.
    ▸ Circle the ending –*es*.
    ▸ Say the ending sound in the new word. /iz/

14. Erase the board and repeat the activity with the following sentence pair:

    ▸ *fox*   The fox is red.
    ▸ *foxes*   The foxes are red. /iz/

15. Guide students if they have difficult identifying the base word. Have them

    ▸ Finger stretch the sounds in the base word.
    ▸ Touch and say the word.

    TIP Students may recall that adding the letter *s* to the end of some words makes the new words mean "more than one." If they ask you if *sits* and *runs* mean "more than one," tell them that adding the letter *s* to the end of some words makes the new words tell what someone is doing.

Build Riddle Rhymes

Have students identify and build words that rhyme by playing a riddle game.

1. Place the following letter tiles at the top of students' whiteboard: *b, ck, d, e, es, h, i, ll, s, sh, ss,* and *u.*

2. **Say:** We are going to play a riddle game. I will think of a word and give you some clues. You will guess the word and solve the riddle. Next you will use letters and sounds to build the rhyming word that I am thinking of. Then you will write and say the word. I'll do the first one for you.

    ▸ It quacks. It rhymes with *truck.*

3. **Say:** The word is *duck.* I will find the letters for the word *duck.*

4. Build the word *duck* on students' whiteboard.

5. Say and write the word *duck* for students.

6. Give students clues to the words. Have them say each word, build it, and then say and write it. Use these clues and words:

    ▸ A snake does this. It rhymes with *kisses. hisses*
    ▸ You eat on these. It rhymes with *fishes. dishes*
    ▸ You can ring these. It rhymes with *tells. bells*

Try It . . . .

"Tom's Pet"

Have students read "Tom's Pet" on page 1 of *K¹² PhonicsWorks Readers Basic 11*.

　　Students should read the story silently once or twice before reading the story aloud. When students miss a word that can be sounded out, point to it and give them three to six seconds to try the word again. If students still miss the word, tell them the word so the flow of the story isn't interrupted.

　　After reading the story, make a list of all the words students missed, and go over those words with them. You may use letter tiles to show students how to read the words.

Objectives

- Read aloud grade-level text with appropriate automaticity, prosody, accuracy, and rate.
- Decode words by applying grade-level word analysis skills.
- Track text from left to right.
- Turn pages sequentially.

 **20 minutes**

REVIEW: Endings –s and –es

Students will work online independently to

▶ Practice the endings *–s* and *–es*.

Help students locate the online activities and provide support as needed.

Objectives

- Identify ending sounds in words.
- Read, write, and spell words containing the ending *–s*.
- Read, write, and spell words containing the ending *–es*.

Offline Alternative

No computer access? Read the following words to students: *hat*, *rock*, *run*, *wish*, and *buzz*. Have students add the ending *–s* or *–es* to each word, spell the word aloud, and say the ending sound in the new word: *hats*, /s/; *rocks*, /s/; *runs*, /z/; *wishes*, /iz/; and *buzzes*, /iz/.

Getting Stronger: Endings –*ff*, –*ll*, –*ss*, –*zz*, and –*all*

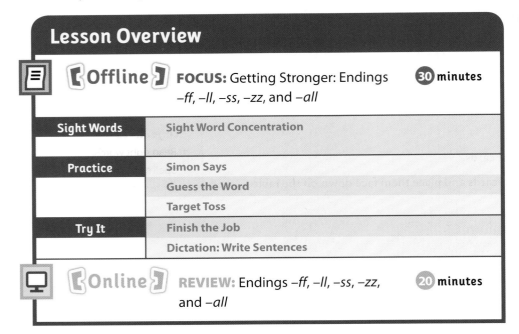

Lesson Overview

Offline FOCUS: Getting Stronger: Endings –*ff*, –*ll*, –*ss*, –*zz*, and –*all* **30** minutes

Sight Words	Sight Word Concentration
Practice	Simon Says
	Guess the Word
	Target Toss
Try It	Finish the Job
	Dictation: Write Sentences

Online REVIEW: Endings –*ff*, –*ll*, –*ss*, –*zz*, and –*all* **20** minutes

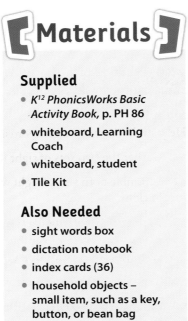

[Materials]

Supplied
- *K¹² PhonicsWorks Basic Activity Book*, p. PH 86
- whiteboard, Learning Coach
- whiteboard, student
- Tile Kit

Also Needed
- sight words box
- dictation notebook
- index cards (36)
- household objects – small item, such as a key, button, or bean bag

Advance Preparation

Gather two sets of the sight word cards students have yet to master.

Go to Target Toss for the lists of words. Print the words in each word list on index cards, using one card per word.

 **Offline** **30** minutes

FOCUS: Getting Stronger: Endings *–ff*, *–ll*, *–ss*, *–zz*, and *–all*

Work **together** with students to complete offline Sight Words, Practice, and Try It activities.

Sight Words

Sight Word Concentration

Help students review sight words.

1. Gather the two sets of sight word cards.

2. Scramble both sets of sight word cards and place them face down on the table or floor.

3. Turn over two cards at a time; take turns with students. If the cards match, the person turning over the matching cards reads the word and uses it in a sentence. If the cards don't match, the person turns them back over.

4. Remove and save the matching cards.

5. Continue the activity until all the cards are paired.

6. Have students read all the words.

7. Take the stack of words that students read correctly and dictate each word to them.

8. Have students write each word or spell it aloud.

TIP If students have difficulty with any sight words, let them work at their own pace to really master these words.

> **Objectives**
> - Read sight words.
> - Spell sight words.
> - Write sight words.

Practice

Simon Says

Play a game with students to help them recognize words that rhyme.

1. **Say:** We're going to play a Simon Says sound game. Listen carefully for words that rhyme with the Simon Says word. Today the Simon Says word is *ball*. Say *ball*.

   ▸ I'm going to say a word and do something. You will repeat the word.
   ▸ If the word rhymes with *ball*, you will copy the action I made.
   ▸ If the word doesn't rhyme with *ball*, then you will be still. We'll do two together.

2. Touch your nose as you say *call*.

3. **Say:** We both say *call* and touch our nose because *call* rhymes with *ball*.

4. Stomp your foot as you say *fuzz*.

> **Objectives**
> - Identify words that rhyme.
> - Identify ending sounds in words.
> - Identify and use ending *–all*.
> - Identify and use ending *–ff*.
> - Identify and use ending *–ll*.
> - Identify and use ending *–ss*.
> - Identify and use ending *–zz*.

5. **Say:** The word is *fuzz*. Repeat the word.

> ▸ We won't stomp our foot when we say *fuzz* because *fuzz* doesn't rhyme with *ball*.
> ▸ Let's begin. Remember, the Simon Says word is *ball*. The new word is *stall*.

6. Repeat the procedure with each of the following words and actions:

> ▸ *stall*   clap your hands
> ▸ *whiff*   pull your ear
> ▸ *all*   stomp your foot
> ▸ *fall*   touch your cheek
> ▸ *mess*   touch your chin

(TIP) If students cannot tell which words rhyme, break each word into its onset and rime (for example, /p/ . . . *itch* and /st/ . . . *itch*).

Guess the Word

Have students use word meaning and sentence structure to choose a word that best completes a sentence.

1. Write the following words on students' whiteboard: *buzz, miss, pass, off,* and *fell*. Make sure students know the meaning of all the words on their whiteboard before you do this activity.

2. **Say:** We're going to play a guessing game. I'm going to read a sentence with a word missing. Your job is to look at the words on your whiteboard and decide which one is the right word to complete the sentence.

> ▸ Listen to this sentence: "When you are not here, I will _____ you."
> ▸ You will tell me what word makes sense in the blank of the sentence. This time the word would be *miss*.
> ▸ The complete sentence would be, "When you are not here, I will *miss* you." Now you try it.

3. Continue the procedure with the following sentences:

> ▸ *I stood by the flowers and heard the bees _____ . buzz*
> ▸ *I cannot reach the juice. Please _____ it to me. pass*
> ▸ *Last night snow _____ and covered everything. fell*
> ▸ *Turn the water _____ so we don't waste it. off*

Target Toss

Play a game with students to help them review double-letter endings. The following word lists will be used in this game:

> ▸ **List 1** (/l/): *dull, ball, catch, tall, fell, quell, toss, hill, pill*
> ▸ **List 2** (/f/): *Jeff, till, miff, buff, mess, cuff, whiff, biff, tiff*
> ▸ **List 3** (/s/): *quack, boss, fuss, miss, kiss, less, mess, bass, gull*
> ▸ **List 4** (/z/): *fuzz, buzz, fizz, pass, fall, hitch, rush, jazz, whack*

1. Gather the word cards you created for list 1 and organize the cards face up in a rectangular grid that measures approximately 1½ feet on one side and 1 foot on the other side. Make the grid on a tabletop or on the floor.

2. Gather a small household object, such as a key, button, or bean bag.

3. **Say:** I am going to say a special ending sound. The first sound is /l/, as in *hull*. Try to toss this object onto a card that shows a word with the sound /l/, as in *hull*.

4. Have students toss the small object onto a card on the grid and read the word on the card where it lands.

5. Give students one point for each word that the object lands on and that they can read that contains the target ending sound.

6. Keep track of students' points. When they score five points, replace the cards in the grid with the cards from list 2.

7. Repeat the activity using the cards from lists 2 through 4.

TIP This game can be played outdoors. Just use chalk to make the grid on the sidewalk or driveway and write the words inside the boxes.

Try It

Finish the Job

Have students complete page PH 86 in *K¹² PhonicsWorks Basic Activity Book* for more practice with the endings *–ff, –ll, –ss,* and *–zz*. Have students choose a word from the box and write that word in the sentence to complete it. Have them read the completed sentences aloud.

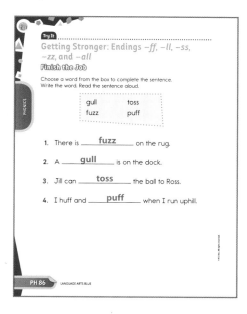

Objectives
- Identify ending sounds in words.
- Identify and use ending *–ff*.
- Identify and use ending *–ll*.
- Identify and use ending *–ss*.
- Identify and use ending *–zz*.
- Read aloud grade-level text with appropriate automaticity, prosody, accuracy, and rate.
- Write words by applying grade-level phonics knowledge.

Dictation: Write Sentences

Use sentences to help students identify individual sounds in words.

1. Gather a pencil and the dictation notebook. Say the sentence, *Toss the ball to Ben.* Then give these directions to students:

   ► Repeat the sentence.
   ► Write the sentence in your notebook.
   ► Read the sentence aloud.

2. When students have finished, write the following sentence on your whiteboard: *Toss the ball to Ben.*

3. Have them compare their answer to your correct version.

4. Repeat this procedure with the following sentences: *This shell is big. Jeff will sell all the bells.*

   ► If students make an error and don't see it, help them correct their mistake by having them finger stretch the sounds in the word they missed.
   ► If students are having difficulty selecting the correct letters or sounds, review those letters or sounds that are confusing them.
   ► If students have difficulty with first, middle, and last sounds, have them finger stretch the sounds in words.

 **20 minutes**

REVIEW: Endings *–ff, –ll, –ss, –zz,* and *–all*

Students will work online independently to

► Practice the endings *–ff, –ll, –ss, –zz,* and *–all.*
► Practice decoding text by reading a story.

Help students locate the online activities and provide support as needed.

Offline Alternative

No computer access? Have students spell words that have the endings *–ff, –ll, –ss, –zz,* and *–all* (for example, *puff, pull, pass, fuzz,* and *wall*).

 Objectives

- Identify ending sounds in words.
- Identify and use ending *–all.*
- Identify and use ending *–ff.*
- Identify and use ending *–ll.*
- Identify and use ending *–ss.*
- Identify and use ending *–zz.*
- Read aloud grade-level text with appropriate automaticity, prosody, accuracy, and rate.
- Decode words by applying grade-level word analysis skills.

Getting Stronger: Compound Words

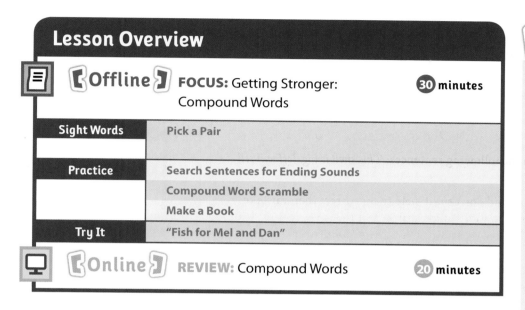

Lesson Overview

Offline 〗 FOCUS: Getting Stronger: Compound Words   30 minutes

Sight Words	Pick a Pair
Practice	Search Sentences for Ending Sounds
	Compound Word Scramble
	Make a Book
Try It	"Fish for Mel and Dan"

Online 〗 REVIEW: Compound Words   20 minutes

〖 Materials 〗

Supplied
- *K¹² PhonicsWorks Readers Basic 11*, pp. 7–14
- whiteboard, Learning Coach
- Tile Kit

Also Needed
- sight words box
- index cards (8)
- paper, construction
- paper, printer
- stapler
- scissors, adult

Advance Preparation

For Compound Word Scramble, print each of the following words on index cards, using one card per word: *laptop, sunset, cannot, uphill, hatbox, bathtub, cobweb,* and *pinball.*

For Make a Book, create a blank book with two sheets of printer paper and a construction paper cover. Fold the pages in half and staple them along the left edge.

 **30 minutes**

FOCUS: Getting Stronger: Compound Words

Work **together** with students to complete offline Sight Words, Practice, and Try It activities.

Sight Words

Pick a Pair

Play a card game with students for more practice with sight words.

1. Gather the sight word cards that students are reviewing. Choose two words and place the cards on the table.

2. Ask questions to help students identify each word. For example, if the words are *or* and *one*, you could ask, "Which word names a number?" If the words are *on* and *but*, you could ask, "Which word is the opposite of *off*?"

3. Continue the activity until students identify all the words.

4. Take the stack of words that students read correctly and dictate each word to them.

5. Have students write each word or spell it aloud.

Objectives
- Read sight words.
- Spell sight words.
- Write sight words.

Practice

Search Sentences for Ending Sounds

Have students practice identifying **ending sounds** in words that are in a sentence.

1. **Say:** I'm going to say a special ending sound that is in a word. You will repeat that sound and the word. The first sound is /k/, as in the word *luck*.

2. Have students say the target sound /k/ and the word *luck*.

3. **Say:** Now I will read a sentence. Repeat the sentence and tell me the word that has the same sound. The first sentence is "Give me back the toy." Which word in the sentence has the special ending sound? *back*

4. Have students repeat the sentence and say the word.

5. Redirect students if they don't name the correct word.

   Say: Let me say the sentence again. Remember, you're listening for the sound [special sound].

6. Guide students if they have difficulty. Say two words from the sentence and have them choose the one with the target ending sound.

7. Use the same procedure with the following words and sentences:

   ▶ /ch/, as in *rich*   *Did Jim eat much?* much
   ▶ /th/, as in *bath*   *Ride your bike on the path.* path
   ▶ /l/, as in *fall*   *Ring the bell in the tower.* bell
   ▶ /z/, as in *jazz*   *Hear the bee buzz.* buzz
   ▶ /sh/, as in *mesh*   *Make a wish.* wish

Objectives
- Identify ending sounds in words.
- Identify complete sentences.
- Capitalize the first word in a sentence.
- Use question marks to end asking sentences.
- Use periods to end telling sentences.
- Decode words by applying grade-level word analysis skills.
- Write words by applying grade-level phonics knowledge.
- Follow three-step directions.

Compound Word Scramble

Have students review and practice building compound words by rearranging individual smaller words.

1. Gather the index cards you prepared and place them face up in front of students.

2. **Say:** You are going to read some compound words and answer some questions. Have students

   ▸ Choose a card.
   ▸ Read the word aloud.
   ▸ Say what the word means.
   ▸ Say how they know the word is a compound word. The word is a compound word because it is made from two smaller words.
   ▸ Name the two smaller words that make up each compound word.

3. After students have read all the words, cut the words in half and scramble them.

4. Arrange two of the cards as follows: *laptop.*

   Say: Now you are going to put two words together to build the compound words you just read. I will lay the cards out for you to see. You will choose two word cards and put them together to make a compound word. Then you will read the compound word. I'll do the first one for you.

5. Point to the word *laptop* and do the following.

   ▸ Read aloud the two smaller words that make the compound word.
   ▸ Read aloud the compound word.

6. Have students continue the procedure to make the remaining compound words.

Make a Book

Have students practice writing compound words and using them in sentences to create a book. Grab your whiteboard and dry-erase marker.

1. **Say:** You are going to make your own book. Let's think of some compound words to write in your book. Name three compound words. I will write those words on my whiteboard.

2. Write the words on the whiteboard.

   Say: Use each compound word in a sentence and write it on your paper.

3. Give students the blank book that you prepared.

   ▸ Have students write "My Book, by [students' name(s)]" on the cover.
   ▸ Have students copy one sentence each on pages 2, 4, and 6.
   ▸ Have students draw a picture for each sentence on pages 3, 5, and 7.
   ▸ Have students illustrate the cover. When they have finished, read the book with them.

4. Help students if they make a spelling mistake. Write the correct spelling above the word and have them make the correction.

Say: That was a good try, but the word is spelled like this.

5. Guide students if they have trouble thinking of or writing sentences. Have them write only a single word on each page and then illustrate it.

 To help students write words that are unfamiliar, tell them the word and help them spell it so that writing becomes a pleasure for them instead of a chore.

 Depending upon the amount of time students have for this activity, you may want to have them finish the illustrations later.

 **Try It** ·

"Fish for Mel and Dan"
Have students read "Fish for Mel and Dan" on page 7 of *K¹² PhonicsWorks Readers Basic 11*.

　　Students should read the story silently once or twice before reading the story aloud. When students miss a word that can be sounded out, point to it and give them three to six seconds to try the word again. If students still miss the word, tell them the word so the flow of the story isn't interrupted.

　　After reading the story, make a list of all the words students missed, and go over those words with them. You may use letter tiles to show students how to read the words.

> **Objectives**
> - Read aloud grade-level text with appropriate automaticity, prosody, accuracy, and rate.
> - Decode words by applying grade-level word analysis skills.
> - Track text from left to right.
> - Turn pages sequentially.

[Online] 20 minutes

REVIEW: Compound Words
Students will work online independently to

▶ Practice compound words.

Help students locate the online activities and provide support as needed.

> **Objectives**
> - Identify and use compound words.
> - Identify individual sounds in words.

Offline Alternative

No computer access? Have students think of compound words, say the two separate words that make each compound word, and use the compound word in a sentence (for example, *nutshell*, *nut* and *shell*, *Give him the nutshell* or *sunfish*, *sun* and *fish*, *He saw a sunfish*).

Unit Checkpoint

Lesson Overview

 【Online】 **REVIEW:** Sentences, Endings, and Compound Words — **20** minutes

【Offline】 **UNIT CHECKPOINT:** Getting Stronger: Sentences, Endings, and Compound Words — **30** minutes

Materials

Supplied
- *K¹² PhonicsWorks Basic Assessments,* pp. PH 199–204

Objectives
- Identify and use ending –*all.*
- Identify and use ending –*ff.*
- Identify and use ending –*ll.*
- Identify and use ending –*ss.*
- Identify and use ending –*zz.*
- Read, write, and spell words containing the ending –*s.*
- Read, write, and spell words containing the ending –*es.*
- Capitalize the first word in a sentence.
- Use periods to end telling sentences.
- Identify and use compound words.
- Identify ending sounds in words.
- Identify individual sounds in words.
- Given the letter, identify the most common sound.
- Given the sound, identify the most common letter or letters.
- Read instructional-level text with 90% accuracy.
- Read aloud grade-level text with appropriate automaticity, prosody, accuracy, and rate.
- Write words by applying grade-level phonics knowledge.
- Write sight words.
- Read sight words.

 **20 minutes**

REVIEW: **Sentences, Endings, and Compound Words**
Students will review sentences, capitalization, and punctuation; the endings –*s,* –*es,* –*ff,* –*ll,* –*ss,* –*zz,* and –*all*; and compound words to prepare for the Unit Checkpoint. Help students locate the online activities and provide support as needed.

 **30 minutes**

UNIT CHECKPOINT: Sentences, Endings, and Compound Words

Explain that students are going to show what they have learned about sounds, letters, and words.

1. Give students the Unit Checkpoint pages for the Getting Stronger: Sentences, Endings, and Compound Words unit and print the Unit Checkpoint Answer Key, if you'd like.

2. Use the instructions below to help administer the Checkpoint to students. On the Answer Key or another sheet of paper, note student answers to oral response questions to help with scoring the Checkpoint later.

3. Use the Answer Key to score the Checkpoint, and then enter the results online.

Part 1. Read Word Parts Have students read across the rows from left to right and say the sounds of each word part. Note any word parts they say incorrectly.

Part 2. Finger Stretching Say each word to students. Have them say each word and finger stretch the sounds. Note any words they finger stretch incorrectly.

19. *fuzz*	23. *bells*
20. *puffs*	24. *less*
21. *catches*	25. *wishes*
22. *miff*	26. *moth*

Part 3. Dictation Say each word to students. Have them repeat and write the word.

27. *dull*	30. *misses*
28. *tells*	31. *tiff*
29. *jazz*	32. *boss*

Part 4. Writing Read each sentence to students. Have them repeat and write the sentence.

33. *Get the boxes for the backpacks.*

34. *Mom misses the bells.*

Part 5. Read Aloud Listen to students read the sentences aloud. Count and note the number of words they read correctly.

Part 6. Say Letters Say each sound. Have students tell you a letter or letters that make that sound. Note any incorrect responses.

36. /ă/	41. /k/
37. /y/	42. /ĭ/
38. /th/	43. /ŏ/
39. /ě/	44. /ŭ/
40. /ch/	

Name _____ Date _____

Unit Checkpoint Answer Key
Getting Stronger: Sentences, Endings, and Compound Words

Part 1. Read Word Parts
Read across the row from left to right. Say the sounds of the word part.

1. –aches	2. –itch	3. –ech
4. –ull	5. –ells	6. –ill
7. –oll	8. –aff	9. –iff
10. –uff	11. –ess	12. –iss
13. –ess	14. –azz	15. –uzzes
16. –ish	17. –ith	18. –oth

1. /ă/ /ch/ /iz/	2. /ĭ/ /ch/	3. /ĕ/ /ch/
4. /ŭ/ /l/	5. /ĕ/ /l/ /z/	6. /ĭ/ /l/
7. /ŏ/ /l/	8. /ă/ /f/	9. /ĭ/ /f/
10. /ŭ/ /f/	11. /ĕ/ /s/	12. /ĭ/ /s/
13. /ĕ/ /s/	14. /ă/ /z/	15. /ŭ/ /z/ /iz/
16. /ĭ/ /sh/	17. /ĭ/ /th/	18. /ŏ/ /th/

Name _____ Date _____

Part 2. Finger Stretching
Listen to the word. Finger stretch the word.

19. /f/ /ŭ/ /z/
20. /p/ /ŭ/ /f/ /s/
21. /c/ /ă/ /ch/ /iz/
22. /m/ /ĭ/ /f/
23. /b/ /ĕ/ /l/ /z/
24. /l/ /ĕ/ /s/
25. /w/ /ĭ/ /sh/ /iz/
26. /m/ /ŏ/ /th/

Name _____ Date _____

Part 3. Dictation
Listen to the word. Repeat the word, and then write it.

27. dull
28. tells
29. jazz
30. misses
31. tiff
32. boss

Name _____ Date _____

Part 4. Writing
Listen to the sentence. Repeat the sentence, and then write it.

33. Get the boxes for the backpacks.
34. Mom misses the bells.

Name _____ Date _____

Part 5. Read Aloud
Read the sentences aloud.

35.
| Jen wishes for a laptop. |
| Why is her doll in there? |
| The pigs cannot get in the pigpen. |
| Are you on the hilltop? |

Name _____ Date _____

Part 6. Say Letters
Listen to the sound. Say the letter or letters that make that sound.

36. a	39. e	42. i
37. y	40. ch or tch	43. o
38. th	41. c, k, or ck	44. u

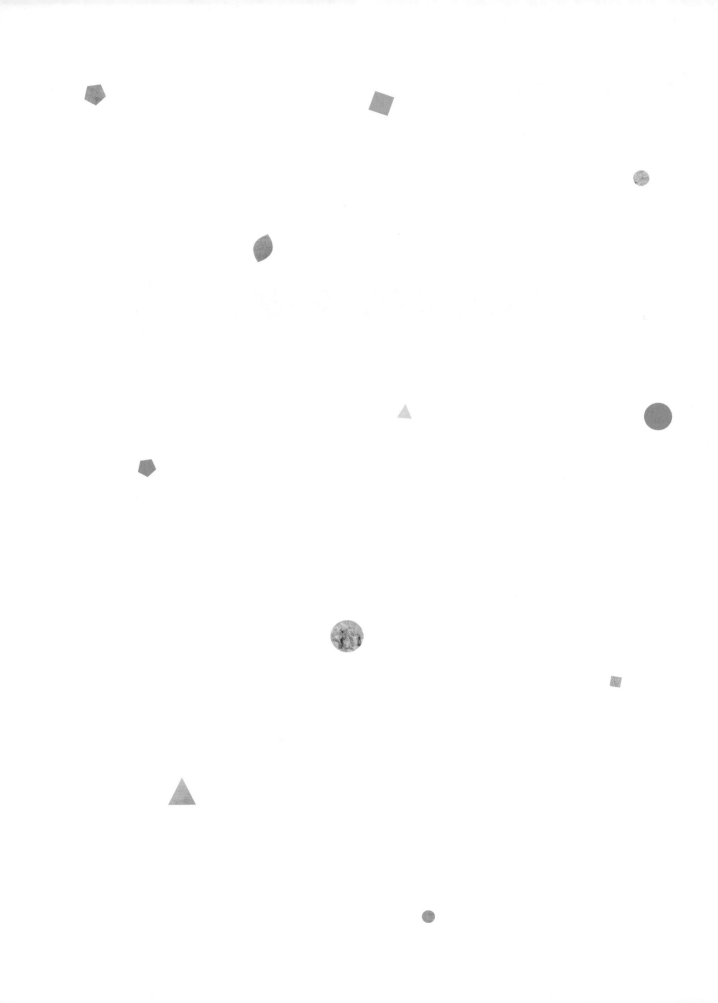

Read and Write Words

Unit Overview

In this unit, students will
- ▶ Review sight words.
- ▶ Create sentences using correct capitalization and punctuation.
- ▶ Review the letters and sounds.
- ▶ Practice reading and writing.

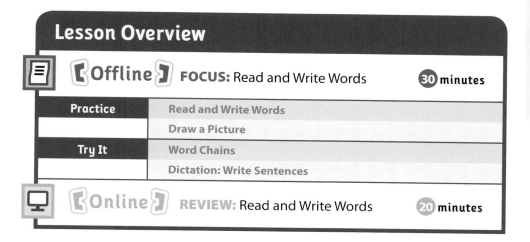

Lesson Overview

[Offline] FOCUS: Read and Write Words		30 minutes
Practice	Read and Write Words	
	Draw a Picture	
Try It	Word Chains	
	Dictation: Write Sentences	

[Online] REVIEW: Read and Write Words — 20 minutes

Materials

Supplied
- *K¹² PhonicsWorks Basic Activity Book*, p. PH 87
- whiteboard, Learning Coach

Also Needed
- dictation notebook
- index cards (12)
- crayons

Advance Preparation

For Read and Write Words, gather 30 index cards with any of the words you prepared in the PhonicsWorks course.

For Draw a Picture, print each of the following words on index cards, using one card per word: *bat, dash, nap, catch, pitch, sip, dig, wish, run, hop, fall,* and *lick.*

 **30** minutes

FOCUS: **Read and Write Words**

Work **together** with students to complete offline Practice and Try It activities.

Practice ●

Read and Write Words

Have students practice reading and writing words.

1. Gather the index cards and the dictation notebook.

2. Shuffle the cards and place them face down in a stack on the table.

3. Have students pick a word and read it to you.

4. If they read it quickly and correctly, put the card in one stack. If they hesitate or do not read the word correctly, put it in another stack. The second stack should have words that they will review again.

5. After students read all 30 words, have them read the difficult words again. Continue the procedure until they read all the words without hesitating.

6. Select five words at random and dictate them to students. Have students write the words in their dictation notebook.

7. Have them check their spelling against the spelling on the card.

Objectives
- Identify individual sounds in words.
- Read aloud grade-level text with appropriate automaticity, prosody, accuracy, and rate.
- Write words by applying grade-level phonics knowledge.

Draw a Picture

Help students practice reading and writing words by having them draw pictures to match the word.

1. Gather the index cards you prepared, the crayons, and the dictation notebook.

2. **Say:** Let's read some words.
   ► If you read the word correctly the first time, put it in one stack.
   ► If a word takes you more than one try, put it in another stack.

3. Have students read each word on the cards.

4. Help students read the words from the stack of words that took them more than one try.

5. Dictate the words to students and have them write the words in their notebook.

6. Have them select two words and use crayons to draw a picture of each word on the back of the card.

TIP If students have trouble reading the words, have them break them into syllables. Then help students finger stretch the sounds in each syllable.

Try It

Word Chains

Have students complete page PH 87 in *K¹² PhonicsWorks Basic Activity Book* for more practice with reading words. Have students read each word, moving down the column, and color the box for the letter that is changed in the next word.

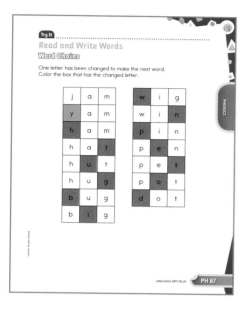

Objectives

- Identify the new word when one sound is changed in a word.
- Write words by applying grade-level phonics knowledge.
- Follow three-step directions.

Dictation: Write Sentences

Use sentences to help students identify individual sounds in words.

1. Gather a pencil and the dictation notebook. Say the sentence, *Mr. Fitch pitches the ball and Sam catches it.* Then give these directions to students:

    ▸ Repeat the sentence.
    ▸ Write the sentence in your notebook.
    ▸ Read the sentence aloud.

2. When students have finished, write the following sentence on your whiteboard: *Mr. Fitch pitches the ball and Sam catches it.*

3. Have them compare their answer to your correct version.

4. Repeat this procedure with the following sentence: *Were Mr. and Mrs. Hill at the picnic with Seth?*

    ▸ If students make an error and don't see it, help them correct their mistake by having them finger stretch the sounds in the word they missed.
    ▸ If students are having difficulty selecting the correct letters or sounds, review those letters or sounds that are confusing them.
    ▸ If students have difficulty with first, middle, and last sounds, have them finger stretch the sounds in words.

 **20** minutes

REVIEW: **Read and Write Words**

Students will work online independently to

▶ Practice reading and making words.

▶ Practice reading sight words.

▶ Practice decoding text by reading a story.

Help students locate the online activities and provide support as needed.

Offline Alternative

No computer access? Have students select a favorite story from any volume of the *K¹² PhonicsWorks Readers Basic* and read the story aloud. Choose five words from the story and dictate those words to students. Have them write the words in their dictation notebook.

 Objectives

- Identify individual sounds in words.
- Blend sounds to create words.
- Read sight words.
- Spell sight words.
- Read aloud grade-level text with appropriate automaticity, prosody, accuracy, and rate.
- Decode words by applying grade-level word analysis skills.

Letters and Sounds

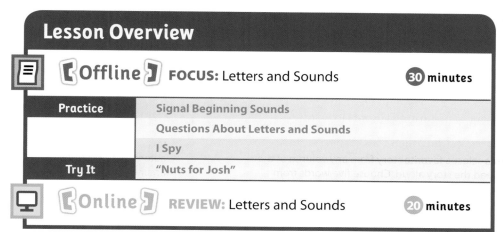

Lesson Overview

Offline **FOCUS:** Letters and Sounds — **30** minutes

Practice	Signal Beginning Sounds
	Questions About Letters and Sounds
	I Spy
Try It	"Nuts for Josh"

Online **REVIEW:** Letters and Sounds — **20** minutes

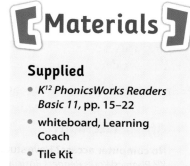

Materials

Supplied

- *K¹² PhonicsWorks Readers Basic 11*, pp. 15–22
- whiteboard, Learning Coach
- Tile Kit

Advance Preparation

For Questions About Letters and Sounds, place lowercase letter tiles in alphabetical order; the digraphs *ch*, *–ck*, *sh*, *th*, and *wh*; trigraph *–tch*; and the double-letter endings *–ff*, *–ll*, *–ss*, and *–zz* on your whiteboard.

 **30 minutes**

FOCUS: Letters and Sounds

Work **together** with students to complete offline Practice and Try It activities.

Practice

Signal Beginning Sounds

Use a special signal to help students identify **beginning sounds** in words.

1. **Say:** I'm going to tell you a special sound, and then I'll say some words. Repeat each word I say and make a special signal to tell me where the special sound is. If the special sound is at the beginning of the word, touch your nose. If the special sound is **not** at the beginning of the word, just smile at me.

   ▶ For example, if I ask you to listen for the sound /ĕ/ and I say the word *edge*, you'll repeat the word *edge* and touch your nose because *edge* has the sound /ĕ/ at the beginning.

   ▶ If I say the word *itch*, you'll repeat the word *itch* and smile at me because *itch* has the sound /ĭ/, not /ĕ/, at the beginning.

2. Say the sound and group of words. Have students make the special signal to identify the beginning sound.

   ▶ /ĕ/: *echo, insect, orange, elbow, exit, edge, umbrella, extra* touch nose: *echo, elbow, exit, edge, extra*

   TIP If students can't identify the beginning sound of each word, say the word again and emphasize the beginning sound by repeating it three times (for example, /t/ /t/ /t/, *taste*). You can also draw out the beginning sound when you say the word (for example, *mmmommy*). If necessary, have students look at your mouth while you repeat the sounds.

Questions About Letters and Sounds

To help students master the letters and sounds of the alphabet, digraphs, trigraph –*tch*, and double-letter endings, have them practice identifying and naming them. Grab your whiteboard with letters placed in alphabetical order, the digraphs, the trigraph –*tch*, and double-letter endings. Have students do the following steps.

1. Touch all the consonants in the first row and tell me their sounds. Answers will vary.

2. Touch and tell me the sound for each letter that is a vowel. /ă/, /ĕ/, /ĭ/, /ŏ/, /ŭ/

3. Say the letter that always has a *u* after it? *q*

4. Touch all the digraphs and say their sounds. *ch, –ck, sh, th, wh* for sounds /ch/, /k/, /sh/, /th/, /th̲/, /w/

Objectives
- Identify beginning sounds in words.
- Identify letters of the alphabet.
- Given the letter, identify the most common sound.
- Given the sound, identify the most common letter or letters.
- Identify short vowel sounds.
- Identify individual sounds in words.

5. Touch the trigraph –*tch* and say the sound the letters make. /ch/

6. Touch all the letters that spell the sound /k/. *c, ck, k*

7. Touch all the letters that spell the sound /w/. *w, wh*

8. Touch the letters that are almost always doubled at the end of a one-syllable word if they follow a short vowel? *–ff, –ll, –ss, –zz*

I Spy

Have students name and use common objects to help them recognize individual sounds in words.

1. Explain to students that you will be playing I Spy and show them how to use the thumb and index finger to make a circle, simulating a spyglass.

2. **Say:** I say, "I spy, with my little eye, something that starts with the sound /l/." Your job is to guess what I spy. What I had in mind was the *light*. *Light* begins with the sound /l/.

3. Repeat Step 2 with a different object in the room.

4. **Say:** Are you ready to begin? I spy, with my little eye, something that starts with the sound [target sound]. Can you guess what it is?

5. After students have guessed the object, repeat Step 4 until you have spied six objects, or until students tire of the game. Possible words to use are: *chair, window, door, box, sheet, refrigerator, magazine, sink, carpet, bowl, mat, newspaper, towel, basket, key,* and *napkin*.

6. Redirect students if they name an object with an incorrect sound.

   Say: The sound that begins the word [word] is [sound]. We're looking for something that begins with the sound [target sound]. What is a word that begins with that sound? Now look around the room. What do you see that begins with that sound?

7. Narrow down the search to a certain part of the room if students become frustrated. If they continue to have trouble, narrow down the search to two objects.

   Say: What is the beginning sound of [target word]? What is the beginning sound of [another word]? Which one starts with the sound [target sound]?

Try It •

"Nuts for Josh"

Have students read "Nuts for Josh" on page 15 of *K¹² PhonicsWorks Readers Basic 11.*

Students should read the story silently once or twice before reading the story aloud. When students miss a word that can be sounded out, point to it and give them three to six seconds to try the word again. If students still miss the word, tell them the word so the flow of the story isn't interrupted.

After reading the story, make a list of all the words students missed, and go over those words with them. You may use letter tiles to show students how to read the words.

> **Objectives**
> - Read aloud grade-level text with appropriate automaticity, prosody, accuracy, and rate.
> - Decode words by applying grade-level word analysis skills.
> - Track text from left to right.
> - Turn pages sequentially.

 **20 minutes**

REVIEW: **Letters and Sounds**

Students will work online independently to

- ▸ Practice letters and sounds.
- ▸ Practice reading sight words.

Help students locate the online activities and provide support as needed.

> **Objectives**
> - Identify letters of the alphabet.
> - Given the letter, identify the most common sound.
> - Given the sound, identify the most common letter or letters.
> - Read sight words.
> - Spell sight words.
> - Identify individual sounds in words.

Offline Alternative

No computer access? Have students practice the letters and sounds in the alphabet. You might have them spell consonant-vowel-consonant words and state what letter is the vowel (for example, *ham, a; cob, o; tin, i; get, e;* and *tub, u*).

Create Words

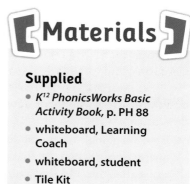

Lesson Overview

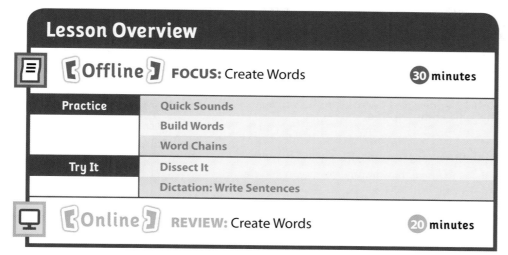

Offline **FOCUS:** Create Words — **30** minutes

Practice	Quick Sounds
	Build Words
	Word Chains
Try It	Dissect It
	Dictation: Write Sentences

Online **REVIEW:** Create Words — **20** minutes

Materials

Supplied
- *K¹² PhonicsWorks Basic Activity Book*, p. PH 88
- whiteboard, Learning Coach
- whiteboard, student
- Tile Kit

Also Needed
- dictation notebook

 **30 minutes**

FOCUS: Create Words

Work **together** with students to complete offline Practice and Try It activities.

Practice •

Quick Sounds

Help students name words that have the same **ending sound**.

1. **Say:** I'm going to say some sounds that end a word. Your job is to think of as many words as you can that end with those same sounds. Let's see how many you can name. The first sound is /f/, as in *laugh*. How many words can you say that end with /f/?

   ▸ If students have trouble thinking of words, have them look around the room and find objects that end with that sound.

2. Continue this procedure with the following sounds:

   ▸ /g/, as in *peg*
   ▸ /sh/, as in *wash*
   ▸ /th/, as in *path*
   ▸ /l/, as in *fall*

   TIP You can get a book and have students find pictures of things that end with that sound.

> **Objectives**
> - Identify ending sounds in words.
> - Given the letter, identify the most common sound.
> - Given the sound, identify the most common letter or letters.
> - Identify individual sounds in words.
> - Blend sounds to create words.
> - Write words by applying grade-level phonics knowledge.
> - Identify the new word when one sound is changed in a word.

Build Words

Help students use letters and sounds to build words.

1. Place the following letter tiles at the top of students' whiteboard: *a, a, b, ck, ck, es, h, i, ll, m, p, s, sh, tch, u, w,* and *x.*

2. Draw seven horizontal lines across the middle of students' whiteboard to represent the sounds in a word.

3. **Say:** Let's use letters and sounds to build the word *backpacks.*

4. Have students finger stretch the sounds in *backpacks.*

5. Have students

   ▸ Identify the first, next, and last sounds in *backpacks.*
   ▸ Choose the corresponding letter tile for each of the sounds.
   ▸ Move the letters to the correct lines on their whiteboard.

6. Guide students with these questions:

   ▸ What is the first sound in *backpacks*? /b/
     Which line does the letter for that sound go on? the first one
   ▸ What is the next sound in *backpacks*? /ă/
     Which line does the letter for that sound go on? the second one

▶ What is the next sound in *backpacks*? /k/
Which line do the letters for that sound go on? the third one

▶ What is the next sound in *backpacks*? /p/
Which line does the letter for that sound go on? the fourth one

▶ What is the next sound in *backpacks*? /ă/
Which line does the letter for that sound go on? the fifth one

▶ What is the next sound in *backpacks*? /k/
Which line do the letters for that sound go on? the sixth one

▶ What's the last sound in *backpacks*? /s/
Which line does the letter for that sound go on? the last one

7. Redirect students if they select the incorrect letter.

   Say: That sound is in the word [word], and it is the [first, second, third, fourth, fifth, sixth, seventh] sound. We want the sound [target sound].

   Continue until students select the correct letter.

8. Have students touch and say the word.

9. Have them say the word as they use a dry-erase marker to write the word on the whiteboard.

10. Help students if they spell a word incorrectly, but the sounds they spell are correct (such as *ruf* for *rough*).

    Say: You have the sounds and letters right, but that word doesn't follow our spelling rules. Try another word.

11. Draw horizontal lines across the middle of students' whiteboard that represent the number of sounds in each word. Repeat the activity to build the following words:

    ▶ *wishes* /w/ /ĭ/ /sh/ /iz/
    ▶ *matches* /m/ /ă/ /ch/ /iz/
    ▶ *uphill* /ŭ/ /p/ /h/ /ĭ/ /l/
    ▶ *axes* /a/ /ks/ /iz/

Word Chains

Have students build words by adding and changing letters to help them recognize and use individual sounds in words.

1. Place the following letter tiles at the top of students' whiteboard: *a, b, c, ch, ck, i, m, o, p, sh, t, tch,* and *th.*

2. **Say:** I am going to build the first word in a chain. The word is *shim.*

   ▶ I will pull down the letters for the sounds /sh/, /ĭ/, and /m/ to spell the word *shim.*
   ▶ I will touch and say *shim.* To change *shim* to *ship,* I will think about what sound is changed from the word *shim* to *ship.* I will need to replace the letter *m* with the letter *p.*
   ▶ Touch and say the word *ship.* Now it's your turn to change *ship* to *shop.* You can spell *shop* by making only one change. Touch and say the new word.

3. Redirect students if they select the incorrect letter for any sound.

   Say: That letter is for the sound [incorrect sound]. We want the letter for the sound [target sound]. What letter makes that sound? Answers will vary.

4. Redirect students if they name the sound incorrectly.

   Say: To change the word [first word] to [target word], we need the letter for the sound [target sound].

   Show students how to make the change. Have them touch and say the new word after they move the letters.

5. Follow this procedure to make the following words: *chop, chip, chap, chat, that, bat, back, batch, match, mash, cash.*

6. For every new word, have students add, replace, or remove only one letter tile.

   TIP If students struggle, review the sounds and letters that are confusing them.

Try It

Dissect It

Have students complete page PH 88 in *K¹² PhonicsWorks Basic Activity Book* for more practice with words. Have students find words in each sentence that start with the digraphs *ch–, sh–, th–,* or *wh–* and write those words to complete the sentences. Have them read the sentences and words aloud.

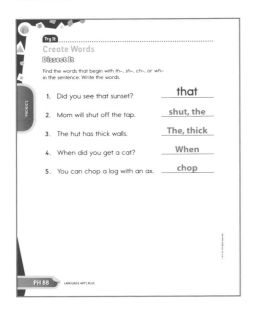

Try It
Create Words
Dissect It

Find the words that begin with *th–, sh–, ch–,* or *wh–* in the sentence. Write the words.

1. Did you see that sunset? — that
2. Mom will shut off the tap. — shut, the
3. The hut has thick walls. — The, thick
4. When did you get a cat? — When
5. You can chop a log with an ax. — chop

PH 88   LANGUAGE ARTS BLUE

Objectives
- Identify ending sounds in words.
- Identify and use the digraph *ch*.
- Identify and use the digraph *sh*.
- Identify and use the digraph *th*.
- Identify and use the digraph *wh*.
- Read aloud grade-level text with appropriate automaticity, prosody, accuracy, and rate.
- Write words by applying grade-level phonics knowledge.
- Follow three-step directions.

Dictation: Write Sentences

Use sentences to help students identify individual sounds in words.

1. Gather a pencil and the dictation notebook. Say the sentence, *Mitch will chop the logs with the big ax.* Then give these directions to students:

   ▸ Repeat the sentence.
   ▸ Write the sentence in your notebook.
   ▸ Read the sentence aloud.

2. When students have finished, write the following sentence on your whiteboard: *Mitch will chop the logs with the big ax.*

3. Have them compare their answer to your correct version.

4. Repeat this procedure with the following sentences: *A ship is at that dock. Which chap is your chum?*

   ▸ If students make an error and don't see it, help them correct their mistake by having them finger stretch the sounds in the word they missed.
   ▸ If students are having difficulty selecting the correct letters or sounds, review those letters or sounds that are confusing them.
   ▸ If students have difficulty with first, middle, and last sounds, have them finger stretch the sounds in words.

 **minutes**

REVIEW: Create Words

Students will work online independently to

▸ Practice making words.
▸ Practice reading sight words.
▸ Practice decoding text by reading a story.

Help students locate the online activities and provide support as needed.

Offline Alternative

No computer access? Have students look around them and name people, places, or things that they know. Have them spell those words aloud and write them in their dictation notebook.

 Objectives
- Identify individual sounds in words.
- Blend sounds to create words.
- Read sight words.
- Spell sight words.
- Read aloud grade-level text with appropriate automaticity, prosody, accuracy, and rate.
- Decode words by applying grade-level word analysis skills.

Read and Write Sentences

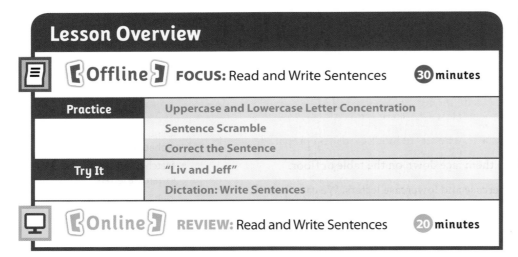

Lesson Overview

Offline FOCUS: Read and Write Sentences **30** minutes

Practice	Uppercase and Lowercase Letter Concentration
	Sentence Scramble
	Correct the Sentence
Try It	"Liv and Jeff"
	Dictation: Write Sentences

Online REVIEW: Read and Write Sentences **20** minutes

Materials

Supplied
- K[12] *PhonicsWorks Readers Basic 11*, pp. 23–30
- whiteboard, Learning Coach
- whiteboard, student
- Tile Kit

Also Needed
- dictation notebook
- index cards (22)

Advance Preparation

For Uppercase and Lowercase Letter Concentration, print matching pairs of 6 uppercase and lowercase letters on 12 individual index cards, using one card per letter. Select letters that students need to review.

For Sentence Scramble, print each of the following words on index cards, using one card per word: *Jeff, misses, pitches, the, ball, will, fun, have, does,* and *catch.*

 **30 minutes**

FOCUS: Read and Write Sentences

Work **together** with students to complete offline Practice and Try It activities.

Practice

Uppercase and Lowercase Concentration

Help students practice pairing uppercase and lowercase letters.

1. Gather the uppercase and lowercase letter pairs of index cards you prepared.

2. Mix up the index cards and place them face down on the table or floor.

3. **Say:** Let's practice matching uppercase and lowercase letters. We can also call these letters big letters and small letters.

4. **Say:** You'll turn over the cards two at a time. If you turn over a card that has a lowercase letter and a card that has the uppercase form of the same letter, the cards match and you can keep them. If the cards don't match, turn them back over.

5. Continue the activity until all the cards are paired.

Sentence Scramble

Have students build sentences by rearranging words to help them learn the meaning of words and phrases.

1. Gather the index cards you prepared, a pencil, and the dictation notebook.

2. Place the index cards in front of students.

3. Point to each word and have students read it aloud with you.

4. Arrange five of the cards as follows: *will Jeff catch the ball.*

5. Have students say if the words make sense. Tell them that the words make an asking sentence.

6. Write the words as a sentence on students' whiteboard. Be sure to capitalize the first letter in *will* and insert the proper punctuation at the end of the sentence.

7. Point out the capital letter and the question mark in the sentence.

8. Read the sentence with students.

9. **Say:** I am going to put these words back with the others. Choose some word cards and put them together to make a different sentence. Read the words in the order you put them.

   ▶ Does your sentence make sense? Is it an asking or a telling sentence?
   ▶ Now write the sentence. Be sure to start with a capital letter. Remember to put a period or a question mark at the end.

Objectives

- Identify letters of the alphabet.
- Match capital letters to lowercase letters.
- Identify ending sounds in words.
- Read aloud grade-level text with appropriate automaticity, prosody, accuracy, and rate.
- Decode words by applying grade-level word analysis skills.
- Use context and sentence structure to determine meaning of words, phrases, and/or sentences.
- Follow three-step directions.
- Write words by applying grade-level phonics knowledge.
- Identify complete sentences.
- Capitalize the first word in a sentence.
- Use question marks to end asking sentences.
- Use periods to end telling sentences.

10. Return the words to the original group, and repeat the steps so that students can create and write one or more sentences.

11. Help students if they have difficulty arranging the words correctly to make a sentence.

    Say: Read the sentence aloud. Does it make sense?

12. Point to any word that seems out of place and state the following:

    ▸ What is this word?
    ▸ Find a word that would make better sense.
    ▸ Switch the words. Now read the sentence.
    ▸ Does it make sense now?

Correct the Sentence

Have students practice correcting capitalization and punctuation in sentences. Grab your whiteboard and dry-erase marker.

1. Write the following sentence on your whiteboard without using capitalization or punctuation: *i will get off this ship.*

2. Have students read the sentence aloud. Have them

    ▸ Cross out the lowercase letter at the beginning of the first word and write the capital letter.
    ▸ Add punctuation to the end of the sentence.

3. **Say:** Read the sentence again. How do you know this sentence is correct? The sentence is correct if it follows the rules. To begin any sentence, use a capital letter in the first word. To end a telling sentence, add a period to mark the end of the sentence. To end an asking sentence, add a question mark to the end of the sentence.

4. Repeat the procedure for each of the sentences.

    ▸ does a duck quack *Does a duck quack?*
    ▸ my doll fell off the bed *My doll fell off the bed.*
    ▸ who can toss the ball *Who can toss the ball?*
    ▸ pass your pen to Jill *Pass your pen to Jill.*
    ▸ Josh pitches the ball *Josh pitches the ball.*

5. Help students if they have difficulty identifying what is wrong with the sentence. Ask the following questions:

    ▸ What is special about the first word in a sentence?
    ▸ Does the first word in this sentence start with a capital letter?
    ▸ How can you change the sentence so it begins with a capital letter?
    ▸ What is special about the mark at the end of a sentence?

6. Guide students by asking one of the following questions if they continue having difficulty:

    ▸ Is this sentence a telling or asking sentence?
    ▸ Is the last word in the sentence followed by a period or a question mark?
    ▸ What mark do you put at the end of [a telling or an asking] sentence?

Try It •

"Liv and Jeff"

Have students read "Liv and Jeff" on page 23 of *K¹² PhonicsWorks Readers Basic 11*.

Students should read the story silently once or twice before reading the story aloud. When students miss a word that can be sounded out, point to it and give them three to six seconds to try the word again. If students still miss the word, tell them the word so the flow of the story isn't interrupted.

After reading the story, make a list of all the words students missed, and go over those words with them. You may use letter tiles to show students how to read the words.

Objectives

- Read aloud grade-level text with appropriate automaticity, prosody, accuracy, and rate.
- Decode words by applying grade-level word analysis skills.
- Track text from left to right.
- Turn pages sequentially.
- Write words by applying grade-level phonics knowledge.
- Follow three-step directions.

Dictation: Write Sentences

Use sentences to help students identify individual sounds in words.

1. Gather a pencil and the dictation notebook. Say the sentence, *Jeff will sell caps.* Then give these directions to students:

    ▸ Repeat the sentence.
    ▸ Write the sentence in your notebook.
    ▸ Read the sentence aloud.

2. When students have finished, write the following sentence on your whiteboard: *Jeff will sell caps.*

3. Have them compare their answer to your correct version.

4. Repeat this procedure with the following sentences: *Foxes are on the hill. They want the maps.*

    ▸ If students make an error and don't see it, help them correct their mistake by having them finger stretch the sounds in the word they missed.
    ▸ If students are having difficulty selecting the correct letters or sounds, review those letters or sounds that are confusing them.
    ▸ If students have difficulty with first, middle, and last sounds, have them finger stretch the sounds in words.

 Online ⓴ minutes

REVIEW: Read and Write Sentences

Students will work online independently to

▸ Practice reading and making sentences.
▸ Practice reading sight words.

Help students locate the online activities and provide support as needed.

Offline Alternative

No computer access? Say telling and asking sentences to students, such as *The cat was fat.* and *Was the cat fat?* Have students tell you which word in each sentence should begin with a capital letter. Have them say where the period or question mark should go. You might also have students write short telling and asking sentences in their dictation notebook, on their whiteboard, or on a piece of paper. Make sure students begin each sentence with a capital letter and place a period or question mark at the end.

Objectives

- Read aloud grade-level text with appropriate automaticity, prosody, accuracy, and rate.
- Read sight words.
- Spell sight words.
- Identify complete sentences.
- Capitalize the first word in a sentence.
- Use question marks to end asking sentences.
- Use periods to end telling sentences.
- Write words by applying grade-level phonics knowledge.

Unit Checkpoint

Lesson Overview

🖥	**Online** REVIEW: Words, Letters & Sounds, and Sentences	**20** minutes
📄	**Offline** UNIT CHECKPOINT: Words, Letters & Sounds, and Sentences	**30** minutes

Materials

Supplied

- *K¹² PhonicsWorks Basic Assessments,* pp. PH 205–210

⭐ Objectives

- Identify complete sentences.
- Capitalize the first word in a sentence.
- Use question marks to end asking sentences.
- Use periods to end telling sentences.
- Identify and use compound words.
- Given the letter, identify the most common sound.
- Given the sound, identify the most common letter or letters.
- Identify ending sounds in words.
- Identify individual sounds in words.
- Read instructional-level text with 90% accuracy.
- Read aloud grade-level text with appropriate automaticity, prosody, accuracy, and rate.
- Write words by applying grade-level phonics knowledge.
- Write sight words.
- Read sight words.

Online **20** minutes

REVIEW: Words, Letters & Sounds, and Sentences

Students will review letters, sounds, words, and sentences to prepare for the Unit Checkpoint. Help students locate the online activities and provide support as needed.

 **30 minutes**

UNIT CHECKPOINT: Words, Letters & Sounds, and Sentences

Explain that students are going to show what they have learned about sounds, letters, words, and sentences.

1. Give students the Unit Checkpoint pages for the Words, Letters & Sounds, and Sentences unit and print the Unit Checkpoint Answer Key, if you'd like.

2. Use the instructions below to help administer the Checkpoint to students. On the Answer Key or another sheet of paper, note student answers to oral response questions to help with scoring the Checkpoint later.

3. Use the Answer Key to score the Checkpoint, and then enter the results online.

Part 1. Read Word Parts Have students read across the rows from left to right and say the sounds of each word part. Note any word parts they say incorrectly.

Part 2. Finger Stretching Say each word to students. Have them say each word and finger stretch the sounds. Note any words they finger stretch incorrectly.

19. *jazz*	23. *well*
20. *off*	24. *kisses*
21. *batch*	25. *rich*
22. *duck*	26. *math*

Part 3. Dictation Say each word to students. Have them repeat and write the word.

27. *catch*	30. *hiss*
28. *deck*	31. *huffs*
29. *buzzes*	32. *toss*

Part 4. Writing Read each sentence to students. Have them repeat and write the sentence.

33. *Shut the latch on the shed.*

34. *Which pet is sick?*

Part 5. Read Aloud Listen to students read the sentences aloud. Count and note the number of words they read correctly.

Part 6. Say Letters Say each sound. Have students tell you the letter or letters that make that sound. Note any incorrect responses.

36. /ŏ/	41. /ch/
37. /j/	42. /ŭ/
38. /sh/	43. /ĭ/
39. /ă/	44. /ĕ/
40. /w/	

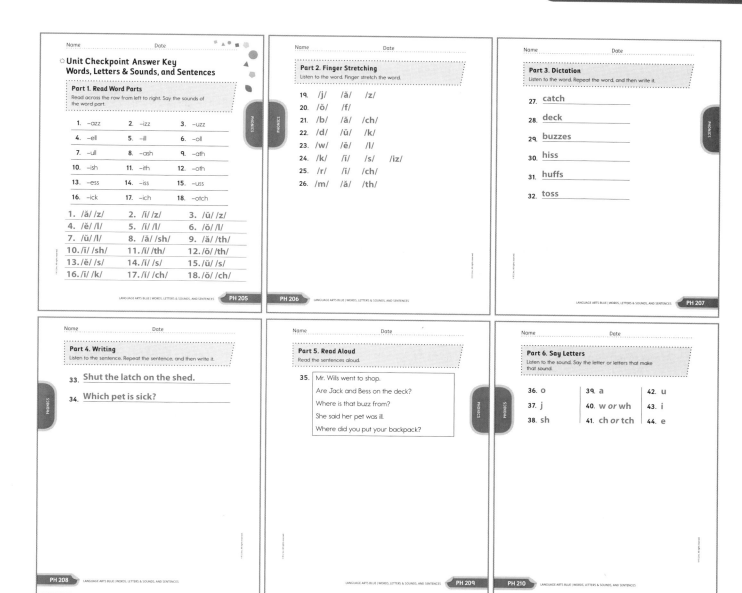

Name _____ Date _____

Unit Checkpoint Answer Key
Words, Letters & Sounds, and Sentences

Part 1. Read Word Parts
Read across the row from left to right. Say the sounds of the word part.

1. –azz	2. –izz	3. –uzz
4. –ell	5. –ill	6. –oll
7. –ull	8. –ash	9. –ath
10. –ish	11. –ith	12. –oth
13. –ess	14. –iss	15. –uss
16. –ick	17. –ich	18. –otch

1. /ă/ /z/	2. /ĭ/ /z/	3. /ŭ/ /z/
4. /ĕ/ /l/	5. /ĭ/ /l/	6. /ŏ/ /l/
7. /ŭ/ /l/	8. /ă/ /sh/	9. /ă/ /th/
10. /ĭ/ /sh/	11. /ĭ/ /th/	12. /ŏ/ /th/
13. /ĕ/ /s/	14. /ĭ/ /s/	15. /ŭ/ /s/
16. /ĭ/ /k/	17. /ĭ/ /ch/	18. /ŏ/ /ch/

LANGUAGE ARTS BLUE | WORDS, LETTERS & SOUNDS, AND SENTENCES **PH 205**

Name _____ Date _____

Part 2. Finger Stretching
Listen to the word. Finger stretch the word.

19. /j/ /ă/ /z/
20. /ŏ/ /f/
21. /b/ /ă/ /ch/
22. /d/ /ŭ/ /k/
23. /w/ /ĕ/ /l/
24. /k/ /ĭ/ /s/ /iz/
25. /r/ /ĭ/ /ch/
26. /m/ /ă/ /th/

PH 206 LANGUAGE ARTS BLUE | WORDS, LETTERS & SOUNDS, AND SENTENCES

Name _____ Date _____

Part 3. Dictation
Listen to the word. Repeat the word, and then write it.

27. catch _____
28. deck _____
29. buzzes _____
30. hiss _____
31. huffs _____
32. toss _____

LANGUAGE ARTS BLUE | WORDS, LETTERS & SOUNDS, AND SENTENCES **PH 207**

Name _____ Date _____

Part 4. Writing
Listen to the sentence. Repeat the sentence, and then write it.

33. Shut the latch on the shed. _____
34. Which pet is sick? _____

PH 208 LANGUAGE ARTS BLUE | WORDS, LETTERS & SOUNDS, AND SENTENCES

Name _____ Date _____

Part 5. Read Aloud
Read the sentences aloud.

35. Mr. Wills went to shop.
Are Jack and Bess on the deck?
Where is that buzz from?
She said her pet was ill.
Where did you put your backpack?

LANGUAGE ARTS BLUE | WORDS, LETTERS & SOUNDS, AND SENTENCES **PH 209**

Name _____ Date _____

Part 6. Say Letters
Listen to the sound. Say the letter or letters that make that sound.

36. o	39. a	42. u
37. j	40. w or wh	43. i
38. sh	41. ch or tch	44. e

PH 210 LANGUAGE ARTS BLUE | WORDS, LETTERS & SOUNDS, AND SENTENCES